DEBATE OF THE *ROMANCE OF THE ROSE*

A Series Edited by Margaret L. King and Albert Rabil Jr.

RECENT BOOKS IN THE SERIES

MADELEINE DE L'AUBESPINE
Selected Poems and Translations: A Bilingual Edition
Edited and Translated by Anna Kłosowska

EMILIE DU CHÂTELET
Selected Philosophical and Scientific Writings
Edited with an Introduction by Judith P. Zinsser, Translated by Isabelle Bour and Judith P. Zinsser

PRINCESS ELISABETH OF BOHEMIA AND RENÉ DESCARTES
The Correspondence between Princess Elisabeth of Bohemia and René Descartes
Edited and Translated by Lisa Shapiro

CATHARINA REGINA VON GREIFFENBERG
Meditations on the Incarnation, Passion, and Death of Jesus Christ
Edited and Translated by Lynne Tatlock

MARÍA DE GUEVARA
Warnings to the Kings and Advice on Restoring Spain: A Bilingual Edition
Edited and Translated by Nieves Romero-Díaz

HORTENSE MANCINI AND MARIE MANCINI
Memoirs
Edited and Translated by Sarah Nelson

MARGUERITE DE NAVARRE
Selected Writings: A Bilingual Edition
Edited and Translated by Rouben Cholakian and Mary Skemp

LUCREZIA MARINELLA
Enrico; or, Byzantium Conquered: A Heroic Poem
Edited and Translated by Maria Galli Stampino

CHIARA MATRAINI
Selected Poetry and Prose: A Bilingual Edition
Edited and Translated by Elaine Maclachlan, With an Introduction by Giovanna Rabitti

ANA DE SAN BARTOLOMÉ
Autobiography and Other Writings
Edited and Translated by Darcy Donahue

SARRA COPIA SULAM
Jewish Poet and Intellectual in Seventeenth-Century Venice
Edited and Translated by Don Harrán

MARÍA DE ZAYAS Y SOTOMAYOR
Exemplary Tales of Love and Tales of Disillusion
Edited and Translated by Margaret R. Greer and Elizabeth Rhodes

Christine de Pizan et al.

DEBATE OF THE *ROMANCE OF THE ROSE*

Edited and Translated by David F. Hult

THE UNIVERSITY OF CHICAGO PRESS
Chicago & London

Christine de Pizan, 1365–1430?

David F. Hult is professor of French at the University of California, Berkeley, and the author of *Self-Fulfilling Prophecies: Readership and Authority in the First "Roman de la Rose"* (1986). He has published essays on Chrétien de Troyes, Jean de Meun, Christine de Pizan, Alain Chartier, medieval allegory, and editorial methodology. He is also the editor or coeditor of six books, most recently of *La Mort du roi Arthur* (2009).

The University of Chicago Press, Chicago 60637
The University of Chicago Press, Ltd., London

Printed in the United States of America

19 18 17 16 15 14 13 12 11 10   1 2 3 4 5

ISBN-13: 978-0-226-67012-6 (cloth)
ISBN-13: 978-0-226-67013-3 (paper)
ISBN-10: 0-226-67012-0 (cloth)
ISBN-10: 0-226-67013-9 (paper)

Library of Congress Cataloging-in-Publication Data
Debate of the Romance of the rose / edited and translated by David F. Hult.
p. cm. — (Other voice in early modern Europe)
In English; translated from documents in Old French or Latin.
Includes bibliographical references and index.
ISBN-13: 978-0-226-67012-6 (cloth : alk. paper)
ISBN-13: 978-0-226-67013-3 (pbk. : alk. paper)
ISBN-10: 0-226-67012-0 (cloth : alk. paper)
ISBN-10: 0-226-67013-9 (pbk. : alk. paper)
1. Guillaume, de Lorris, fl. 1230. Roman de la rose. 2. Christine, de Pisan, ca. 1364–ca. 1431—Correspondence. 3. Jean, de Montreuil, 1354–1418—Correspondence. 4. Romances—History and criticism. 5. Feminism and literature—France. 6. Courtly love in literature. I. Hult, David F., 1952– II. Christine, de Pisan, ca. 1364–ca. 1431. Correspondence. Selections. III. Jean, de Montreuil, 1354–1418. Correspondence. Selections. IV. Series: Other voice in early modern Europe.
PQ1529.D44 2010
841'.1—dc22
2009042968

♾ The paper used in this publication meets the minimum requirements of the American National Standard for Information Sciences—Permanence of Paper for Printed Library Materials, ANSI Z39.48-1992.

CONTENTS

ACKNOWLEDGMENTS

My special thanks to Andrea Tarnowski for her meticulous reading of the introduction and large portions of the translation as well as suggestions for maintaining fidelity to the Middle French while adhering to something resembling English syntax. Nicholas Paige helped me to clarify some murky passages in the Volume Editor's Introduction. Two anonymous readers for the Press provided excellent advice on both Middle French and Latin translations. Discussions with Sylvie Lefèvre and Danielle Bohler helped iron out some difficult passages. Heather Bamford wrote an interesting essay on the structure of the Bancroft manuscript copy of the *Debate* that I found very useful in thinking about the different versions of the *Debate*. I thank Susan Tarcov for a great copy-editing job, which helped correct numerous infelicities and made me rethink some of my translations one final time. Finally, I am grateful to Tony Bliss and the rest of the staff of the Bancroft Library at Berkeley for their help and for graciously allowing me access to materials in their collection.

David F. Hult

THE OTHER VOICE IN EARLY MODERN EUROPE: INTRODUCTION TO THE SERIES

Margaret L. King and Albert Rabil Jr.

THE OLD VOICE AND THE OTHER VOICE

In western Europe and the United States, women are nearing equality in the professions, in business, and in politics. Most enjoy access to education, reproductive rights, and autonomy in financial affairs. Issues vital to women are on the public agenda: equal pay, child care, domestic abuse, breast cancer research, and curricular revision with an eye to the inclusion of women.

These recent achievements have their origins in things women (and some male supporters) said for the first time about six hundred years ago. Theirs is the "other voice," in contradistinction to the "first voice," the voice of the educated men who created Western culture. Coincident with a general reshaping of European culture in the period 1300–1700 (called the Renaissance or early modern period), questions of female equality and opportunity were raised that still resound and are still unresolved.

The other voice emerged against the backdrop of a three-thousand-year history of the derogation of women rooted in the civilizations related to Western culture: Hebrew, Greek, Roman, and Christian. Negative attitudes toward women inherited from these traditions pervaded the intellectual, medical, legal, religious, and social systems that developed during the European Middle Ages.

The following pages describe the traditional, overwhelmingly male views of women's nature inherited by early modern Europeans and the new tradition that the "other voice" called into being to begin to challenge reigning assumptions. This review should serve as a framework for understanding the texts published in the series The Other Voice in Early Modern Europe. Introductions specific to each text and author follow this essay in all the volumes of the series.

TRADITIONAL VIEWS OF WOMEN, 500 B.C.E.–1500 C.E.

Embedded in the philosophical and medical theories of the ancient Greeks were perceptions of the female as inferior to the male in both mind and body. Similarly, the structure of civil legislation inherited from the ancient Romans was biased against women, and the views on women developed by Christian thinkers out of the Hebrew Bible and the Christian New Testament were negative and disabling. Literary works composed in the vernacular of ordinary people, and widely recited or read, conveyed these negative assumptions. The social networks within which most women lived—those of the family and the institutions of the Roman Catholic Church—were shaped by this negative tradition and sharply limited the areas in which women might act in and upon the world.

GREEK PHILOSOPHY AND FEMALE NATURE. Greek biology assumed that women were inferior to men and defined them as merely childbearers and housekeepers. This view was authoritatively expressed in the works of the philosopher Aristotle.

Aristotle thought in dualities. He considered action superior to inaction, form (the inner design or structure of any object) superior to matter, completion to incompletion, possession to deprivation. In each of these dualities, he associated the male principle with the superior quality and the female with the inferior. "The male principle in nature," he argued, "is associated with active, formative and perfected characteristics, while the female is passive, material and deprived, desiring the male in order to become complete."[1] Men are always identified with virile qualities, such as judgment, courage, and stamina, and women with their opposites—irrationality, cowardice, and weakness.

The masculine principle was considered superior even in the womb. The man's semen, Aristotle believed, created the form of a new human creature, while the female body contributed only matter. (The existence of the ovum, and with it the other facts of human embryology, was not established until the seventeenth century.) Although the later Greek physician Galen believed there was a female component in generation, contributed by "female semen," the followers of both Aristotle and Galen saw the male role in human generation as more active and more important.

1. Aristotle, *Physics* 1.9.192a20–24, in *The Complete Works of Aristotle,* ed. Jonathan Barnes, rev. Oxford trans., 2 vols. (Princeton, 1984), 1:328.

In the Aristotelian view, the male principle sought always to reproduce itself. The creation of a female was always a mistake, therefore, resulting from an imperfect act of generation. Every female born was considered a "defective" or "mutilated" male (as Aristotle's terminology has variously been translated), a "monstrosity" of nature.[2]

For Greek theorists, the biology of males and females was the key to their psychology. The female was softer and more docile, more apt to be despondent, querulous, and deceitful. Being incomplete, moreover, she craved sexual fulfillment in intercourse with a male. The male was intellectual, active, and in control of his passions.

These psychological polarities derived from the theory that the universe consisted of four elements (earth, fire, air, and water), expressed in human bodies as four "humors" (black bile, yellow bile, blood, and phlegm) considered, respectively, dry, hot, damp, and cold and corresponding to mental states ("melancholic," "choleric," "sanguine," "phlegmatic"). In this scheme the male, sharing the principles of earth and fire, was dry and hot; the female, sharing the principles of air and water, was cold and damp.

Female psychology was further affected by her dominant organ, the uterus (womb), *hystera* in Greek. The passions generated by the womb made women lustful, deceitful, talkative, irrational, indeed—when these affects were in excess—"hysterical."

Aristotle's biology also had social and political consequences. If the male principle was superior and the female inferior, then in the household, as in the state, men should rule and women must be subordinate. That hierarchy did not rule out the companionship of husband and wife, whose cooperation was necessary for the welfare of children and the preservation of property. Such mutuality supported male preeminence.

Aristotle's teacher Plato suggested a different possibility: that men and women might possess the same virtues. The setting for this proposal is the imaginary and ideal Republic that Plato sketches in a dialogue of that name. Here, for a privileged elite capable of leading wisely, all distinctions of class and wealth dissolve, as, consequently, do those of gender. Without households or property, as Plato constructs his ideal society, there is no need for the subordination of women. Women may therefore be educated to the same level as men to assume leadership. Plato's Republic remained imaginary, however. In real societies, the subordination of women remained the norm and the prescription.

2. Aristotle, *Generation of Animals* 2.3.737a27–28, in *The Complete Works,* 1: 1144.

The views of women inherited from the Greek philosophical tradition became the basis for medieval thought. In the thirteenth century, the supreme Scholastic philosopher Thomas Aquinas, among others, still echoed Aristotle's views of human reproduction, of male and female personalities, and of the preeminent male role in the social hierarchy.

ROMAN LAW AND THE FEMALE CONDITION. Roman law, like Greek philosophy, underlay medieval thought and shaped medieval society. The ancient belief that adult property-owning men should administer households and make decisions affecting the community at large is the very fulcrum of Roman law.

About 450 B.C.E., during Rome's republican era, the community's customary law was recorded (legendarily) on twelve tablets erected in the city's central forum. It was later elaborated by professional jurists whose activity increased in the imperial era, when much new legislation was passed, especially on issues affecting family and inheritance. This growing, changing body of laws was eventually codified in the *Corpus of Civil Law* under the direction of the emperor Justinian, generations after the empire ceased to be ruled from Rome. That *Corpus,* read and commented on by medieval scholars from the eleventh century on, inspired the legal systems of most of the cities and kingdoms of Europe.

Laws regarding dowries, divorce, and inheritance pertain primarily to women. Since those laws aimed to maintain and preserve property, the women concerned were those from the property-owning minority. Their subordination to male family members points to the even greater subordination of lower-class and slave women, about whom the laws speak little.

In the early republic, the *paterfamilias,* or "father of the family," possessed *patria potestas,* "paternal power." The term *pater,* "father," in both these cases does not necessarily mean biological father but denotes the head of a household. The father was the person who owned the household's property and, indeed, its human members. The *paterfamilias* had absolute power—including the power, rarely exercised, of life or death—over his wife, his children, and his slaves, as much as his cattle.

Male children could be "emancipated," an act that granted legal autonomy and the right to own property. Those over fourteen could be emancipated by a special grant from the father or automatically by their father's death. But females could never be emancipated; instead, they passed from the authority of their father to that of a husband or, if widowed or orphaned while still unmarried, to a guardian or tutor.

Marriage in its traditional form placed the woman under her husband's authority, or *manus*. He could divorce her on grounds of adultery, drinking wine, or stealing from the household, but she could not divorce him. She could neither possess property in her own right nor bequeath any to her children upon her death. When her husband died, the household property passed not to her but to his male heirs. And when her father died, she had no claim to any family inheritance, which was directed to her brothers or more remote male relatives. The effect of these laws was to exclude women from civil society, itself based on property ownership.

In the later republican and imperial periods, these rules were significantly modified. Women rarely married according to the traditional form. The practice of "free" marriage allowed a woman to remain under her father's authority, to possess property given her by her father (most frequently the "dowry," recoverable from the husband's household on his death), and to inherit from her father. She could also bequeath property to her own children and divorce her husband, just as he could divorce her.

Despite this greater freedom, women still suffered enormous disability under Roman law. Heirs could belong only to the father's side, never the mother's. Moreover, although she could bequeath her property to her children, she could not establish a line of succession in doing so. A woman was "the beginning and end of her own family," said the jurist Ulpian. Moreover, women could play no public role. They could not hold public office, represent anyone in a legal case, or even witness a will. Women had only a private existence and no public personality.

The dowry system, the guardian, women's limited ability to transmit wealth, and total political disability are all features of Roman law adopted by the medieval communities of western Europe, although modified according to local customary laws.

CHRISTIAN DOCTRINE AND WOMEN'S PLACE. The Hebrew Bible and the Christian New Testament authorized later writers to limit women to the realm of the family and to burden them with the guilt of original sin. The passages most fruitful for this purpose were the creation narratives in Genesis and sentences from the Epistles defining women's role within the Christian family and community.

Each of the first two chapters of Genesis contains a creation narrative. In the first "God created man in his own image, in the image of God he created him; male and female he created them" (Gn 1:27). In the second, God created Eve from Adam's rib (2:21–23). Christian theologians relied principally on Genesis 2 for their understanding of the relation between man and woman, interpreting the creation of Eve from Adam as proof of her subordination to him.

The creation story in Genesis 2 leads to that of the temptations in Genesis 3: of Eve by the wily serpent and of Adam by Eve. As read by Christian theologians from Tertullian to Thomas Aquinas, the narrative made Eve responsible for the Fall and its consequences. She instigated the act; she deceived her husband; she suffered the greater punishment. Her disobedience made it necessary for Jesus to be incarnated and to die on the cross. From the pulpit, moralists and preachers for centuries conveyed to women the guilt that they bore for original sin.

The Epistles offered advice to early Christians on building communities of the faithful. Among the matters to be regulated was the place of women. Paul offered views favorable to women in Galatians 3:28: "There is neither Jew nor Greek, there is neither slave nor free, there is neither male nor female; for you are all one in Christ Jesus." Paul also referred to women as his coworkers and placed them on a par with himself and his male coworkers (Phlm 4:2–3; Rom 16:1–3; 1 Cor 16:19). Elsewhere, Paul limited women's possibilities: "But I want you to understand that the head of every man is Christ, the head of a woman is her husband, and the head of Christ is God" (1 Cor 11:3).

Biblical passages by later writers (although attributed to Paul) enjoined women to forgo jewels, expensive clothes, and elaborate coiffures; and they forbade women to "teach or have authority over men," telling them to "learn in silence with all submissiveness" as is proper for one responsible for sin, consoling them, however, with the thought that they will be saved through childbearing (1 Tm 2:9–15). Other texts among the later Epistles defined women as the weaker sex and emphasized their subordination to their husbands (1 Pt 3:7; Col 3:18; Eph 5:22–23).

These passages from the New Testament became the arsenal employed by theologians of the early church to transmit negative attitudes toward women to medieval Christian culture—above all, Tertullian (*On the Apparel of Women*), Jerome (*Against Jovinian*), and Augustine (*The Literal Meaning of Genesis*).

THE IMAGE OF WOMEN IN MEDIEVAL LITERATURE. The philosophical, legal, and religious traditions born in antiquity formed the basis of the medieval intellectual synthesis wrought by trained thinkers, mostly clerics, writing in Latin and based largely in universities. The vernacular literary tradition that developed alongside the learned tradition also spoke about female nature and women's roles. Medieval stories, poems, and epics also portrayed women negatively—as lustful and deceitful—while praising good housekeepers and loyal wives as replicas of the Virgin Mary or the female saints and martyrs.

There is an exception in the movement of "courtly love" that evolved in southern France from the twelfth century. Courtly love was the erotic love between a nobleman and noblewoman, the latter usually superior in social rank. It was always adulterous. From the conventions of courtly love derive modern Western notions of romantic love. The tradition has had an impact disproportionate to its size, for it affected only a tiny elite, and very few women. The exaltation of the female lover probably does not reflect a higher evaluation of women or a step toward their sexual liberation. More likely it gives expression to the social and sexual tensions besetting the knightly class at a specific historical juncture.

The literary fashion of courtly love was on the wane by the thirteenth century, when the widely read *Romance of the Rose* was composed in French by two authors of significantly different dispositions. Guillaume de Lorris composed the initial four thousand verses about 1235, and Jean de Meun added about seventeen thousand verses—more than four times the original—about 1265.

The fragment composed by Guillaume de Lorris stands squarely in the tradition of courtly love. Here the poet, in a dream, is admitted into a walled garden where he finds a magic fountain in which a rosebush is reflected. He longs to pick one rose, but the thorns prevent his doing so, even as he is wounded by arrows from the god of love, whose commands he agrees to obey. The rest of this part of the poem recounts the poet's unsuccessful efforts to pluck the rose.

The longer part of the *Romance* by Jean de Meun also describes a dream. But here allegorical characters give long didactic speeches, providing a social satire on a variety of themes, some pertaining to women. Love is an anxious and tormented state, the poem explains: women are greedy and manipulative, marriage is miserable, beautiful women are lustful, ugly ones cease to please, and a chaste woman is as rare as a black swan.

Shortly after Jean de Meun completed *The Romance of the Rose,* Mathéolus penned his *Lamentations,* a long Latin diatribe against marriage translated into French about a century later. The *Lamentations* sum up medieval attitudes toward women and provoked the important response by Christine de Pizan in her *Book of the City of Ladies.*

In 1355, Giovanni Boccaccio wrote *Il Corbaccio,* another antifeminist manifesto, although ironically by an author whose other works pioneered new directions in Renaissance thought. The former husband of his lover appears to Boccaccio, condemning his unmoderated lust and detailing the defects of women. Boccaccio concedes at the end "how much men naturally surpass women in nobility" and is cured of his desires.[3]

WOMEN'S ROLES: THE FAMILY. The negative perceptions of women expressed in the intellectual tradition are also implicit in the actual roles that women played in European society. Assigned to subordinate positions in the household and the church, they were barred from significant participation in public life.

Medieval European households, like those in antiquity and in non-Western civilizations, were headed by males. It was the male serf (or peasant), feudal lord, town merchant, or citizen who was polled or taxed or succeeded to an inheritance or had any acknowledged public role, although his wife or widow could stand as a temporary surrogate. From about 1100, the position of property-holding males was further enhanced: inheritance was confined to the male, or agnate, line—with depressing consequences for women.

A wife never fully belonged to her husband's family, nor was she a daughter to her father's family. She left her father's house young to marry whomever her parents chose. Her dowry was managed by her husband, and at her death it normally passed to her children by him.

A married woman's life was occupied nearly constantly with cycles of pregnancy, childbearing, and lactation. Women bore children through all the years of their fertility, and many died in childbirth. They were also responsible for raising young children up to six or seven. In the propertied classes that responsibility was shared, since it was common for a wet nurse to take over breast-feeding and for servants to perform other chores.

Women trained their daughters in the household duties appropriate to their status, nearly always tasks associated with textiles: spinning, weaving, sewing, embroidering. Their sons were sent out of the house as apprentices or students, or their training was assumed by fathers in later childhood and adolescence. On the death of her husband, a woman's children became the responsibility of his family. She generally did not take "his" children with

3. Giovanni Boccaccio, *The Corbaccio, or The Labyrinth of Love,* trans. and ed. Anthony K. Cassell, rev. ed. (Binghamton, N.Y., 1993), 71.

her to a new marriage or back to her father's house, except sometimes in the artisan classes.

Women also worked. Rural peasants performed farm chores, merchant wives often practiced their husbands' trades, the unmarried daughters of the urban poor worked as servants or prostitutes. All wives produced or embellished textiles and did the housekeeping, while wealthy ones managed servants. These labors were unpaid or poorly paid but often contributed substantially to family wealth.

WOMEN'S ROLES: THE CHURCH. Membership in a household, whether a father's or a husband's, meant for women a lifelong subordination to others. In western Europe, the Roman Catholic Church offered an alternative to the career of wife and mother. A woman could enter a convent, parallel in function to the monasteries for men that evolved in the early Christian centuries.

In the convent, a woman pledged herself to a celibate life, lived according to strict community rules, and worshiped daily. Often the convent offered training in Latin, allowing some women to become considerable scholars and authors as well as scribes, artists, and musicians. For women who chose the conventual life, the benefits could be enormous, but for numerous others placed in convents by paternal choice, the life could be restrictive and burdensome.

The conventual life declined as an alternative for women as the modern age approached. Reformed monastic institutions resisted responsibility for related female orders. The church increasingly restricted female institutional life by insisting on closer male supervision.

Women often sought other options. Some joined the communities of laywomen that sprang up spontaneously in the thirteenth century in the urban zones of western Europe, especially in Flanders and Italy. Some joined the heretical movements that flourished in late medieval Christendom, whose anticlerical and often antifamily positions particularly appealed to women. In these communities, some women were acclaimed as "holy women" or "saints," whereas others often were condemned as frauds or heretics.

In all, although the options offered to women by the church were sometimes less than satisfactory, they were sometimes richly rewarding. After 1520, the convent remained an option only in Roman Catholic territories. Protestantism engendered an ideal of marriage as a heroic endeavor and appeared to place husband and wife on a more equal footing. Sermons and treatises, however, still called for female subordination and obedience.

THE OTHER VOICE, 1300–1700

When the modern era opened, European culture was so firmly structured by a framework of negative attitudes toward women that to dismantle it was a monumental labor. The process began as part of a larger cultural movement that entailed the critical reexamination of ideas inherited from the ancient and medieval past. The humanists launched that critical reexamination.

THE HUMANIST FOUNDATION. Originating in Italy in the fourteenth century, humanism quickly became the dominant intellectual movement in Europe. Spreading in the sixteenth century from Italy to the rest of Europe, it fueled the literary, scientific, and philosophical movements of the era and laid the basis for the eighteenth-century Enlightenment.

Humanists regarded the Scholastic philosophy of medieval universities as out of touch with the realities of urban life. They found in the rhetorical discourse of classical Rome a language adapted to civic life and public speech. They learned to read, speak, and write classical Latin and, eventually, classical Greek. They founded schools to teach others to do so, establishing the pattern for elementary and secondary education for the next three hundred years.

In the service of complex government bureaucracies, humanists employed their skills to write eloquent letters, deliver public orations, and formulate public policy. They developed new scripts for copying manuscripts and used the new printing press to disseminate texts, for which they created methods of critical editing.

Humanism was a movement led by males who accepted the evaluation of women in ancient texts and generally shared the misogynist perceptions of their culture. (Female humanists, as we will see, did not.) Yet humanism also opened the door to a reevaluation of the nature and capacity of women. By calling authors, texts, and ideas into question, it made possible the fundamental rereading of the whole intellectual tradition that was required in order to free women from cultural prejudice and social subordination.

A DIFFERENT CITY. The other voice first appeared when, after so many centuries, the accumulation of misogynist concepts evoked a response from a capable female defender: Christine de Pizan (1365–1431). Introducing her *Book of the City of Ladies* (1405), she described how she was affected by reading Mathéolus's *Lamentations*: "Just the sight of this book . . . made me wonder how it happened that so many different men . . . are so inclined to express both in speaking and in their treatises and writings so many wicked insults about women and their behavior."[4] These statements impelled her to detest herself "and the entire feminine sex, as though we were monstrosities in nature."[5]

The rest of *The Book of the City of Ladies* presents a justification of the female sex and a vision of an ideal community of women. A pioneer, she has received the message of female inferiority and rejected it. From the fourteenth to the seventeenth century, a huge body of literature accumulated that responded to the dominant tradition.

The result was a literary explosion consisting of works by both men and women, in Latin and in the vernaculars: works enumerating the achievements of notable women; works rebutting the main accusations made against women; works arguing for the equal education of men and women; works defining and redefining women's proper role in the family, at court, in public; works describing women's lives and experiences. Recent monographs and articles have begun to hint at the great range of this movement, involving probably several thousand titles. The protofeminism of these "other voices" constitutes a significant fraction of the literary product of the early modern era.

THE CATALOGS. About 1365, the same Boccaccio whose *Corbaccio* rehearses the usual charges against female nature wrote another work, *Concerning Famous Women.* A humanist treatise drawing on classical texts, it praised 106 notable women: ninety-eight of them from pagan Greek and Roman antiquity, one (Eve) from the Bible, and seven from the medieval religious and cultural tradition; his book helped make all readers aware of a sex normally condemned or forgotten. Boccaccio's outlook nevertheless was unfriendly to women, for it singled out for praise those women who possessed the traditional virtues of chastity, silence, and obedience. Women who were active in the public realm—for example, rulers and warriors—were depicted as usually being lascivious and as suffering terrible punishments for entering the masculine sphere. Women were his subject, but Boccaccio's standard remained male.

Christine de Pizan's *Book of the City of Ladies* contains a second catalog, one responding specifically to Boccaccio's. Whereas Boccaccio portrays female virtue as exceptional, she depicts it as universal. Many women in his-

4. Christine de Pizan, *The Book of the City of Ladies,* trans. Earl Jeffrey Richards, foreword by Marina Warner (New York, 1982), 1.1.1, pp. 3–4.

5. Ibid., 1.1.1–2, p. 5.

tory were leaders, or remained chaste despite the lascivious approaches of men, or were visionaries and brave martyrs.

The work of Boccaccio inspired a series of catalogs of illustrious women of the biblical, classical, Christian, and local pasts, among them Filippo da Bergamo's *Of Illustrious Women,* Pierre de Brantôme's *Lives of Illustrious Women,* Pierre Le Moyne's *Gallerie of Heroic Women,* and Pietro Paolo de Ribera's *Immortal Triumphs and Heroic Enterprises of 845 Women.* Whatever their embedded prejudices, these works drove home to the public the possibility of female excellence.

THE DEBATE. At the same time, many questions remained: Could a woman be virtuous? Could she perform noteworthy deeds? Was she even, strictly speaking, of the same human species as men? These questions were debated over four centuries, in French, German, Italian, Spanish, and English, by authors male and female, among Catholics, Protestants, and Jews, in ponderous volumes and breezy pamphlets. The whole literary genre has been called the *querelle des femmes,* the "woman question."

The opening volley of this battle occurred in the first years of the fifteenth century, in a literary debate sparked by Christine de Pizan. She exchanged letters critical of Jean de Meun's contribution to *The Romance of the Rose* with two French royal secretaries, Jean de Montreuil and Gontier Col. When the matter became public, Jean Gerson, one of Europe's leading theologians, supported de Pizan's arguments against de Meun, for the moment silencing the opposition.

The debate resurfaced repeatedly over the next two hundred years. *The Triumph of Women* (1438) by Juan Rodríguez de la Camara (or Juan Rodríguez del Padron) struck a new note by presenting arguments for the superiority of women to men. *The Champion of Women* (1440–42) by Martin Le Franc addresses once again the negative views of women presented in *The Romance of the Rose* and offers counterevidence of female virtue and achievement.

A cameo of the debate on women is included in *The Courtier,* one of the most widely read books of the era, published by the Italian Baldassare Castiglione in 1528 and immediately translated into other European vernaculars. *The Courtier* depicts a series of evenings at the court of the duke of Urbino in which many men and some women of the highest social stratum amuse themselves by discussing a range of literary and social issues. The "woman question" is a pervasive theme throughout, and the third of its four books is devoted entirely to that issue.

In a verbal duel, Gasparo Pallavicino and Giuliano de' Medici present the main claims of the two traditions. Gasparo argues the innate inferiority of women and their inclination to vice. Only in bearing children do they profit the world. Giuliano counters that women share the same spiritual and mental capacities as men and may excel in wisdom and action. Men and women are of the same essence: just as no stone can be more perfectly a stone than another, so no human being can be more perfectly human than others, whether male or female. It was an astonishing assertion, boldly made to an audience as large as all Europe.

THE TREATISES. Humanism provided the materials for a positive counterconcept to the misogyny embedded in Scholastic philosophy and law and inherited from the Greek, Roman, and Christian pasts. A series of humanist treatises on marriage and family, on education and deportment, and on the nature of women helped construct these new perspectives.

The works by Francesco Barbaro and Leon Battista Alberti—*On Marriage* (1415) and *On the Family* (1434–37)—far from defending female equality, reasserted women's responsibility for rearing children and managing the housekeeping while being obedient, chaste, and silent. Nevertheless, they served the cause of reexamining the issue of women's nature by placing domestic issues at the center of scholarly concern and reopening the pertinent classical texts. In addition, Barbaro emphasized the companionate nature of marriage and the importance of a wife's spiritual and mental qualities for the well-being of the family.

These themes reappear in later humanist works on marriage and the education of women by Juan Luis Vives and Erasmus. Both were moderately sympathetic to the condition of women without reaching beyond the usual masculine prescriptions for female behavior.

An outlook more favorable to women characterizes the nearly unknown work *In Praise of Women* (ca. 1487) by the Italian humanist Bartolommeo Goggio. In addition to providing a catalog of illustrious women, Goggio argued that male and female are the same in essence, but that women (reworking the Adam and Eve narrative from quite a new angle) are actually superior. In the same vein, the Italian humanist Mario Equicola asserted the spiritual equality of men and women in *On Women* (1501). In 1525, Galeazzo Flavio Capra (or Capella) published his work *On the Excellence and Dignity of Women*. This humanist tradition of treatises defending the worthiness of women culminates in the work of Henricus Cornelius Agrippa *On the Nobility and Preeminence of the Female Sex*. No work by a male humanist more succinctly or explicitly presents the case for female dignity.

THE WITCH BOOKS. While humanists grappled with the issues pertaining to women and family, other learned men turned their attention to what they perceived as a very great problem: witches. Witch-hunting manuals, explorations of the witch phenomenon, and even defenses of witches are not at first glance pertinent to the tradition of the other voice. But they do relate in this way: most accused witches were women. The hostility aroused by supposed witch activity is comparable to the hostility aroused by women. The evil deeds the victims of the hunt were charged with were exaggerations of the vices to which, many believed, all women were prone.

The connection between the witch accusation and the hatred of women is explicit in the notorious witch-hunting manual *The Hammer of Witches* (1486) by two Dominican inquisitors, Heinrich Krämer and Jacob Sprenger. Here the inconstancy, deceitfulness, and lustfulness traditionally associated with women are depicted in exaggerated form as the core features of witch behavior. These traits inclined women to make a bargain with the devil—sealed by sexual intercourse—by which they acquired unholy powers. Such bizarre claims, far from being rejected by rational men, were broadcast by intellectuals. The German Ulrich Molitur, the Frenchman Nicolas Rémy, and the Italian Stefano Guazzo all coolly informed the public of sinister orgies and midnight pacts with the devil. The celebrated French jurist, historian, and political philosopher Jean Bodin argued that because women were especially prone to diabolism, regular legal procedures could properly be suspended in order to try those accused of this "exceptional crime."

A few experts such as the physician Johann Weyer, a student of Agrippa's, raised their voices in protest. In 1563, he explained the witch phenomenon thus, without discarding belief in diabolism: the devil deluded foolish old women afflicted by melancholia, causing them to believe they had magical powers. Weyer's rational skepticism, which had good credibility in the community of the learned, worked to revise the conventional views of women and witchcraft.

WOMEN'S WORKS. To the many categories of works produced on the question of women's worth must be added nearly all works written by women. A woman writing was in herself a statement of women's claim to dignity.

Only a few women wrote anything before the dawn of the modern era, for three reasons. First, they rarely received the education that would enable them to write. Second, they were not admitted to the public roles—as administrator, bureaucrat, lawyer or notary, or university professor—in which they might gain knowledge of the kinds of things the literate public thought worth writing about. Third, the culture imposed silence on women, considering speaking out a form of unchastity. Given these conditions, it is remarkable that any women wrote. Those who did before the fourteenth century were almost always nuns or religious women whose isolation made their pronouncements more acceptable.

From the fourteenth century on, the volume of women's writings rose. Women continued to write devotional literature, although not always as cloistered nuns. They also wrote diaries, often intended as keepsakes for their children; books of advice to their sons and daughters; letters to family members and friends; and family memoirs, in a few cases elaborate enough to be considered histories.

A few women wrote works directly concerning the "woman question," and some of these, such as the humanists Isotta Nogarola, Cassandra Fedele, Laura Cereta, and Olympia Morata, were highly trained. A few were professional writers, living by the income of their pens; the very first among them was Christine de Pizan, noteworthy in this context as in so many others. In addition to *The Book of the City of Ladies* and her critiques of *The Romance of the Rose,* she wrote *The Treasure of the City of Ladies* (a guide to social decorum for women), an advice book for her son, much courtly verse, and a full-scale history of the reign of King Charles V of France.

WOMEN PATRONS. Women who did not themselves write but encouraged others to do so boosted the development of an alternative tradition. Highly placed women patrons supported authors, artists, musicians, poets, and learned men. Such patrons, drawn mostly from the Italian elites and the courts of northern Europe, figure disproportionately as the dedicatees of the important works of early feminism.

For a start, it might be noted that the catalogs of Boccaccio and Alvaro de Luna were dedicated to the Florentine noblewoman Andrea Acciaiuoli and to Doña María, first wife of King Juan II of Castile, while the French translation of Boccaccio's work was commissioned by Anne of Brittany, wife of King Charles VIII of France. The humanist treatises of Goggio, Equicola, Vives, and Agrippa were dedicated, respectively, to Eleanora of Aragon, wife of Ercole I d'Este, duke of Ferrara; to Margherita Cantelma of Mantua; to Catherine of Aragon, wife of King Henry VIII of England; and to Margaret, Duchess of Austria and regent of the Netherlands. As late as 1696, Mary Astell's *Serious Proposal to the Ladies, for the Advancement of Their True and Greatest Interest* was dedicated to Princess Anne of Denmark.

These authors presumed that their efforts would be welcome to female patrons, or they may have written at the bidding of those patrons. Silent themselves, perhaps even unresponsive, these loftily placed women helped shape the tradition of the other voice.

THE ISSUES. The literary forms and patterns in which the tradition of the other voice presented itself have now been sketched. It remains to highlight the major issues around which this tradition crystallizes. In brief, there are four problems to which our authors return again and again, in plays and catalogs, in verse and letters, in treatises and dialogues, in every language: the problem of chastity, the problem of power, the problem of speech, and the problem of knowledge. Of these the greatest, preconditioning the others, is the problem of chastity.

THE PROBLEM OF CHASTITY. In traditional European culture, as in those of antiquity and others around the globe, chastity was perceived as woman's quintessential virtue—in contrast to courage, or generosity, or leadership, or rationality, seen as virtues characteristic of men. Opponents of women charged them with insatiable lust. Women themselves and their defenders—without disputing the validity of the standard—responded that women were capable of chastity.

The requirement of chastity kept women at home, silenced them, isolated them, left them in ignorance. It was the source of all other impediments. Why was it so important to the society of men, of whom chastity was not required, and who more often than not considered it their right to violate the chastity of any woman they encountered?

Female chastity ensured the continuity of the male-headed household. If a man's wife was not chaste, he could not be sure of the legitimacy of his offspring. If they were not his and they acquired his property, it was not his household, but some other man's, that had endured. If his daughter was not chaste, she could not be transferred to another man's household as his wife, and he was dishonored.

The whole system of the integrity of the household and the transmission of property was bound up in female chastity. Such a requirement pertained only to property-owning classes, of course. Poor women could not expect to maintain their chastity, least of all if they were in contact with high-status men to whom all women but those of their own household were prey.

In Catholic Europe, the requirement of chastity was further buttressed by moral and religious imperatives. Original sin was inextricably linked with the sexual act. Virginity was seen as heroic virtue, far more impressive than, say, the avoidance of idleness or greed. Monasticism, the cultural institution that dominated medieval Europe for centuries, was grounded in the renunciation of the flesh. The Catholic reform of the eleventh century imposed a similar standard on all the clergy and a heightened awareness of sexual requirements on all the laity. Although men were asked to be chaste, female unchastity was much worse: it led to the devil, as Eve had led mankind to sin.

To such requirements, women and their defenders protested their innocence. Furthermore, following the example of holy women who had escaped the requirements of family and sought the religious life, some women began to conceive of female communities as alternatives both to family and to the cloister. Christine de Pizan's city of ladies was such a community. Moderata Fonte and Mary Astell envisioned others. The luxurious salons of the French *précieuses* of the seventeenth century, or the comfortable English drawing rooms of the next, may have been born of the same impulse. Here women not only might escape, if briefly, the subordinate position that life in the family entailed but might also make claims to power, exercise their capacity for speech, and display their knowledge.

THE PROBLEM OF POWER. Women were excluded from power: the whole cultural tradition insisted on it. Only men were citizens, only men bore arms, only men could be chiefs or lords or kings. There were exceptions that did not disprove the rule, when wives or widows or mothers took the place of men, awaiting their return or the maturation of a male heir. A woman who attempted to rule in her own right was perceived as an anomaly, a monster, at once a deformed woman and an insufficient male, sexually confused and consequently unsafe.

The association of such images with women who held or sought power explains some otherwise odd features of early modern culture. Queen Elizabeth I of England, one of the few women to hold full regal authority in European history, played with such male/female images—positive ones, of course—in representing herself to her subjects. She was a prince, and manly, even though she was female. She was also (she claimed) virginal, a condition absolutely essential if she was to avoid the attacks of her opponents. Catherine de' Medici, who ruled France as widow and regent for her sons, also adopted such imagery in defining her position. She chose as one symbol the figure of Artemisia, an androgynous ancient warrior-heroine who combined a female persona with masculine powers.

Power in a woman, without such sexual imagery, seems to have been indigestible by the culture. A rare note was struck by the Englishman Sir Thomas Elyot in his *Defence of Good Women* (1540), justifying both women's participation in civic life and their prowess in arms. The old tune was sung by the Scots reformer John Knox in his *First Blast of the Trumpet against the Mon-*

strous Regiment of Women (1558); for him rule by women, defects in nature, was a hideous contradiction in terms.

The confused sexuality of the imagery of female potency was not reserved for rulers. Any woman who excelled was likely to be called an Amazon, recalling the self-mutilated warrior women of antiquity who repudiated all men, gave up their sons, and raised only their daughters. She was often said to have "exceeded her sex" or to have possessed "masculine virtue"—as the very fact of conspicuous excellence conferred masculinity even on the female subject. The catalogs of notable women often showed those female heroes dressed in armor, armed to the teeth, like men. Amazonian heroines romp through the epics of the age—Ariosto's *Orlando Furioso* (1532) and Spenser's *Faerie Queene* (1590–1609). Excellence in a woman was perceived as a claim for power, and power was reserved for the masculine realm. A woman who possessed either one was masculinized and lost title to her own female identity.

THE PROBLEM OF SPEECH. Just as power had a sexual dimension when it was claimed by women, so did speech. A good woman spoke little. Excessive speech was an indication of unchastity. By speech, women seduced men. Eve had lured Adam into sin by her speech. Accused witches were commonly accused of having spoken abusively, or irrationally, or simply too much. As enlightened a figure as Francesco Barbaro insisted on silence in a woman, which he linked to her perfect unanimity with her husband's will and her unblemished virtue (her chastity). Another Italian humanist, Leonardo Bruni, in advising a noblewoman on her studies, barred her not from speech but from public speaking. That was reserved for men.

Related to the problem of speech was that of costume—another, if silent, form of self-expression. Assigned the task of pleasing men as their primary occupation, elite women often tended toward elaborate costume, hairdressing, and the use of cosmetics. Clergy and secular moralists alike condemned these practices. The appropriate function of costume and adornment was to announce the status of a woman's husband or father. Any further indulgence in adornment was akin to unchastity.

THE PROBLEM OF KNOWLEDGE. When the Italian noblewoman Isotta Nogarola had begun to attain a reputation as a humanist, she was accused of incest—a telling instance of the association of learning in women with unchastity. That chilling association inclined any woman who was educated to deny that she was or to make exaggerated claims of heroic chastity.

If educated women were pursued with suspicions of sexual misconduct, women seeking an education faced an even more daunting obstacle: the assumption that women were by nature incapable of learning, that reasoning was a particularly masculine ability. Just as they proclaimed their chastity, women and their defenders insisted on their capacity for learning. The major work by a male writer on female education—that by Juan Luis Vives, *On the Education of a Christian Woman* (1523)—granted female capacity for intellection but still argued that a woman's whole education was to be shaped around the requirement of chastity and a future within the household. Female writers of the following generations—Marie de Gournay in France, Anna Maria van Schurman in Holland, and Mary Astell in England—began to envision other possibilities.

The pioneers of female education were the Italian women humanists who managed to attain a literacy in Latin and a knowledge of classical and Christian literature equivalent to that of prominent men. Their works implicitly and explicitly raise questions about women's social roles, defining problems that beset women attempting to break out of the cultural limits that had bound them. Like Christine de Pizan, who achieved an advanced education through her father's tutoring and her own devices, their bold questioning makes clear the importance of training. Only when women were educated to the same standard as male leaders would they be able to raise that other voice and insist on their dignity as human beings morally, intellectually, and legally equal to men.

THE OTHER VOICE. The other voice, a voice of protest, was mostly female, but it was also male. It spoke in the vernaculars and in Latin, in treatises and dialogues, in plays and poetry, in letters and diaries, and in pamphlets. It battered at the wall of prejudice that encircled women and raised a banner announcing its claims. The female was equal (or even superior) to the male in essential nature—moral, spiritual, and intellectual. Women were capable of higher education, of holding positions of power and influence in the public realm, and of speaking and writing persuasively. The last bastion of masculine supremacy, centered on the notions of a woman's primary domestic responsibility and the requirement of female chastity, was not as yet assaulted—although visions of productive female communities as alternatives to the family indicated an awareness of the problem.

During the period 1300–1700, the other voice remained only a voice, and one only dimly heard. It did not result—yet—in an alteration of social patterns. Indeed, to this day they have not entirely been altered. Yet the call for justice issued as long as six centuries ago by those writing in the tradition of the other voice must be recognized as the source and origin of the mature feminist tradition and of the realignment of social institutions accomplished in the modern age.

We thank the volume editors in this series, who responded with many suggestions to an earlier draft of this introduction, making it a collaborative enterprise. Many of their suggestions and criticisms have resulted in revisions of this introduction, although we remain responsible for the final product.

Folio 1 (recto) of UCB MS 109, the only extant manuscript copy of the *Debate of the "Romance of the Rose"* in pamphlet form. This manuscript was transcribed by Gontier Col and undoubtedly presented to Jean, duke of Berry, within a few years of the debate. Courtesy of the Bancroft Library, University of California, Berkeley.

VOLUME EDITOR'S INTRODUCTION

THE OTHER VOICE

Christine de Pizan is far from being the first female author in the French literary tradition. One thinks most notably of Marie de France or Clemence, an English nun of Barking, two twelfth-century pioneers.[1] Yet what distinguishes Christine, and in fact defines the significance of the debate over the *Romance of the Rose,* is her adamant staking out of a position as a woman in the male-dominated world of letters. More than a verbal protest against obscenity or misogyny (which it certainly is), the debate is an active counterassault against an entire intellectual establishment to which women were solely the object of discussion, and which greatly limited their ability to take up the subject position in speech. The period of Christine's early career, extending from *The God of Love's Letter* (1399) to the *City of Ladies* (1405), shows her opposing the clerical establishment by her tendentious definition of the female voice as the "other" voice, speaking against a characteristic mistreatment of women. As she has the God of Love say in his rebuke of misogynistic writings, the reason for this state of affairs is that "women did not make the books," adding that "if women had written the books . . . the facts would be different."

1. After the Norman Conquest of 1066, French remained officially the language of the aristocracy in England until the end of the fourteenth century. The French literary tradition of this early period thus includes works written on the Continent and Anglo-Norman works composed in Britain; indeed, through the mid- to late twelfth century, the production of French works in England and their preservation in manuscript were at the forefront of literary activity in the Francophone world. Little is known of Clemence, a French-speaking nun of English birth (unlike Marie who, while probably working in Britain, perhaps at the court of King Henry II, identifies herself as being "from France"), except for her statement at the end of a hagiographical work, the *Life of Saint Catherine:* "I am named Clemence and am a nun from Barking." Many scholars suspect that another, anonymous, work produced at the same convent, a life of Saint Edward the Confessor, was also written by Clemence.

Indeed, Christine constructed a mythology around her assumption of the "other voice" that made of her a privileged, unique female interlocutor, of which the epistolary exchange is perhaps the foundational emblem. Rather than styling herself as "Everywoman," she makes it quite clear that her position is exceptional. The trajectory in the development of this mythology extends from the God of Love's complaint about women's absence in the world of letters, to the visitation of three ladies, Reason, Rectitude and Justice, who come to Christine's study and endow her with the mission of constructing the city made up of the tales of illustrious women from antiquity and recent history in the *City of Ladies,* to Nature's memory of having urged her to give birth to the products of her mind at the beginning of her career (in *Christine's Vision*).

In the context of this trajectory, the *Rose* debate represents more than a statement: it is a crucial *staging* of Christine's movement from disenfranchised woman to female author. From her first intervention in the debate, her letter in response to Jean de Montreuil's now-lost treatise in defense of the *Romance of the Rose* (no. 5 below), she plays with the characteristics of her positioning as female. What are for us her uncomfortable apologies for her intellectual inferiority, frequently associated with her status as a woman ("May [my untrained intellect and uncomplicated sensibility] in no way induce your wisdom to scorn the slightness of my arguments, but rather to consent to make up for their deficiency out of consideration for my feminine weakness"), are belied by the sharpness and precision of her objections to the *Rose.* But what is crucial here is perhaps less the content of her arguments than the fact of establishing a dialogue with her interlocutors from a female perspective. In fact, one of the most intriguing aspects of Christine's intervention is the nature of the position she occupies, which is not fully resolved at the outset. Is she using her position as a woman to attack a male establishment, or is she assuming a male voice as she enters into dialogue with her clerical opponents? Christine frequently relies on the question of experience. Does her having lived as a woman make her more qualified to speak on their behalf? Later in this first letter, she waffles somewhat, stating first that she is speaking not as a woman but on behalf of truth, yet only two lines later, she says that because of her experience as a woman she is "better suited to attest to these matters."

This initial problem underlines a paradox that will occupy Christine throughout this entire period: the struggle between a quest for truth that is independent of individual contingencies and particularities, on the one hand, and the features of personal experience and observation that are themselves conduits to truth, on the other. But inevitably this divide is itself gender-determined, inasmuch as "experience" for Christine is irreducibly tied to her femininity, while the universality of truths is yoked to clerical learning, and therefore a male universe. Hence the striking image Christine gives in the opening section of the *Book of Fortune's Transformation,* in which she describes the physical transformation of her body into that of a man as a metaphor for the change in her life after the death of her husband:

> I felt myself completely transformed. I felt my limbs to be stronger than before, and the great pain and lamentation which had earlier dominated me, I felt to be somewhat lessened. Then I touched myself all over my body, like one completely bewildered. . . . Then I felt myself much lighter than usual and I felt that my flesh was changed and strengthened, and my voice much lowered, and my body harder and faster. . . . Thus I became a true man (this is no fable) . . . I am still a man and I have been for a total of more than thirteen full years, but it would please me much more to be a woman.[2]

Accordingly, one would be underestimating Christine if one simply understood her as advocating a woman's voice in resistance to a male-dominated world. Not only do her various statements about gender suggest a somewhat ambivalent stance on that subject, but she is also quite aware of the complexities of voicing (what we might call authorial ventriloquism, speaking as an other). As early as her *Hundred Ballads* (1399), she intermingles poems in her own voice, sorrowful laments over her widowhood, with poems of indeterminate voice, including ones spoken by men. She even reveals the artifice of her statements of passion in certain of these poems when, in the strategically placed fiftieth ballad, she claims that she is indifferent to love and that these poems thus do not originate in her own feelings—such is, after all, the nature of the poet. Likewise, in the course of the debate, the dismay and outrage of Christine's reaction to the defenders of the *Rose* and, more generally, to clerical misogyny are quite obvious, yet in two places (at the end of her last letter in the debate, the one addressed to Pierre Col [no. 23], and in her dedicatory letter to Guillaume de Tignonville [no. 17]) she stresses the amiable nature of the debate, as a source of diversion.

That the enigma of sincerity may be one that she plays with here is underscored by another circumstance. More than a participant in the debate, Christine was responsible for packaging it and diffusing it to prominent

2. *The Selected Writings of Christine de Pizan,* ed. Renate Blumenfeld-Kosinski, trans. Renate Blumenfeld-Kosinski and Kevin Brownlee (New York: W. W. Norton, 1997), 106–7.

members of the French court, in booklet format.[3] The apparently submissive and victimized position of the female poet is belied by the controlling gesture of the publisher. If one takes the situation as a whole, to insist exclusively upon Christine's seriousness in support of the defense of women is at the same time to discount her cleverness and her control of both the issues and the strategies of rhetorical argumentation. It is to buy into her insistence upon her simplicity, her straightforward style, her lack of sophistication, and her need to defend herself—placing her in the position of helpless female that she constructs for herself, while ignoring the gender transformation that she herself affirms and that is echoed by her ally Jean Gerson, when he calls her "a strong or manly woman" (*virilis illa femina*) or even an "Amazon" (*virago*), both comments made in praise of her debating skills.[4] The ambiguity of Christine's gender positioning, the sincerity of her voice versus its manipulation as a mask, the nature of experience, knowledge, and opinion, the idiosyncratic professionalism of the writer/publisher—these are all tantalizing aspects of Christine's poetic persona that make up an important network of issues opposing her to Jean de Meun, author of the *Romance of the Rose,* an equally inscrutable writer, at the same time that they circumscribe the irreducible fascination of this pioneering literary figure.

CHRISTINE DE PIZAN'S WORLD

Christine de Pizan was born in Venice, Italy, in 1365 but spent her earliest years in the town of Pizzano (near Bologna).[5] Her father, Tommaso da Pizzano (whose name was frenchified as Thomas de Pizan), was a well-known

3. Although we know that she sent copies of the dossier by itself to Isabeau de Bavière and Guillaume de Tignonville, the only extant booklet version of the debate, of which perhaps many were prepared, is University of California, Berkeley, Bancroft Library MS 109, which was owned at one time by the duke of Berry. All other extant copies overseen by Christine are found in the large manuscripts containing her collected works.

4. These terms are both used by Gerson to refer to Christine toward the beginning of his Latin rebuke of Pierre Col's letter (no. 28 below). The terms *virilis* and *virago* have as their root the Latin noun *vir* (man), and therefore designate qualities coded as masculine. The first expression means quite literally "manly woman" whereas the second frequently extends this meaning to refer to a heroine or even to a female warrior, hence "Amazon." Since Gerson uses these two expressions synonymously in one same sentence, I have translated both as "manly woman."

5. Christine's early dates all revolve around the death of her husband: She tells us that he died of the plague on a trip to Beauvais with King Charles VI, that she was twenty-five years old when he died, and that they had been married for ten years. As Reno and Dulac affirm, Etienne's death must have occurred "between October 29 and November 7, 1390," as this was the only trip during that period that the king made to Beauvais (*Le livre de l'advision Christine,* ed. Christine Reno and Liliane Dulac [Paris: Honoré Champion, 2001], 177–78).

doctor and astrologist whose renown brought him to the attention of King Charles V of France. He was summoned to the French court and, three years later, around 1369, the young Christine and her mother came to join him. Christine's father was a greatly admired, handsomely compensated servant to the king, and she spent her childhood and adolescence in the court environs. Her father taught her to read and write, which was quite exceptional for a female at this time. She was married, probably in 1380, to Etienne de Castel,[6] a Picard nobleman who worked as secretary to the king. The next decade brought a series of personal tragedies to Christine, the successive deaths of Charles V (1380) and of her father (some time between 1385 and 1390), both of whom she revered, and of her husband (1390). Christine was left with three children, her mother, and a niece to support; financial exigency led her thereafter to use her nascent literary skills to earn a living.

The world into which Christine was born was a troubling one, burdened by political strife and harsh living conditions. A crisis of royal succession early in the century launched what would be one of the most long-lived and deadly of political conflicts in European history, the Hundred Years' War. In 1328, the last of the three sons of Philip the Fair died on the throne, ending the direct male succession of the Capetian line (which had lasted for over three hundred years). The English kings, dating back to the Norman Conquest, were French speakers and vassals of the king of France; they frequently intermarried with the French royal line. Edward III, who reigned in England from 1327 to 1377, felt he had a legitimate claim to the French throne, as he was the grandson of Philip the Fair through the latter's daughter Isabelle and thus the only direct male heir. But unwritten custom (which would later be formulated as the Salic law) had excluded from the throne not only women but also the succession of their male descendants; consequently, the kingdom went to Philip of Valois, Philip the Fair's nephew, son of his younger brother.

There were ebbs and flows in the course of this conflict, but it was not definitively put to rest until the Aquitaine region was conquered from the English in 1453. The succession crisis inaugurated a lengthy period of warfare, hostage taking, and ransoms, along with a staggering loss of life. In 1356, the father of the future Charles V, King John II, was taken prisoner at the disastrous battle of Poitiers and held for four years until peace was nego-

6. The form of the name of Christine's husband and son is found as *Castel* or *de Castel*, and, probably incorrectly, as *du Castel*. As Antoine Thomas determined long ago ("Jean Castel," *Romania* 21 [1892]: 274), *de Castel* was the "official form, used by the family itself" and was also the way Christine's husband signed official documents as secretary to the king, but in regular usage one seems simply to have used *Castel*.

tiated. The Black Plague struck Europe in the period 1347–50, during which, as most estimates suggest, at least one-third of its population perished. Epidemics recurred regularly after that devastating pestilence. The memories of these events would have been quite alive throughout Christine's youth.

Other rifts put pressure on social cohesion. The papacy had moved from Rome to Avignon early in the fourteenth century, and in 1378 rival claims of the pope in Avignon and a newly chosen Roman pope led to the Great Schism, which would last until 1417. King Charles VI, who succeeded his father Charles V, started showing signs of madness in 1392, and from that moment forward the realm itself was adrift, as it was essentially ruled by the king's uncles, the dukes of Burgundy and of Berry. When the duke of Burgundy, Philip the Bold, died in 1404, he was succeeded by his son John the Fearless, whose rivalry with his cousin the duke of Orléans, the king's brother, led to his assassination of the latter in 1407. Thus was unleashed a relentless, and often bloody, civil dispute (known as the clash between the Burgundians and the Armagnacs) that would last for decades. This civil strife would dovetail with a revival of aggression on the part of the English king, Henry V, just two years after he succeeded to the throne, culminating in one of France's greatest military calamities, the battle of Agincourt in 1415; only a few years later, Charles VI's cession of the throne of France to the English king pushed it to the brink of disaster.

But at the same time, literary and artistic culture was at the very beginning of a movement that we now widely refer to as the Renaissance. Whereas artists of the time in France felt very little influence from Italy, the budding *literati* of the French intellectual milieu in the late fourteenth century were acutely aware of the humanistic movement in Italy, especially under the important influence of Petrarch (perhaps because of the international nature of Latinate culture and the bonds it formed across Europe). Jean de Montreuil and his entourage, who either participated directly in the debate (Pierre and Gontier Col) or simply might have been aware of it (Nicolas de Clamanges), represent the important clerical establishment, having religious training yet working in the secular space of the royal bureaucracy as secretaries, scribes, and ambassadors. Christine's husband had likewise been a secretary to the king, a fact that undoubtedly explains her familiarity with his former colleagues.

The grim realities of life seem to have sent patrons and scholars alike to an inner world dominated by learning and the book. The late fourteenth and first half of the fifteenth century saw the manufacture of some of the most dazzlingly beautiful of any decorated manuscripts produced during the Middle Ages. The members of the royal family, in particular Charles V and the dukes of Burgundy and Berry, are renowned for having been great patrons of the arts, and especially the literary arts. The collection of books put together by Charles V, including copies of books that he commissioned, many of them lavishly illustrated, along with original translations of works from Latin to French, forms the core of what is now one of the greatest manuscript collections in the world, that belonging to the National Library of France. It seems doubtless that Christine had access to the King's library and that much of her early initiation into literary and philosophical writing might have come through her frequentation of his books.

Perhaps as a type of distraction from the political and social woes of the realm, the ideals of chivalry and praise of women and love were being revisited and formulated anew. The "type" of the knight/love poet was likewise revived, as we find notably in an important poetic compilation, the *Hundred Ballads* (1389), the fruit of the collaboration of a small group of these poets, in which an older knight gives advice to a younger one on fidelity in love, only to have his advice contradicted afterward by a woman, who speaks of the virtues of coquettishness. In the closing years of the fifteenth century, official associations devoted to chivalry, love, and the defense of women were formed, most notably the Order of the Golden Shield, founded by Louis de Bourbon in order to "honor ladies and demoiselles and not tolerate slander of them," and the Order of the White Lady with the Green Shield (1400), with which the young knight/poet Boucicault proposed to lift his sword in the service of ladies. The so-called Court of Love of Charles VI, the charter of which has come down to us, was established on Saint Valentine's day 1401 (n.s.) in the Parisian *hôtel* of the duke of Burgundy, likewise for the praise of women and love.[7] Among the hundreds of conservators, ministers, and other officers of the Court of Love are found virtually all the great nobles and knights of the realm, as well as notable squires, chamberlains, and bureaucrats, members of the bourgeoisie and lower nobility—including, among the participants in the debate, Jean de Montreuil, Guillaume de Tignonville, and the brothers Col. In the list of statutes for this group, one of the reasons for its foundation at this time, which coincides

7. The opening lines of the charter specify that the statutes were made public at the *Hôtel* of Artois (otherwise known as the *Hôtel* of Bourgogne), the only vestige of which is the Tower of John the Fearless, built in 1410 and one of the few remaining medieval buildings in present-day Paris. Christine herself adds to this current in her *Dit de la Rose* (Poem of the Rose, dated Saint Valentine's Day 1402 [n.s.]), in which, recalling a celebration that took place at the *hôtel* of the duke of Orléans in January of that year, she is appointed to found the Order of the Rose, reward for knights who protect the honor of women. Not coincidentally, Christine's first version of the debate documents was sent to the queen on February 1, in the period between the founding of the Order of the Rose and Christine's account of it on February 14.

with the beginnings of the *Rose* debate, was "to spend part of the time more pleasantly and to find once again a renewal of joy," for this was a period, it says, of "unpleasant and deadly pestilence arising from an epidemic at present overrunning this very Christian realm."[8] Indeed for three years, starting in 1399, a dangerous epidemic once again struck France. It is hard not to see in this backdrop a phenomenon comparable to the setting of Boccaccio's *Decameron,* during the Black Death, in which the ten protagonists retire to a country retreat, where storytelling was initiated as a source of pleasure and consolation. Given these circumstances, it is quite plausible that the debate over the *Rose,* in addition to being a serious exchange on moral, religious, and intellectual matters, served as a form of diversion during these profoundly troubling times.

CHRISTINE DE PIZAN'S CAREER

Although Christine speaks of herself and her life in many of her works, the most detailed intellectual autobiography is contained in *Christine's Vision,* written in 1405. The death of her husband in 1390 marked the beginning of her professional career, for she needed to earn money to support her family. This need, however, turned into an opportunity for, as Lady Philosophy tells her by way of consolation, she would never have been able to discover the world of the mind had it not been for her tragic loss. But it was not until 1399 that Christine de Pizan began to produce what would be a swift succession of works extending into the first decade of the fifteenth century. Her first volume, part of which was certainly written by the mid-1390s, was probably her poetry collection, the *Hundred Ballads,* on a variety of topics, including some famous ones devoted to the sorrows of her widowhood. It is scarcely possible to separate Christine's career as an author from her personal publication initiatives, as she makes clear in an important passage from *Christine's Vision:*

> Then I began to forge pretty things, at the beginning of a lighter nature, and just like a craftsman who becomes more and more skillful the more he works, by studying different subject matters my mind filled more and more with new things, improving my style by more subtleness and nobler subject matter. Between the year 1399 when I began writing and the present year, 1405, during which I am still writing, I

8. Carla Bozzolo and Hélène Loyau, *La cour amoureuse dite de Charles VI,* vol. 1: Étude et Édition critique des sources manuscrites (Paris: Le Léopard d'Or, 1982), 36.

> have compiled fifteen major works, without counting some smaller works, which together are contained in seventy large-size quires, as one can see clearly.[9]

For not only did Christine begin writing in 1399, she started copying the first of her major manuscripts of her collected works, which was completed three years later, in June 1402. The works contained in this manuscript are instructive about the first phase of her career, as she describes it in the above passage. Not only do many of them deal with the topic of love and courtliness, which Christine clearly considers to be on the "lighter" side, but nearly the entire volume is devoted to works in verse. If, as many scholars believe, the order of the works roughly follows their chronology, then it would seem that her very earliest writings, in addition to the *Hundred Ballads,* were likewise short, fixed-form lyric genres, such as *rondeaux, virelays,* and *lays.* Following the lyrics are a series of works of courtly inspiration, including the *God of Love's Letter* (1399; excerpted below as no. 1), *The Debate of Two Lovers* (1400; excerpted as no. 3), and the *Dit de la Rose* (1402), along with some pious works, such as *A Prayer to Our Lady* (1402), and some didactic ones, including what was probably Christine's most popular work during her lifetime, *Othea's Letter* (1400–1402), in which she evokes in verse quatrains one hundred mostly mythological characters, followed by moralizing glosses and religious allegorizations in prose—her first use of that form. The result was thus Christine's first work of some complexity and undoubtedly the movement toward "more subtleness" to which she refers three years later in *Christine's Vision.*

During the period described in that work, 1399–1405, not only was Christine's production of new works rapid and increasingly more ambitious, but she also actively sought out patrons through her successful publication ventures. As she summarizes, "And thus my books were discussed and circulated in many different regions and lands."[10] Among the fifty-odd surviving manuscripts of *Othea's Letter* (an exceptionally large number, betokening considerable success), for instance, there is evidence in the dedications that she offered copies to at least four noble patrons: the dukes of Orléans, Burgundy, and Berry, and King Henry IV of England. We have mentioned Christine's enterprising packaging of the debate documents for public consumption, which scandalized Jean de Montreuil. But as part of Christine's building of a reputation, it also may have provoked envy in her opponents, as Pierre

9. *Selected Writings,* 194.

10. Ibid.

Col seems to reveal in his letter of October 1402 (no. 21 below), referring to Christine's presumption through the fable of the fox and the crow. The period of the debate seems thus to coincide with a move away from her initial courtly period and toward an increasing interest in didactic, moralizing, and political issues. The "other things" she tells Pierre Col she is occupied with in her letter in response to his criticisms of her (no. 22 below) and of Jean Gerson are none other than her two most ambitious and lengthy narrative poems: the six-thousand-line *Long Road of Learning* (1402–3), in which she uses a journey to the heavens guided by the Cumaean Sybil to comment upon the current war-torn situation in France and the need for leadership; and *The Book of Fortune's Transformation* (completed late in 1403), in which she illustrates the importance and effects of Fortune in her own life and in universal history in nearly twenty-four thousand lines of verse.

Closing the period discussed by *Christine's Vision* are her first two extensive works entirely in prose, *The Book of the Deeds and Good Conduct of the Wise King Charles V,* which had been commissioned by the duke of Burgundy soon before his death, and the work for which she is most renowned today, the *Book of the City of Ladies* (1405; see excerpts below, no. 31), in which, in order to counter the rampant misogyny of her time, she recounts the construction of a glorious city reserved for the great ladies of ancient history, mythology, early Christianity, and recent times, and built upon their stories. The *City of Ladies,* coupled with its companion piece, *The Book of the Three Virtues, or the Treasure of the City of Ladies,* a work of moral instruction for women, closes Christine's years devoted to the cause of women but also marks a turn in a new direction with its move to prose, a form she certainly considered more serious than verse. Indeed, with the exception of her *Hundred Ballads of a Lover and a Lady* (1409–10), which Christine says she would not have written but for the request of a noble patron, and her final work, a brief poem celebrating Joan of Arc (1429), from then on she abandoned poetic verse.

In the period after *Christine's Vision,* she was increasingly concerned about political issues and ways of addressing them. In 1405 she wrote a letter to the queen of France, entreating her to work for peace in view of the increasing tensions between the duke of Orléans and other nobles of the realm, whom she portrays as the bickering children of their mother, the queen. Her *Book of the Body Politic* (1406–7) is a manual of instruction for the monarch, intended for the dauphin, Louis de Guyenne. In the decade following this work, Christine was somewhat less prolific than during the preceding period but also resolutely turned her attention to France's political and social miseries: the *Book of Deeds of Arms and of Chivalry* (1410), a manual of technical instruction on warfare and legal issues raised by it; the *Lamentation on the Ills of France* (1410), likewise concerned about violence tearing apart the country; the *Book of Peace* (1412–14), which continued pleas for peace with instruction for the prince; and one of her last works before returning to Joan of Arc over a decade later, the *Epistle on the Prison of Human Life* (1418), a work of consolation for grieving women following upon the disastrous battle of Agincourt (1415).

Christine tells us in the opening lines of her *Poem of the Maid [Joan of Arc]* that, having fled Paris in 1418, the year the Burgundians took over Paris and unleashed a bloodbath in their struggle against the Armagnacs, she spent the following eleven years in a "closed abbey," undoubtedly the convent in Poissy where her daughter was a nun. She exercised her poetic talents one last time to celebrate Joan of Arc's military exploits, including the crowning of the dauphin as King Charles VII in mid-July 1429 in the cathedral of Rheims. Swiftly following these contemporary events, she completed her last work in honor of the "female sex" on July 31 of that same year. Christine undoubtedly died soon thereafter, perhaps in 1430.

THE DEBATE

The *Romance of the Rose* had been composed more than a century before the debate it inspired. An author known as Guillaume de Lorris started the work, a first-person dream narrative in which the protagonist, also the narrator and the dreamer, falls in love with a rose in a landscape populated by a profusion of personified qualities (Love, Jealousy, Shame, and so forth). The psychological state of the narrator/lover, as well as the personified qualities, are all taken from the vocabulary of passionate love as developed in the lyric poetry of the troubadours and the trouvères, which concentrates on the longing of the Lover for his Lady, the object of his desire, and the obstacles that distance him from her, arising either in the Lady herself or from others who attempt to hinder the affair. Undoubtedly written in the 1230s, the dream narrative was left a fragment, amounting to slightly more than four thousand lines of verse. Some forty years later, a second author, Jean de Meun, took it upon himself to continue and bring to a close the narrative, adding a text more than four times the length of his predecessor's work. While completing the narrative line (the Lover eventually manages, with the help of an army of personifications headed by the God of Love and Venus, to acquire the rose and, in the concluding lines of the continuation, wakes up from his dream), Jean inserted lengthy digressions on a variety of topics, most placed in the mouths of a handful of seemingly authoritative personified abstractions such as Reason and Nature. Much of the material contained in these digressions consists of passages from learned Latin authors, both classical and medieval (e.g., Ovid, Juvenal, Boethius, Alan of Lille, John of Salisbury). But the text was also quite provocatively laced with misogynistic, antireligious, and obscene passages. The work became a huge success, a "best-seller" that dominated and influenced the literary world of the fourteenth and fifteenth centuries, both in France and beyond its borders.

By the time of the debate, Jean de Meun would appear to have acquired a near-cult following. Certainly, one of the factors that accounted for the work's success was the access Jean provided to a number of Latin authors in translation for an audience little experienced in, or ignorant of, Latin. The personal attention readers lavished on Jean as an author-figure was based upon his immense erudition but also upon his self-presentation, in the course of the narrative, as a cunningly manipulative writer—a factor that would be very much at issue in the debate.

We know from works previous to the debate that Christine read the *Romance of the Rose* and was significantly influenced by it. But she was also opposed to its misogynistic treatment of women, as she makes clear through the voice of Cupid in the *God of Love's Letter* (no. 1 below), which she completed two years before the debate, in 1399. The reasons for her disapproval of the *Rose* broadened considerably over the next two years, but it was her reading of Jean de Montreuil's enthusiastic encomium of both work and author (specifically Jean de Meun) that moved her to lay out her arguments in writing. Since we do not have Jean de Montreuil's text to compare with the letter she sent in response to it in 1401, it is difficult to say to what extent her criticisms are independent of it or simply answering what he had said, though she does occasionally quote some of his statements. In any event, following are the issues raised (and critiqued) by Christine in the letter addressed to Jean de Montreuil, after an introductory section in which she speaks of her experience reading the *Rose,* as well as her general feeling that the work does not merit praise because of its lack of any moral or social redeeming value: (1) the indecency (and impropriety) of Reason's use of a dirty word in the course of her discussion with the Lover; (2) Reason's immoral statement that it is better to deceive than to be deceived; (3) the objectionable "way of speaking" of the Old Woman, who has only improper lessons for young ladies, and of the Jealous Man, owing to his outrageous statements, both misogynous and misogamous; (4) the blasphemy of the figure of Genius, who is portrayed as a priest, yet misleadingly presents sexual activity as the way to attain heaven; (5) Genius's misogynous statements, directing men to flee women, to avoid confiding in them because they are untrustworthy, in addition to his general indictment of all women; (6) the obscenity of the poem's ending; and (7), as a general conclusion, the work's uselessness and, more important, its danger for innocent readers who, inherently susceptible, could be led to sin by reading it. It should be obvious that the relatively short amount of space Christine devotes to the defense of women in this letter, countering statements made by the Jealous Husband and Genius, scarcely justifies placing women at the center of her interests, and that it is rather issues condemned by Christian morality—obscenity, blasphemy, immorality, pornography, deceit, carnality—that largely frame her criticisms of the text. However much she may have pursued the defense of women in her later work, whatever subsequent critics may have seen as her protofeminist tendencies, these forward-looking stances need to be reviewed against the backdrop of her fundamentally conservative views of women's roles in society and her adherence to a narrow moral outlook.

Jean de Montreuil seems not to have answered Christine's letter, so there never would have been a "debate" if Christine had not made the extraordinary gesture (at least as extraordinary as her addressing herself on an equal plane to members of the clerical establishment) of putting together a collection of documents in which her own letter occcupied the central place and her sharp rejoinder to Gontier Col provided the "last word."

The second phase of the debate was inadvertently initiated by what might be considered the surprising intervention of one of the most prominent theologians of the time, Jean Gerson, who published a treatise against the *Romance of the Rose* (no. 20 below) some four months after Christine compiled her first collection of documents. Whereas Christine, in her first letter, tackles directly the moral and religious issues raised by the second author of the *Romance of the Rose*, Jean de Meun (who becomes the single target of her criticisms), Gerson creates a fictional framework, an allegorical dream vision featuring a legal trial, that significantly complicates the issues of agency and authorial responsibility. He does indeed start his treatise with a sequence of specific reprisals, in the form of eight articles submitted by Lady Chastity, who considers her position to be threatened by the *Rose*: (1) the author of the work incites young girls to lascivious behavior; (2) he decries marriage and encourages men not to enter into it; (3) he says it is not natural for young men to enter religion; (4) he uses lascivious words to excite people and to eradicate chastity; (5) he defames Reason by making her speak of shameful things; (6) he mixes together dissolute words and sacred matters; (7) he promises paradise to the promiscuous; and (8) he describes sinful acts as though they were sacred, while using deceit in order to trick people into committing sins. These accusations, several of which intersect with those of Christine, clearly are based upon moral teachings of the sort that Gerson included in his sermons.

However, the bulk of Gerson's treatise is devoted to a lengthy speech of the advocate for the court, Theological Eloquence, who focuses more closely upon what one might call an ethics of speech and the identity politics of slander. Is the Foolish Lover a designation of the protagonist inscribed in the dream narrative of the *Rose*, or a slightly disguised figuration of Jean de Meun, or perhaps a conflation of the two? All of these are possible, as Gerson is scarcely consistent. But the point is that Gerson makes the question of who is speaking and who is responsible a center of attention, just as he makes the use of dirty language and a morality of expression—itself a component of Christine's and Chastity's previous critiques—the principal focus of his criticisms. Moreover, whereas Christine's criticisms were directly aimed at the author, Jean de Meun, Theological Eloquence takes the interesting approach of exonerating the author (Jean's name is never provided, and he is tacitly associated with the "Foolish Lover") because he is supposed to have repented for his follies later in life. Instead, through his allegorical personification, Gerson attacks the work itself, which merits punishment (that is, destruction by fire), and those of his contemporaries (among whom we may include Jean de Montreuil and his colleagues) who abusively strive to defend both author and work.

Many of Theological Eloquence's remarks concentrate upon the strategies of deceptive speech and their noxious effects. Key among these concerns is the troubled relation between a speaker/writer and his intention. The principal problem with Jean de Meun's work is that not only does what the personifications say not cohere with their named quality (Reason is not reasonable, etc.), but even within their discourses there is a mixture of good and deviant teaching that cannot easily be differentiated. The issue of the work's dual authorship is also called upon in this regard. The culmination of Theological Eloquence's frustration comes in a sudden burst:

> I truly wish that the Foolish Lover had not used these characters except as Holy Scripture does, that is, in order to reprove evil, and in such a way that everyone would perceive the reproach of evil and the approval of good—and, what is most important, without an excess of frivolity. But that is not at all what he does. Everything seems to be said in his person; everything seems as true as the Gospel, especially to the naïve, foolish lovers he is addressing. What distresses me most

is that everything feeds the flames of lust, especially when he seems to be reproaching it. (No. 20 below)

Not only can one not distinguish Jean's voice from those of the characters he introduces, but the intention of the words is always evil, even when the words support the good.

Pierre Col's response, which is addressed to Christine, but which responds both to her letter and to Gerson's treatise, is important at the very least because it is the only part of the debate that has come to us representing the specific arguments of the defenders of Jean de Meun. But it does much more, for in addition to rebutting the points made by the two detractors, it continues the game of voices begun by Gerson. Just as Gerson coyly erased the identity of Jean de Meun behind the character of the Foolish Lover, knowing full well of whom he was speaking, Pierre Col maintains an identical ironic stance: he shows that he knows the identity of the treatise's author but prefers to address his comments to the principal character, Theological Eloquence, an ironic stance furthered by the fact that his other interlocutor is not a personification but . . . Christine de Pizan. The gesture has the effect of attenuating the limit between living author and fictional creation, thus putting into practice the critical problem of expression and intention that, *pace* Jean de Meun, he develops throughout his letter. At the same time, feminizing the voice of Gerson, along with other references by Col to the theologian's lack of experience with love and carnal relations, could even be read as a questioning of his manhood.[11]

Whatever the questionable bases and inconsistencies of some of Pierre Col's arguments, as commentators have pointed out,[12] his assimilation of the hermeneutic maneuvers of Jean de Meun is flawless. For one must not forget that a part of Jean de Meun's strategy in the *Rose* is to push to the limits his satire of certain religious orders and their hypocritical ways, on the one hand, and of misogyny and prudish behavior, on the other. Jean even includes in the midst of his lengthy composition an intriguing apology aimed at potential critics of his antireligious and misogynistic views, calling into question such criticisms based upon the intention lying behind them: are the critics motivated by an objective judgment of Jean's ideas or rather by a

11. See Alastair Minnis, *Magister Amoris: The* Roman de la Rose *and Vernacular Hermeneutics* (New York: Oxford University Press, 2001), 213.

12. For example, Rosalind Brown-Grant, *Christine de Pizan and the Moral Defence of Women: Reading beyond Gender* (Cambridge: Cambridge University Press, 1999), 39–43.

need to censor because they recognize themselves? Speaking specifically of his attack on religious hypocrisy, Jean uses the metaphor of the arrow, claiming that he aims at no one in particular but that if someone wishes to place himself in the arrow's path, that is not his fault: "for I can strike no one who wants to protect himself as long as he knows how to see where he stands."[13] One could say that the terms characterizing especially the second wave of the debate were themselves put into place by Jean de Meun. As Eric Hicks cogently notes, "If the *Romance* [*of the Rose*] fit so easily into the debate, it is because the debate was already in the romance."[14] He later calls Jean's taking over of Guillaume de Lorris's poem a "collaboration posthume" (posthumous collaboration), a characterization that could equally well be applied to the intervention of Pierre Col in the debate.

In any event, Pierre Col likewise pursues a path in the course of which he attempts not only to address the substance of the issues but to call into question the motivations of the *Rose*'s critics. Christine said, for instance, that the ending of the poem—the taking of the castle, recounted in scarcely disguised terms suggesting the mechanics of sexual intercourse—was so disgusting as to make honorable women blush. Why, says Pierre Col, would women blush unless "they felt they were guilty"? As for the critics themselves, he queries whether it is envy of Jean de Meun's elevated status or some kind of personal hatred that motivates them. But then he comes to the most insidious suggestion: perhaps they attack the *Rose* only to draw attention to it and thereby to encourage people to read it. In this case, he says, "the accusers ought to be considered completely pardoned, for their goal and their intention would be good, whatever means might have been used." In short (this is certainly the way Gerson will take it), the critics are hypocrites. Col further attempts to put Christine in her place, as we mentioned earlier, by suggesting that a kind of arrogance (the result of her brilliant professional success at this crucial moment in her career) risks assimilating her to the crow of the well-known fable: "because people praised his song, [he] began to sing louder than was his custom and let his mouthful drop."

These allegations are not without their effect on both Christine and

13. Guillaume de Lorris and Jean de Meun, *Le roman de la rose,* ed. Félix Lecoy, 3 vols. (Paris: Champion, 1965–70), ll. 15254–56: "car je ne puis nullui ferir / qui du cop se veille garder, / s'il set son estat regarder." English trans.: *The Romance of the Rose by Guillaume de Lorris and Jean de Meun,* trans. Charles Dahlberg (Princeton: Princeton University Press, 1971), 260.

14. *Le débat sur le Roman de la Rose,* ed. Eric Hicks, Bibliothèque du XVe siècle, 43 (Paris: Honoré Champion, 1977), xix ("Si le *Roman* s'est installé si aisément dans le débat, c'est donc que le débat existait déjà dans le roman"). The Hicks edition is the basis for all translations, except where noted.

Gerson. The suggestion of presumptuousness elicits from Christine a statement of humility and a denial of any manipulation, including a disavowal of any active attempt on her part to solicit noble patronage or to acquire personal fame:

> It is quite possible that by frequenting the solitary life of study I have gathered some of the low-lying little flowers of the delightful garden, rather than climbing into the tall trees. . . . But on account of the fragrance of even the little flowers, out of which I had made slender garlands, those who wanted to obtain them (to whom I would not have dared or had the capacity to refuse them) were astounded by my labor, not for any greatness to be found there, but because of its novelty, which is out of the ordinary. So they did not keep quiet about it—even though it had been concealed for a long time, and I promise you that it was not made public at my request. And if you are suggesting that I might have composed some things in consideration of certain individuals, this happened after it was already common knowledge (I do not say this to make any excuses, for there is no need for any, but in order to dispel any opinion that I was assuming some kind of authority through my actions). (No. 22 below)

As for Gerson, Pierre Col's suggestion provoked a dramatic response:

> You were never able to glorify my modest standing so much with your panegyrics as you disparage it when what may be called the liberty you take in speaking with me claims falsely that I said the things I said so that a more intense flame might engulf men, who we know gravitate toward what is forbidden, and incite them to repeat the reading of this book—as though, in other words, I would have transformed my profession into a sham, and it were my function to act deceptively in the teaching of morals and be in disaccord with my very self (or rather, with the Christian religion!), speaking both sincerely and insincerely, in the manner of your author. I would sooner die than ever be found cloaked in deception of this kind. (No. 28 below)

The *Rose* debate does not simply represent a quaint affair in which Christine de Pizan nobly stood up for the cause of women and what is frequently considered an outdated Christian morality. Not only does it revealingly display the terms used in debates over obscene speech and censorship that retain their currency in our own twenty-first century, but it more profoundly suggests that debating is itself not totally based upon substance, ideas, or moral convictions. It is important to note that the wide array of positions called into play are dictated by both individual sensibilities and professional concerns: Christine's deeply held beliefs as well as her professional preoccupations of the moment; Gerson's need, as a theologian and a high-profile preacher, to improve public morals, but also his personal foibles and obsessions; the playful humor of the protohumanist intellectuals of the chancery, who delighted in Jean de Meun's outrageous misogyny and obscenity, even though they themselves would not have indulged in them; finally, Jean de Meun's profile as a *provocateur* and satirist of the first order, one who seems to have come back once again from beyond the grave (as he had done just a few years before in Honoré Bovet's 1398 *Apparicion de Jehan de Meung* [The Apparition of Jean de Meun]) in order, himself, to launch France's first literary debate.

Judging from the relatively meager manuscript legacy, it would not appear that the debate had a direct lasting influence over discussions of women or of obscenity. Of the eight manuscripts containing documents that can be considered to transmit what we call the *Debate,*[15] six were copied within a decade of the events and the other two were copies made in the first half of the fifteenth century based undoubtedly upon manuscripts the transcription of which Christine de Pizan supervised. Only two of the manuscripts were copied outside of Christine's influence and anthologize the debate with works other than hers. The situation suggests that the debate documents primarily circulated among the noble patrons for whom Christine made copies, but scarcely beyond that entourage. There exists only one printed version, a sixteen-folio pamphlet entitled *Le Contre Rommant de la Rose* (The Anti-Romance of the Rose), which contains no publication information, no date, and no authorial attribution. However, it is highly likely that the issues debated among the members of the king's chancery continued to circulate and inspire later authors. Alain Chartier (c. 1385–1430), a secretary to the king and younger contemporary of Christine, in 1424 wrote the *Belle Dame sans Mercy,* a poem that could very well have been inspired by ideas circulating about women in the preceding generation. The work was wildly successful and spawned a series of poetic responses for and against the freedom of a woman to refuse the advances of a suitor, constituting a second "debate" that affected generations of love poets. One must perhaps consider that the debate lived on through this indirect sequence of influences that

15. On the manuscript transmission of the documents, see the following section, "The Documents of the Debate."

would lead to the more fully developed debates over women that arose during the Renaissance.[16]

THE DOCUMENTS OF THE DEBATE

What we call the debate over the *Romance of the Rose*, if we consider a "debate" to be something like an exchange of ideas focused on a particular theme or topic, does not precisely describe the letters, sermons, and fictional works brought together below. Only a few of them can be said to enter into this category: Christine de Pizan's letter to Jean de Montreuil (no. 5), Pierre Col's letter to Christine (no. 21) responding both to the letter she had written Montreuil and to Jean Gerson's treatise (no. 20), Christine's reply to Pierre (no. 22), Pierre's fragmentary reply to Christine (no. 23), and Jean Gerson's severe letter (in Latin) to Pierre Col (no. 28) are the only items that can be considered to be part of a debate according to the above definition. What I have attempted to do is bring together in chronological order the various letters, sermons, and fictional works that either participate in or surround the so-called debate and that scholars have been discussing for some time now. This might seem transparent, but it is not the method that recent translators have used.[17]

This translation is based for most of the texts upon the very good edi-

16. For a pioneering overview, see Joan Kelly, "Early Feminist Theory and the *Querelle des Femmes: 1400–1789*," *Signs* 8 (1982): 4–28. See also the series editors' introduction.

17. The first English translation of the debate documents, published by Joseph L. Baird and John R. Kane some thirty years ago, is accessible only in university libraries, having gone out of print some time ago (*La querelle de la Rose: Letters and Documents*, ed. and trans. Joseph L. Baird and John R. Kane [Chapel Hill: North Carolina Studies in the Romance Languages and Literatures, 1978]). The Baird/Kane translation of the debate texts (which includes 22 of the 33 included herein) follows a principle of chronological ordering similar to the one in this volume, though since they based their chronology upon the flawed scheme of Peter Potansky (*Der Streit um den Rosenroman* [Munich: Wilhelm Fink Verlag, 1972]) and without the benefit of the more or less definitive reordering by Hicks and Ezio Ornato ("Jean de Montreuil et le débat sur le *Roman de la Rose*," *Romania* 98 [1977]: 34–64, 186–219), which was summarily reproduced in Hicks's edition (lii–liv), their placement of the letters of Jean de Montreuil differs significantly from what is found here.

Two translations, one in French and one in English, have appeared very recently: the first, that of Virginie Greene (Traductions des Classiques du Moyen Âge, 76. [Paris: Champion, 2006]), and the second, by Christine McWebb and Earl Jeffrey Richards (*Debating the Roman de la Rose: A Critical Anthology* [New York/London: Routledge, 2007]). The latter came to my attention only after the bulk of my own work on this volume had been completed; it is thus not mentioned in notes to the translation. Greene translates the Hicks volume exactly as the texts are found in it; the McWebb/Richards volume contains a large number of texts around the debate divided into several sections, but also follows the "documentary" approach, at least in its presentation of Christine's revised version of her initial collection addressed to the queen of France (see the second item in the list of manuscript sources below).

tion of the primary texts published by Eric Hicks some thirty years ago.[18] The intended audience of Professor Hicks's edition was the scholarly community, principally specialists of Christine de Pizan, and so he took an approach that can best be described as "documentary." In fact, not only was the "debate" as contained in the present volume never conceived of by contemporaries as a single event, but these writings were never collected together in any single place. Any edition or translation of the writings risks therefore being an artificial and anachronistic collection. Hicks, wanting to maintain the scholarly integrity of his undertaking, decided that he would edit manuscript collections rather than abstract texts from them. There are several sources for the latter, with little or no connection among them:

1. First and foremost, Christine de Pizan single-handedly manufactured a small collection of letters that she sent to the queen of France: this was the first "Debate of the *Romance of the Rose*," which showcased her response to Jean de Montreuil's French treatise defending the work and included two letters of Gontier Col as attestations of the animosity or stance of her opponents, but contained no substantial arguments counter to hers. She unfortunately did not include the treatise to which she was responding, but it is this publication of the letters that transformed the debate from a private into a public event. Four manuscripts transmitting this first version have survived.

2. Christine produced a second "version" of this collection after she wrote a response to Pierre Col's critique of her letter and of Jean Gerson's treatise; she added her response, but neither of these other texts to which she nonetheless refers, to the collection; the only other change in the manuscripts she supervised was that the dedicatory letter to Guillaume de Tignonville (no. 17 below) was dropped in the last of them, British Library MS Harley 4431, since the provost of Paris had fallen out of grace by the time of its compilation, probably around 1410. Three surviving manuscripts contain this version of the debate.

3. Jean de Montreuil's Latin letters have survived in one of the two manuscript collections that he himself compiled to give to close friends and that were not meant to be circulated publicly.

4. An intriguing (and unique) manuscript, BnF fr. 1563, which Hicks attributes to a "rhodophile" (lover of the *Rose*) and dates to the opening of the fifteenth century (thus, soon after the debate), collects with several texts attributed to Jean de Meun (the *Romance of the Rose, Testament, Codicil,* and the translation of Vegetius's *Art of Chivalry*) an alternative version of the debate

18. See above, n. 14.

accenting its second phase, which Hicks believes might previously have circulated separately in pamphlet form,[19] although there is no evidence for this. The debate documents contained in this manuscript include, in the following order: Christine's response to Jean de Montreuil's treatise (no. 5);[20] Jean Gerson's *Treatise against the Romance of the Rose* (no. 20); Pierre Col's response to both of the preceding documents (no. 21); Christine's response to Pierre Col (no. 22); and Pierre Col's fragmentary response to Christine (no. 23). The compiler of this manuscript would have put some effort into collecting these texts from diverse sources: Christine's letters from one of the collections listed above (neither of Christine's letters is otherwise transmitted outside of manuscripts supervised by her); and Gerson's treatise from one of the manuscripts of his works. This is, moreover, the only surviving manuscript containing Pierre Col's letters, which, in the absence of Jean de Montreuil's French treatise, remain the only developed argument originating from the pen of a supporter of Jean de Meun that has survived.

5. Jean Gerson's treatise has come down to us in seven medieval manuscripts representing a wide variety of contexts (by itself, associated with miscellaneous didactic works, or with other of Gerson's vernacular compositions), but in only one case (the preceding manuscript by the "lover of the *Rose*") has it been transmitted along with any other texts connected with the debate.

6. The sermons of Jean Gerson are collected together with others of his sermons, both in French and in Latin.

7. Pierre d'Ailly's *The Devout Soul's Garden of Love,* clearly very popular, as it has survived in seventeen manuscripts and four early printed editions, extending from 1476 to 1528, is attributed to him in two of these manuscripts and one of the editions, while it is attributed to Gerson in one of the other manuscripts (the balance of the copies do not provide an authorial name). It was long thought to be by Gerson (the most recent edition of his complete works includes it along with Gerson's French treatises), but in an important article published in 1976, Pierre-Yves Badel demonstrated conclusively that Pierre d'Ailly was its author.

The core of Hicks's edition presents essentially three of these manuscript documents edited fairly conservatively: first, Christine's original col-

19. *Le débat,* ed. Hicks, lxiii.

20. It is to be noted that because of Hicks's approach, as outlined above, he prints two versions of this letter in his edition: the first found in one of the manuscripts Christine herself supervised (and which we have translated here as no. 5); and the second contained in this "rhodophile" manuscript, which provides a shorter, manifestly corrupt version.

lection of the letters, dating to February 1, 1402 (n.s.) (one of the manuscripts under [1] above); then, the letters of Jean de Montreuil that concern the debate, taken from the autograph manuscript that contains them; finally, the dossier of the "lover of the *Rose*" (the entire contents of the debate portion of manuscript 4 above). However informative these might be for the specialist, they present a somewhat confusing series of texts that are difficult to understand when one is approaching the *Debate* for the first time. A presentation of the various writings in their most likely chronological sequence is more accessible for use in the classroom. It also provides a sense of the dynamic of the positions of the participants, with most notably Jean de Montreuil's letters not simply separated from the other documents but integrated among them so as to show, for instance, how important Christine's publicizing of the debate in February 1402 turned out to be. Inclusion of Christine's references to the *Romance of the Rose* prior to the *Debate* and in the works she wrote afterward offers an intriguing glimpse of her various opinions of that work during her career. The following is a schematic rendering of the documents as ordered here, including various events relevant to the debate[21]:

I. Christine and the Rose *before the Debate*

1. Christine de Pizan, *The God of Love's Letter* (May 1, 1399)
2. Christine de Pizan, *Moral Teachings* (1399 or 1402?)
3. Christine de Pizan, *The Debate of Two Lovers* (1400?)

II. The Debate: First Phase

Jean de Montreuil composes a treatise on the Romance of the Rose *(now lost), which he sends to a "noteworthy cleric," undoubtedly Nicolas de Clamanges and, subsequently, to Christine de Pizan (May 1401).*

4. Jean de Montreuil, *Épître 103* (Cum ut dant) to Pierre d'Ailly, accompanying above treatise (end May 1401)

5. Christine de Pizan, *Epître* (Reverence, honneur) to Jean de Montreuil (June–July 1401)

6. Jean de Montreuil, *Épître 118* (Quo magis) to a lawyer, probably the same addressee as no. 9 (July–August 1401)

7. Jean de Montreuil, *Épître 119* (Ex quo nugis) to a prelate, accompanying above treatise (July–August 1401)

21. The numbers attributed to Jean de Montreuil's letters are those found in the critical edition of his correspondence edited by Ezio Ornato, vol. 1 (First Part): "Epistolario" (Turin: G. Giappichelli, 1963).

8. Jean de Montreuil, *Épître 120* (Scis me) to Gontier Col, sent with copy of no. 6 (July–August 1401)

9. Jean de Montreuil, *Épître 121* (Mee an fuerit) to a prelate, probably the same addressee as no. 7, sent with a copy of no. 6 and a draft of no. 8 (July–August 1401)

10. Jean de Montreuil, *Épître 122* (Etsi facundissimus) to "vir insignis," certainly the lawyer to whom no. 6 was addressed (July–August 1401)

11. Pierre d'Ailly, *The Devout Soul's Garden of Love* (summer 1401?)

12. Jean Gerson delivers the sermon "Considerate lilia" (August 25, 1401)

13. Gontier Col, *Épître* (Femme de hault et eslevé entendement) to Christine (September 13, 1401)

Christine sends a copy of item 5 to Gontier Col (September 13–15, 1401).

14. Gontier Col, *Épître* (Pour ce que la divine Escripture) to Christine (September 15, 1401)

15. Christine de Pizan, *Épître* (O clerc subtil) to Gontier Col (late September 1401)

16. Christine de Pizan, *Épître* (Tres haulte, tres puissant et tres redoubtee dame) to the queen of France, Isabeau de Bavière, accompanying Christine's first collection of the *Rose* documents (February 1, 1402)

17. Christine de Pizan, *Épître* (A vous mon seigneur le prevost de Paris) to Guillaume de Tignonville, accompanying Christine's first collection of the *Rose* documents (February 1, 1402)

18. Christine's brief narrative account of the events leading to the debate (February 1, 1402)

Christine sends her first dossier of the Debate documents to the queen of France and, undoubtedly at the same time, to Guillaume de Tignonville. The dossier as she had it transcribed in her manuscripts included, in the following order, items 16, 17, 18, 13, 5, 14, and 15 (February 1, 1402).

Christine publishes the Dit de la Rose, *intended to commemorate a celebration at the Hotel of the Duke of Orléans in January 1402, at which the Order of the Rose was founded (February 14, 1402).*

III. The Debate: Second Phase

19. Jean de Montreuil, *Épître 154* (Ut sunt mores) to a great poet, perhaps Eustache Deschamps or Honoré Bouvet, accompanying Jean de Montreuil's initial treatise (February–March/July–August 1402)

20. Jean Gerson, *Treatise against the* Romance of the Rose (May 18, 1402)

Christine de Pizan completes the first manuscript containing her collected works, including the initial set of documents relative to the debate, as noted above (June 23, 1402).

21. Pierre Col, *Épître* (Aprés ce que je oÿ parler) to Christine (late summer 1402)

22. Christine de Pizan, *Épître* (Pour ce que entendement humain) to Pierre Col (October 2, 1402)

23. Pierre Col, *Épître* (Combien que tu aies proposé) to Christine (November 1402)

IV. Aftermath

24. Jean Gerson, sermons of the *Poenitemini* series (December 17, 24, 31, 1402)

25. Christine de Pizan, *Ballade* (Redoubtee, excellent), addressed to Isabeau de Bavière, accompanied by a new version of the debate documents, supplemented by no. 22 (January 1, 1403)

26. Christine de Pizan, *Rondeau* (Mon chier seigneur) addressed to a noble lord, perhaps Guillaume de Tignonville, addressee of no. 17, and perhaps accompanied by the new version of the debate, as was no. 25 (January 1, 1403)

27. Christine de Pizan, *Ballade* (Jadis avoit en la ville) (January 1, 1403?)

28. Jean Gerson, *Épître* (Talia de me) to Pierre Col (winter 1402–3)

29. Jean de Montreuil, *Épître 152* (Ex quo nuge) to a high-ranking prelate, accompanying Montreuil's now-lost treatise and item no. 6 (1403–4)

V. Christine's Later Mentions of the Romance of the Rose

30. *Book of Fortune's Transformation* (November 1403)
31. *Book of the City of Ladies* (1405)
32. *Christine's Vision* (1405)
33. *Book of Deeds of Arms and of Chivalry* (1410)

A NOTE ON THE TRANSLATION

The texts translated here represent various forms. Most are in French, but several are in Latin (the letters of Jean de Montreuil [nos. 4, 6–10, 19, and 29], the sermon *Considerate lilia* of Gerson [no. 12], and Gerson's letter to

Pierre Col [no. 28]). Of the French texts, the early ones by Christine de Pizan not directly connected to the debate are in verse (nos. 1, 2, 3, 25, 26, 27, and 30), but all the rest are in prose, which she pointedly tells Guillaume de Tignonville (no. 17) was used in her letters in order to "imitate the style" of her assailants. Since the uniform translation into English largely erases these linguistic differences, I have clearly indicated at the beginning of each document its language, Latin or French, and its form, verse or prose. Where Latin words have been inserted into a French text, I have maintained the Latin in the translation in order to convey the linguistic distancing, providing a gloss in a note. In my translations, I have respected the division into verses only in the lyric poems (Pierre d'Ailly's lyric conclusion to his *The Devout Soul's Garden of Love* [no. 11] and the ballades and rondeau of Christine [nos. 25, 26, and 27]), inasmuch as the verse form used in Christine's early narrative poems (nos. 1, 2, 3, and 30), rhyming octosyllabic and decasyllabic couplets—a staple for the composition of fiction and even history dating back to the twelfth century—had a status somewhere between what we consider "poetry" and its converse, narrative prose. Fifteenth-century French prose is notoriously difficult, partly because of very complex syntactic structures, with numerous subordinate and coordinate clauses and its imitation of Latinate periodic construction, and partly owing to an inclusion of Latinate vocabulary. This is especially the case for Christine de Pizan, who clearly attempted to develop and cultivate a "more elevated vernacular register,"[22] which does not necessarily guarantee, or even strive for, clarity of expression. Even Christine, in her semi-autobiographical *Christine's Vision* (no. 32), admits to the difficulty of her writing. I have tried to provide a translation that is as close as possible to the original sentence structures without presenting an opaque, or unreadable, text. In certain cases, where a sentence is simply too complicated, owing to subordinated or imbedded clauses, I have broken it down into smaller and clearer syntactic units.

Pronouns are frequently used for which the references are unclear or ambiguous. Rather than simply replace the pronoun with the noun for which it stands, I have tried to maintain the text as written and either clarify through syntactic manipulation or proper names in brackets, or explain the nature of the difficulty in a note.

22. See Thelma Fenster, "'Perdre son latin': Christine de Pizan and Vernacular Humanism," in *Christine de Pizan and the Categories of Difference,* ed. Marilynn Desmond, Medieval Cultures, 14 (Minneapolis: University of Minnesota Press, 1998), 103.

VOLUME EDITOR'S BIBLIOGRAPHY

EDITIONS AND TRANSLATIONS OF THE DEBATE DOCUMENTS

Debating the Roman de la Rose: A Critical Anthology. Ed. Christine McWebb. New York: Routledge, 2007.

Le débat sur le Roman de la Rose. Ed. Eric Hicks. Bibliothèque du XVe siècle, 43. Paris: Honoré Champion, 1977. (French trans. by Virginie Greene, Traductions des Classiques du Moyen Âge, 76 [Paris: Champion, 2006].)

"The Epistles on the Romance of the Rose and Other Documents in the Debate." Ed. Charles Frederick Ward. Ph.D. diss., University of Chicago, 1911.

La querelle de la Rose: Letters and Documents. Ed. and trans. Joseph L. Baird and John R. Kane. Chapel Hill: North Carolina Studies in the Romance Languages and Literatures, 1978.

SELECTED WORKS OF CHRISTINE DE PIZAN

[As Angus Kennedy has noted in the second supplement to his initial bibliography devoted to Christine de Pizan (first volume 1984; second supplement 2004; see below), the amount of work devoted to the medieval author has increased exponentially in the past decade or two. Any bibliography is likely to be superseded the instant it appears, so I have not made an attempt to be comprehensive. I have listed here editions and translation of works that are mentioned in the introduction and in the course of the translation. I have limited myself to works that I consider relevant to the *Debate*; my goal is not to provide a complete list of the works produced by Christine.]

Cent ballades d'amant et de dame. Ed. Jacqueline Cerquiglini. Paris: 10/18, 1982.

Le chemin de longue étude. Ed. and trans. Andrea Tarnowski. Paris: Livre de Poche (Lettres Gothiques), 2000.

"Christine de Pizan's *Epistre à la reine* (1405)." Ed. Angus Kennedy. *Revue des Langues Romanes* 92 (1988): 253–64.

La città delle dame (The City of Ladies). Ed. Earl Jeffrey Richards. Italian trans. Patrizia Caraffi. Milan: Luni, 1997. (English translations, *The Book of the City of Ladies,* trans. Earl Jeffrey Richards, rev. ed. [New York: Persea Books, 1998]; *The City of Ladies,* trans. Rosalind Brown-Grant [New York: Penguin Books, 1999]; French translation, *La cité des dames,* trans. Thérèse Moreau and Eric Hicks [Paris: Stock, 1986].)

Debate of Two Lovers. In *An Anthology of Medieval Love Debate Poetry,* ed. and trans. R. Barton Palmer and Barbara K. Altmann. Gainesville: University Press of Florida, 2006.

Epistre Othea. Ed. Gabriella Parussa. Textes Littéraires Français, 517. Geneva: Droz, 1999.

"The *Livre de la Cité des Dames* of Christine de Pisan: A Critical Edition." Ed. Maureen Cheney Curnow. Ph.D. diss., Vanderbilt University, 1975.

Le livre de l'advision Christine. Ed. Christine Reno and Liliane Dulac. Études christiniennes, 4. Paris: Honoré Champion, 2001. (English translations, *Christine's Vision,* trans. Glenda K. McLeod, Garland Library of Medieval Literature, series B, vol. 68 [New York, 1993]; *The Vision of Christine de Pizan,* trans. Glenda McLeod and Charity Cannon Willard [Cambridge, Eng.: D. S. Brewer, 2005].)

Le livre de la mutacion de Fortune. Ed. Suzanne Solente. 4 vols. SATF. Paris: Picard, 1959–66.

Le livre des fais d'armes et de chevalerie. In Christine Moneera Laennec, "Christine *antygrafe:* Authorship and Self in the Prose Works of Christine de Pizan with an Edition of B.N. MS 603 'Le livre des fais d'armes et de chevallerie.'" 2 vols. Ph.D. diss., Yale University, 1988. (English translation, *The Book of Deeds of Arms and of Chivalry,* trans. Sumner Willard [University Park: Pennsylvania State University Press, 1999].)

Le livre des fais et bonnes meurs du sage roy Charles V. Ed. S. Solente. 2 vols. Paris: Honoré Champion, 1936–40. (French translation by Eric Hicks and Thérèse Moreau [Paris: Stock, 1997].)

Le livre des trois vertus. Ed. Eric Hicks. Introduction and notes by Charity Cannon Willard. Bibliothèque du XVe siècle, 50. Paris: Honoré Champion, 1989. (English translations, *The Treasure of the City of Ladies, or the Book of the Three Virtues,* trans. Sarah Lawson, rev. ed. [New York: Penguin, 2003]; *A Medieval Woman's Mirror of Honor: The Treasury of the City of Ladies,* trans. Charity Cannon Willard, ed. Madeleine Pelner Cosman [New York: Persea Books, 1989].)

Le livre du corps de policie. Ed. Angus J. Kennedy. Études Christiniennes, 1. Paris: Champion, 1998. (English translation, *The Book of the Body Politic,* trans. Kate Langdon Forhan [Cambridge: Cambridge University Press, 1994]).

The Love Debate Poems of Christine de Pizan (Le livre du débat de deux amans, Le livre des trois jugemens, Le livre du dit de Poissy). Ed. Barbara Altmann. Gainesville: University Press of Florida, 1998.

Œuvres poétiques de Christine de Pisan. Ed. Maurice Roy. 3 vols. SATF. Paris: Firmin Didot, 1886–96. Rpt. New York: Johnson Reprint Corporation, 1965.

Poems of Cupid, God of Love: Christine de Pizan's Epistre au Dieu d'Amours and Dit de la Rose, Thomas Hoccleve's The Letter of Cupid, with George Sewell's The Proclamation of Cupid. Ed. and trans. Thelma S. Fenster and Mary Carpenter Erler. Leiden: Brill, 1990.

The Selected Writings of Christine de Pizan. Ed. Renate Blumenfeld-Kosinski. Trans. Renate Blumenfeld-Kosinski and Kevin Brownlee. New York: W. W. Norton, 1997.

The Writings of Christine de Pizan. Ed. Charity Cannon Willard. New York: Persea Books, 1994.

OTHER PRIMARY WORKS

Abaelart, Pierres, and Heloys sa Fame. *La Vie et les Epistres.* Thirteenth-century translation attributed to Jean de Meun with a new edition of the Latin texts according to Troyes, BM MS 802. Ed. Eric Hicks. Vol. 1. Paris: Honoré Champion, 1991. (English translation, *The Letters of Abelard and Heloise,* trans. Betty Radice [Harmondsworth: Penguin Books, 1974].)

Alan of Lille. "Alan of Lille, 'De Planctu naturae.'" Ed. Nikolaus M. Häring. *Studi Medievali,* 3rd ser., vol. 19, no. 2 (1978): 797–879. (English translation, *The Plaint of Nature,* trans. James J. Sheridan, Medieval Sources in Translation, 26 [Toronto: Pontifical Institute of Mediaeval Studies, 1980].)

Andeli, Henri d'. *Le lai d'Aristote.* Ed. A. Héron. Société Rouennaise de Bibliophiles. Rouen: Imprimerie Léon Gy, 1901.

Aristotle. *The Complete Works: The Revised Oxford Translation.* Ed. Jonathan Barnes. 2 vols. Bollingen Series, 71. Princeton: Princeton University Press, 1984.

Augustine, Saint. *On Christian Doctrine.* Trans. D. W. Robertson Jr. Indianapolis: Bobbs-Merrill, 1958.

Boccaccio, Giovanni. *Famous Women* [*De mulieribus claris*]. Ed. and trans. Virginia Brown. I Tatti Renaissance Library. Cambridge: Harvard University Press, 2001.

Boethius. "Boethius' *De Consolatione* by Jean de Meun." Ed. V. L. Dedeck-Héry. *Mediaeval Studies* 14 (1952): 165–275.

———. *Le livre de Boece de consolacion.* Ed. Glynnis M. Cropp. Textes Littéraires Français, 580. Geneva: Droz, 2006.

Bonet [Bovet], Honoré. *L'Apparicion Maistre Jehan de Meun et le Somnium super Materia Scismatis.* Ed. Ivor Arnold. Publications de la Faculté des Lettres de l'Université de Strasbourg, fasc. 28. Paris: Les Belles Lettres, 1926.

Chartier, Alain, Baudet Herenc, and Achille Caulier. *Le cycle de* La Belle Dame sans Mercy. Ed. David F. Hult, with the collaboration of Joan E. McRae. Champion Classiques, 8. Paris: Honoré Champion, 2003.

Cicero. *De inventione, De optimo genere oratorum, Topica.* Trans. H. M. Hubbell. Cambridge: Harvard University Press, 1949.

———. *De natura deorum—Academica.* Trans. H. Rackham. Rev. ed. Cambridge: Harvard University Press, 1951.

———. *De officiis.* Ed. and trans. Walter Miller. Cambridge: Harvard University Press, 1913.

———. *De oratore, Books I, II.* Trans. E. W. Sutton. Rev. ed. Cambridge: Harvard University Press, 1948.

———. *De senectute, De amicitia, De divinatione.* Ed. and trans. William Armistead Falconer. Cambridge: Harvard University Press, 1923.

———. *In Catilinam I–IV—Pro Murena—Pro Sulla—Pro Flacco.* Trans. C. Macdonald. Rev. ed. Cambridge: Harvard University Press, 1977.

Claudian. Vol. 1. Trans. Maurice Platnauer. Cambridge: Harvard University Press, 1922.

Deschamps, Eustache. *Œuvres complètes.* Ed. Marquis de Queux de Saint-Hilaire (vols. 1–6), then Gaston Raynaud (vols. 7–11). 11 vols. SATF. Paris: Firmin-Didot, 1878–1903.

The Distichs of Cato: A Famous Medieval Textbook. Ed. Wayland Johnson Chase. University of Wisconsin Studies in the Social Sciences and History, 7. Madison: University of Wisconsin Press, 1922.

Gerson, Jean. *Œuvres complètes.* Ed. Mgr. Glorieux. 10 vols. in 11. Paris: Desclée, 1960–73.

———. "Le traité contre le *Roman de la Rose.*" In Ernest Langlois, "Le Traité de Gerson contre le Roman de la Rose." *Romania* 45 (1918–19): 23–48.

Horace. *Satires, Epistles and Ars Poetica.* Ed. and trans. H. Rushton Fairclough. Rev. ed. Cambridge: Harvard University Press, 1929.

Hugh of Saint Victor. *Didascalicon: De studio legendi.* Ed. Brother Charles Henry Buttimer. Catholic University of America Studies in Medieval and Renaissance Latin,. 10. Washington, DC: Catholic University Press, 1939. (English translation, *The* Didascalicon *of Hugh of St. Victor: A Medieval Guide to the Arts,* trans. Jerome Taylor [New York: Columbia University Press, 1961].)

Joinville, Jean, sire de. *Histoire de Saint Louis, Credo, et Lettre à Louis X.* Ed. Natalis de Wailly. Paris: Firmin Didot, 1874.

———. *Vie de Saint Louis.* Ed. and trans. Jacques Monfrin. Paris: Classiques Garnier, 1995.

Juvenal and Persius. Ed. and trans. Susanna Morton Braund. Cambridge: Harvard University Press, 2004.

Le Fèvre de Ressons, Jehan. *Les lamentations de Matheolus et le livre de Leesce.* Ed. A.-G. Van Hamel. 2 vols. Bibliothèque de l'École des Hautes Études, 95–96. Paris: Émile Bouillon, 1892–95.

Le Seneschal, Jean, with the collaboration of Phillippe d'Artois, Comte d'Eu, of Boucicault le jeune and of Jean de Crésecque. *Les cent ballades, poème du XIV*[e] *siècle.* Ed. Gaston Raynaud. SATF. Paris: Firmin-Didot, 1905.

Livy. [*Ab urbe condita*]. Vol. 1. Ed. and trans. B. O. Foster. Cambridge: Harvard University Press, 1919. Vol. 10. Trans. Evan T. Sage. Cambridge: Harvard University Press, 1935.

Lorris, Guillaume de, and Jean de Meun. *Le Roman de la Rose.* Ed. Ernest Langlois. 5 vols. SATF. Paris: Firmin-Didot (vols. 1–2) and Champion (vols. 3–5), 1914–24. (English translation, *The Romance of the Rose by Guillaume de Lorris and Jean de Meun,* trans. Charles Dahlberg [Princeton: Princeton University Press, 1971].)

———. *Le Roman de la Rose.* Ed. Félix Lecoy. 3 vols. Paris: Champion, 1965–70.

Machaut, Guillaume de. *Le livre de la fontaine amoureuse.* Ed. and French trans. Jacqueline Cerquiglini-Toulet. Paris: Éditions Stock, 1993.

Map, Walter. *De nugis curialium* (Courtiers' Trifles). Ed. and trans. M. R. James. Rev. C. N. L. Brooke and R. A. B. Mynors. Oxford: Clarendon Press, 1983.

Meun, Jean de. *Le Testament maistre Jehan de Meun: un caso letterario.* Ed. Sylvia Buzzetti Gallarati. Alessandria: Edizioni dell'orso, 1989.

Montreuil, Jean de. *Opera.* Ed. Ezio Ornato. Vol. 1 (First Part): "Epistolario." Turin: G. Giappichelli, 1963.

Ovid. *The Art of Love and Other Poems.* Trans. J. H. Mozley. Rev. G. P. Goold. 2nd ed. Cambridge: Harvard University Press, 1979.

———. *Fasti.* Ed. and trans. Sir James George Frazer. Rev. G. P. Goold. 2nd ed. Cambridge: Harvard University Press, 1989.

———. *Heroides and Amores*. Trans. Grant Showerman. Rev. G. P. Goold. 2nd ed. Cambridge: Harvard University Press, 1977.

———. *Metamorphoses*. Trans. Frank Justus Miller. Rev. G. P. Goold. 2 vols. Cambridge: Harvard University Press, 1977 (vol. 1) and 1984 (vol. 2).

———. *Tristia ex Ponto*. Ed. and trans. A. L. Wheeler. Rev. G. P. Goold. 2nd ed. Cambridge: Harvard University Press, 1988.

Patrologiae Cursus Completus, Series Latina (PL). Ed. J. P. Migne. 221 vols. in 222. Paris: Migne, 1844–1864. (Also available as *Patrologia Latina: The full Text Database*. An electronic resource. London: Chadwyck-Healey, 1996.)

Petrarch. *Rerum senilium libri* (Letters of Old Age). In *Librorum Francisci Petrarche Impressorum Annotatio*. Venice: n.p., 1501.

Quintilian. *Institutio oratoria*. Ed. and trans. H. E. Butler. 4 vols. Cambridge: Harvard University Press, 1920.

Recueil général des Isopets. Ed. Julia Bastin. Vol. 1. SATF. Paris: Champion, 1929.

Seneca. *Ad Lucilium epistulae morales* (Moral Epistles to Lucilius). Trans. Richard M. Gummere. 3 vols. Vols. 4–6 of *The Works of Seneca*. Cambridge: Harvard University Press, 1917–25.

———. *De tranquilitate animae* (On Tranquility of Mind). In *Moral Essays*, vol. 2. Vol. 2 of *The Works of Seneca*. Ed. and trans. John W. Basore. Rev. ed. Cambridge: Harvard University Press, 1935.

———. *Naturales quaestiones*. Trans. Thomas H. Corcoran. 2 vols. Vols. 7 and 10 of *The Works of Seneca*. Cambridge: Harvard University Press, 1971–72.

Terence. *Terence*. Ed. and trans. John Barsby. 2 vols. Cambridge: Harvard University Press, 2001.

Valerius Maximus. *Memorable Doings and Sayings*. Ed. and trans. D. R. Shackleton Bailey. 2 vols. Cambridge: Harvard University Press, 2000.

Virgil. *Eclogues, Georgics, Aeneid 1–6* (vol. 1) and *Aeneid 7–12, Appendix Vergiliana* (vol. 2). Ed. and trans. H. Rushton Fairclough. Rev. G. P. Goold. Rev. ed. 2 vols. Cambridge: Harvard University Press, 1999–2000.

SECONDARY SOURCES

Altmann, Barbara K., and Deborah L. McGrady, eds. *Christine de Pizan: A Casebook*. New York: Routledge, 2003.

Badel, Pierre-Yves. "Pierre d'Ailly, auteur du *Jardin amoureux*." *Romania* 97 (1976): 369–81.

———. *Le Roman de la Rose au XIVe siècle: Étude de la réception de l'œuvre*. Publications Romanes et Françaises, 153. Geneva: Droz, 1980.

Baird, Joseph L. "Pierre Col and the *Querelle de la Rose*." *Philological Quarterly* 60 (1981): 273–86.

Baird, Joseph L., and John R. Kane. "*La Querelle de la Rose*: In Defense of the Opponents." *French Review* 48, no. 2 (1974): 298–307.

Blamires, Alcuin. *The Case for Women in Medieval Culture*. Oxford: Clarendon Press, 1997.

Blumenfeld-Kosinski, Renate. "Christine de Pizan and the Misogynistic Tradition." *Romanic Review* 82, no. 3 (1990): 279–92.

———. "Jean Gerson and the Debate on the *Romance of the Rose*." In *A Companion to Jean Gerson*, ed. Brian Patrick McGuire. Brill's Companions to the Christian Tradition, 3. Leiden: Brill, 2006. 317–56.

Bozzolo, Carla, and Hélène Loyau. *La cour amoureuse dite de Charles VI*. Vol. 1: Étude et Édition critique des sources manuscrites. Paris: Le Léopard d'Or, 1982.

Brown, Cynthia J. "The Reconstruction of an Author in Print: Christine de Pizan in the Fifteenth and Sixteenth Centuries." In *Christine de Pizan and the Categories of Difference*, ed. Marilynn Desmond. Medieval Cultures, 14. Minneapolis: University of Minnesota Press, 1998. 215–35.

Brown-Grant, Rosalind. *Christine de Pizan and the Moral Defence of Women: Reading beyond Gender*. Cambridge: Cambridge University Press, 1999.

———. "Christine de Pizan as a Defender of Women." In *Christine de Pizan: A Casebook*, ed. Barbara K. Altmann and Deborah L. McGrady. New York: Routledge, 2003. 81–100.

———. "A New Context for Reading the 'Querelle de la *Rose*': Christine de Pizan and Medieval Literary Theory." In *Au Champ des Escritures*, ed. Eric Hicks, with Diego Gonzalez and Philippe Simon. Essays from the Third International Colloquium on Christine de Pizan. Études Christiniennes, 6. Paris: Honoré Champion, 2000. 581–95.

Brownlee, Kevin. "Discourses of the Self: Christine de Pizan and the *Romance of the Rose*." *Romanic Review* 79 (1988): 199–221.

Cerquiglini-Toulet, Jacqueline. *The Color of Melancholy: The Uses of Books in the Fourteenth Century*. Trans. Lydia G. Cochrane. Baltimore: Johns Hopkins University Press, 1997. [French orig., 1993.]

———. "L'étrangère." *Revue des Langues Romanes* 92, no. 2 (1988): 239–51. (English translation in *The Selected Writings of Christine de Pizan*, ed. Renate Blumenfeld-Kosinski, trans. Renate Blumenfeld-Kosinski and Kevin Brownlee [New York: W. W. Norton, 1997], 265–74.)

Combes, André. *Jean de Montreuil et le Chancelier Gerson: Contribution à l'histoire des rapports de l'humanisme et de la théologie en France au début du XVe siècle*. Études de Philosophie Médiévale, 32. Paris: Vrin, 1942.

Coville, A. *Gontier et Pierre Col et l'humanisme en France au temps de Charles VI*. Paris: Librairie E. Droz, 1934.

Cropp, Glynnis M. "Boèce et Christine de Pizan." *Le Moyen Âge* 87, nos. 3–4 (1981): 387–417.

Desmond, Marilynn, ed. *Christine de Pizan and the Categories of Difference*. Medieval Cultures, 14. Minneapolis: University of Minnesota Press, 1998.

———."The *Querelle de la Rose* and the Ethics of Reading." In *Christine de Pizan: A Casebook*, ed. Barbara K. Altmann and Deborah L. McGrady. New York: Routledge, 2003. 167–80.

Di Stefano, Giuseppe. *Dictionnaire des locutions en moyen français*. Bibliothèque du Moyen Français, 1. Montreal: Editions CERES, 1991.

Fenster, Thelma. "'Perdre son latin': Christine de Pizan and Vernacular Humanism." In *Christine de Pizan and the Categories of Difference* ed. Marilynn Desmond. Medieval Cultures, 14. Minneapolis: University of Minnesota Press, 1998. 91–107.

Fleming, John V. "The Moral Reputation of the *Roman de la Rose* before 1400." *Romance Philology* 18, no. 4 (1965): 430–35.

Guenée, Bernard. *Between Church and State: The Lives of Four French Prelates in the Late Middle Ages*. Trans. Arthur Goldhammer. Chicago: University of Chicago Press, 1991. [French orig. 1987.]

Hasenohr, Geneviève. Review of Hicks, *Le débat*. *Romania* 100 (1979): 126–32.

Hassell, James Woodrow, Jr. *Middle French Proverbs, Sentences, and Proverbial Phrases*. Subsidia Mediaevalia, 12. Toronto: Pontifical Institute of Mediaeval Studies, 1982.

Hicks, Eric. "The 'Querelle de la Rose' in the *Roman de la Rose*." *Les Bonnes Feuilles* 3, no. 2 (1974): 152–69.

Hicks, Eric, ed., with Diego Gonzalez and Philippe Simon. *Au Champ des Escriptures*. Essays from the Third International Colloquium on Christine de Pizan. Études Christiniennes, 6. Paris: Honoré Champion, 2000.

Hicks, Eric, and Ezio Ornato. "Jean de Montreuil et le débat sur le *Roman de la Rose*." *Romania* 98 (1977): 34–64, 186–219.

Hill, Jillian M. L. *The Medieval Debate on Jean de Meung's* Roman de la Rose: *Morality Versus Art*. Studies in Mediaeval Literature, 4. Lewiston, NY: Edwin Mellen Press, 1991.

Horowitz, Maryanne Cline. *Seeds of Virtue and Knowledge*. Princeton: Princeton University Press, 1998.

Hult, David F. "The *Roman de la Rose*, Christine de Pizan, and the *querelle des femmes*." In *The Cambridge Companion to Medieval Women's Writing*, ed. Carolyn Dinshaw and David Wallace. Cambridge: Cambridge University Press, 2003. 184–94.

———. "Words and Deeds: Jean de Meun's *Romance of the Rose* and the Hermeneutics of Censorship." *New Literary History* 28, no. 2 (1997): 345–66.

Huot, Sylvia. "Confronting Misogyny: Christine de Pizan and the *Roman de la Rose*." In *Translatio Studii: Essays by His Students in Honor of Karl D. Uitti for His Sixty-fifth Birthday*, ed. Renate Blumenfeld-Kosinski, Kevin Brownlee, Mary B. Speer, and Lori J. Walters. Amsterdam: Rodopi, 2000. 169–87.

———. *The Romance of the Rose and Its Medieval Readers: Interpretation, Reception, Manuscript Transmission*. Cambridge: Cambridge University Press, 1993.

———. "Seduction and Sublimation: Christine de Pizan, Jean de Meun and Dante." *Romance Notes* 25 (1985): 361–73.

Kelly, Douglas. *Christine de Pizan's Changing Opinion: A Quest for Certainty in the Midst of Chaos*. Cambridge, Eng.: D. S. Brewer, 2007.

Kennedy, Angus J. *Christine de Pizan: A Bibliographical Guide*. London: Grant & Cutler, 1984. Supplement 1, London: Grant & Cutler, 1994. Supplement 2, Rochester, NY: Tamesis, 2004.

Laidlaw, James. "Christine and the Manuscript Tradition." In *Christine de Pizan: A Casebook*, ed. Barbara K. Altmann and Deborah L. McGrady. New York: Routledge, 2003. 231–49.

———. "Christine de Pizan—An Author's Progress." *Modern Language Review* 78 (1983): 532–50.

———. "Christine de Pizan—A Publisher's Progress." *Modern Language Review* 82 (1987): 35–75.

———. "Christine de Pizan, the Earl of Salisbury and Henry IV." *French Studies* 36, no. 2 (1982): 129–43.

———. "L'unité des 'Cent Ballades.'" In *The City of Scholars: New Approaches to Christine de Pizan*, ed. Margarete Zimmerman and Dina De Rentiis. Berlin: De Gruyter, 1994. 97–106.

Lerner, Robert E. *The Heresy of the Free Spirit in the Later Middle Ages.* Berkeley: University of California Press, 1972

Lieberman, M. "Chronologie gersonienne, X: Le Sermon *Memento Finis.*" *Romania* 83 (1962): 52–89.

Marchello-Nizia, Christiane. *La langue française aux XIV*[e] *et XV*[e] *siècles.* Rev. ed. Paris: Nathan, 1997.

McWebb, Christine. "The *Roman de la Rose* and the *Livre des trois vertus:* The Never-Ending Debate." In *Au Champ des Escritures,* ed. Eric Hicks, with Diego Gonzalez and Philippe Simon. Essays from the Third International Colloquium on Christine de Pizan. Études Christiniennes, 6. Paris: Honoré Champion, 2000. 309–24.

Minnis, Alastair. *Magister Amoris: The* Roman de la Rose *and Vernacular Hermeneutics.* Oxford: Oxford University Press, 2001.

———. "Theorizing the Rose: Commentary Tradition in the *Querelle de la Rose.*" In *Poetics: Theory and Practice in Medieval English Literature.* Cambridge: D. S. Brewer, 1991. 13–36.

Monahan, Jennifer. "*Querelles:* Medieval Texts and Modern Polemics." In *Contexts and Continuities.* Proceedings of the Fourth International Colloquium on Christine de Pizan, Glasgow, July 21–27, 2000, published in honour of Liliane Dulac, ed. Angus J. Kennedy, with Rosalind Brown-Grant, James C. Laidlaw, and Catherine M. Müller. Vol. 2. Glasgow: University of Glasgow Press, 2002. 575–84.

Morawski, Joseph. *Proverbes français antérieurs au XV*[e] *siècle.* CFMA 47. Paris: Librairie Ancienne Édouard Champion, 1925.

Mourin, Louis. *Jean Gerson, Prédicateur français.* Rijksuniversiteit te Gent, Werken uitgegeven door de Faculteit van de Wijsbegeerte en Letteren, 113. Bruges: De Tempel, 1952.

———. *Six sermons français inédits de Jean Gerson: Étude doctrinale et littéraire suivie de l'édition critique et de remarques linguistiques.* Études de Théologie et d'Histoire de la Spiritualité, 8. Paris: Vrin, 1946.

Ornato, Ezio. *Jean Muret et ses amis, Nicolas de Clamanges et Jean de Montreuil: Contribution à l'étude des rapports entre les humanistes de Paris et ceux d'Avignon (1394–1420).* Geneva: Droz, 1969.

Ouy, Gilbert. "La plus ancienne œuvre retrouvée de Jean Gerson: *Le brouillon inachevé d'un traité contre Juan de Monzon (1389–90).*" *Romania* 83 (1962): 433–92.

Piaget, Arthur. "Chronologie des épistres sur le *Roman de la Rose.*" In *Études romanes dédiées à Gaston Paris.* Paris: Émile Bouillon, 1891. 114–22.

———. "La cour amoureuse dite de Charles VI." *Romania* 20 (1891): 417–54.

Potansky, Peter. *Der Streit um den Rosenroman.* Münchener Romanistische Arbeiten. Munich: Wilhelm Fink, 1972.

Richards, Earl Jeffrey. "Christine de Pizan and Jean Gerson: An Intellectual Friendship." In *Christine de Pizan 2000; Studies on Christine de Pizan in Honour of Angus J. Kennedy,* ed. John Campbell and Nadia Margolis. Faux Titre, 196. Amsterdam: Rodopi, 2000. 197–208.

Schibanoff, Susan. "Taking the Gold out of Egypt: The Art of Reading as a Woman." In *Gender and Reading: Essays on Readers, Texts, and Contexts,* ed. Elizabeth A. Flynn and Patrocinio P. Schweickart. Baltimore: Johns Hopkins University Press, 1986. 83–106.

Solente, Suzanne. "Christine de Pisan." *Histoire Littéraire de la France.* Ouvrage commencé par des Religieux Bénédictins de la Congrégation de Saint-Maur et continué par les Membres de l'Institut. Vol. 40. Paris: Imprimerie Nationale, 1974. 335–422.

Solterer, Helen. "Fiction versus Defamation: The Quarrel over the *Romance of the Rose.*" *Medieval History Journal* 2 (1999): 111–41.

———. "Flaming Words: Verbal Violence and Gender in Premodern Paris." *Romanic Review* 86, no. 2 (1995): 355–78.

———. *The Master and Minerva: Disputing Women in French Medieval Culture.* Berkeley: University of California Press, 1995.

South, Helen Pennock. "The Upstart Crow." *Modern Philology* 25, no. 1 (1927): 83–86.

Sullivan, Karen. "At the Limit of Feminist Theory: An Architectonics of the Querelle de la Rose." *Exemplaria* 3, no. 2 (1991): 435–66.

———. "The Inquisitorial Origins of Literary Debate." *Romanic Review* 88, no. 1 (1997): 27–51.

Thomas, Antoine. "Jean Castel." *Romania* 21 (1892): 271–74.

I
CHRISTINE AND THE *ROSE* BEFORE THE DEBATE

1. FROM CHRISTINE DE PIZAN, *THE GOD OF LOVE'S LETTER* (*L'EPISTRE AU DIEU D'AMOURS*, MAY 1, 1399)[1]

FRENCH VERSE (RHYMING DECASYLLABIC COUPLETS)

[*Cupid, the god of love, addresses this letter to all who are in his service. Presiding over his court, he has received a complaint from an unspecified group of women, concerning the large number of insincere and devious men who attempt to get their favors but who do nothing but slander women, whatever the outcome. Cupid condemns such men but praises those who are loyal and sincere in their love. He then launches into the more general topic of how men treat women.*]

Still I say that a man who says defamatory, offensive, or disgraceful things about women in an effort to scold them (be it one woman, or two, or categorically) is acting contrary to nature. And even if we assume that there are some foolish ones or ones full of many vices of different sorts, lacking faith, love, or any loyalty, domineering, wicked, or full of cruelty, or with little sense of constancy, fickle and changeable, crafty, furtive, and deceptive, must one, on that account, challenge all of them[2] and assert that they

1. This passage has been translated from *Œuvres poétiques de Christine de Pisan*, ed. Maurice Roy, 3 vols., SATF (Paris: Firmin Didot, 1886–96; rpt. New York: Johnson Reprint Corporation, 1965), 2:7–14 (ll. 181–422). English translations of the complete work are available in *Poems of Cupid, God of Love: Christine de Pizan's Epistre au Dieu d'Amours and Dit de la Rose, Thomas Hoccleve's The Letter of Cupid, with George Sewell's The Proclamation of Cupid*, ed. and trans. Thelma S. Fenster and Mary Carpenter Erler (Leiden: Brill, 1990), 34–75; and *The Selected Writings of Christine de Pizan*, ed. Renate Blumenfeld-Kosinski, trans. Renate Blumenfeld-Kosinski and Kevin Brownlee, 16–29.

2. The expression used here is *mettre en fermaille*, the meaning of which is not immediately obvious, although the general sense of the sentence is clear, referring to the idea, repeated elsewhere, that all women are being slandered and mistreated indiscriminately by men. In its literal sense, a *fermaille* is a buckle or a clasp; the few uses of the word I have found in a figurative

are all worthless? When God on high created and formed the angels, the cherubim, seraphim, and the archangels, were there not some of them whose acts were evil? Must one for that reason call the angels wicked? Instead, if someone knows an evil woman, let him watch out for her, without defaming one-third or one-fourth of them, or reprimanding all of them without exception and besmirching their female behavior; for there have been, are, and will be many of them[3] who, kindly and beautiful, are to be praised and in whom virtuous qualities are to be found, their discernment and merit having been proven by their benevolence.

But as concerns those who scold those women who are of but little worth, I still say that they are at fault if they name them and say who they are, where they live, what their deeds are, and of what sort. For one must not defame the sinner, this God tells us, or reprimand him in public. As the text where I read this asserts, one can certainly blame vices and sins harshly, without naming those who are tainted by them or defaming anyone. There are large numbers of people who speak like this, but such a vice is disgraceful in noble men. I say this to those who are guilty of it and not at all to those who have not sinned in this way, for there are many noble men so worthy that they would rather forfeit their possessions than in any way be accused or reproached for such deeds or be caught in the act of performing them.

But the injurious men I am talking about, who are good neither in deed nor in intention, do not follow the example of the good Hutin de Vermeilles,[4] in whom there was such an ample measure of goodness that no one ever had any reason to reproach him, nor did he ever value a slur meant

---

sense provide the sense of an agreement or an accord (such as a marriage betrothal) or, more frequently, a wager of some kind, typically involving some kind of dispute or challenge. The online Middle French Dictionary (ATILF, Nancy Université and CNRS, Dictionnaire du Moyen Français, http://www.atilf.fr/dmf, hereafter DMF) provides one example of the reflexive verb *soi mettre en fermaille,* meaning "to engage oneself, to bind oneself by one's word." I have translated the expression according to the latter sense, which suggests that men make all women prove their innocence by swearing to it or by putting up some kind of defense.

3. This is a tacit rejoinder to the famous, highly misogynistic, couplet attributed to the Jealous Husband in the *Rose:* "Toutes estes, serez et fustes, / de fet ou de volenté, pustes" (All you women are, will be, or have been, in deed or intention, whores) (*Rose,* ed. Lecoy, ll. 9125–26; trans. Dahlberg, 165 [altered]).

4. Hutin de Vermeilles was a well-known figure in the late fourteenth century, renowned for his chivalric deeds and his courtly qualities; he is best represented in the *Cent Ballades* (One Hundred Ballads), a poetic narrative written in 1389 by a small group of nobles, of whom Jean Le Sénéchal was the principal poet. Hutin is there portrayed as a wise, older knight who gives advice on chivalry and on manners to a younger knight identified as Jean Le Sénéchal. In addition to having had a brilliant military career (he was at the battle of Poitiers in 1356 and fought other battles against the Black Prince), he was related to the royal family through his marriage to Marguerite de Bourbon and served as a chamberlain to the king until his death in 1390.

to defame. He was exceptional in the honor he bestowed upon women, and he was incapable of listening to accusatory or dishonorable things said about them. He was a brave, wise, and beloved knight, and this is why he was and will continue to be glorified. The good, the valiant Oton de Grandson,[5] who ventured out exerting himself so much for military causes, was in his time courtly, noble, brave, handsome, and kind—may God receive his soul in heaven!—for he was a knight with many good qualities. Whoever acted ill toward him I consider to have committed a sin; Fortune, however, did him harm, but she commonly brings suffering to good men.[6] For in all circumstances I consider him to have been loyal, and braver in military deeds than Ajax, son of Telemon. He never took pleasure in defaming anyone, he strove to serve, praise, and love women. Many others were good and valiant and ought to serve as examples for those who fall short; there still are many of them, there truly is need of them, those who follow the good paths of valiant men. Honor trains them, virtue leads them there; they put effort into acquiring renown and praise; they take pride in the noble manners with which they are endowed; their merits are manifested in their brilliant deeds in this kingdom, in others, and beyond the seas. But I will refrain from naming their names here, for fear that someone might say this was meant to flatter, or that it risk turning into a boast.[7] And this is indeed how men of noble breeding must by right behave. Otherwise that very nobility would be lacking in them.[8]

5. Oton de Grandson (1340/1350–1397) was the emblematic figure of the knight/poet in the late fourteenth century. He had a very full military career during the Hundred Years' War. A noble from Savoy whose earlier allegiances were with the kings of England, Oton was later pardoned by the king of France. His fame as a love poet was even greater than that as a knight, and his works remained popular to the end of the fifteenth century. Hutin de Vermeilles and Oton de Grandson are also mentioned by Christine in the *Débat de deux amants* (Debate of Two Lovers), in *Œuvres poétiques de Christine de Pisan,* 2:97 (ll. 1615–19).

6. Oton de Grandson did indeed come to a tragic end. Caught up in some complicated political maneuvers in the 1390s, he was accused of being an accomplice to murder, and, ultimately sentenced to participate in a judicial duel in order to prove his guilt or innocence, he was killed in 1397.

7. One can sense here the dual presence of Christine and the God of Love in this fictional letter. Christine has reason to be sensitive about flattery, an issue that will be brought out later in the debate, but it is the God of Love who is cautious about boasting (worthy men in love being a sign of Cupid's success).

8. What I have translated as "in them" is the indirect object pronoun *y,* which can in Old and Middle French refer to animate or inanimate nouns. It could conceivably be referring to the aforementioned "kingdom" or more generally to the "world," meaning that if noble men do not act in this way nobility would disappear. However, a form of the same word is being used for "noble"/"nobility" (*gentil/gentillece*) in the last two sentences of this paragraph, which would suggest that this sentence is referring pointedly back to the statement in the previous one.

But the above-mentioned ladies complain of several clerics[9] who accuse them of blameworthy conduct, composing literary works, lyric poems, works in prose and in verse, defaming their behavior with a variety of expressions; then they give these materials to beginning students—to their new, young pupils—to serve as a model and as instruction, so that they will retain such advice into their adulthood. They say in their poetry, "Adam, David, Samson, and Solomon, along with a mass of others, were deceived by women morning and night. What man will manage to protect himself from this?" Another cleric says that they are most deceitful, wily, treacherous, and of little value. Others say that they are exceedingly mendacious, fickle, unstable, and flighty. Others accuse them of several serious vices and blame them ceaselessly, never excusing them for anything. It is in this manner that day and night clerics compose their poems, now in French, now in Latin, and they base themselves upon I don't know what books that tell more lies than a drunken man.

Ovid said a lot of nasty things about them (I consider that he did much harm by this) in a book he wrote, which he called the *Remedia amoris* (Remedies for Love)[10] and in which he accuses them of repulsive behavior—foul, ugly, and full of disgrace. That they might possess such vices, this I dispute with him, and I make my pledge to defend this in battle against all those who would like to throw down the gauntlet; I am of course referring to honorable women, for I do not take any account of worthless ones. Thus the clerics have studied this little book since their childhood in their earliest learning of grammar,[11] and they teach it to others with the goal that their pupils not

9. Here and elsewhere in this volume, I translate the French term *clerc* as "cleric," which indicated throughout the Middle Ages a man who had received some measure of learning (in matters both secular and religious) and had some connection with a religious institution, typically marked by the tonsure. The words "lay" and "cleric" designated a major social distinction, the former often associated with a lack of learning and illiteracy (but incorrectly so, as many aristocrats knew how to read but were members of the laity), while the latter (as a group, known as the *clergie*) formed the intelligentsia, functioning not only in religious circles but in the secular world, as teachers, for instance, or as bureaucrats within the royal administration. All of the men participating in the debate with Christine are members of this group.

10. Although it is Ovid's *Art of Love* that is usually cited for its misogynistic perspectives, as later in this passage, here Christine has the God of Love refer to Ovid's retraction of his earlier text. Part of the advice Ovid gives to the lover who wishes to rid himself of his feelings is to disparage his lady's physical charms and behavior, which is undoubtedly what is being referred to here.

11. The study of grammar, one of the three sciences of language, along with logic and rhetoric, known throughout the Middle Ages as the *trivium*, had become a very sophisticated discipline in the universities, stretching into the domains of philosophy and epistemology. Here, Christine is thinking of the more modest place of grammar in pre-university training, which often used snippets of classical Latin texts as exemplars.

endeavor to love a woman. But as far as this is concerned, they are foolish and wasting their time: to prevent such love would be nothing if not futile. For between myself and Lady Nature, as long as the world lasts we will not allow women not to be cherished and loved, in spite of all those who would like to reproach them, nor will we prevent them from seizing, removing, and making off with the hearts of several of those very people who rebuke them the most[12]—this without any deceit and without any blackmail, but just by ourselves and the impression we make on the mind: men will never be so informed by skilled clerics [as to resist it], not even for all their poems, notwithstanding the fact that many books speak of women and blame them, for they have very little effect in this matter.

And if someone says that one must believe the books that were made by men of great renown and of great learning, who did not give their consent to lies—those who proved the wickedness of women—I respond to them that those who wrote this down in their books did not, I think, seek to do anything else in their lives but deceive women; these men could not get enough of them, and every day they wanted new ones, without remaining loyal, even to the most beautiful of them. What was the result for David and King Solomon? God became angry with them and punished their excess. There have been many others, and especially Ovid, who desired so many of them and then thought he could defame them. Indeed, all the clerics who have spoken so much about them were wildly attracted to them much more than other people—not to a single one, but to a thousand! And if people like this had a mistress or a wife who did not do absolutely all they wanted or who might have attempted to deceive them, what is surprising about that? For there is no doubt that when a man thrusts himself into such an abject state, he does not go looking for worthy ladies or good and respected noblewomen. He neither knows them nor has anything to do with them. He does not want any others than those who are of his station: he surrounds himself with strumpets and commoners. Does such a man deserve to possess anything of value, a skirt chaser who adds all women to his list and then, when he is no longer capable of anything and is already an old man, thinks he can successfully cover up his shame by blaming women with his clever arguments? However, were someone to blame only those women who have given themselves over to vice and who have led a dissolute life, and advise them not

12. The syntax of this very long sentence is tricky. The God of Love's point is that whatever the clerics say, he and Nature will prevail: men will love women and women will steal men's hearts, in spite of what they read. The sentence reads in the original: "we will not allow them not to be cherished . . . and not to seize the hearts." Since this is rather awkward, I have reformulated the second part with the verb "prevent" and a positive verb, which says roughly the same thing.

to continue as they have done, he could truly succeed in his enterprise; and it would be a very reasonable thing, a worthy, just, and praiseworthy teaching, devoid of defamatory statements about all women indiscriminately.

And to say something about trickery, I am incapable of imagining or conceiving how a woman could deceive a man: she neither goes looking for him nor hunts him down; she does not go to his home to beg him or woo him; she does not think of him or even remember him when the man comes to deceive and tempt her. To tempt her how? Truly, he gives the appearance that there is no torment that is not easy for him to endure, nor burden to bear. He doesn't take pleasure in any other activity than in striving to deceive them, having committed his heart, his body, and his wealth to it. This suffering, along with the pain, lasts a long time and is often repeated, even though such lovers' plans often fail, in spite of their effort. And it is of these men that Ovid speaks in his treatise on the art of love; for on account of the pity that he had for these men he compiled a book in which he writes to them and teaches them clearly how they will be able to deceive women with tricks and obtain their love. And he called the book *The Art of Love*; however, he does not teach behaviors or morals having to do with loving well, but rather the opposite. For a man who wants to act according to this book will never love, however much he is loved, and this is why the book is poorly named. For it is a book on the *Art of Great Deception*—this is the name I give it—*and of False Appearances.*

How is it then—since women are weak and frivolous, easy to sway, naïve and scarcely upright, as some clerics claim—that these men have need for so many ruses in their effort to procure this goal? And why do these women not give in instantly without there being any need for skill or cunning in order to capture them? For once a castle has been taken there is no need to start a war. And especially for a poet as clever as Ovid, who was later exiled, and Jean de Meun in the *Romance of the Rose*—what a drawn-out affair! what a difficult thing! He puts in it much erudition, both clear and obscure, and impressive stories! But how many characters are introduced into it and consulted, and so many exertions and tricks invented, in order to deceive just one young girl—and that's the goal of it, by means of fraud and ruse! Is a great assault thus necessary for an unprotected place? What's the use of making a great leap when one is so close? I do not see or understand why great effort, skill or wit, or great cunning would be necessary to take an undefended site. It thus necessarily follows from this that since skill, great ingenuity, and considerable effort are needed to deceive a noble or common woman, they are not at all so fickle as some say or so changeable in their affairs.

Yet if people tell me that the books are full of these things—this is a response that many make and that I deplore—I respond to them that women did not make the books and that they did not put in them the things that we read there against women and their morals; and those who plead their case without an opponent go on talking to their hearts' content, make no concessions, and take the lion's share for themselves, for combative people easily injure those who do not defend themselves. But if women had written the books, I know in truth that the facts would be different, for they know well that they have been wrongly condemned and that the shares have not been divided equitably: the stronger ones take the biggest portion and he who slices the pieces keeps the best for himself . . .

2. FROM CHRISTINE DE PIZAN, *MORAL TEACHINGS* (*LES ENSEIGNEMENS MORAUX*, 1399 OR 1402?)[13]

FRENCH VERSE (RHYMING OCTOSYLLABIC COUPLETS ORGANIZED IN QUATRAINS)

[*Christine wrote this work to provide teachings to her young son, who had a lengthy stay in England from 1399 to 1402; it is normally assumed that she either gave it to him before his departure or wrote it after he returned in the spring of 1402. In any event, it was written before June 1402, inasmuch as it is included in Christine's first manuscript collection, which was completed in that month. The work consists of a sequence of 113 quatrains, each providing a specific moral lesson or bit of advice concerning such things as dress, speech, charity, and so forth.*]

XXXVIII. Do not believe all the defamatory statements that some books make about women, for there exist many good women; this, experience shows you.

XLI. Flee rowdy company and women who lack modesty, deceivers, people who ridicule and slander, as well as those who harm others.

XLIV. Listen to this lesson and note it down. Do not fall madly in love with a stupid woman if you want true love, for your moral fiber would be degraded by it.

XLVII. Do not be a deceiver of women; honor them and do not defame them. Limit yourself to loving a single one and do not quarrel with any.

LI. If you wish to take a woman as a wife, observe the mother and you can ascertain her moral qualities; this said, there are undoubtedly few rules that do not on occasion prove wrong.

13. Translated from *Œuvres poétiques de Christine de Pisan,* 3:33–41.

LV. If you have a good and wise wife, believe her on the state of the household and trust her word, but do not speak in confidence to a foolish one.

LXVII. Do not reveal your secret to anyone without cause, and do not tell tales of others when there is no point in doing so, for he who reveals his thoughts is enslaved.

LXXIII. Flee idleness if you want to acquire honor, possessions, a reputation, and land; beware of worthless pleasures, and avoid disreputable deeds.

LXXVI. If you wish to flee the domination of love and totally cast it away, distance yourself from the person to whom your heart is most inclined.

LXXVII. If you wish to live well and chastely, do not read the book of the *Rose* or Ovid's *Art of Love,* for their example merits reproach.

LXXX. If your desire is pointed toward love and you wish to love in order to be more worthy, do not work up such a passion in your heart that you might end up being worth less.

LXXXV. If you feel your passions making you impulsive, have Reason take you into her school and teach you to put your feelings in order; in this way you can restrain yourself.

XCI. To the extent that you can, clothe your wife honorably and let her be next to you as the lady of the house, not a servant; make your household serve her.

XCIV. Make your wife fear you as necessary, but make sure never to beat her, for if she's good it would make her resentful, and if she's bad, she'd just get worse.

3. FROM CHRISTINE DE PIZAN, *THE DEBATE OF TWO LOVERS* (*LE DÉBAT DE DEUX AMANS,* 1400?)[14]

FRENCH VERSE (QUATRAINS FORMED BY THREE DECASYLLABLES FOLLOWED BY A FOUR-SYLLABLE LINE, WITH THE RHYME SCHEME *AAAB, BBBC, CCCD,* ETC.)

[*The first-person narrator, identifiable with Christine, presents to Louis, duke of Orléans, this debate between two lovers that she claims to have witnessed, and she asks him to offer his*

14. Translated from ibid, 2:76–79 (ll. 909–1000). A complete English translation is available in *An Anthology of Medieval Love Debate Poetry,* ed. and trans. R. Barton Palmer and Barbara K. Altmann (Gainesville: University Press of Florida, 2006), 257–305.

judgment of it. At a gracious party in a Parisian dwelling in the month of May, the narrator begins a conversation on the topic of love with a knight and a squire. In order to be able to talk more privately, they go outside to an orchard, but the narrator insists on having a "lady . . . who hates slander and reproach" (l. 386) and a bourgeois woman accompany them, so that there will be no possibility for slanderers to wag their tongues. The debate, on whether love brings happiness or sorrow to lovers, is opened by the knight, who provides a lengthy exposé on the torments of love.]

When the affable and courtly knight had finished his noteworthy speech, which most people would take to be the truth, and expertly delivered, expressed with some nice touches, neither too slow nor too hurried, the lady, who had listened closely to the speech, then started afresh and said: "If I have understood your discourse, the god of Love provides harsh schooling to lovers, neither soothing nor tender, or so it seems to me; without reason, he drives many a man mad. But as for me, I do not think that there are hordes of lovers trapped in such a prison, in spite of the fact that many go around delivering this line to women, sometimes here, sometimes there; nonetheless, their heart is not in it nor do they ever pause in one single place,[15] however much they go on thoroughly wasting their words with endless speeches. But I do not believe that a single one is so seriously enslaved by it nor that he would ever serve Love and his lady so loyally and with such submissive hope. And, begging your pardon, I do not believe, by my soul, that any man is so inflamed by such a fire that he would experience such painful suffering for a woman; rather, it is a quite a common tale that men tell women in order to inspire trust, whereas the whole thing amounts to nothing. But she who lends credence to such a discourse is in the end held to be rather unwise. As for me, I maintain that it has just become a habit to speak of love in this way, in jest and to pass the time.

And if what I have just heard were true, that lovers in ancient times were sincere in the way you describe, then to my mind it has been more than a hundred years since this has happened, for neither today nor yesterday have lovers been thus afflicted. However, lovers do know how to satisfy their needs through argumentation and eloquence. And even if long ago they died and languished on account of love and endured many painful ills—even the most fortunate of them, as you tell[16]—I believe that nowadays

15. Not pausing or stopping in a single place, or not depositing one's heart there, is a common way of referring to the lover's fickleness.

16. In his discourse, the unhappy lover had provided a list of unhappy lovers from myth, romance, and history: Paris and Helen; Pyramus and Thisbe; Hero and Leander; Achilles and Po-

their pains are slight. In spite of this, these pains continue to be found written down in abundance in romances and meticulously described at length. The *Romance of the Rose* spoke of it well in drawn-out expositions, and thus provided something of a gloss on the sort of love you have just expressed here, in the chapter of Reason, who forcefully gives directives to the foolish lover, who has been ensnared by such a love. She states all too well that the greatest joy arising from this love is worth little and passes quickly; she gives him advice on the path one must take in order to extricate oneself from it and likewise says that it is a thing that leads lovers astray, a severe affliction, adding that it is loyal disloyalty, and loyalty that is very disloyal,[17] a great peril for noblemen and royalty: all people are doomed if they approach it. That's what she said, but I think that few people are caught up in this kind of feeling;[18] rather, all desire nothing except money and living comfortably. But also who could live in the wretchedness that you have described? I believe, by Saint Nicaise, that there is not a man alive (may no one be displeased by this) who, however sturdy he might be, would be able to bear the ills that I hear you tell of here without tasting death.

But I have never heard tell where the cemeteries are in which are buried those whom pure love has put to death and who, for such a reason, have been confined to bed or might be carried in a stretcher to the saint from whom the illness comes.[19] So, whatever many people say, I believe that no one loves unless it is for his pleasure. I do not say this to contradict your statement and your lament, with all due respect, nor am I debating that this

---

lixena; Essacus, son of Priam, and Hesperia; Iphis and Anaxarete; Tristan and Iseut; Cahedin, also from the *Tristan*; the Châtelain de Coucy and the dame de Faël; the Châtelaine de Vergy.

17. Christine here quotes from Reason's list of contraries, itself translated from Alan of Lille's *Complaint of Nature*, that articulates the paradoxical nature of love (*Rose*, ed. Lecoy, ll. 4265–66; trans. Dahlberg, 94: "Love is . . . disloyal loyalty and loyal disloyalty").

18. Thus, according to this lady, Reason's cautions are unnecessary, for no one loves in this way.

19. There would seem to be here a reference to a tradition used by Achille Caulier, a poet who followed upon the success of Christine's contemporary, Alain Chartier, probably in the 1430s. In his *Cruelle femme en amour* (Cruel Lady in Matters of Love), he speaks of a temple of Venus where sick lovers go to be cured, next to which is a cemetery of great lovers; he expands this vision in his later *Hospital of Love*, which has still another famous cemetery scene (cf. Alain Chartier, Baudet Herenc, Achille Caulier, *Le cycle de* La Belle Dame sans Mercy, ed. David F. Hult, with the collaboration of Joan E. McRae, Champion Classiques, 8 [Paris: Honoré Champion, 2003], 260–65 and 362–69). On the cemetery of love as an important image characteristic of fourteenth- and fifteenth-century literature, see Jacqueline Cerquiglini-Toulet, *The Color of Melancholy*, trans. Lydia G. Cochrane (Baltimore: Johns Hopkins University Press, 1997), 127–40.

could not be, but I believe that those who have such a poor recovery from having loved too much are few and far between."

[The squire follows with an impassioned response in which he speaks of the joys of love. After a brief restatement of their irreconcilable positions, the two men attempt to find a judge who will decide the dispute, but since it is impossible to pick a judge, it is left in the hands of the narrator (Christine), who proposes to turn the decision over to the duke of Orléans. The two debaters ask Christine to make a poem of the event, and that is the form in which she presents it to the duke.]

II
THE DEBATE: FIRST PHASE

4. JEAN DE MONTREUIL TO PIERRE D'AILLY (LATE MAY 1401)[1]

LATIN PROSE

As things go, since it happens that there is nothing better that I might write, my most reverend father, nor would I wish to be a spreader of rumors[2] (for this is beyond and in violation of our office), I was beginning, so to speak, to till new fields; then recently, here you have Gontier urging me—or rather ordering me!—to take a look at the *Romance of the Rose*: I ran off and read it as eagerly as possible. Then I described, in a French work, the author's genius,

1. Translated from *Le débat*, ed. Hicks, 28. Pierre d'Ailly (1351–1420) was an important theologian of the late fourteenth and early fifteenth centuries, deeply involved in papal politics during the time of the Schism. He preceded his former disciple and close ally, Jean Gerson, as chancellor of the University of Paris and then rose rapidly in the Church hierarchy, becoming the bishop of Cambrai (1396) and later a cardinal and papal legate. He was also a prolific writer of theological and philosophical works, including some written in French, and a master at the Collège de Navarre, which was a breeding ground for many members of the Parisian intelligentsia, the milieu of the male participants in the debate, including Gerson and Jean de Montreuil. Although this letter, like most of those by Jean de Montreuil included here, does not contain the name of its addressee, Hicks and Ezio Ornato ("Jean de Montreuil et le débat sur le *Roman de la Rose*," 42–49) argue convincingly that it was Pierre d'Ailly. It is generally assumed now that Pierre d'Ailly's "answer" to Jean de Montreuil's treatise on the *Rose*, which accompanied this letter, was the French rereading of the *Rose* overlaid with the biblical Song of Songs, his "The Devout Soul's Garden of Love" (no. 11 in this volume). See Pierre-Yves Badel, "Pierre d'Ailly, auteur du *Jardin Amoureux*," *Romania* 97 (1976): 369–81; and Bernard Guenée, *Between Church and State: The Lives of Four French Prelates in the Late Middle Ages*, trans. Arthur Goldhammer (Chicago: University of Chicago Press, 1991), 199.

2. The documentation and detailed discussion by Hicks and Ornato, "Jean de Montreuil et le débat sur le *Roman de la Rose*," 42–64, suggest that the "rumors" (*rumores*) refer to state secrets: Jean de Montreuil had recently returned from a diplomatic mission to Germany and he seems to be indicating that he preferred busying himself with some other activity during his "down time," rather than indiscriminately revealing any of these confidential affairs.

including as much as it was possible to pull together and my great enthusiasm could express, just as you will see, very reverend father, in the attachment to the present letter.[3]

It will therefore be up to you to decide, my lord, whether I have praised the author more or less than is due, or in proper measure; and this notwithstanding, also to let this adoptive son of yours know, provided that your other occupations permit, whether a certain reply sent by me several days ago to our treasurer of Langres[4] has reached the attention of your Excellency.

Be well and do approve.

5. CHRISTINE DE PIZAN TO JEAN DE MONTREUIL (JUNE–JULY 1401)[5]

FRENCH PROSE

To a most considerable and learned person, Master Jean Johannes, secretary to the king our lord

Reverent and respectful greetings to you, my lord provost of Lille, most cherished lord and master, wise in behavior, a lover of knowledge, immersed in clerical learning and expert in rhetoric, from me, Christine de Pizan, a woman of untrained intellect and uncomplicated sensibility. May these factors in no way induce your wisdom to scorn the slightness of my arguments, but rather to consent to make up for their deficiency out of consideration for my feminine weakness. It has pleased you to do the good deed of sending me—for which I thank you—a short treatise prepared with impressive eloquence and plausible arguments (which is made up of your own com-

3. This "attachment," Jean de Montreuil's French treatise in praise of the *Romance of the Rose,* has unfortunately not survived and is therefore not one of the documents included in this volume. See above, volume editor's introduction, p. 12.

4. The treasurer of Langres is the humanist colleague of Jean de Montreuil, Nicolas de Clamanges, who is most likely to have been the "noble cleric" to whom Jean de Montreuil initially sent his treatise on the *Rose,* according to Christine's account (see below, n. 6). Whereas she claims that the treatise was written in order to "convert" this cleric to his side, Montreuil states here that he wrote it spontaneously and without an addressee in mind.

5. Translated from *Le débat,* ed. Hicks, 11–22. A cautionary note: Hicks prints two versions of this letter in his edition: the one I have translated, taken from one of Christine de Pizan's manuscripts and therefore copied under her supervision; and the one contained in the manuscript of the "Lover of the Rose" (49–57). The latter contains a text that shortens some passages, displaces others, and occasionally mangles parts of the original; it is likely to be related to the version of the letter to which Pierre Col responded (see below, no. 21) but does not seem to have fundamentally altered the content of Christine's arguments.

ments, intended to reproach, as it seems to me, some critics of certain parts of the compilation known as the *Romance of the Rose,* and to champion the work while sanctioning it along with its authors, in particular Meun). I have read and pondered your aforementioned prose essay and understood the gist of it, within the confines of my meager intellect. But even though it neither is addressed to me nor requires a response, I, stirred up by an opinion that runs counter to your writings, concur with the preeminent, shrewd cleric to whom the letter in question is addressed[6] and wish to state, proclaim, and maintain publicly that, with all due respect, it is most wrongly and without justification that you have given such unalloyed praise to the work in question, which may in my judgment more appropriately be labeled pure idleness than useful work.[7]

And however much you reproach its opponents, claiming that "it is thus a difficult thing to understand what another text expresses; he [Meun] has better constructed and proposed, through much study and at great length, etc.," may the fact that I dare to repudiate and reproach such a celebrated and clever author not be attributed to presumptuousness on my part, but rather be credited to the firm and serious conviction that motivates me to oppose certain details contained within the work. After all, something stated as an opinion and not dictated by Law can be accused of error without harm.[8] And although I am not steeped in learning or familiar with subtle

6. This cleric is never named. Hicks and Ornato ("Jean de Montreuil et le débat sur le *Roman de la Rose,*" 50) float the name of Nicolas de Clamanges (see above, n. 4) as a good possibility, but only affirm that this "noble cleric" was a member of Jean de Montreuil's close circle of friends and someone of comparable social rank. Pierre-Yves Badel (*Le Roman de la Rose au XIVe siècle: Étude de la réception de l'œuvre,* Publications Romanes et Françaises, 153 [Geneva: Droz, 1980], 412) concurs with somewhat more certainty that it is "probably" Nicolas de Clamanges. In no.18, her introductory outline of the genesis of the debate, Christine says, "the said provost sent to the said Christine the copy of a letter he had sent to a friend of his, a noble cleric, who, motivated by reason, was of the same opinion as the said Christine against the said romance; in order to convert him, the said provost had written the said letter, most remarkably embellished with beautiful rhetoric, and in order to kill two birds with one stone, he sent it to her."

7. As Baird and Kane have suggested (*La querelle de la Rose,* 47), the use of the word "idleness" (*oysiveté*) to refer to the *Rose* is certainly an ironic reference to the personified character Idleness (*Oiseuse*) in the poem, who is the gatekeeper of the garden: both the garden and the poem are condemned by the same argument.

8. Christine here makes a distinction she will use elsewhere (see the opening to her letter to Pierre Col, no. 22), between opinion, which is variable and lacking any authority, and the truth, which for her has the value of "law" (by which she may be thinking of Christian orthodoxy). "Law" is capitalized in this passage and elsewhere to indicate the specificity of Christine's reference to God's law. For Christine, Jean de Montreuil and the other supporters of the *Rose* are in error when they consider it to be the statement of eternal truths. As Badel has pointed out (*Le Roman de la Rose au XIVe siècle,* 436–47), "opinion" is for Christine a stage of knowledge that

language, which would enable me to use sophisticated structures and finely arrayed, polished words that would make my arguments dazzling, I will nonetheless not refrain from stating concretely and in plain vernacular the conviction I have formed in my mind, even though I may not be capable of expressing it with precision by means of ornate words.

Now why did I say before that the work "may better be called idleness"? It seems to me without doubt that anything lacking value, however great the labor and effort with which it may have been conceived, composed, and brought to completion, can be called idle, or worse than idle the more that evil results from it. And since I had already long ago wanted to see the aforementioned romance because of its great and widespread reputation, once my learning made me somewhat able to understand subtle matters I read and evaluated it from one end to the other as best I could understand it. It is true that regarding material that in some parts was not to my taste, I skipped over it like a rooster over hot embers, so I did not see it in its entirety. Nevertheless, there remained in my memory certain topics it treats that my judgment severely condemned and still cannot approve, in spite of the praise of other people that says quite the contrary. It is indeed true that my meager understanding finds in it considerable charm, and in some sections there is quite serious treatment of what he wants to express, with very beautiful terms and in elegant verses with rich rhymes;[9] and what he desired to expound could not be expressed more subtly or in more skillful strokes. However, I agree with the opinion that you contradict: without any doubt, it seems to me, he speaks most inappropriately in some parts, especially through the character he calls Reason, who names the private parts plainly by name.[10] And as

---

is contingent and transitory; in her later *Christine's Vision*, the personified Opinion, daughter of Ignorance and Desire-to-Know, claims to be the inspiration for the debate (see no. 32 below). In retrospect, therefore, Christine acknowledges that her position in the debate itself participates in the contingency that characterizes all intellectual exchanges, in spite of her references to the truth of experience and of faith.

9. The word used here is *leonime*, which had been used as early as the twelfth century (cf. the prologue to *Guillaume d'Angleterre*, attributed by some to Chrétien de Troyes) to refer to rhymes involving two or as many as three syllables repeated. In his *Art of Poetry (Art de Dictier)*, Christine's contemporary Eustache Deschamps uses a stanza of one of his ballads to illustrate the poetic effect: "This ballad is *leonine*, because in every line it [the rhyme] comprises an entire syllable, as in *dolente* and *presente*, *concepcion* and *constellacion*" (*Oeuvres complètes*, ed. Gaston Raynaud [Paris: Firmin-Didot, 1878–1903], 7:274). In both cases the rhymes contain more than the minimal requirement for a simple rhyme (in the first case, the mute *e* following the rhyme, and in the second, the preceding consonantal sound in addition to the two syllables of the *io* sound). Whatever Christine thinks about the content of the *Rose*, she has praise for Jean de Meun's artistry.

10. Cf. *Rose*, ed. Lecoy, ll. 5507, 7081–82, 7086–87 (trans. Dahlberg, 113, 135). By using antiseptic Latinate terms such as "testicle" to translate the raunchier terms used by Jean de Meun, Dahlberg's translation obscures the provocative intention of the medieval author. Here as elsewhere, in Christine's letter as well as in Pierre Col's, the genitals are referred to with the phrase

to your support of his opinion, you who concur that it is only reasonable to act thus, claiming that there is no ugliness in the things God has made and that, consequently, their names should not be avoided, I declare and profess that God truly did create all things pure and clean coming from himself and that it would thus not have been an offense to name them in the state of innocence; but by the pollution of sin man became impure, and because of this original sin has remained with us up to the present moment (to this, Holy Scripture testifies). By way of comparison I can propose the following: God made Lucifer beautiful above all the angels and gave him a very solemn and appealing name, but he was later reduced to horrible ugliness on account of his sin; whence the name, albeit very attractive in itself, nonetheless arouses horror in those who hear it because of the impression made by the person.

Furthermore, you propose that Jesus Christ, "in speaking of women sinners, calls them *meretrix*," etc.[11] As far as his calling them by this name is concerned, I can refute you by explaining that using the word *meretrix* is not at all inappropriate, in view of the vileness of the thing—in fact, it could be said even more shamefully in Latin. And as for the idea that modesty ought to be shunted aside when one speaks publicly of things about which even Nature blushes with shame, I state, with all due respect to the author and to you, that you are both committing a great wrong against the noble virtue of modesty, which by its nature inhibits ribaldry and licentiousness in words and deeds. Moreover, that it is a great vice and outside the order of respectable rules of behavior and good morals is made clear in many places in the Holy Scripture.[12] Furthermore, [as to your statement] that the word should not be

---

secréz membres (literally, "secret members"). I have preferred to translate it throughout as "private parts," finding it faithful to the Middle French but somewhat more colloquial.

11. Mt 21:31–32: "Amen dico vobis, quia publicani et meretrices præcedent vos in regnum Dei. Venit enim ad vos Joannes in via justitiae, et non credidistis ei: publicani autem et meretrices crediderunt ei" (Amen I say to you, that the publicans and the harlots shall go into the kingdom of God before you. For John came to you in the way of justice, and you did not believe him. But the publicans and the harlots believed him); Lk 15:30: "Sed postquam filius tuus hic, qui devoravit substantiam suam cum meretricibus, venit, occidisti illi vitulum saginatum" (But as soon as this thy son is come, who hath devoured his substance with harlots, thou hast killed for him the fatted calf). Biblical quotations and English translations throughout have been taken from *Biblia Sacra juxta Vulgatam Clementinam: Editio Electronica*, ed. Michaele Tvveedale (London: n.p., 2005): http://vulsearch.sourceforge.net/html. The translation included on this site is the Douay-Rheims Bible. Of the versions of the Vulgate available from numerous venues, the Clementine version seems closest to the biblical text used by the debate participants.

12. As Hicks notes, Christine will later, in her *Book of the Deeds and Good Conduct of the Wise King Charles V* (1404), use the following quotation from 1 Cor 15:33: "Les paroles mauvaises courrompent les bonnes meurs" (Evil words corrupt good manners) (*Le livre des fais et bonnes meurs du sage Roy Charles V*, ed. S. Solente, 2 vols. [Paris: Honoré Champion, 1936–40], 1:85). The same text is quoted by Gerson in his sermon *Considerate lilia* (no. 12).

rejected "any more than if they were called relics,"[13] I profess to you that the name does not create the indecency of the thing, but that the thing makes the name indecent. Because of this, in my humble opinion, they must be spoken about soberly—and only when necessary—with a view toward some particular case, such as an illness or some other respectable exigency. Just as our first parents hid them instinctually, so must we do in deed and in word.

Moreover, I cannot remain silent about the following, at which I feel deep displeasure: that the function of Reason, whom he [Jean de Meun] even calls the daughter of God, should be to put forward a proposition (and in the form of a proverb!) of the sort that I found in the same chapter, where she says to the Lover that "in the war of love . . . it is better to deceive than to be deceived."[14] Indeed I dare say that the Reason of Master Jean de Meun renounced her father with this dictum, for he provided a totally different teaching. And if the one were to be better than the other, it would follow that both were good, which cannot be. I myself maintain a contrary opinion: that it is, to speak truthfully, less evil to be deceived than to deceive.

Now let's go on to consider the subject matter or the manner of speaking, which, in the fine opinion of many, merit reproach. Dear Lord God! What dreadfulness! What indecency! And what a profusion of reprehensible teachings he includes in the chapter about the Old Woman![15] For God's sake, who will be able to find anything there except specious exhortations replete with filth and reminders of the most ignoble things. Hey there! Those of you who have beautiful daughters and wish to introduce them to an honorable way of living, give them, yes, seek out and give them *The Romance of the Rose* in order to teach them to distinguish good from evil—what am I saying!—rather evil from good! What is the use or the profit to those who hear so many outrageous statements? Then, in the chapter on Jealousy,[16] my God!

13. This is apparently a quotation from Montreuil's now-lost treatise, in which he recapitulates the argument already contained in Reason's speech: "se je, quant mis les nons aus choses / que si reprendre et blasmer oses, / coilles reliques apelasse / et reliques coilles clamasse, / tu, qui si m'en morz et depiques, / me redeïsses de reliques / que ce fust lez moz et vilains" (*Rose,* ed. Lecoy, ll. 7079–85) (if, when I put names to things that you dare to criticize thus and blame, I had called testicles relics and had declared relics to be testicles, then you, who criticize me and goad me on account of them, would reply that 'relics' was an ugly, base word) (trans. Dahlberg, 135).

14. *Rose,* ed. Lecoy, ll. 4369–71; trans. Dahlberg, 96.

15. The bawdy character of the Old Woman provides advice on love to Fair Welcoming, the personification representing allegorically the Lady's favorable disposition, much of which is taken from Ovid's *Art of Love. Rose,* ed. Lecoy, ll. 12710–14688; trans. Dahlberg, 221–51.

16. The personification of Jealousy does indeed figure in both parts of the *Rose,* but here Christine is referring to the figure of the Jealous Husband, quoted at great length by Friend and used as an illustration of the misfortunes of marriage and the violent abuses caused by jealousy. *Rose,* ed. Lecoy, ll. 8437–9330; trans. Dahlberg, 156–68.

What great benefits can be discovered there? What need is there to record the improprieties and the foul words that are quite common in the mouths of the unfortunate people afflicted with this illness? What sort of good example or "introduction" to the subject can this be? And as for the filth that is written there about women, many people say, in order to excuse him [Jean de Meun], that it is the Jealous Man who is speaking, claiming that he is in truth acting as did God who spoke through the mouth of Jeremiah.[17] Yet it is certain that whatever additional lies he may have included there, these lies are incapable of weakening or doing any harm, thank God, to the various conditions of women. Ha! When I think of the deceitful tricks, the hypocrisy, and the dissimulations attributed to marriage and other conditions one can recall from this treatise, you can be sure that I deem these statements very fine and profitable to hear!

But the character he calls Genius, the priest, says amazing things;[18] surely the works of Nature would have come to a complete halt a long time ago if he had not so strongly praised them! For God's sake, is there someone capable of clarifying or explaining to me what profit can be derived from this lengthy development full of vituperation (which he calls a sermon, as though out of derision for holy preaching) that he says this Genius delivers? In it there is found an excess of indecencies, specious names, and words meant to inflame passions for Nature's secrets; yet these must be kept quiet and not be named, inasmuch as no one has observed an interruption in such activity which, as per the general order of things, cannot fail. If it were otherwise, it would be good, for the benefit of human generation, to invent and use arousing and inflaming words and terms, in order to stimulate man to continue this activity.

Yet the author did even more, if my memory is correct, and regarding this I cannot stop wondering to what purpose. For in the aforementioned sermon he tacks on, as a type of allegory, paradise and its joys. He does well to say that the virtuous will go there, and then he concludes that all men and women, without exception, should be intent upon accomplishing and train-

17. Jer 1:7–9: "quoniam ad omnia quæ mittam te ibis, et universa quaecumque mandavero tibi loqueris . . . Et misit Dominus manum suam, et tetigit os meum, et dixit Dominus ad me: Ecce dedi verba mea in ore tuo" (for thou shalt go to all that I shall send thee: and whatsoever I shall command thee, thou shalt speak . . . And the Lord put forth his hand, and touched my mouth: And the Lord said to me: Behold I have given my words in thy mouth).

18. Genius is the confessor of Nature and delivers a mock sermon, containing what the narrator refers to as the "definitive meaning" (*Rose,* ed. Lecoy, l. 19474; trans. Dahlberg, 322), to the allegorical combatants besieging the castle just before the conclusion of the *Rose* (*Rose,* ed. Lecoy, ll. 19465–20637; trans. Dahlberg, 322–38). The characters of Nature and Genius are adapted from Alan of Lille's late-twelfth-century *Complaint of Nature,* a condemnation of vicious behavior, especially sodomy, and an urging to "straight," procreative sexuality.

ing themselves in the works of Nature; but he does not make any exception based on Law, as if he wished to say—indeed, he says it plainly!—that they will be saved.[19] And in this way it seems that he wishes to maintain that the sin of lust is no sin at all, but rather a virtue—which is an error and contrary to the Law of God. Ha! what seed he sows and what doctrine! How many great benefits can result from it! I believe that many have retired from the world and entered religion because of it, or become hermits on account of this holy reading experience, or withdrawn from an evil way of life and existence, having been saved by such exhortation, which doubtlessly—this I dare say no matter who might be displeased by it—had no other source than a corrupt spirit, one totally given over to dissolution and vice, something that can be the cause of great misfortune and sin.

And yet, for God's sake, let us look a bit further: in what way can it be of value or to good purpose that he so excessively, impetuously, and mendaciously accuses, blames, and defames women regarding several grave vices, at the same time asserting that their behavior is full of every type of perversity? But with so many accusations placed in the mouths of almost all his characters, he still can't get his fill. For even if you wish to tell me that the Jealous Man speaks this way because he is deeply tormented, I cannot understand how such an attitude pertains to the function of Genius, who recommends and exhorts at such length that one should sleep with women and not fail to accomplish the activity he praises so highly. Yet this same character, more than all the others, makes many profoundly vituperative statements about women, and in fact says: "Flee! Flee! Flee the venomous serpent!"—and then he says that one should go after them assiduously without giving up.[20]

19. Christine seems to be thinking of the concluding advice provided by Genius but singles out the questions of sexual activity and leaves out the other types of behavior that are being urged: "Concentrate on honoring Nature and doing her service by laboring well [Genius is here referring to procreative sexual activity]; and if you have someone else's belongings, give them back if you know how; and if you cannot give back those goods that are spent or played away, have the good will to do so when you have plenty of good things. May no one come close to murder, keep your hands and mouth clean. Be loyal, be compassionate: then you will go to the pleasurable field [allegorical figure for Paradise]" (*Rose*, ed. Lecoy, ll. 20607–18; my translation).

20. Genius's highly misogynous rant occurs some three thousand lines before the abovementioned sermon urging sexual activity, during our first encounter with him and Nature (*Rose*, ed. Lecoy, ll. 16284–676; trans. Dahlberg, 276–81). This quotation is not exact, as Genius says, somewhat more extensively (over some thirty lines): "Fly, fly, fly, fly, fly, my children; I advise you and urge you without deception or guile to fly from such an animal. Note these verses of Virgil, but know them in your heart so that they cannot be drawn out therefrom: O child who gathers flowers and fresh, clean strawberries, here lies the cold serpent in the grass. Fly, child, for he poisons and envenoms every person that comes near . . . No herb or root is worth anything against it. The only medicine is flight" (*Rose*, ed. Lecoy, ll. 16552–86; trans. Dahlberg,

Here there is a glaring contradiction: he orders one to flee what he wants one to pursue, and to pursue what he wants one to flee. But since women are so perverse, he should not order men to approach them at all: for he who fears misfortune ought to avoid it.

But then he so strenuously forbids a man to tell his secrets to a woman.[21] As he tells it, she is terribly anxious to find out his secret, but I don't know where the devil he found so much rubbish and wasted verbiage that he assembled there in such a lengthy demonstration. Yet I beg all those who consider this argument authoritative and who are convinced by it that they might see fit to tell me how many men they have seen accused, murdered, hanged, or reproached in the streets as a result of their wives' accusation.[22] I do indeed believe that they will find them to be few and far between. This notwithstanding the fact that it would be good and praiseworthy advice for everyone to keep their secrets in order to be more secure, for there are underhanded people among the general public;[23] and it wasn't long ago, as I hear tell, that someone was accused and subsequently hanged because he revealed his thoughts to a friend whom he trusted; but I do believe that few outcries or complaints have been brought before justice relating to such horrible crimes, the great betrayals and diabolical acts that he claims women know how to commit so maliciously and covertly—it really is covert when no one notices! And as I said some time ago about this topic in a poem of mine entitled *The God of Love's Letter:* where are the countries or kingdoms that have been ravaged by women's great iniquities?[24] But without speaking just

279–80). But in the following line, Genius says nearly the opposite: "However, I do not say, and it was never my intent to say, that you should not hold women dear or that you should flee from them and not lie with them" (*Rose,* ed. Lecoy, ll. 16587–91; trans. Dahlberg, 280). The Virgilian text in question is *Eclogue* 3.92–93: "Qui legitis flores et humi nascentia fraga, / frigidus, o pueri, fugite hinc, latet anguis in herba" (Ye who cull flowers and low-growing strawberries, away from here, lads; a chill snake lurks in the grass).

21. The leitmotif running through nearly all of Genius's speech against women consists in the danger men risk if they entrust their secrets to them.

22. Christine is undoubtedly thinking of the moment in Genius's misogynistic speech to Nature when he warns men not to tell any incriminating secrets to their wives, for "if, just one single time he ever dares grouch at her or scold her or get angry, he puts his life in danger—if he deserved death for his deed—that she will have him hanged by the neck, if the judges can catch him, or secretly murdered by friends" (*Rose,* ed. Lecoy, ll. 16350–57; trans. Dahlberg, 277).

23. See Christine's *Moral Teachings* LV and LXVII (no. 2 above).

24. "et ne portent domage / Aux royaumes, aux duchiez, n'aux empires; Mal ne s'ensuit gaires, meismes des pires" (Nor do they inflict damage on kingdoms, duchies, or empires; there is scarcely ever a bad result, even from the worst of them) (*The God of Love's Letter,* in *Œuvres poétiques de Christine de Pisan,* 2:21 [ll. 650–52]).

to please myself, let us talk about what kind of great crimes one can accuse even the worst and the most deceitful of them of having committed. What are they capable of, and in what ways do they deceive you? If these women ask you to take money out of your purse, then they are not stealing from you or robbing you: don't give them anything if you don't want to! Do they pursue you at your home, beg you or take you by force? It would be good to know how they mislead you.[25]

What's more, he spoke so superficially and spitefully about married women who deceive their husbands—a state about which he could not have known anything through experience, and therefore spoke in such a general manner. What positive goal could he have had, what good could he have expected to come from what he said? I don't see anything in it but an impediment to the good and to peace, making husbands who hear such babble and rubbish suspicious and disinclined to love their wives, if they lend credence to those words. My God, what exhortation! How profitable it is! But in truth, since he blamed all women in general, I am forced to believe for that very reason that he never had any acquaintance or relation with honorable or virtuous women, but rather, by keeping company with many dissolute women of wicked ways—as lustful men commonly do—he believed, or pretended to know, that all women were this way; for he had no knowledge of any others. And if he had only reproached indecent women and advised that one flee them, it would have been a good and just teaching. But no! Instead, he accuses all women without exception. But if the author, venturing so far beyond the bounds of reason, took it upon himself to accuse women or judge them erroneously, blame should be imputed not to them but rather to the person who tells lies at such a distance from the truth and so lacking in credibility, inasmuch as the opposite is patently evident. For even if he and all his accomplices had solemnly sworn that this was the truth, may it not distress any of them when I declare that there already have been, are, and will be[26] many women more worthy, more honorable, better trained, and even more learned, and from whom greater good has resulted in the world than ever he accomplished in his person—women very well educated, particularly with regard to conduct in the world and virtuous morals; and there are many who have been responsible for the resolution of their husbands' affairs, and who have borne

25. See no. 1 above.

26. This is certainly meant to echo ironically one of the most violently misogynous lines in the *Rose*, placed in the mouth of the Jealous Husband: "Toutes estes, serez et fustes, / de fet ou de volenté, pustes" (All you women are, will be, and have been whores, in fact or in desire) (*Rose*, ed. Lecoy, ll. 9125–26; trans. Dahlberg, 165). Cf. *The God of Love's Letter* (see ch. 1, n. 3).

their difficulties, their secrets, and their illnesses patiently and confidentially, however much their husbands might have been brutal or lacking in love.[27] One finds ample proof of this in the Bible and in other ancient histories, such as those of Sarah, Rebecca, Esther, Judith, and many others.[28] And even in our times we have seen in France a number of worthy women, our greatest ladies of the realm and many others—the holy devout Queen Jeanne; Queen Blanche; the duchess of Orleans, daughter of the king of France; the duchess of Anjou, who is now called the queen of Sicily—all of whom, along with a host of others, possessed great beauty, chastity, dignity, and wisdom.[29] And there are worthy gentlewomen of a lesser rank, such as the very praiseworthy Madame de la Ferté, the wife of Monsieur Pierre de Craon,[30] and numerous others about whom it would take too long to say any more.

27. Christine uses the rather vague expression *cause du reconciliement de leurs maris,* which has been translated here as "responsible for the resolution of their husbands' affairs." It would seem that the idea of "reconciliation" is meant to address the accusation that men should mistrust their wives and never divulge their secrets or personal affairs for fear of being betrayed by them, as indicated by reference to these wives' discretion and support in the latter part of the sentence. In the following passage listing illustrious ladies from the Bible and from the recent past, one can see the germ of Christine's later *City of Ladies.*

28. Stories of these four biblical women are included in the *City of Ladies:* Sarah (book 2, chap. 38) and Rebecca (book 2, chap. 39) for the great deeds they performed; Esther (book 2, chap. 32) and Judith (book 2. chap. 31) for their virtue.

29. The first three of these ladies are, as Hicks points out, Jeanne d'Evreux (1310–71), the third wife of Charles IV, the last of the Capetian kings (Jeanne produced only daughters, who could not succeed to the throne); Blanche de Navarre (1331–98), the second wife of King Philip VI, first king of the Valois line; and Blanche de France (1328–93), posthumous daughter of Charles IV and Jeanne d'Evreux, who married Philip, duke of Orléans, who was the younger son of Philip VI (*Le débat,* 202). Hicks neglects to mention the fourth woman in the list, Marie of Blois (1343–1404), who married Count Louis of Anjou (a younger brother of King Charles V) in 1360, who later that year became the duke of Anjou and, later still, King Louis I of Sicily (1383). Marie clearly kept the title "Queen of Sicily" until her death. All four ladies are mentioned in a passage from the *City of Ladies* (*The Book of the City of Ladies,* trans. Earl Jeffrey Richards, rev. ed. [New York: Persea Books, 1998], 34–35 [book 1, chap. 13]). In addition to being women related in some way to the royal line and having lived in the recent past, they are perhaps all mentioned because Christine de Pizan would have come into contact with them (in the *City of Ladies,* Reason says to Christine, with regard to Jeanne d'Evreux, who died some thirty years before the writing of this letter, "you yourself saw [her] in your childhood"). As Solente pointed out some time ago (*Le livre des fais et bonnes meurs du sage Roy Charles V,* 1:55), the *City of Ladies* erroneously identifies Queen Blanche as the wife of King Jean II: the wife of the latter was Bonne de Luxembourg, who died in 1349. If the Queen Blanche in our letter and that of the *City of Ladies* are to be identified with the one who appears in the *Book of the Deeds and Good Conduct of the Wise King Charles V,* it must be Blanche de Navarre and not, by some scribal error, the wife of Jean II, who was long dead by the time of the events recounted therein.

30. Identified by Hicks (*Le débat,* 203) as "Jeanne de Chastillon, third daughter of Gaucher de Châtillon, lady of Le Rosay in Thériache [who] married Pierre de Craon, lord of Sablé and of La Ferté-Bernard."

But do not believe, dear sir (and may no other person be of this opinion), that I have stated or enumerated the aforementioned justifications, or that they are predicated upon biased excuses, because I am a woman; for in truth my motivation stems from nothing other than simply advocating pure truth, since by proven knowledge I know this truth to be contrary to the statements I have refuted. But insofar as I am in fact a woman, I am better suited to attest to these matters than he who, not having had this experience, speaks instead through conjecture and in a haphazard manner.

But after all these things, for the love of God, may the ending of the treatise in question be examined. For as a proverb says, "All things are determined by the end."[31] Let it thus be seen and observed what the usefulness of this very horrible and shameful conclusion[32] might be. Shameful? What am I saying! Rather it is so indecent that I dare say that no one loving virtue and honor will listen to it without being totally confounded by shame and filled with abomination, hearing in this way—clearly described, dissected, and expressed under the cover of immoral fictions—things the very thought of which reason and modesty must suppress in upright people. Going still further, I dare say that even the Goliards would be horrified to read it or hear it in public in respectable places and in front of people they considered to be virtuous.[33] And therefore what is the use of praising a work that one could not permit to be read or spoken of in a proper manner[34] at the tables of queens, princesses, or worthy gentlewomen—who would be obliged to cover their faces, blushing with shame? And if you wish to make excuses for

31. There are several variants for this proverb: "A la bone fin veit tout" (everything leads to a good end) (Joseph Morawski, *Proverbes français antérieurs au XVe siècle* [Paris: Librairie ancienne Édouard Champion, 1925], no. 44); "La fin loe l'oeuvre" (the end recommends the work) (Morawski, no. 1002); "La fin couronne l'œuvre" (the end crowns the work) (James W. Hassell, *Middle French Proverbs, Sentences and Proverbial Phrases* [Toronto: Pontifical Institute of Mediaeval Studies, 1982], 115 [F89]).

32. The conclusion of the *Rose* portrays the narrator as a sort of pilgrim striving to attain the "relics" contained in the besieged castle, which turns into a barely disguised description of sexual intercourse, if not rape.

33. The name "Goliard" is applied somewhat loosely to clerics who, from as early as the twelfth century, wrote Latin lyrics that were often highly satirical and parodic. The Goliards came to have a reputation, abusively so, of being drunken ribalds who frequented taverns and had loose morals. It is this reputation to which Christine is referring.

34. The expression used here, *en propre forme* (literally, "in proper form"), is somewhat ambiguous, as it could be referring to the exactness of the reading (that is, one would have to use circumlocutions or otherwise avoid reading out the text as written) or alternately, as I have translated it, to the propriety of the situation, which would preclude reading the text at all. It would seem to be the latter that Christine intended, for when she recalls this statement in her letter to Pierre Col, she cites it approximately and, in place of this expression, uses the adverb *honnestement* (decently).

the author by saying that it pleased him to use these metaphors in a fanciful tale to express the goal of love, I respond to you that he is not telling us anything out of the ordinary! Don't we know how men couple with women by nature? If he were to recount how it happens with bears or lions or birds or some other unfamiliar creature, it would be material worthy of laughter on account of the fable, but when he says this he does not tell us anything new. And without any doubt he could have accomplished what he wanted more graciously, more gently, and with a more refined vocabulary, which would have particularly appealed to elegant and honorable lovers, as well as to every other virtuous person.

Thus, within the limits of my meager capability and feeble discernment, and without being more verbose, in spite of the fact that much more could be said, and said better, I cannot deem this treatise to have any usefulness, though I believe that great effort was made—just without any profit. Nonetheless my judgment admits that Master Jean de Meun is a very great cleric, subtle and eloquent, and he could have produced a much better work, more profitable and with a more elevated sensibility, if he had applied himself to it, so it's a pity he did not do so. But I suppose that perhaps the great lasciviousness with which he was filled made him move more in the direction of his desire than toward the production of something useful and beneficial, since it commonly occurs that people's inclinations are made known by their actions. In spite of this, I certainly do not reprove all the parts of the *Romance of the Rose*, for there are without any doubt some good things that are pleasingly expressed. But so much the greater is the peril: for the more authentic the good found therein, the more credence is lent to the evil; and it is in this way that many subtle thinkers have on occasion sown great errors: they mix them together with bits of truth and virtue and thereby palliate them. But just as his priest Genius says, "Flee! Flee woman, that evil serpent hidden in the grass!" I can say, "Flee! Flee the wickedness concealed in the shadow of goodness and virtue!"

This is why I say to you in conclusion, dearest sir, to you and to all your allies and associates who praise the *Rose* so highly and want to glorify it to such an extent that you wish, and even dare, to diminish the status of nearly all other books in comparison, I say that it is not worthy of praise, with all due respect to you; and you do great wrong to works of value, for a work without usefulness, and lacking in either general or particular benefit, does not deserve praise—even supposing that it is delightful and the result of great labor and expense. And inasmuch as in ancient times the triumphant Romans would not attribute praise or honor to anything whatsoever if it did not contribute to the utility of the republic, let us examine their example to see whether we can crown this romance.[35] But it truly seems to me that in view of the aforementioned arguments and many others, this work should more fittingly be engulfed in a shroud of fire than crowned with laurel, even though you call it "a mirror of the good life, an example to all classes for political self-conduct and for living religiously and wisely."[36] On the contrary; begging your pardon, I say that it is an exhortation to vice that encourages a dissolute life, a doctrine full of deceit, a path to damnation, a purveyor of public defamation, a cause of suspicion and distrust, a source of shame to many people, and perhaps a seed of heresy.

Nonetheless, I well know that concerning this point you will make excuses for the work, replying to me that it is urged therein that people do good and shun evil. But I can answer you with a superior argument, namely, that human nature, which is inherently inclined to evil, doesn't need anyone to point out which foot it is limping on in order to walk straighter. And as for the talk about all the good that can be discovered in the book in question, it is certain that many more virtuous things, better stated, more authoritative,[37] and more profitable—namely, with regard to the conduct of a civilly responsible and moral life—are found in a number of other volumes written both by philosophers and by scholars of our faith, such as Aristotle, Seneca, Saint Paul, Saint Augustine, and others, as you are well aware. And they more adequately and straightforwardly testify to and teach the virtues, while counseling the avoidance of vice, than Jean de Meun could have. But these books are not usually studied or remembered so willingly by the carnal men of this world, because the thirsty invalid is delighted when the doctor gives him permission to drink copiously, and because of his gluttonous desire to drink he most willingly convinces himself that it will never do him any harm.[38] I thus profess that I am certain that once you (may God grant it!) and all the others have by the grace of God been brought back to the lucidity and purity of a clean conscience, without the stain or pollution of sin or sinful in-

35. Christine's admiration of the Roman republic as a political model is made particularly obvious in her treatise on the "role of the monarchy and the moral and political education of the dauphin [Louis de Guyenne]" (*The Book of the Body Politic [Le livre du cors de policie]* [1406–7], ed. Angus Kennedy [Paris: Champion, 1998], xxvi).

36. This quotation from Jean de Montreuil's lost French treatise echoes a phrase that he includes in one of his later letters (see no. 19), "a mirror or discourse of human life."

37. As Hicks notes (*Le débat,* 203), the use of the technical term *auttentique* here refers specifically to doctrine that has received official approval and that is taught in the schools.

38. Cf. Ovid, *Amores,* 3.4.17–18 (*Heroides and Amores,* trans. Grant Showerman, rev. G. P. Goold, 2nd ed. [Cambridge: Harvard University Press, 1977], 460–61): "nitimur in vetitum semper cupimusque negata; / sic interdictis imminet aeger aquis" (We ever strive for what is forbid, and ever covet what is denied; so the sick man longingly hangs over forbidden water).

tent, and have been cleansed by the prick of contrition (which performs so as to make one see clearly the secrets of conscience and condemns self-will as a judge of truth), you will render another judgment upon the *Romance of the Rose* and might perhaps even wish that you had never seen it.

This is enough for now. Finally, may it not be attributed to folly, arrogance, or presumption that I, a woman, dare to reprimand and refute so subtle an author and to divest his work of its renown, when he, just one man, dared undertake to defame and condemn without exception an entire sex.

6. JEAN DE MONTREUIL TO A LAWYER (JULY–AUGUST 1401)[39]

LATIN PROSE

O very wise man, the more I examine the weights of the mysteries and the mysteries of the weights of this profound work of celebrated memory produced by Master Jean de Meun, the more clearly does the genius of that author reveal itself; indeed, I am entirely moved to surprise and roused up at the thought of what impulse, what whim, or what cast of mind has led you in particular—you who every day are engaged in civil suits (which depend in the highest degree upon sound judgment and where it is advised to pronounce a sentence on issues with seriousness and careful consideration)—to judge that this most eloquent and most learned author spoke too frivolously, improperly, and like a buffoon. And, as though you were arguing a case in the palace, three days ago you quarreled in a rage, speaking words against a dead man, at the same time showing by far a preference for Guillaume de Lorris in terms of originality, clarity, propriety, and elegance. At that time, moved by purposeful consideration, I chose not to speak out and I forgo doing so now.

Yet if henceforth you admit to having said this in earnest, "tell me what pledge you propose to put up in our struggle: I will come," as Virgil said, "to whatever place you name."[40] I say this as someone who will not abandon my master or benefactors till the final, sobbing breath or allow their honor to be

39. Translated from *Le débat,* ed. Hicks, 28–30. As is not uncommon in Jean de Montreuil's transcription of his letters, the addressee is not named. His use of the informal *tu* (on which see below, n. 122) suggests that this "very wise man" is a friend or colleague, or at least at the same professional and social level. The reference a few lines below about his participating in judicial proceedings suggests that he is a lawyer, but there are no other clues to his identity. He is probably the same as the addressee of no. 10.

40. Virgil, *Eclogue* 3, ll. 31 and 49: "tu dic, mecum quo pignore certes . . . veniam, quocumque vocaris" (Now tell me, for what stake you will match me . . . Wherever you call me, I will meet you [translation altered]). The context is a singing contest between two young shepherds.

damaged as long as I am able. But if in truth, as I am more inclined to believe, you produced this as a joke, or perhaps under the influence of someone else, we are not headstrong to such a degree that we would refuse to acknowledge the sort of freedom to be found in debate, or would not know how to be indulgent with a switch of position: On the contrary, because truth is known through debate "as gold is tested in the furnace,"[41] I admit the possibility of debate over the innate talent of this brilliant scholar—yet only on the condition that you cease to make vehement pronouncements against our poet with such obstinacy.[42]

Be well, and let me know what you intend to do about this. For if you go on any further saying evil things about our teacher, there is nothing about which we might be able to keep quiet. From this moment on, take this as a challenge. For there are, lest you have some doubt, not a few fighters and champions who will defend this cause, to the extent possible, with writing, with speech, and likewise with their hands.

7. JEAN DE MONTREUIL TO A PRELATE (JULY–AUGUST 1401)[43]

LATIN PROSE

Since such worth has been attributed to my trifles, reverend father, that your Eminence deigns to look upon them and has requested them, here they are, as it is suitable for me to comply with your bidding and it would be an immense arrogance on my part to refuse. I am sending you such trifles with the following stipulation, my father most worthy of confidence: that they

41. Prov 27:21: "Quomodo probatur in conflatorio argentum et in fornace aurum, sic probatur homo ore laudantis" (As silver is tried in the fining-pot and gold in the furnace: so a man is tried by the mouth of him that praiseth).

42. The word found here is *imitatorem,* which would not seem to apply to Jean de Meun, and therefore would not seem to accord with the context. Is it, as suggest Baird and Kane, that it might be referring to "some disciple of his, who had written in support of the *Roman de la Rose* and been harshly criticized for that fact" (*La querelle de la Rose,* 43)? This is possible, but the writing of such a disciple is never mentioned. Geneviève Hasenohr suggests (review of Hicks, *Le débat, Romania* 100 [1979], 130) that *imitatorem* resulted from a copying error for *instructorem,* but, as she admits, this would be odd given that this is an autograph manuscript (and that the word *imitator,* clearly designating Jean de Meun, is likewise used in no. 8). The problem disappears, however, if one considers that the word *imitator* undoubtedly continues to have the valence of the Greek *mimesis,* according to which all arts, including poetry, are mimetic arts. One need only think of Hugh of Saint Victor's well-known scheme, according to which all works created by man are imitative: "the human work . . . is not nature but only imitative [*imitatur*] of nature" (*Didascalicon* 1.9).

43. Translated from *Le débat,* ed. Hicks, 30–32. Given the words used to refer to the addressee, and Jean's use of the formal *vos,* he must be a high-ranking prelate. He is certainly the same person to whom Jean sent subsequently no. 9.

be communicated to no one. For I could be reprimanded or reproached by some for the rudeness and lack of ornamentation of the style; by others for the material (which might provoke antipathy in some people on account of its truth)[44] or for its superficiality or buffoonery, since it was produced in the vulgar tongue—but chiefly because human nature is accustomed to find ambiguities perverse rather than to take them in the most positive way. But there is nothing I would not submit to the prudence of your Faithfulness, in all things just like another myself.

Be well, most faithful father, and since you have oftentimes put up with my acts of verbal foolishness, in the same way tolerate with benevolence these literary follies.

8. JEAN DE MONTREUIL TO GONTIER COL (JULY–AUGUST 1401)[45]

LATIN PROSE

Most circumspect master and brother, you know that under your continual urging and instigation I have taken a look at that noble work of Master Jean de Meun, called the *Romance of the Rose* in the vernacular. And because I stand with you regarding his admirable artistry, genius, and teaching—and I confess that I will persist in this unwaveringly—I am being poorly treated and bitterly accused, more than you would believe, by many learned men of no little authority, with the result that if I endeavor to put up more of a defense, they intend quite simply to prove me, as they say, a heretic. Nor is it any use for you and so many other worthy and learned scholars to allege that what he did is of such consequence that you nearly worship him, to such an extent that you would rather do without your shirt than do without him; it is no less useless to point out to our critics that his rivals were of such great stature that they would by no means have allowed his book to survive one hour if it contained the slightest fault. It is moreover of no use to beseech them, as every sense of justice demands, to look first at, and to take note of, for what reason, by what cause, and on what occasion he says certain things and introduces certain characters, instead of condemning so great an author. But scarcely do I venture to move my lips than they instantly intercept my

44. Hicks (*Le débat,* 205) adduces here a line from Terence's *Andria* (The Woman from Andros) (*Terence,* 2 vols., ed. and trans. John Barsby [Cambridge: Harvard University Press, 2001], 1:56 (l. 68): "veritas odium parit" (the truth makes you unpopular).

45. Translated from *Le débat,* ed. Hicks, 32–34.

words and break them to pieces: they well-nigh threaten me with the scandal of excommunication and judge me worthy of the death penalty.

What do you want me to say? What galls me more, "they pursue" our master "with curses," to such an extent that they claim he deserves flames[46] more than he deserves to be read: "and they esteem themselves to be contaminated by an inexpiable sin if they should hear the slightest part of it; but on the other hand, by the law of humanity, I more modestly request that they not condemn before they have become thoroughly acquainted with everything," and I declare that "the ability to defend oneself should be granted even to sacrilegious and poisonous traitors," and also that "it is not permitted for anyone whomsoever to be condemned beforehand for an unknown reason." Yet we accomplish nothing, my very honored brother, other than to lash out at the air in vain, wasting time, "nor is there anything that we might hope to be able to accomplish, so great is the obstinacy of men." This is their behavior, this their madness! "For they are afraid lest, having been refuted by us, the truth itself having been proclaimed, they be compelled to surrender at some point. Therefore, they make a clamor," as Lactantius says, "and they disrupt so as not to hear. They shut their eyes so as not to see the light we bring forth,"[47] following the behavior of the Jews against our Savior, in whose power "the enemies became judges."[48]

46. Jean is likely thinking of Christine de Pizan's response, in which she says that the *Rose* deserves to "be engulfed in a shroud of fire" (no. 5). It is likewise possible that he is thinking of it when he mentions people's desire to prove him a heretic, as she uses the word *erreur,* which can mean "error, mistake, or heresy." However, as some have suggested, this could be referring to Jean Gerson's sermon *Considerate lilia* (excerpted as no. 12 in this volume), in which Gerson accuses the character of Reason of spreading the heresy of the Beghards and the Turlupins.

47. The passages here in quotation marks are an adaptation of a passage from Lactantius's *Divine Institutions* (5.1.1ff.): "[He] inveighs against him with curses and casts him down, perhaps having scarcely read the beginning, so as to banish him, thinking that he might bring a curse upon himself, being corrupted and bound by an inexpiable sin if he either reads or hears it patiently. From this, however, if something can come about by the law of humanity, we demand that one not condemn before one has become thoroughly acquainted with everything. For if the ability to defend oneself should be granted even to sacrilegious and poisonous traitors, it is not permitted for anyone whatsoever to be condemned beforehand for an unknown reason. May we not appear to demand unjustly that if there is someone who finds himself in such circumstances, if he will read, let him read thoroughly; if he will hear, let him defer judgment till the end. But I have come to know the obstinacy of men; never will we accomplish this. For they are afraid lest, refuted by us, the truth itself having been proclaimed, they be compelled to surrender. Therefore they make a clamor and disrupt, so as not to hear, and they shut their eyes, so as not to see the light we bring forth" (quoted in Jean de Montreuil, *Opera,* ed. Ezio Ornato [Turin: G. Giappichelli, 1963], 1:181; translation mine).

48. Deut 32:31: "et inimici nostri sunt judices" (our enemies themselves are judges). Referring this quotation to the judgment of Christ of course removes it from its context. Hicks (*Le débat,*

Thus is our most eminent teacher condemned, completely innocent, without a hearing—something that all laws prohibit—by those who certainly would not have ventured to make a sound if he were before their eyes, alive. Yet, what is more vexing, our critics ignominiously disdain him, curse him, and impugn him, having poorly read, noted, and examined him. Oh, what arrogance, what temerity, what audacity! These men who have declared openly that they read it superficially, neither in context nor in its entirety, all of a sudden reproach and condemn so great a work, elaborated and produced over so many days and nights with so much toil and careful application; and they do so after the fashion of those who at table, in a drunken stupor, berate all things as they please and as the impulse moves them—placing so great a work on the scales, as though having little more weight than the song of a jongleur, the work of a single day!

Because of this display of theirs, I inveighed against another of these lawyers in writing, as you will see by the letter this porter has carried to you. It will therefore be up to you, as leader, chief, and director of this undertaking, to defend this most praiseworthy and beloved poet[49] of yours, to crush underfoot those irrational and foolish people, as well as to strengthen, adorn, and overlay my slight and disorganized reasoning with the keenness of your eloquence, seeing that I entered this battlefield relying upon my trust in your support and upon the wealth of your talents, but would not otherwise have done so. For I know that when your sleeping senses awaken, and your indolent pen moves forward, these enemies of truth "will not prevail against us";[50] rather, I have no doubt that, when you wish, you will turn them into gentle sheep and make them mute on all topics, just like tree stumps.

Farewell, and to the extent that you are able may you not allow your friends to be destroyed so unjustly, cunningly, perniciously, and unfairly.

---

206) points out that this same quotation is used by Peter Abelard to refer to the condemnation of his own treatise (*The Letters of Abelard and Heloise,* trans. Betty Radice [Harmondsworth: Penguin Books, 1974], 79). Perhaps not coincidentally, Jean de Meun was a translator of this correspondence, and the only surviving copy of his translation was copied by none other than Gontier Col (see *La vie et les epistres Pierres Abaelart et Heloys sa fame,* ed. Eric Hicks [Paris: Honoré Champion, 1991]). Jean de Montreuil is also known to have had a copy of the correspondence, certainly in Latin (cf. Hicks, ibid.).

49. The word is *imitatorem,* as in n. 42, above.

50. Ps 12:5: "nequando dicat inimicus meus: Prævalui adversus eum" (lest at any time my enemy say: I have prevailed against him); Mt 16:18: "Et ego dico tibi, quia tu es Petrus, et super hanc petram ædificabo Ecclesiam meam, et portæ inferi non prævalebunt adversus eam" (And I say to thee: That thou art Peter; and upon this rock I will build my church, and the gates of hell shall not prevail against it).

9. JEAN DE MONTREUIL TO A PRELATE (JULY–AUGUST 1401)[51]

LATIN PROSE

My very excellent father, you yourself should judge whether it was my dull thoughtlessness or confidence in your goodness that made me speak to you about my trifles and unpolished essays—I, a mediocre person speaking to a great one, an inexperienced to a highly skilled one, an uneducated to a very learned one, and, finally, a coarse to an exceptionally circumspect one. I have gone on and applied myself so that you might have in writing something I would not have shared with any mortal. But so it is, reverend father, one error leads easily to another one, and as Claudian said, "Presumption exhorts to extravagance."[52] Moreover, in the manner of children, wherever (as the proverb says) a friendly countenance greets me, there I go and there I am—I remain there perpetually to the point of being a nuisance. And, heedless, "my tongue manifesting itself up front,"[53] whatever suggests itself I blurt out, laying bare my soul in every respect just as to my own confessor.

Thus it has once again come into my mind to send your Reverence a letter, the one in the form of a satirical invective, about which we had a conversation yesterday at your home—not in order that it should be copied (this I pray, beseech, implore, and request you not to do), but only so that your Eminence might examine it and consider whether it seems overly hurtful (which I fear), biting, or insolent, and, in the manner of a corrector or editor, note any faults in the margin. For I know that because I have little sense of moderation, I am inclined to be entirely too impetuous, moved in one direction or the other according to my whims, since, as Ter-

51. Translated from *Le débat,* ed. Hicks, 36. Hicks and Ornato ("Jean de Montreuil et le débat sur le *Roman de la Rose,*" 194–95) consider it "probable" that this prelate is the same as the addressee of no. 7.

52. Cf. Claudian, *Panegyric on the Fourth Consulship of the Emperor Honorius,* 262–64 (ed. and trans. Maurice Platnauer [Cambridge: Harvard University Press, 1976], 1: 304–5): "proclivior usus / in peiora datur suadetque licentia luxum / inlecebrisque effrena favet" (The easier way often trod leads to worse; liberty begets license and, when uncontrolled, leads to vice).

53. E. Ornato (Jean de Montreuil, *Opera,* 1:352) says that this expression, used several times in Jean de Montreuil's correspondence, is attributed by him to Saint Jerome, but he states that he has not been able to find its source. He does quote an analogous expression from Petrarch: "nichil fingere, sed in lingua atque in fronte animum habere" (to feign nothing, but to place one's soul in one's tongue and in one's countenance). I have translated the expression *in fronte* (literally, "on one's brow or forehead," and by extension "in one's expressions or countenance") as "up front."

ence describes the reason: "our judgment is clouded by excesses of joy or sorrow."[54] And, very dear father—something that does not lessen the rashness of my behavior—behold, the messenger is also delivering to your Eminence this draft letter on the same topic, addressed to a certain colleague of mine (although it has not as yet been sent to him).[55] Let it be attributed not to my arrogance but to the boldness instilled in me by your knowing benevolence.

10. JEAN DE MONTREUIL TO A LAWYER (JULY–AUGUST, 1401)[56]

LATIN PROSE

Although you are not only extremely well-spoken, copious in expression, and overflowing with eloquence, but also ("and this is the source of writing")[57] wise, my distinguished colleague, I see, however, that having been conquered by the truth and tormented by conscience, there is nothing more that you "dare mutter"[58] or are able to argue against that rigorous satirical writer Master Jean de Meun; indeed, so great is the power of the truth he articulates that the diligent effort of no rhetorician can compare with it, to which the author who said the following gave his assent: "The truth will remain eternally,"[59] "false things do not last."[60]

Reconcile yourself, therefore, with this very dear master and teacher, and do not fear because you flew off the handle with so little hesitation. For

54. Terence, *Heauton Timorumenos* (The Self-Tormentor),ll. 505–6: "an eo fit quia in re nostra aut gaudio sumus praepediti nimio aut aegritudine?" (Is it because in our own affairs our judgment is clouded by excesses of joy or sorrow?) *Terence,* trans. Barsby, 1:230.

55. Hicks and Ornato ("Jean de Montreuil et le débat sur le *Roman de la Rose,*") establish that the first letter being sent, the satirical invective, is our no. 6 (the letter to a lawyer), while the draft to a colleague is our no. 8 (the letter to Gontier Col). Hicks makes an error in his note (*Le débat,* 206), when he says that the satirical invective refers to the "following" letter (our no. 10), for he indicates otherwise in his summary of the documents.

56. Translated from *Le débat,* ed. Hicks, 38–40.

57. Horace, *The Art of Poetry,* l. 309: "Scribendi recte sapere est et principium et fons" (Of good writing the source and fount is wisdom) (*Satires, Epistles and Ars Poetica,* ed. and trans. H. Rushton Fairclough, rev. ed. [Cambridge: Harvard University Press, 1929], 476).

58. Terence, *Andria* (The Woman from Andros), l. 505: "nil iam muttire audeo" (I daren't utter a word). *Terence,* trans. Barsby, 1:106–7.

59. Ps 116:2: "et veritas Domini manet in æternum" (And the truth of the Lord remaineth for ever).

60. Seneca, *Moral Epistles to Lucilius* 120.19: "Vero tenor permanet, falsa non durant" (It is indeed consistency that abides; false things do not last) (trans. Richard M. Gummere, *The Works of Seneca* [Cambridge: Harvard University Press, 1925], 6:392–93).

immediately, when you want, having obtained our indulgence you will be one of us, provided that, following upon your sincere promise, there remain no doubt among us with regard to your repentance. We are not unaware of the extent to which unbridled freedom in debate can progress, nor that the argument of the morning oftentimes contradicts that of the evening. You know as well, O man of great experience, that Origen, together with Lactantius, erred, and likewise that Augustine and many of great reputation, as well as other famous and erudite men, recanted.

May it therefore not cause shame, when one merits punishment, to correct things stated too freely and intended as an attack. Perhaps, in fact, those verses that you condemn you looked at perfunctorily and not recently. These two great factors corrupted your judgment and drove you headlong into error . . . an error not of faith, unreasonableness, or ill will but from which several of the aforementioned (having only superficially looked at a verse of de Meun himself) tumble down with you. May you not take lightly this present admonition of ours or reckon that it is lacking in fraternal affection, or that I in my previous letter gratuitously called to your attention the matter of the fervent admirers and defenders of the philosopher under examination. For there are among them those whose spurs gleam with gold, possessing offices of great importance, who, in defense of our argument, "seek," as Virgil says, "amid wounds a glorious death."[61] Nor do they think they can do anything more pleasing to God than rush in to attack those who refute our teacher on the basis of only a petty syllable or mark of punctuation.

Be that as it may, do you want me to advise you what to do? I strongly urge you to say that which he who was simultaneously prophet and king was not ashamed to confess humbly: "I made my crime known to you, and did not hide my injustice."[62] But if then, in the meantime, you were to compose a treatise, I beg you in the name of our friendship that you not at all neglect out of weariness to send to this director of yours a dutiful response,

61. Virgil, *Georgics* 4.217–18: "et saepe attollunt umeris et corpora bello / obiectant pulchramque petunt per volnera mortem" (Often they lift him on their shoulders, for him expose their bodies to battle, and seek amid wounds a glorious death; *Eclogues, Georgics, Aeneid 1–6*, trans. H. Rushton Fairclough, rev. G. P. Goold [Cambridge: Harvard University Press, 1999], 234–35); and *Aeneid* 11.646–47: "dant funera ferro / certantes pulchramque petunt per vulnera mortem" (they deal carnage, clashing with the sword, and seek amid wounds a glorious death) (*Aeneid 7–12, Appendix Vergiliana*, trans. H. R. Fairclough, rev. G. P. Goold [Cambridge: Harvard University Press, 2000], 280–81; translation slightly modified).

62. Ps 31:5: "Delictum meum cognitum tibi feci, et injustitiam meam non abscondi." The "prophet and king" is of course David, to whom many of the psalms are attributed.

which might serve chiefly as an alleviation of our wait and an announcement of your intention. As the Psalmist says, "I will rejoice in your eloquence, as someone who has found great spoils."[63]

Be well.

11. PIERRE D'AILLY, *THE DEVOUT SOUL'S GARDEN OF LOVE* (SUMMER 1401?)[64]

FRENCH PROSE (FOR THE NARRATIVE) AND VERSE (CLOSING SONG OF LOVE)

[This work was long thought to be by Jean Gerson (indeed the edition of it that serves as the base for my translation is included in the collected works of Gerson), but in an important article published in 1976, Pierre-Yves Badel established, by comparison with a sermon delivered by Pierre d'Ailly, that the latter was the author of both, since there are numerous identical passages. The sermon was written for Pentecost, but the year is not certain: Badel leans toward 1401, in which Pentecost fell on May 22. The chronology he suggests, which I follow here, is that Pierre d'Ailly, who clearly knew the Romance of the Rose *very well, disagreed with the treatise Jean de Montreuil wrote in support of it and that he had sent to him in May 1401 (no. 4 in this volume). He would have conceived the present work, predicated upon the structure and the figures of the* Rose *(the enclosed garden, the personifications, the pictures on the wall, the concentration on the definition of love), as a counterargument, in which the love of God is substituted for the carnal, "courtly love" of Guillaume de Lorris and Jean de Meun. He seems to have used sections from his previously delivered sermon to reinforce certain didactic points. Although it does not participate directly in the debate (as does Gerson's treatise [no. 20], for instance), it does reflect part of the variety of responses to the* Rose *in this milieu and may be likened to Gerson's reference to the character Reason in his sermon "Considerate lilia" [no. 12]).]*

In the abbey founded on devout religion

In this desert of the world is found the Amorous Garden where the real God of love lives: It is the gracious garden where sweet Jesus lives and to which he calls his beloved when he says in the book of amorous little songs: *Veni in*

63. Ps 118:162: "Laetabor ego super eloquia tua, sicut qui invenit spolia multa."

64. Translated from Jean Gerson, *Œuvres complètes*, ed. Mgr. Glorieux, 10 vols. in 11 (Paris: Desclée, 1960–73), vol. 7.1, 144–54. I have used the title found in the Avignon manuscript (see Badel, "Pierre d'Ailly," 372), which is one of only two manuscripts to attribute the work to Pierre d'Ailly. Even though Glorieux's edition is based upon this manuscript, he leaves out the word *devote* (devout) in his title.

ortum meum, soror mea, sponsa mea.[65] Come, he says, into my garden, my sweet sister and my dear wife. Jesus Christ sings this little love song with this sweet voice—the loyal lover, calling to himself the sacred soul that is in love with him through ardent goodness; and in it he names his sister and his wife: his sister through the semblance of human nature that he assumed in the Virgin Mary, and his wife through the beauty of divine grace that the soul takes from God the Father . . . his sister through natural lineage and his wife through spiritual marriage. She[66] must certainly be praised and blessed who is of his lineage and in such an exalted marriage that she is called sister and wife of the great king of the heavens and the exalted emperor of the world. Here are thus meager words but full of great meaning, blazing with ardent love and sprinkled with amorous sweetness.

The second chapter of the holy soul that hears the voice of its beloved says:

When the sacred soul, the beloved of sweet Jesus Christ, is thus lovingly called by her beloved, upon hearing his soothing song she opens her ears with diligent purpose and wakes up her heart through fervent reflection and lifts up her head out of great admiration. Oh, God, she says, I have heard the voice of my beloved; I have heard the sound of my beloved. Oh, very dear Jesus, your voice sounded in my ears and the sound of you has awakened my weary heart: Where will I search for you, where will I find you? Then she runs with the feet of good affection, and seeks out the path of righteous proceedings, and comes to the garden of true perfection. And because of the great warmth she has from running, seeking, and entering, she shivers, shudders, and staggers; because of the ardent desire she has to find her beloved, her heart sighs, her eyes tear up, and her face goes pale. For her amorous desire does not permit her to wait a long time for her beloved without torment or to conceal her impatience over her so lengthy delay. But she can neither run as easily nor seek as completely nor find as rapidly as her heart desires, for her feet are weak and tired, the path is rough and narrow, and

65. This is a quotation from the Song of Songs (also known as the Canticle of Canticles) inserted in Latin in this French work, which I have maintained in order to give the same sense of linguistic disruption: Sg 5:1: "veni in hortum meum, soror mea, sponsa" (Come into my garden, my sister, my spouse; translation altered). The Song of Songs, one of the most popular books of the Bible, is known for its sensual language, which the Church Fathers interpreted as an allegory of Christ's love for humanity or for the Church. It serves as a biblical basis for much of what follows in this work, which can therefore be seen as a conflation between that text and the *Romance of the Rose.*

66. In his edition (Jean Gerson, *Œuvres complètes*), Glorieux begins this sentence with "Helas" (Alas!), which does not fit the context, so I have eliminated it.

the garden is firmly enclosed and closely shut.[67] Now listen how, you who are deeply in love.

The third [chapter] is about the feet of the sacred soul that are weak and tired

The feet of the sacred soul that is the beloved of Jesus Christ are the thoughts and the emotions that attract her toward her beloved, but they are weak and tired if they are not well anointed and comforted by the soothing oil of grace, for they are often wounded and thrust against the hard stones of the various temptations that the three adversaries of the soul throw in front of her in order to make her feet stumble. These three adversaries are the world, the flesh, and the devil. The world throws the stones of earthly wealth, the flesh throws the stones of corporeal delights, and the devil throws the stones of spiritual fallacies. Alas, scarcely can anyone pass over these stones without wounding his feet and limping or stumbling, regarding which the prophet says in his lament that the just man[68] falls seven times a day; and because of this hindrance the sacred soul is delayed in going toward her beloved and in running as easily as her heart desires.

The fourth chapter is about the path to the garden, which is narrow and rough

But when, with the safe conduct of God, she can escape from the paths of the world, the flesh, and the devil and withdraw her feet from the stones of their temptations, she looks for the path of righteous proceedings and finds it narrow and rough because of its strict mortification. For this path is enclosed and surrounded by a hedge composed of hawthorn bushes and replete with prickles. This is the path of true penitence which is sharp through contrition, but it is in bloom through confession and bearing fruit through salvation. What an extraordinary hedge and precious hawthorn bush that so lavishly flowers and bears fruit, for it bears the true fruits of penitence which because of their powerful medicine are recommended and praised in the Holy Gospel. O little thorn, little thorn, how sweet is your prick, for the deeper it pierces the heart the sooner it brings recovery. This fruit that can heal the wound and cure the sickness of every mortal sin is very full of grace. No pilgrim can pass over this path without tasting this fruit,

67. The two expressions here represent a chiasmatic structure that is not easily transferred into English: "fermement enclos et clozement fermez." This is, according to Edith Brayer (see Badel, "Pierre d'Ailly," 378), a characteristic trait of Pierre d'Ailly's preaching style.

68. Glorieux prints "il" (he), but I have preferred a variant from MS b, which makes more sense.

for he needs it in order to cure his sickness, restore his health, and sustain his life. And it is very sweet and full of grace when it is truly savored, even though at the beginning it tastes acidic and bitter.

The fifth chapter is about the garden's enclosure

When the sacred soul has entered the path of righteous proceedings and has tasted the fruit of penitence in order to obtain refection in her spiritual pilgrimage, she then comes to the garden of true perfection in order to find her beloved and experience with him the solace of virtue. But this garden is firmly enclosed and closely shut, for it is enclosed and surrounded by a solid wall: this is the wall of harsh austerity, built upon profound humility, erected by dignified poverty, fortified with patience and kindness, in order to put up resistance against the blows of adversity and the winds of prosperity. The sacred soul marvels greatly before the solidity and the height of this wall; and when she feels exhausted and overcome, not seeing how she can get past it and enter the garden, she sits down at the base of the wall and cries and lets out sighs and manifests great sorrow. But once she has given her body a bit of rest, her heart takes consolation and she gets up, seeking and searching until through her diligence she comes to the door.

The sixth chapter is about the custodian of the garden

There she finds an awe-inspiring lady, worthy of great respect, who was made aware of her arrival by certain signs and, in her courtliness, opened the door to her. This is Lady Obedience, who is the custodian of the garden and holds the keys of discretion, the staff of correction, and the rod of punishment: the keys serve to open and close, to make the good enter and the bad exit; the staff and the rod, to correct and punish misdeeds and to thrust out foolish idleness[69] and villainous sin with all their companions. This staff and this rod are unpleasant to the arrogant but gracious and pleasing to the humble, and so the holy prophet said that this staff and this rod brought him consolation.

The seventh chapter is about the four maidens of Lady Obedience

When the sacred soul sees Lady Obedience, her condition and her manner, she fears her tremendously and humbly submits herself and bows down to her. And she asks her: "Who are you who come here and what cause leads you?"

"I am," she replies, "a poor pilgrim who has heard the voice of my beloved and come to obey him."

69. This is an obvious reference to, and rejection of, the *Romance of the Rose,* given that the gatekeeper of the garden in the latter work is the allegorical personification Lady Idleness.

"Are you thus," says the lady, "the one who is loved by the God of love and summoned into his garden? If it is thus, welcome."

Then she takes her by the right hand and makes her swear and promise that she will live in obedience and will do nothing without authorization and permission; and she promises her gladly and gives herself joyfully over to her teaching and her discipline. The lady receives her instantly with tenderness and gives her four maidens to accompany her: These are the four noble cardinal virtues, namely, Prudence to teach her, Temperance to advise her, Fortitude to maintain her, Justice to govern her. Then these four beautiful maidens take her under their protection and authority and with neither difficulty nor refusal permit her to pass through the door and enter the garden.

The eighth chapter is about the great beauty of the garden in general

When the sacred soul sees that she has entered inside, she is very happy and full of joy; she is so impatient and full of longing to find her beloved that she can scarcely control her expression and her bearing. But the maidens accompanying her compel her to show moderation and make her walk tranquilly and proceed in proper order through all the sections of the garden in order to look at its beauty and contemplate its merit. Then she sees the bright paintings, the verdant plants, the resplendent flowers, the fortifying fruits, the bubbling springs, the singing birds, men and women full of affection, joyously disporting themselves.

The ninth chapter is specifically about the garden's paintings

But of all the things in the garden that are so beautiful and so pleasing, the sacred soul looks first at, and contemplates assiduously, the noble paintings that are skillfully depicted on the wall of the garden. There she sees the works of divine wisdom, the marvels of the Holy Scriptures, the stories of the Bible, the teachings of the Gospels, the miracles of Jesus Christ, the acts of the apostles, the victories of the martyrs, the qualities of confessors, the merits of virgins, the lives of the Fathers, the sayings of holy men, the examples of the wise; in general, she can view there all that belongs to the spiritual doctrine of her salvation. Oh, what noble paintings there are here, containing teaching of a sort with which neither earthly philosophy nor whatever human knowledge can be compared.

The tenth chapter, about the plants, the flowers, the trees, and the fruits

After the sacred soul is sufficiently instructed by these paintings, she proceeds farther into the garden in order to smell the delightful odor of the plants and the flowers and the very great sweetness of the trees and fruits.

There she sees the land of our mortal corruption sowed with spiritual correction, diligently plowed by the exercise of virtue, and gently watered by divine inspiration. In this land spring up the plants of humble meditation, the trees of lofty contemplation, the flowers of respectable behavior, the fruits of holy perfection, and, in general, the good actions of grace grow there in such great abundance that human understanding could barely number them nor could language describe them. Among these good actions, the sacred soul finds gentle pasture for her full refection. She sits upon the green expanse of the lawns, she rests in the shade of the trees, she gathers flowers, tastes the fruits, and especially, out of all the flowers and fruits, she picks the violet of true charity that grows among the new grass of submissive humility; then she makes a garland out of it to adorn herself and better please her beloved. This garland is very beautiful and gracious and, among all other adornments, is pleasing to the God of love and especially since the fine grass is gathered and is interwoven with the tender violet in order to enhance the beauty of the delicately red rose of fleshly virginity and the sweetly white rose of spiritual purity. O very sweet God! She must really be praised and blessed who can offer to her beloved such a garland and surround him with such delicate flowers. This is the present that he requests from the women who adore him when he says in the book of the Canticles: "Daughters of Jerusalem, provide me with dainty flowers, surround me with little apples, for I am languishing over my fleeting loves."[70] Oh, what a gracious request and what a very amorous lament! Alas, alas, the heart would be cruel and disdainful indeed that would not present this gift to this loyal lover who is languishing for having loved.

The eleventh chapter is about the tree of the cross

And this is why the sacred soul takes great pains and strives to find her beloved in order to offer and give to him the gracious gift of the beautiful flowers of decency and the good fruits of sanctity. She searches and seeks until she finds the precious tree of life. It is the tree of the holy cross where the God of love languished from an amorous martyrdom and suffered a bitter death. It is where he stretched out his arms and offered his mouth to embrace and kiss his beloved. It is where he opened his heart and shed his blood in order to show and elucidate his love. There, the sacred soul sees the manifest signs and the amorous languor and the languorous pain of her beloved. And when she realizes that he thus painfully died for love of her, then she is inspired, more than ever before, with love and more inflamed by

70. Sg 2:5: "fulcite me floribus, stipate me malis, quia amore langueo" (Stay me up with flowers, compass me about with apples: because I languish with love).

it, for she is struck in the heart and deeply wounded by the amorous arrow, which is to say by amorous compassion for sweet Jesus Christ, over whom she sighs, moans, and breaks out in tears and sobs; while weeping, she falls to the foot of the cross. And thus, as though faltering, she pitifully laments and wails out loud: "Woe is me! Alas," she says, "where will I find consolation since my beloved is dead? Alas, that was my life; how will I be able to live, then, since my life is dead? O tree of the cross, why are you called the tree of life? You should rather be called the tree of death, since the life of mortals has died in you. O immortal and everlasting life, how have you been thus handed over to death? O dearest Jesus and most glorious martyr of love, you paid too dearly for my life when, for having truly loved, you languished in a bitter death. O languorous death, the memory of you is terribly bitter since you have taken from me the sweetness of my life. O Jesus, my very tender love and my very amorous sweetness; alas, where will I find you in order to make a gift to you of the dainty and good-smelling flowers of good love, and of the good-tasting little apples that I heard you request in order to console your pain and your fatal languor? O sorrowful languor of my beloved, you make me languish too sorrowfully if you do not make me die shortly, for I do not wish to live without him a single day."

The twelfth chapter is about the three ladies who console the sacred soul over the death of her beloved

Thus laments the sacred soul over her beloved; and when the God of love hears her lament, he has pity for her pain and sends to her three ladies to comfort her. They are the three theological virtues; which is to say Faith to fortify her, Hope to assist her, and Charity in order to provide her solace. And then these three noble ladies console her very tenderly. Friend, they say, we are messengers from your beloved and will tell you good news of him. He is up there in the heavens and sends us to you down on the earth. He sends word to you through us that you should no longer feel distress over his languor or his death, for through his death you will have life, through languor you will have joy, through his suffering you will have solace, and through his woes you will have eternal rest. And if at present you do not see him, nor do you possess him as you desire, you must not be impatient over this. For if he is physically absent from you and you do not see him now except in an unclear image, you will see him afterward face to face, clearly.[71] Be consoled now, be happy and display your joy, for Faith attests to you, Hope promises you, and Charity assures you that if you love your

71. 1 Cor 13:12: "Videmus nunc per speculum in ænigmate: tunc autem facie ad faciem" (We see now through a glass in a dark manner; but then face to face).

beloved loyally and if you preserve for him the amorous present up to the end of your mortal life, finally you will see his dear countenance and you will kiss his sweet mouth, and you will have joy without end with him, everlasting joy, soothing joy secure from all ills, life without death and supplied with all good things. For he himself says in the Holy Scripture that no eye ever saw, no ear ever heard, no heart can give or even comprehend the good things that he has prepared for the loyal men and women who love him.[72] When the sacred soul hears these tidings: "Alas," she says, "and when will death come, when will the day come that will separate me from my body? I truly desire to be separated from the body and be with Jesus Christ."[73]

The thirteenth chapter is about the springs and streams of the garden

But when these three ladies, with their ardent speeches and their amorous promises, have inflamed the sacred soul and set her on fire with ardent desire and an amorous flame, then they direct her to the sweet springs of the garden in order to refresh her and sprinkle water on her great heat, and in order to pacify and refresh the ardent thirst of her desire. And there she finds the sweet spring of Grace, from which gush and spring seven streams, which are the seven sacraments of Jesus Christ, and seven others, which are the seven gifts of the Holy Spirit. There she finds the sweet spring of Compassion, which multiplies and divides into seven streams that are seven spiritual works, and into seven others that are seven corporeal works. And when these streams consisting of seven works of Compassion pass through the spring of Grace, there spouts from it and gushes a very fast-flowing and beautiful river, clear and limpid. It is the active water surging into everlasting life, just as Jesus Christ said to the Samaritan woman.[74]

O God, what a great leap, a great rise from low to high when a human creature, in order to perform works of compassion in this poor mortal life, rises to the noble life of the kingdom of heaven. O very sweet Jesus, they will be truly blessed, as you promise in the Gospel, those who will be called

72. 1 Cor 2:9: "Sed sicut scriptum est: Quod oculus non vidit, nec auris audivit, nec in cor hominis ascendit, quæ præparavit Deus iis qui diligunt illum" (But, as it is written: That eye hath not seen, nor ear heard, neither hath it entered into the heart of man, what things God hath prepared for them that love him).

73. Cf. Phil 1:23: "Coarctor autem e duobus: desiderium habens dissolvi, et esse cum Christo, multo magis melius" (But I am straitened between two: having a desire to be dissolved and to be with Christ, a thing by far the better).

74. Jn 4:14: "sed aqua quam ego dabo ei, fiet in eo fons aquæ salientis in vitam æternam" (But the water that I will give him, shall become in him a fountain of water, springing up into life everlasting).

by you to perform such works in order to come to the lofty kingdom that has been prepared for them since the beginning of the world.[75] O sovereign king, how can this water of grace and of compassion which flows down here on earth rise and leap up there to the kingdom of heaven? How can the water that springs so low surge so high, and how can the earthly work of the human creature ascend to the celestial realm of God the Creator? Certainly, this could not be done except by the great power of your infinite bounty, for the springs and streams of grace and compassion originate from you and descend from the heavens to the earth, from you who are good beyond measure, from you who are the source of all good things; and you make them ascend by your power from low to high and return to you, who are their original and principal place of birth.

Now the springs are very sweet: the streams that flow and arise from you, who are full of true tenderness, are very gentle. And this is why the sacred soul is gently sprinkled with water and abundantly drenched; she is watered there in order to refresh the great heat; she is sprinkled with water there in order to alleviate her ardent thirst; and from this there comes to her the sweet dew of merciful compassion; from this flows down to her the gentle rain of perfect devotion; there she feels the mild drop of divine inspiration; there she sees and drinks the sweet water of true consolation.

The fourteenth chapter is about the little birds that fly and sing in the garden

It is thus that the sacred soul takes her gentle refection in the springs and streams of this gracious garden; but her pleasure and joy are increased by the sweet song of the birds that are flying and singing. This is what devout souls do when they fly from low on high, ascending from the active to the contemplative life, abandoning the lowly things of the earth in order to attain the celestial ones. This is what the little birds do when they fly from the earth to the heavens, extracting the feathers of their laborious thoughts from earthly pursuits and flapping the wings of their emotions with divine meditations.[76] Thus the devout souls fly effortlessly and ascend to the heights.

75. Mt 25:34: "Tunc dicet rex his qui a dextris ejus erunt: Venite benedicti Patris mei, possidete paratum vobis regnum a constitutione mundi" (Then shall the king say to them that shall be on his right hand: Come, ye blessed of my Father, possess you the kingdom prepared for you from the foundation of the world).

76. I have translated the Middle French word *cogitations* as "laborious thoughts"; as the on-line Middle French Dictionary (DMF; http://www.atilf.fr/dmf/) specifies, in a spiritual context *cogitation* is considered to designate a kind of "vague, slow, laborious, and inefficient thought," inferior to meditation and contemplation. Here, as elsewhere, Pierre d'Ailly has translated this hierarchy into allegorical terms.

But as they fly and ascend they sing very sweetly and amorously chant spiritual songs, giving praise and exaltation to the God of love, while delivering thanks and blessings. It is the sweet and amorous chant of flawless prayer made in true devotion, which begins with the low voice of private confession, then a middle voice sounding out loud with discreet exultation, culminating with perseverance in a tone of jubilation. This song is quite melodious for it is sung very sweetly more through divine grace than natural ability; there is no disharmony or excess, neither false nor simulated music, but rather a total agreement between the heart and the mouth and a perfect concord between voice and thought.

The fifteenth chapter is about the beloved women and the men, lovers, who joyously learn the art of love

At the sound of this melody, the beloved women and the men, lovers, come to disport themselves joyously, manifesting a spiritual joy, without unseemly merriment. There the lovers assemble their amorous company and lead a joyous life thinking and speaking of love; there they get down on their knees to pay homage to the God of love, giving themselves over obediently to his amorous service; there they come to his school to hear the amorous law, where the art of loving is completely enclosed.[77] It is the school of Jesus Christ where he teaches the divine law, which contains the art and doctrine of loving God above all things and one's neighbor as oneself. It is the art of loving well, which no human creature can know through native reasoning unless it has been disciplined and taught by the word of divine Scripture. This art was never known by Virgil or Ovid or the others who taught how to love foolishly and deceptively and to foolishly honor Cupid, the false god of love, and his wanton mother, Venus.

Faith, the mistress of true love, urges and disposes us firmly to flee this false love: "Flee, flee," she says, "flee, loyal lovers, flee the perilous teaching, flee the false and mendacious art, flee the perverse doctrine that teaches that hateful love full of sin and filth. Instead, come to sweet Jesus Christ who calls you to his school; come to the sovereign master who teaches you to love well, out of a loyal love lacking dishonor." Then come the good pupils, who leave every love of this world in order to acquire divine love. But they are not all equal in their discipline or in their perfection. Rather,[78] they

77. This is an explicit quotation of part of the most well-known couplet of the *Romance of the Rose*: "This is the *Romance of the Rose* / where the art of love is completely enclosed" (*Rose*, ed. Lecoy, 37–8; trans. Dahlberg, 31 [altered]).

78. As Badel points out ("Pierre d'Ailly," 377 n. 1), Glorieux prints in error *Ainsi* (thus) instead of *Ains* (rather).

are very different in their adequacy and their status, for some are beginners, others making progress, and others perfect.[79] The beginners attend[80] school out of fear of punishment, those making progress out of an ardor for acquiring a recompense, and the perfect out of pure love and absolute affection. These are the three stations of the true students of love who apply themselves and are intent upon loving God entirely with their heart, their soul, and their thought.

The sixteenth chapter is about the sacred soul who out of joy sings the praises of the God of love

When the sacred soul sees this beautiful company thus in love with her beloved, she is very pleased and delighted, for she is not filled with foolish jealousy, but rather desires that her beloved be loved by all and that all be loved by him as herself. And in order to be able to attract amorous hearts to this love, she takes pains and makes an effort to praise her beloved and deliver her sweet praises to him; and because of the joy she feels in praising her beloved and in recounting the great benefits that come from loving him, she is compelled to sing this amorous little song:

In order to earn the amorous crown
of which the God of love makes an amorous present
to lovers, all must praise him,
love him, serve him most amorously,
for through the love of his absolute will,
through the tenderness of his noble nature,
everything was planned in his art,
and out of nothing he formed the form
  of every creature.

Love made him create the beautiful world
and adorn the firmament with stars;
he made the elements harmonize

79. This is the identical division given by Gerson in his sermon *Considerate lilia* (no. 12 in this volume), which is not surprising, inasmuch as this was a "classic" distinction at the time (cf. Badel, "Pierre d'Ailly," 374 n. 1).

80. As Badel notes ("Pierre d'Ailly," 377 n. 2), Glorieux's edition has here the verb *fuient* (flee), which is clearly the opposite of what the context would require, for what ought to be *suient* (follow, pursue, adhere to). This is a common scribal error, as the only distinction between *f* and the common form of *s* found in medieval manuscripts is the stroke through the middle of the former letter.

as he appeased their contrariety;
In plants he rejuvenated the greenery,
he made beasts see to procreation;
by him force was given to things,
by him worth was bequeathed to them
    in equitable measure.

Love made him form man and woman
and distribute generously to them all good things:
to participate in life with plants;
in natural feeling with beasts;
and in reason, sense, and righteousness with the angels.
This was the noble portrait of God,
for his image was imprinted on him.
Never was there made or imagined
    a more beautiful figure.

Love made him humble his power
When he was born as a human of a woman
who was a virgin and a mother without contradiction,
she who conceived in a divine fashion God and man.
Divinity then took on a fleshly garb,
eternity took on a mortal covering,
immensity was then measured,
infinity was then confined
    within a small enclosure.

Love made him have his body hanged and bound,
and die on the cross with great anguish
in order to release his friends from prison
to give them the alleviation of love.
Thus he shattered the murky dungeon of hell
and reopened the fortress of heaven.
Our sickness was treated by him,
our health was restored by him
    through a merciful cure.

Love made him promulgate among lovers
the law of grace in a gentle commandment

that makes the human heart be bound by itself
and love God fittingly more than itself.
It is a firm bond and a perfect joining.
In this instance, there is no insight stemming from nature,
for nature is in love with herself
above all things; she is certainly suspected of this
  in the Holy Scripture.

Love made him fashion the crown
of which I spoke, which he presents to his people.
It is the present so worthy of being prized,
the prize of love that is so noble and fine.
This is where the attention of true lovers should direct itself,
it is a flawless gift, it is a good thing that lasts without end,
it is total glory and secure joy;
it is a sound life, it is health protected
  from every injury.

It is a sweet thing to love loyally
since love is the foundation of all good things.
There is in good love sweetness without gall
for those who know how to maintain it gently;
for sweet pleasure greatly assures its gift[81]
and sweet hope feeds its desire:
If such sweetness is fully tasted,[82]
true lovers can find in it
  sweet nourishment.

Let us now have the warmth of this love.
Let us love him who is beautiful without foulness;
let us love the beautiful one who is loved by him,
let us love for his sake all created beauty
  lacking vulgar filth.

81. I have substituted for the text Glorieux printed for the last part of this line the variant reading he lists from one of his control manuscripts, BnF fr. 24865 (MS b).

82. I have emended Glorieux's text, which doesn't make too much sense, using one of his variants.

12. FROM JEAN GERSON, *CONSIDERATE LILIA* (SERMON, AUGUST 25, 1401)[83]

LATIN PROSE

[*After a lengthy elaboration of the image of the lilies of the field, Gerson concludes his sermon with three separate orations directed to the three principal groups into which he divides his audience: beginning students* (incipientes), *those advanced in their studies* (proficientes), *and the mature men who have completed their training* (perfectos). *Following is the first oration, in which Gerson concentrates on the topic of education of the young and professors' duties.*]

First oration. I now address my speech to you, O noble young men. And if you wish to be noble and not unworthy, learned and not fools, then obey what Christ commands. What does Christ command? Consider the lilies of the field and how they grow.[84] But consider them without noise and disruption, and pay heed to your whispering, since these are the conditions that will be most suitable for the first shoots of the virtuous lilies to grow in the field of your young mind. Indeed, certain shoots of the virtues are grafted onto you by the actions of infallible nature, as though in conformity with the seminal judgments that Cicero calls the seed-plots of the virtues,[85] which, if we were to allow them to grow and acquire strength, would lead us off to the blessed life (he says). Nor was the Philosopher silent about them in his second book of *Ethics*.[86] Do not stifle these seeds with vicious shoots or destroy them with anything else. And although you are to hold in dread at different moments the cold frost of stupefying inactivity, the fire of exceedingly violent desire, cankerworms, envy, and the other vile diseases standing in opposition to the growth of the spiritual lilies, nonetheless it is necessary to apply

83. This passage has been translated from Gerson, *Œuvres complètes*, 5:160–64 (the entire sermon occupies pp. 151–68). The sermon was delivered before the professors and students in theology at the Collège de Navarre in celebration of the birthday of Saint Louis, king of France.

84. The sermon takes as its point of departure and theme the image of the lilies of the field, as found in Christ's Sermon on the Mount. Cf. Mt 6:28 and Lk 12:27.

85. The image of the "seeds of the virtues" (*semina virtutum*), developed into that of the "seed-plots of the virtues" (*seminaria virtutum*), apparently was inspired by Cicero and filtered through Saint Augustine and Saint Thomas Aquinas; used to express the notion that the development of human intellect and the acquisition of virtues are comparable to natural physical growth, it was further refined by a late-thirteenth-century Franciscan named Matthew of Aquasparta, who was a disciple of Bonaventure (see M. C. Horowitz, *Seeds of Virtue and Knowledge* [Princeton: Princeton University Press, 1998], 51–52).

86. A reference, of course, to Aristotle and his *Nicomachean Ethics*, book 2, chap. 1 (1103a).

oneself principally to study for the purpose of maintaining a suitable stronghold fortified by the wall of instruction: when this wall has not been put into place or has been demolished, the lilies are completely done for. They are trampled down and perish. Wherefore, take hold of education as did the person who said to God: "And your instruction itself will teach me."[87]

But why am I speaking to the young men? Perhaps they close their ears or do not take up carefully enough the things that are being said. That's what it is! The chattering of certain of them reveals this: undoubtedly, they are less capable of observing attentively, on account of either the dull obscurity of ignorance or the disorder of the passions and of youthful longings, which transport their thoughts and reflections elsewhere. Or maybe it is because they bring to this place a lack of discipline that they practice elsewhere.

For that reason reflect carefully on their account, you, their teachers and venerable masters; I turn to you, who have chosen to take the lead in guiding such young men and who, in doing so, have indeed set out to rule a difficult province, as Terence puts it.[88] May the stronghold of your instruction enclose them. Under its protection, set their morals in order and form them according to the precepts of the Christian religion. Indeed, what a great shame it is in the case of Christians that their young people do not partake of Christian doctrine, do not know the precepts of God, and are profoundly ignorant about what they should do, what they should give up, what they should believe, and what they should fear and hope for. What a shame it is that they speak and read only about either what does not benefit their character or what injures rather than improves their nature. It is shameful that up to the present day, on the contrary, Jewish boys are instructed from the beginning in their own law as the Lord appears to have commanded. Deuteronomy 4.[89]

87. Ps 17:36: "et disciplina tua ipsa me docebit."

88. Gerson may here be referring to Terence's *The Brothers*, which deals with two brothers who have two quite different philosophies of education, and the complications that ensue.

89. Moses' command to the Jews that they teach God's law to their children is found in Deut 4:9–10: "Custodi igitur temetipsum, et animam tuam sollicite. Ne obliviscaris verborum, quæ viderunt oculi tui, et ne excidant de corde tuo cunctis diebus vitae tuæ. Docebis ea filios ac nepotes tuos, a die in quo stetisti coram Domino Deo tuo in Horeb, quando Dominus locutus est mihi, dicens: Congrega ad me populum, ut audiant sermones meos, et discant timere me omni tempore quo vivunt in terra, doceantque filios suos." (Keep thyself therefore, and thy soul carefully. Forget not the words that thy eyes have seen, and let them not go out of thy heart all the days of thy life. Thou shalt teach them to thy sons and to thy grandsons, from the day in which thou didst stand before the Lord thy god in Horeb, when the Lord spoke to me, saying: Call together the people unto me, that they may hear my words, and may learn to fear me all the time that they live on the earth, and may teach their children.)

See how at this moment the same young men, more than usual, flock together in multitudes from the entire kingdom of France to the very flourishing garden of the University of Paris; they intend to be educated in its elementary and grammatical subjects, whereas not long ago those who had been accustomed to arrive were already trained in just such subjects. As to why this is happening and whether it might be a favorable sign, I have not endeavored to examine. We know that in a mortal being the breath of life flows to the heart. This one thing I am able to say, that a greater amount of care and attention must be given to it in this very distinguished university lest—should the wall of instruction that ensures the protection of these young people be destroyed and neglected—there sprout from the soil not the fragrant and pure white lilies of the virtues, but instead "luckless darnel and sterile oats," as Virgil says;[90] also brambles and flintstones and all sorts of noxious plants of the vices, working not only toward the destruction of these individuals but toward the public destruction of the Church, lest the field be one such as Jeremiah saw, full of abominations. Jeremiah 13.[91]

O tempora, o mores![92] How many and what great abominations fill the minds and bodies of certain young people! Moreover, these abominations spread gradually among them with impious contamination, but no one looks closely, no one restrains them, no one eradicates them; if only there were no one instigating them or in any way hindering access to those who would endeavor to extirpate them. And, alas, a heap of evils! They do not abhor their own abominations, as does the prophet, saying: "I have hated and abhor injustice."[93] But what does it mean to abhor injustice? Assuredly, it is to spew it out or cast it away through the words of confession. Truly, with this purpose in mind it is necessary to act in such a way that the closed and mute mouth is opened more frequently. For scarcely ever is this very foul and repulsive poison, which is contrary to nature, extricated, unless it is in the manner of the parable of Scripture: "Let the tortuous serpent spring forth by

90. *Georgics* 1.154: "infelix lolium et steriles avenae."

91. Jer 13:27: "Adulteria tua, et hinnitus tuus, scelus fornicationis tuae: super colles in agro vidi abominationes tuas. Vae tibi, Ierusalem! Non mundaberis post me: usquequo adhuc?" (I have seen thy adulteries, and thy neighing, the wickedness of thy fornication; and thy abominations, upon the hills in the field. Woe to thee, Jerusalem, wilt thou not be made clean after me: how long yet?)

92. A phrase often used by Cicero, e.g., *Oratio in Catilinam* (Speech against Lucius Sergius Catiline) 1.2: "O tempora, o mores!" (O the times, O the morals). Expression also used by Jean de Montreuil (no. 19 in this volume).

93. Ps 118:163: "Iniquitatem odio habui, et abominatus sum."

the midwifery of the learned confessor's hand."[94] Why therefore be astonished if many are suffocated by this noxious venom that has been retained inside and irremediably go to ruin?

At least this will be left from the cure, namely, that if the senses and thoughts of man are inclined to evil from adolescence, just as the voice of Scripture[95] and experience confirm it all too much to be the case, this remnant, I say, will be that they will abhor these abominations they have contracted, because in abhorring them, that is, by spewing them out through confession, they will be cured and the field will cease to be full of abominations; very clearly, since it is said: It is human to sin but diabolical to persevere.

This is why it is clear to what extent the guardianship of the new fields that we call young people, especially during the period when they are of a tender age, is a necessary precondition for instruction; indeed, "strong is habit in tender years,"[96] so says Virgil. Let there be an enclosure of instruction over them and may the very best form of living be furnished, as pleasant as custom provides.

If in truth there are some masters who neither consider carefully in this way nor act with respect toward their students, whether this happens by dishonest neglect or perverse contempt or by greedy fear (lest their pupils leave and go off elsewhere), or by their corrupt example of an evil life, here is what should be proclaimed about them: for every one of those masters who should be called not "instructors" of the spiritual fields but rather "destroyers" ought to have saved those fields and yet they ruin them. Moreover, it also happens often that the licentiousness of one young person that has neither been controlled nor utterly driven out, as is necessary, risks dragging away the other unblemished plantings toward the uncultivated, degenerate liquors and illegitimate fruits of moral conduct, so much so that, not without the appearance of reason, Quintilian seems to have wondered whether

94. Gerson has slightly altered the quotation for his own purpose here. Job 26:13: "Spiritus ejus ornavit cælos, et obstetricante manu ejus, eductus est coluber tortuosus" (His spirit hath adorned the heavens, and his obstetric hand brought forth the winding serpent).

95. Gen 8:21 (God speaking to Noah after the flood): "Nequaquam ultra maledicam terræ propter homines: sensus enim et cogitatio humani cordis in malum prona sunt ab adolescentia sua: non igitur ultra percutiam omnem animam viventem sicut feci" (I will no more curse the earth for the sake of man: for the imagination and thought of man's heart are prone to evil from his youth: therefore I will no more destroy every living soul as I have done).

96. *Georgics* 2.272: "adeo in teneris consuescere multum est." Virgil is here speaking of the transplanting of young vines. Trans. Fairclough, 1:155.

it was useful for young people to be taught together in schools or whether it wouldn't better be done individually in their homes.[97] And since the recollection of Quintilian, who was a celebrated teacher of the young, is brought to mind, it seems appropriate to single out these few things from his principles of instruction which he attributes to the office of the teacher:

First, he says, let him assume before all things the disposition of a parent with regard to his students and let him consider that he is taking the place of those by whom the children have been intrusted to him. Teachers have therefore the obligation to address their students with the same words full of religious and maternal piety with which the mother of Saint Louis exhorted the illustrious young man: "I would rather, dear son, that you incur a temporal death than that you offend your Creator owing to some mortal sin."[98]

Second, the instructor should neither possess nor tolerate vice. A famous expression from the mouth of a pagan, Juvenal, who was a contemporary of Quintilian and who wrote about this, gives the reason for it: that domestic examples corrupt us all the more swiftly and readily since they penetrate the mind with the sanction of great authority.[99] For that reason he adds that the greatest respect is owed to the child,[100] namely, that nothing obscene or lewd, no sort of example tempting to evil be presented before innocent eyes and minds; for their angels always behold the face of the Father in heaven;[101] and he who leads one of these little ones to sin, it would be better for him, etc.[102] And one example of wickedness would do more harm

97. Quintilian, *Institutio oratoria* 1.2.1: "Hoc igitur potissimum loco tractanda quaestio est, utiliusne sit domi atque intra privatos parietes studentem continere an frequentiae scholarum et velut publicis praeceptoribus tradere" (This therefore is the place to discuss the question as to whether it is better to have him educated privately at home or hand him over to some large school and those whom I call public instructors). Trans. H. E. Butler (Cambridge: Harvard University Press, 1920), 38–39.

98. Gerson here recalls an anecdote recorded by Jean de Joinville in his *Vie de Saint Louis* (ed. Jacques Monfrin [Paris: Classiques Garnier, 1995], 36 [par. 71]: "[Saint Louis] recordoit que sa mere li avoit fait aucune foiz a entendre que elle ameroit miex que il feust mort que ce que il feist un pechié mortel" (Saint Louis remembered that his mother let him know from time to time that she would prefer him to die rather than commit a mortal sin). We are reminded that the birthday of the holy king was the occasion upon which Gerson delivered this sermon.

99. Juvenal, *Satires* 14.31–33: "velocius et citius nos / corrumpunt vitiorum exempla domestica, magnis cum subeant animos auctoribus" (Bad examples in the home corrupt us more speedily and quickly, because they creep into our minds with powerful authority). *Juvenal and Persius,* trans. Susanna M. Braund (Cambridge: Harvard University Press, 2004), 460–61.

100. Ibid., 14.47 (462–63): "maxima debetur puero reverentia" (A child deserves the utmost respect).

101. Mt 18:10: "quia angeli eorum in cælis semper vident faciem Patris mei, qui in cælis est."

102. Mt 18:6: "qui autem scandalizaverit unum de pusillis istis, qui in me credunt, expedit ei ut suspendatur mola asinaria in collo ejus, et demergatur in profundum maris" (But he that shall

than ten of goodness would bring profit; for a child, as though of wax, may be bent toward vice, and even without a teacher evils are learned.

Third, may there neither be disagreeable harshness nor lax affability in a teacher, lest, for the first cause, hatred for him should arise, or, for the second cause, contempt. Wherein it is to be observed that excessive affability does less harm than harshness among young men of a good natural disposition, who, guided by kindnesses, are more rapidly domesticated, in the manner of those birds which they call noble, than attracted by threats; may it just be noted that these kindnesses should lack any inward shamelessness of mind and body. Whereby Quintilian himself concludes that children must not be beaten with lashes. I leave out his reasoning.

Fourth, may speech to the child be chiefly about virtue and the good. Against those who not only dare to name the shameful parts of the body and abominable acts not only with overt impudence but who, with even more shameless vehemence, maintain that according to the character of Reason such speech should be permitted,[103] they do not consider that by saying these things they are falling into the error of the Beghards and the Turlupins, who said that one need not blush over anything bestowed naturally,[104] just as the philosophers known as the Cynics said that one ought to go about stark naked and make use of the privy parts in public as dogs do, which things Cicero faults in *De officiis* (Of Duties), discussing what is beautiful

---

scandalize one of these little ones that believe in me, it were better for him that a millstone should be hanged about his neck, and that he should be drowned in the depth of the sea).

103. As M. Lieberman noted in an important article ("Chronologie gersonienne, X: Le Sermon *Memento Finis*," *Romania* 83 [1962], 67–77), although a few of the doctrines featured in the *Romance of the Rose* are criticized or condemned by Gerson prior to this time without his mentioning the work, this is the first time that a specific reference to the *Rose* is made by Gerson in a public declaration. Lieberman calls this Gerson's "first intervention" in the debate, and a "frontal attack," even though the *Rose* is not explicitly named; he also considers that Gerson's mention of the people he opposes ("Against those who . . .") refers specifically to Jean de Montreuil and the Col brothers.

104. "Beghards" and "Beguines" were names given, respectively, to lay men and women who, as early as the twelfth century, chose to live a *vita apostolica* (apostolic life), following the ideals of poverty and mendicancy and, for the women, chastity. They gave rise to much hostility, as did members of the mendicant orders generally, and were regularly persecuted as heretics through the thirteenth and fourteenth centuries. The term "Turlupin," generally associated with these two groups, designated a sect that was associated with the "Free Spirit" movement and that Gerson more specifically condemned for its outrageous behavior, including dirty language, public nudity, and indiscriminate sexual relations. As Lieberman states ("Chronologie gersonienne," 74–75), Gerson fulminated against them his entire career; he specifically condemns them in at least twenty-four places in his writings, extending from 1401 to 1427. As recently as 1372, the books and belongings of a sect of Turlupins, along with one of its members, had been burned in the Place de Grève (now the Place de l'Hôtel de Ville) in Paris.

and proper;[105] and Seneca teaches that you should not say filthy things, for little by little modesty regarding these things is unlearned through using the words for them;[106] and the Apostle Paul says: "perverse conversations corrupt good morals."[107]

Fifth, may the teacher be minimally irritable, yet not a dissembler regarding those things that ought to be chastised. On this, there are the examples of Plato and Plutarch and many others.

Sixth, let him be straightforward in teaching. On this, the famous line from the ancient law can be excerpted: "Do not sow the field with dissimilar seeds."[108] Indeed, usually a variety of methods in teaching does harm and so does, as a consequence, a changing of masters, first these and then those.

Seventh, may he endure his charge patiently. Eighth, let him respond willingly to questions. Ninth, let him on the other hand interrogate those who do not ask questions of their own accord. Tenth, let him be neither niggardly nor extravagant toward those responses of students deserving praise,

105. Cicero, *De officiis,* 1. 35.126–28 (trans. Walter Miller [Cambridge: Harvard University Press, 1913], 129–31: "And in outward, visible propriety there are three elements—beauty, tact, and taste . . . the parts of the body that are given us only to serve the needs of Nature and that would present an unsightly and unpleasant appearance she [Nature] has covered up and concealed from view. Man's modesty has followed this careful contrivance of Nature's; all right-minded people keep out of sight what Nature has hidden and take pains to respond to Nature's demands as privately as possible; and in the case of those parts of the body which only serve Nature's needs, neither the parts nor the functions are called by their real names. To perform these functions—if only it be done in private—is nothing immoral; but to speak of them is indecent. And so neither public performance of those acts nor vulgar mention of them is free from indecency. But we should give no heed to the Cynics (or to some Stoics who are practically Cynics) who censure and ridicule us for holding that the mere mention of some actions that are not immoral is shameful, while other things that are immoral we call by their real names."

106. As Lieberman notes, the passage from Seneca to which Gerson refers here is now known to be the work of Martin of Braga, an influential sixth-century churchman: "Turpia ne dixeris, paulatim enim pudor per verba discutitur" (may you not say indecent things, for one's modesty is gradually destroyed by words); *Libellus de Moribus* (Pamphlet on Morals), *Patrologiae Cursus Completus, Series Latina (PL),* ed. J. P. Migne (Paris, 1841–55), vol. 72, col. 31. It is also mentioned in the *Treatise against the Romance of the Rose* (no. 20 in this volume) and in the third and fourth sermons of the *Poenitemini* series (included in no. 24).

107. 1 Cor 15:33: "corrumpunt mores bonos colloquia mala" (evil communications corrupt good manners). The texts quoted by Gerson here recur at other moments when he refers to the Beghards and Turlupins. As Lieberman cogently remarks ("Chronologie gersonienne," 73), Gerson had a strong association of ideas, extending from the *Romance of the Rose* to illicit sexuality, to lascivious language, to nudism, to dogs, to the impudence of the Cynics, to Cicero, Seneca, and Saint Paul, ending with the heresy of the Turlupins and the Beghards. The thought of the *Romance of the Rose* seemed to trigger one or several of the other terms. It is to be noted that the Turlupins were also known by the slang term *Cagnards,* from the common noun *cagne,* which meant, first, "dog," then "prostitute."

108. Lev 19:19: "Agrum tuum non seres diverso semine."

because the one produces in the pupil an aversion for his exertion, and the other produces carelessness.

Eleventh, in improving work that needs to be corrected, let him be neither sharp nor in the slightest insulting; for the fact that certain people scold in this manner, just as though out of hatred, truly chases many away from the determination to study.

Twelfth, let him say something, or rather many things, daily that might themselves refer back to things that have already been heard. For while it is permissible for him to furnish enough examples from their reading for them to imitate, the living voice, as it is said, nourishes more fully, and especially the voice of the teacher, whom the students love and revere, provided that they are taught in the correct manner. Moreover it can scarcely be said how much more willingly we imitate those whom we favor. Above all things, I would like this rule to be observed by teachers of our time, be it in a village of straw huts or in private homes: in place of the ordinary trifling tales and fictitious narratives they are requested to tell, let them recount salutary and pleasing ones, because, as Horace attests: "He has won every vote who has blended profit and pleasure."[109] Thus it was, for instance, with Master Reginald Gobart. A trustworthy report affirmed to me that he scarcely if ever read out loud or listened to a reading in the presence of his students without mixing in some words about salvation and ardently inculcating it into them, to such a point that a great portion of his students turned out to be distinguished and religious men.

Thirteenth, let teachers wish to be attentively listened to and in an orderly manner. If this were to be observed in the schools, the attentiveness and orderliness of students would be different when listening to the word of God, which would certainly have to be heard with the greatest reverence and knowledge, and nowhere less than when in the presence of the sacrosanct mystery of the body of Christ. For so said Aristotle, as reported by Seneca: never should we show more restraint and respect than when we speak with God;[110] and also while we listen.

However, the following actions are fitting for students: first, that they love their teachers no less than their studies; second, that they believe them

109. *The Art of Poetry* 343: "omne tulit punctum qui miscuit utile dulci." *Satires, Epistles, and Ars Poetica*, trans. Fairclough, 478–79.

110. Seneca, *Naturales quaestiones* 7.30.1: "Egregie Aristoteles ait numquam nos uerecundiores esse debere quam cum de diis agitur" (Aristotle has said excellently that we should never be more reverent than when a subject deals with the gods) (trans. Thomas H. Corcoran, 2 vols. [Cambridge: Harvard University Press, 1972], 2:290–91). Cf. Aristotle's *Nicomachean Ethics*, book 1, chap. 12 (1101b).

to be as their parents—certainly not of the body but of the mind. This dutiful conduct brings much to their study, for they will listen gladly and will trust in their words and will aspire to be like them.

If these things are observed with respect to the care and instruction of young men, their field will be germinating with the white lilies of those same virtues until they burst forth by growing into great strength. And so it will be in such a way as in that passage in which Christ commands: consider the lilies of the field, how they grow.

13. GONTIER COL TO CHRISTINE DE PIZAN (SEPTEMBER 13, 1401)[111]

FRENCH PROSE

To the prudent, honored, and wise demoiselle Christine

Woman of high and exalted intellect, worthy of honor and the greatest compliments. I have heard tell from the mouths of several prominent clerics that among your other meditations and virtuous works, all worthy of praise, (as I understand it from their report) you have recently written a sort of invective more or less counter to what my master, teacher, and friend, the late Master Jean de Meun, wrote down and compiled in the book of the *Rose*—he, a sincere Catholic, a celebrated master, and, in his time, a doctor of holy theology, a very profound and excellent philosopher, possessing the knowledge of all that is available to human understanding; his glory and reputation live and will live in the ages to come in the minds of those who have been lifted up by his merits.[112] Moreover, as those who have spoken about and reported on this matter affirm, you endeavor and take great pains to reproach him and accuse him of errors in the above-mentioned new work of yours. This matter causes me great astonishment and comes to me as a complete surprise;

111. Translated from *Le débat,* ed. Hicks, 9–11.

112. Gontier Col may well be thinking principally of three doctrinally oriented, moralizing works attributed to Jean de Meun at this time and the attribution of which would not have been doubted: the *Testament* and the *Codicil* (both of which scholars now agree to have been composed by Jean), and the *Tresor* (Treasure), which is now known to have been composed by an author named Jean Chapuis. However, it is clear from the supporters of Jean de Meun that they considered the *Romance of the Rose* to be replete with philosophical and moral instruction. Hicks (*Le débat,* 198) notes that the expression "possessing the knowledge of all that is available to human understanding" roughly translates a part of the epitaph alleged to have been placed on Peter Abelard's tomb.

indeed, my firsthand knowledge of you and your activities moves me not to believe it, on account of your having known, read, and understood him in the book in question and in his other writings in French, as well as many other diverse doctors, authors, and poets.

And since those who have denounced this work, some of them perhaps envious of the writings of the aforementioned Jean de Meun, consider and view your invective as a unique and magnificently composed work, constructed and carried out in accord with their wishes and viewpoint, so much so that I cannot obtain a copy of the original from them, I beg and request you, by the love you have for learning, to consent to send me the work in question in its present state by means of this messenger of mine or of some other one that suits you, in order that I may toil over it and apply myself to defending my master and his works. But there would never be any need for me or any other mortal to get involved in this if he were alive: indeed, I would have preferred him to have lived during my lifetime over being at this very moment emperor of the Romans.

And in order to lead you back to the real truth, so that you may learn more about, and better acquaint yourself with, the works of the aforementioned Meun, I am sending you, with honest intentions and in haste, a bit of his *Treasure* which he assembled to be made known to those who were envious of him, as well as others, upon his death.[113] (What I am sending is riddled with errors owing to the fault of the scribe, who did not understand it, or so it seems, and I did not have the time or leisure to look it over or correct it at length on account of the urgency I feel and my fervor to see the above-mentioned work of yours; and especially because it is to be assumed that you will be capable of deciphering and correcting the scribal errors in this collection.) This, at the risk of giving you or your acolytes[114] material to write even more against him if it please you—they who pushed you into this endeavor because they either did not dare to touch it

113. To anyone put off by the misogyny and comic indecency of the *Romance of the Rose,* the sober tone of the *Treasure* would seem to vindicate the putative author of the two works (see the previous note).

114. This paragraph consists of one very rambling, syntactically complex sentence, the principal verb of which is "I am sending." What I have translated as "This, at the risk of," along with all that follows to the end of the paragraph, is actually placed toward the beginning of the paragraph, as a subordinate clause. The basic structure of the sentence would most literally say, "in order to lead you back . . . and in order to give you material to write even more against . . .," which is contradictory. This suggests that the second clause, along with the references to Christine's "acolytes," is dripping with irony. The word used by Christine, *satalites,* would have denoted either mercenary soldiers or devoted followers, hence my translation.

or weren't capable of doing so, but who want to make of you, as it were, a raincoat,[115] in order to claim that they would know how to do it better than a woman and to inhibit more effectively the unflagging renown of such a man among mortals.

Insofar as you have chosen, or rather dared, to accuse, correct, and reproach him, as people say, for what he accomplished in the book of the *Rose,* where there are a large number of extraordinary and diverse words and ideas,[116] there is one thing I do not wish to forget or leave unmentioned: that if you do not reverse your position and disavow what you have said, I shall undertake to come to his defense against your writings and any other ones whatsoever, being confident in good and true justice, and certain that truth, which does not retreat into hiding,[117] will be with me. This in spite of the fact that I am right now, and have been recently, pressured by other serious affairs.

Written in haste, in the presence of Master Jehan de Quatre Mares, Jehan Porchier, counselors, and Guillaume de Neauville, secretary of our lord the king,[118] Tuesday, the thirteenth day of September, in the year 1401.

Yours, to the extent that the law of friendship can allow,
Gontier Col
Secretary of the king our lord

115. The expression used here is a *chappe a pluie,* a *chappe* being a loose-fitting overgarment with long sleeves: hence, such a cloak meant to protect from the rain. But of course the meaning here is figurative, suggesting that Christine is being used as a form of protection, a buffer, or even a decoy by the otherwise unnamed "satellites." The expression is used in the *Rose* (ed. Lecoy, l. 8481; trans. Dahlberg, 156), where the Jealous Husband accuses his philandering wife of using him as a "rain-coat"; Lecoy interprets this in his glossary to mean that her married status protects her from being criticized for her wanton behavior. Could Gontier Col be ironically transferring this statement to refer to Christine's situation?

116. As Hasenohr notes (review of Hicks, *Le débat,* 129), Hicks's punctuation of this sentence is infelicitous, but her way of understanding the syntax is not much of an improvement. Clearly the reading from the B manuscripts is preferable ("Quant en ce que" instead of "Quant ad ce que"), as it provides a transparent understanding; I have adopted that reading in my translation.

117. This is a very well-known proverb, found in the form, as here, "verité ne quiert angles" (truth does not seek out hiding places), or "verité n'a cure d'angles" (truth does not care about hiding places). It is in fact found twice in the *Romance of the Rose* (ed. Lecoy, ll. 11404 and 16546). Cf. Morawski, *Proverbes français,* no. 2468; Hassell, *Middle French Proverbs,* 247 (V68); and Giuseppe di Stefano, *Dictionnaire des locutions en moyen français* (Montreal: Editions CERES, 1991), 25–26.

118. Jean de Quatremares and Jean Porchier were counselors at the Parlement of Paris, while Guillaume de Neauville, like Jean de Montreuil and Gontier Col, was a secretary and notary to the king.

14. GONTIER COL TO CHRISTINE DE PIZAN (SEPTEMBER 15, 1401)[119]

FRENCH PROSE

ITEM,[120] *When the said Christine had sent the copy of the aforementioned letter to Master Gontier Col, he sent back to her the following letter:*

To a woman of lofty understanding, demoiselle Christine

The divine Scripture teaches and orders us to correct and reprimand one's friend at first in private when one sees him go astray or make a mistake, but that if he does not wish to improve himself on that occasion one should correct him in public; and if he does not wish to correct himself after that, then one should consider him *tanquam eunucus et publicanus.*[121] Now, I bear you loyal affection on account of your virtues and merits, and because of this I exhorted, advised, and implored you initially, in a letter that I sent you the day before yesterday, to correct and redress your stance with regard to that manifest error, folly, or senselessness that came to you as a result of presumption and arrogance—you being a woman passionately engaged in this matter. May it not displease you if I speak the truth. Following the divine commandment, I beg, advise, and request you for the second time, by means of this document of mine, to agree to correct, disown, and make amends for your above-mentioned error with respect to that very excellent and irreproachable doctor of holy divine Scripture, a lofty philosopher and a cleric very deeply learned in all the seven liberal arts (whom you so outrageously dare and presume to correct, indeed reproach, at his considerable expense), as well as with respect to his true and loyal disciples, my lord the provost of Lille, myself, and others. I likewise entreat you to confess your error, and we will have pity on you and grant you mercy by giving you salutary penance.

And with regard to this matter, along with a reply to my other letter, may it please you to let me know at your leisure and convenience your in-

119. Translated from *Le débat,* ed. Hicks, 23–24. In this and the following letter, I have italicized Christine's identification of this document contained in the dossier she sent to the queen of France, thus connecting it with the narrative account of no. 18. Gontier Col's first letter (no. 13) follows immediately upon the narrative account of the debate in no. 18.

120. The word "ITEM" here indicates a continuation of the list in no. 18.

121. Whether by intention or by copying error, this is a misquotation of the biblical text "sicut ethnicus et publican" (as an heathen man and a publican [tax collector]) (Mt 18:17). The opening of this letter replicates the teaching of Christ in this biblical passage (Mt 18:15–17).

tention before I begin writing in opposition to the false (with all due respect) texts that you have chosen to write about him.

And if now, and when I write to you in the future, I address you in the singular, may it not displease you, nor should you attribute it to arrogance or haughtiness on my part, for this is and always has been my manner when I have written to my friends, especially when they are learned.[122]

May God in short order see fit to bring your heart and understanding back to the true light and knowledge of the truth! For it would be unfortunate if you remained any longer in such error under the shadows of ignorance.

Written this Thursday, the fifteenth day of September.

15. CHRISTINE DE PIZAN TO GONTIER COL (LATE SEPTEMBER 1401)[123]

FRENCH PROSE

After this there follows the response sent to the said Master Gontier Col.

To the very notable and considerable person, Master Gontier Col, secretary of the king our lord

O cleric subtle in philosophical understanding, accomplished in the sciences, nimble in polished rhetoric and refined poetic skill, please do not allow a zealous error to lead you to blame and to reproach my rightful opinion that is motivated by a sense of what is just, even if it doesn't suit you. Since I learned from the first letter you sent me that you wanted to have a copy of a short treatise in the form of an epistle that I had sent some time ago to that eminent cleric, my lord the provost of Lille (in which is treated and developed at length, within the confines of my limited wit, the opinion held by me, contrary to his, regarding the great praise that he confers upon the compilation of the *Romance of the Rose,* as it became clear to me in a work of his

122. Gontier Col is here referring to the use of *tu* as opposed to *vous* (indicating either a difference in number [singular/plural] or a level of formality [informal/formal]) in medieval French and Latin, as well as in modern French, a distinction that does not exist in English. One might take this as a sign of condescension on his part, given the tone of his letter, but in fact this was a usage that Gontier and his circle (including Jean de Montreuil and Nicolas de Clamanges) had recently adopted from the Italian humanists, principally Petrarch and Coluccio Salutati (cf. Ezio Ornato, *Jean Muret et ses amis* [Geneva: Droz, 1969], 19–24). Both letters of Gontier Col use *tu,* and among Jean de Montreuil's letters in Latin included in this volume, nos. 6, 8, 10, and 19 (addressed to friends or professional peers) use the familiar form, whereas nos. 4, 7, 9, and 29 (all addressed to prelates of a certain stature) maintain the formal pronoun.

123. Translated from *Le débat,* ed. Hicks, 24–26.

addressed to one of his friends, a subtle and learned cleric,[124] who disagreed with his said opinion, and with whose opinion my own was in accord), I sent it to you in order to satisfy your honest request. Thereupon, after having looked it over and spent some time with it, you found your error punctured and struck down by the truth, and in a fit of impatience you wrote me your much more injurious second letter, reproaching my feminine sex (which you consider to be, as though by nature, afflicted by powerful emotions[125] and motivated by folly and presumption in daring to correct and reproach a doctor as exalted, as honored, and as important as you claim the author of this work to be). And with regard to this matter, you exhort me vehemently to reject this position and to repent, in which case heartfelt mercy will still be extended to me; but if not, I shall be treated as was the publican, etc.

Ha! What a lofty and clever judgment! Do not allow your own whims to shut down the penetration of your mind! Gaze straight ahead following the most excellent path of theology, and not only will you not condemn my ideas as I have written them, but you will reconsider whether praise is appropriate for the specific passages they reprove; be that as it may, you should in all instances take note of which things I condemn and which I do not. And if you discount my arguments to such a degree on account of the meagerness of my faculties (for which you reproach me when you say "being a woman," etc.), you should know that I do not in truth consider this at all a reproach or slander, because of the consolation arising from the noble memory and continued experience of a great abundance of noble women who have been and still are most worthy of praise and accustomed to every virtuous activity. I would rather resemble them than be made rich by all the goods of fortune.

However, if you still wish at all costs to belittle my vehement arguments for this reason, may it please you to recall that the small point of a dagger or a penknife can puncture a large sack full of, indeed distended by, material things; and don't you know that a small weasel attacks a great lion and sometimes puts him to rout? So do not think in the slightest that I may be

124. This is the cleric mentioned by Christine in her letter to Jean de Montreuil (see above, n. 6) and in her narrative account of the genesis of the debate (no. 18).

125. The word used here is *passioné,* which Gontier Col had used to describe Christine in the previous letter ("you being a woman passionately engaged in this matter"). Whereas *passion* is typically used to refer either to torment (as in the passion of Christ) or to a vice or defect, it seems here to be closer to our modern meaning of "emotion, affection," though it maintains a negative valence. As Hicks notes (*Le débat,* 204), Christine might very well be recalling this negative remark in the first lines of her *Book of the Body Politic:* "Se il est possible que de vice puist naistre vertu, bien me plaist en ceste partie estre passionnee comme femme" (If it is possible for virtue to be produced from vice, I am truly happy at this point to be *passionnee* like a woman) (1). Not atypically, Christine turns an admission of a defect to an advantage by proclaiming that it is precisely this "passion" that has given her the courage to produce this work.

shaken or discouraged by a faintness of will that would make me quickly recant—in spite of the fact that while saying vile things to me, you menace me with your subtle arguments, which are tactics that commonly terrify the cowardly. But in order that you may be reminded briefly of what I have previously written about at length, I declare once again and repeat it a second and a third time—as many times as you wish—that although there might be some good things in the poem entitled *The Romance of the Rose,* the more the good found in it is authentic, the greater the peril is, as I have said before. And, insofar as human nature is excessively inclined to evil, it can be the source of a wicked and perverse instigation to very abominable behavior encouraging the dissolute life: a doctrine full of deceit, a path to damnation, a public defamer, a cause of suspicion and distrust and shame to many people, and perhaps of heresy, and, in many parts, a most indecent reading experience. And all this I endeavor and dare to hold and maintain everywhere and before all people, and prove it by the book itself, as I defer to and rely upon the judgment of all equitable wise men, theologians and true Catholics, in addition to people of an honorable and salutary life.

Yours,
Christine de Pizan

HERE END THE LETTERS ON THE ROMANCE OF THE ROSE[126]

16. CHRISTINE DE PIZAN TO ISABEAU DE BAVIÈRE, QUEEN OF FRANCE (DEDICATORY LETTER, FEBRUARY 1, 1402)

FRENCH PROSE

Here begin the letters of the debate on The Romance of the Rose *among noteworthy people: Master Gontier Col, general counsel to the king, Master Johan Johannez [Jean de Montreuil], and Christine de Pizan*[127]

To the most excellent, most eminent, and most revered princess, my lady Isabeau de Bavière, by the grace of God queen of France

Most noble, most powerful, and most revered lady, before all else accept my very humble esteem. And inasmuch as I have heard that your very noble Excellency delights in hearing works on topics that are both full of virtue and

126. This italicized conclusion was used by Christine to close the initial dossier she sent to the queen of France, in which her response to Gontier Col is the "last word."

127. Translated from *Le débat,* ed. Hicks, 5–6. I have italicized this introductory comment intended for the collection of documents Christine sent to the queen of France, of which the letter she addressed to her is the first item.

well expressed, a pastime that itself increases the virtue and good morals of your noble person (for, as a wise man said, "Virtues added to virtues, wisdom added to nobility, make a person venerable"—which can be taken to mean "having achieved moral and spiritual perfection"), well, my very revered lady, since such virtue is found in your very noble judgment, it is appropriate that works on select topics be presented to you as befits a sovereign. Accordingly, I, simple and uncultivated among women, your humble lady-in-waiting at your command, wishing to serve you if I could aspire to the confidence of your gracious modesty, am impelled to send you the accompanying letters, in which, my very revered lady—if it pleases you to so honor me that you might deign to listen to them—you will be able to take note of the diligence, desire, and will with which my scant power strives to stand up against certain opinions that run counter to decency, and also to support the honor and praise of women (which many clerics and others have endeavored to belittle through their writings—something one is not allowed to tolerate or endure). However weak I may be in shouldering the burden of opposing such cunning masters, nonetheless, moved by the truth—since I know with absolute certainty that their[128] legitimate rights are worthy of defense—my limited intelligence has wanted and still wishes to devote itself to debating their adversaries and accusers, as is evident here and in other works of mine. So I beg you humbly, your worthy Highness, both to lend credence to my rightful arguments, even though I do not know how to develop and carry them out in as beautiful language as another might, and to approve my saying more if I am able. And let it all be done under your wise and gracious oversight.

My most revered lady, most dignified and most excellent, I pray that the true Trinity grant you a good and a long life, along with the fulfillment of all your good wishes.

Written on the eve of Candlemas, in the year 1401.[129]

Your most humble and totally devoted servant,[130]
Christine de Pizan

128. The possessive adjective in the expression *leur bon droit* could be taken to refer to the plural noun immediately preceding this clause, "masters," but the meaning would be twisted at best, whereas referring it further back, to "women," makes perfect sense. This reading is confirmed later in the same sentence when "their" (in "their adversaries and accusers") is unambiguously referring back to the aforementioned women.

129. The Feast of Candlemas, which commemorates the presentation of Jesus Christ at the temple and the purification of the Virgin, falls on February 2. It was custom in France at least until the end of the fifteenth century to begin the New Year on Easter Day and not January 1, so the actual date of this letter is February 1, 1402.

130. The Middle French word is *creature,* which usually refers to a living being, human, created by God; it typically designates other created beings only when juxtaposed with a human being.

17. CHRISTINE DE PIZAN TO GUILLAUME DE TIGNONVILLE, PROVOST OF PARIS (FEBRUARY 1, 1402)[131]

FRENCH PROSE

To my very dear lord, noble, and wise knight, Messire Guillaume de Tignonville, provost of Paris

To you, my lord the provost of Paris, elected to such a worthy position and office as the guardian of high justice by the grace of God and the prudent management of your own good sense, go in first place due consideration and homage from me, Christine, of feeble intelligence and the least among those women desiring an honorable life. I inform you that, assured of your wisdom and merit, I am impelled to communicate to you the amiable, and not spiteful, debate motivated by contrary opinions among worthy people: Master Gontier Col, currently general counsel to our lord the king, and Master Jehan Johannes, the provost of Lille and secretary of the said lord. You will be able to hear the background of this debate from the letters exchanged among us and from the recollections[132] that make reference to it hereinafter. With regard to this, very wise provost, I implore you that out of deference to me, and in spite of the laborious preoccupations of greater and more urgent affairs, it may please you, by way of solace, to agree to hear the reasons for our disagreements. Along with this, I ask that through fair and circumspect reflection, you might devote your wisdom to an examination of the affair and side favorably with the rightfulness of my opinion, even though I am not able to express it vividly or put it in terms that are harmonious and propitious to the defense of my aforementioned rightfulness, as some other person would be better able to do.

This is why I ask, O very learned man, that out of compassion for my female ignorance, your humility might be so inclined as to espouse my righ-

---

When one identifies oneself as someone's *creature* (e.g., je sui vo creature), it means that one is obliged to someone to whom one is devoted.

131. Translated from *Le débat,* ed. Hicks, 7–8. Guillaume de Tignonville had been chamberlain of the king's household from 1395 and was named provost of Paris in May 1401. After a public disgrace in 1408, he worked in the royal Chamber of Accounts. He was also a man of letters, translator into French of a work entitled *Moral Sayings of the Philosophers,* which had great success throughout the fifteenth century. He was also one of the original twenty-four ministers of the "Amorous Court" of King Charles VI, founded on Saint Valentine's Day 1401 (n.s.) in order to honor women and advance the cultivation of poetry.

132. These "recollections" refer undoubtedly to Christine's brief third-person narrative account of the beginnings of the debate, no. 18 in this volume.

teous opinions, so that your wisdom might serve as strength, help, defense, and support for me against such respected and distinguished masters, whose clever arguments would soon have brought down my just cause because of my failure to know how to uphold it; in this way, inasmuch as a legitimate cause needs a helping hand,[133] with your alliance I might be more boldly inspired to continue the war undertaken against the aforementioned powerful and strong men. Moreover, may it not please you to refuse my plea upon consideration of their great stature and my own, which is slight, since your good sense knows by experience that it is incumbent upon your office to support in all cases the weakest party, providing that the cause is just.

Also, dear lord, since I have been in the habit of putting my other works into rhyme, do not be surprised that this work is in prose.[134] For since the subject matter does not require it to be done in this way, it is fitting for me to imitate the style of my assailants, however little my scant knowledge matches their beautiful eloquence.

May he who created all things grant you paradise.

18. CHRISTINE DE PIZAN, ACCOUNT OF THE DEBATE (FEBRUARY 1, 1402)[135]

FRENCH PROSE

It has already been some time since words were exchanged between my lord the provost of Lille, Master Jehan Johannes, and Christine de Pizan touching upon treatises and books dealing with several subjects, in the course of which discussion the said provost mentioned *The Romance of the Rose*, attributing to it very considerable and singular merit and great dignity, to which the said Christine replied and submitted several arguments, saying that with all due respect, it did not in her opinion deserve such great praise:

133. "Bon droit a bon mestier d'aide" (a good cause has much need of favor): This was a well-known proverb through the fourteenth and fifteenth centuries, quoted by such authors as Machaut, Froissart, and Villon. Cf. Hassell, *Middle French Proverbs*, 98 (D125); Morawski, *Proverbes français*, no. 604; di Stefano, *Dictionnaire des locutions*, 274.

134. Indeed, even though prose would become the vehicle for several of Christine's later works, the only work preceding the debate containing prose was her very successful didactic *Letter of Othea* (1400–1401), which alternated sections in prose and in verse.

135. Translated from *Le débat*, ed. Hicks, 8–9. In Christine's dossier, this brief narrative is placed immediately after the dedicatory epistles to Isabeau de Bavière and Guillaume de Tignonville (nos. 16 and 17) and followed by Gontier Col's first letter (no. 13), which it introduces in its closing line, Christine's letter to Jean de Montreuil (no. 5), Gontier Col's second letter (no. 14), and, as concluding document, Christine's response to Gontier Col (no. 15).

ITEM, after several days the said provost sent to the said Christine the copy of a letter he had sent to a friend of his, a noble cleric,[136] who, motivated by reason, was of the same opinion as the said Christine against the said romance; in order to convert him, the said provost had written the said letter, most remarkably embellished with beautiful rhetoric, and in order to kill two birds with one stone, he sent it to her;

ITEM, the said Christine, having read and pondered the said letter, wrote back to the said provost, as can be seen hereinafter;

ITEM, after these things, it came to the attention of a notable person, Master Gontier Col, that the said Christine had written against *The Romance of the Rose*; he, incited to oppose her, wrote her the present letter, as follows:

136. Although it was long thought that the reference here to a "noble cleric," friend of Jean de Montreuil, was to none other than Jean Gerson, Hicks and Ornato (with whom P.-Y. Badel concurs) have convincingly shown that it is probably to Nicolas de Clamanges (c. 1363–1437), a humanist and frequent correspondent of Jean de Montreuil and others in this closely knit circle. See Hicks and Ornato, "Jean de Montreuil et le débat sur le *Roman de la Rose*," and Badel, *Le Roman de la Rose au XIV*[e] *siècle*. Cf. above, nn. 4 and 6.

III
THE DEBATE: SECOND PHASE

19. JEAN DE MONTREUIL TO A GREAT POET (EUSTACHE DESCHAMPS OR HONORÉ BOVET?) (EITHER FEBRUARY/MARCH OR JULY/AUGUST 1402)[1]

LATIN PROSE

I would like to communicate to you some unfortunate revelations with regard to how variable the manners and emotions of men are. You will hear, O illustrious man, and at the same time you will see, in the context of a certain text of mine in the vernacular, how inequitably and unjustly, and with what extraordinary arrogance, some people inveigh and cry out against the most eminent Master Jean de Meun, in particular a certain woman by the name of Christine, given that she now circulates her writings in public. And although she is not lacking in intelligence within the limits of her female capacity, it seemed to me nevertheless that I was hearing the Greek whore Leontium, who, as Cicero reports, "dared to write against so great a philosopher as Theophrastus."[2] The above-mentioned detractors claim that this very brilliant man erred in several passages of that most illustrious work of his on the *Rose* and appeared to speak insolently and with impudence: to be precise, first in the chapter of Reason, making her speak in a manner incompatible with the function of her character; after that, making the Jeal-

1. Translated from *Le débat,* ed. Hicks, 42–44. For the question of dating this letter, see below, n. 8.

2. Cicero, *De natura deorum* (On the Nature of the Gods) 1.33.93: "sed meretricula etiam Leontium contra Theophrastum scribere ausa est" (but actually emboldened a loose woman like Leontium to contradict Theophrastus). Trans. H. Rackham (Cambridge: Harvard University Press, 1951], 90–91 (altered). It would appear that Jean de Montreuil got this quotation from a text of Petrarch (Jean de Montreuil, *Opera,* ed. Ornato, 221–22; *Le débat,* ed. Hicks, 207).

ous Husband speak extravagantly; and in the conclusion of his treatise or book, where the Lover expresses his juvenile passions disgracefully, excessively, and, as they add, licentiously. "O tempora! o mores!"[3] "I am beside myself," as Terence says.[4] I observe so great a work, such a man—our era has not produced his equal, nor, as I predict, will any later periods do so—being slashed to ribbons by the claws of slander, and these most unreflecting people quarrel with a dead man who, if he were living, would crush them entirely with a single gesture. They do not distinguish the variety of characters, nor do they notice by what passions they are motivated, with what emotions they are endowed, or to what end, in what context or why they speak; nor do they consider that this teacher is precisely taking up the role of a satirist, by virtue of which many things are permitted that are prohibited to other authors.

Indeed, I would cry out against those slanderers most gladly, if I had not learned with certainty that all the most eminent men of the military and clerical profession, wherever they were born, have always had to undergo the stain of such an assault. Nor is it the case that lofty minds avoid the barking of dogs or, likewise, the bites of the envious: he who was at once king and prophet attested that it is not possible "to close the mouth of those who speak iniquities."[5] In truth, according to the saying of Livy, "the greater the glory, the more it was exposed to jealousy."[6] But it really irritates me that among our detractors certain of them have examined this romance, which must rather be called a mirror of or discourse on human life, superficially, or read it in a hurry, as they admit;[7] others, in truth, although they have studied it with care, are, believe me, scarcely capable of understanding so great a thing or open to its mysteries. And even grant

3. As Hicks and Ornato both mention in their editions, this exclamation recurs in several parts of Cicero's corpus. Cf. above, ch. 2, n. 92.

4. *Andria* (The Woman from Andros), l. 937: "vix sum apud me." *Terence*, trans. Barsby, 1:161.

5. Ps 62:12: "rex vero lætabitur in Deo; laudabuntur omnes qui jurant in eo: quia obstructum est os loquentium iniqua" (the king shall rejoice in God, all they shall be praised that swear by him: because the mouth is stopped of them that speak wicked things). Oddly, Jean's quotation of this passage uses it to say exactly the opposite.

6. Livy, *Ab urbe condita* (From the Founding of the City), 35.10.5: "maior gloria Scipionis, et quo maior, eo propior invidiam" (The greater fame was Scipio's, and the greater it was, the more it was exposed to jealousy). Trans. Evan T. Sage (Cambridge: Harvard University Press, 1935), 10:26–27. As with the quotation from Cicero (above, n. 2), Ornato (Jean de Montreuil, *Opera*, 222) thinks that Jean got this text from Petrarch.

7. Jean is here referring to remarks made in Christine's first letter (no. 5) sent to him. He likewise had mentioned it in his previous letter to Gontier Col (no. 8).

that one of them will have read this work more attentively and thrown himself impulsively into its study with all the force of his mental faculties, in such a way that it must be admitted that he understood it. Nonetheless, the vocation owing to his station leads him, or his profession of faith orders him, to speak about it otherwise than the way he judges it. Or, if you prefer, he is perhaps of the sort who cannot properly perpetuate the human species, which is the point of the book.[8] Who therefore would not immediately reject the judgment of such people who surely, as Petrarch says, "reproach in others what they do not know or what does not matter to them"?[9]

It is for these reasons, very dear brother, that I would like to ask for your active assistance, in order that you, who, it seems to me, revere, esteem, and honor, as is merited, this man, at once a philosopher and a brilliant poet, and who rise above the others of this realm in his type of writing, may speak out loudly against these slanderers with your forcefully sublime muse. In this way, you can defend this exceptional teacher of morals with the cudgel of your eloquence, so that they may recognize what it means to speak against a man defended by so many learned disciples and glorified by so many powerful friends (assuming that their mind may be lifted up by the senses).

Farewell, and recommend me humbly to my teacher, Master Jean Le Veneur,[10] and forgive me for having boldly spoken to you with the familiar form *tu*. For I learned it from my reading of the ancients: a single person is not to be addressed in the plural.

8. I concur with Hicks (*Le débat,* 208) that this evocation possibly refers to Gerson; it could be the result of having heard of Gerson's disapproval of the *Rose* orally (as in his sermon of August 1401), which allows this letter to be dated soon after Christine's publication of the first version of the dossier, perhaps in February or March 1402. But if it is referring to Gerson's treatise (no. 20), written in late May 1402, then it would have to be dated in the summer of 1402.

9. The quotation, as Hicks notes (*Le débat,* 208), comes from one of Petrarch's *Rerum senilium libri* (Letters of Old Age, book 17, letter 3): "hominum genus et insolens et ignavum qui quicquid ipsi vel nolunt vel nesciunt vel non possunt in aliis reprehendunt" (the kind of insolent and lazy men who blame in others whatever they don't know, are unwilling to learn, or incapable of doing so). It is a letter he wrote to Boccaccio after having read the latter's *Decameron* and having decided to translate the last tale, that of Griselda, into Latin, so that those who did not read Italian could profit from the story. The context of the quotation arises from the attacks against that work and Boccaccio's defense.

10. The name *Johannes Venator* (literally "John Hunter") appears in a cartulary of the University of Paris (see Hicks, *Le débat,* 208), but is otherwise unknown.

20. JEAN GERSON, TREATISE AGAINST THE *ROMANCE OF THE ROSE* (MAY 18, 1402)[11]

FRENCH PROSE

On a morning not long ago, as I lay awake, it seemed to me that my agile heart flew off—thanks to the feathers and wings of diverse thoughts—from one place to another, all the way to the holy court of Christianity.[12] Canonical Justice, the defender of the law, was in that place, sitting on the throne of fairness, backed up by Mercy on one side and Truth on the other. Justice held in her right hand the scepter of reward and in her left the sharp sword of punishment: She had bright eyes, worthy of respect and more resplendent than the beautiful morning star, or even than the sun. Her company was magnificent, for she had her very wise council on one side and all around were gathered the most noble of her knights and a barony composed of all the Virtues (who are the daughters of God himself and of Free Will), such as Charity, Fortitude, Temperance, Humility, and others in great number. The head of the council and acting chancellor was Penetrating Judgment, joined in close companionship with Lady Reason, the wise; his secretaries were Prudence and Knowledge. Faith the good Christian and Wisdom divine and celestial were part of this tightly knit council: to provide them assistance there were Memory, Providence, Good Sense, and many others. Theological Eloquence, who was of moderate and tempered language, stood as advocate for the court. The promoter of lawsuits was called Conscience, for there is nothing that she doesn't know and report.

As I was taking pleasure in gazing with great admiration at the impressive magnificence of this court of Christianity and righteous Justice, I had

11. Translated from *Le débat*, ed. Hicks, 59–87. It is unclear whether or not Gerson gave a title to this work, which he elsewhere refers to as an *oratio* (no. 28, below). The MS edited by Hicks provides the title "Treatise regarding a Vision written against the *Romance of the Rose*"; E. Langlois used the same MS, along with two others, for his edition ("Le Traité de Gerson contre le Roman de la Rose," *Romania* 45 [1918–19]: 23–48). Of Langlois's other two MSS, one does not provide a title, while the other calls it simply "The Treatise of Master Jean Gerson against the *Romance of the Rose*," which is what has been adapted for the title here.

12. The *Romance of the Rose* had established the dream vision as a privileged narrative framework for didactic and amorous tales. Following in that tradition, Guillaume de Machaut had popularized an important variation, according to which the narrator is in a dreamlike state midway between sleep and wakefulness, what he calls in the *Fontaine amoureuse* "dorveille" (l. 63), a state that accentuates the inability to tell whether the events being recounted really happened or not. Gerson, by using this framework, is slyly turning the techniques of allegory against the author he is criticizing. For an excellent account of the rich tradition of dream visions in the fourteenth century, see Badel, *Le Roman de la Rose au XIVe siècle*, 331–409.

the impression that Conscience, whose duty was to set in motion the court's lawsuits, made a move to stand up with Law, who serves as master of requests. Conscience held in her hand and in her bosom numerous entreaties, among others one that contained verbatim (I remember it well) the following pitiful complaint lodged by the very beautiful and very pure Chastity, who had never consented to allow any ignoble filth even to cross her mind:

"To Justice, defender of the law, who occupies the place of God on earth, and to her devout court, representative of the Christian religion. Chastity, your faithful subject, submits the following plaint and humbly begs that measures be taken and a succinct provisional sentence be pronounced against the intolerable crimes that someone who calls himself the Foolish Lover[13] has committed, and continues to commit, against me. Following are the articles:

"FIRST ARTICLE. This Foolish Lover puts all his effort into driving me from the earth—I, who am not guilty—as well as my faithful guards: Shame, Fear, and Resistance the good gatekeeper, who would not dare or deign to grant even one shameful kiss, or any dissolute glances, or a seductive smile, or a frivolous word. And this he accomplishes through a cursed Old Woman worse than the devil, who teaches and demonstrates with her exhortations how all young girls should sell their bodies at an early age and at a high price without fear or shame; how they should not mind deceiving or lying, provided that they always make off with something; how they should not put up any difficulties or resist abandoning themselves impetuously, for as long as they remain beautiful, to the most base and filthy carnal acts, be it with clerics, lay people, or priests, without distinction.[14]

13. In the *Romance of the Rose,* the character known as the Lover is identified with the Dreamer/Narrator through the shared use of the first-person voice, but this identification, clear in Guillaume de Lorris's part, becomes complicated in Jean de Meun's continuation. By adding the epithet *Fol* (foolish) to the Lover's name (borrowed from a passage of the poem in which the lover admits his folly, "Se je sui fols, c'est mes domages" (*Rose,* ed. Lecoy, l. 7177: If I am a fool, it is my misfortune; trans. Dahlberg, 137), Gerson cunningly transforms the Narrator into an allegorical personification representing not just any lover but one who deserves to be condemned.

14. Shame, Fear, and Resistance are characters introduced in Guillaume de Lorris's first part of the *Rose,* as gatekeepers of the castle Jealousy builds in order to protect the rosebud from the Lover's approach. They appear periodically in Jean de Meun's continuation. Chastity is herself frequently mentioned, not as an active character in the narrative, but as the personification whose duty is to protect the roses from the plundering of Venus. The Old Woman is mentioned briefly by Guillaume de Lorris as the prison guard of Fair Welcoming after the castle is built. Her role is greatly expanded by Jean de Meun, who turns her into the spokesperson for bawdy, manipulative female behavior. It is her doctrine, as elaborated in the lengthy episode devoted to her (*Rose,* ed. Lecoy, ll. 12710–14688; trans. Dahlberg, pp. 221-51), that is the object of the first article.

"SECOND ARTICLE. He wants to forbid marriage, without exception, by means of a Jealous Man who is suspicious, full of hate and vexation, a scoundrel[15]—both on his own and through the words of some of my adversaries.[16] Moreover, he advises one to hang oneself, to drown oneself, or to commit sins that dare not be named, sooner than enter the bonds of matrimony.[17] And he blames all women, with no exception whatever, in order to make them so hateful to all men that no one would wish to pledge his faith in marriage to them.

"THIRD ARTICLE. He censures young men who devote themselves to religion because, he says, by their nature they will always make an effort to escape from it.[18] This is prejudicial to me, for I am especially devoted to religion.

"FOURTH ARTICLE. He spreads everywhere fire more intense and more foul than Greek fire[19] or brimstone: the fire of astonishingly lascivious, dirty, and forbidden words—sometimes in the name of Venus, Cupid, or Genius, but often in his own name[20]—by means of which are burned

15. The word as found in Hicks's edition is *malendrius,* which Hasenohr (review of *Le débat,* 131) glosses as "sickly" (maladif, malade). Given that scribes often confuse *u* and *n,* it is quite possible to construe the word as *malendrins,* a borrowing from the Italian *malandrino* (scoundrel, rogue), which seems to fit the context better.

16. The Jealous Man, or Jealous Husband, is a character who is introduced by Friend and whose monologue, in which he rants and raves about his wayward wife, is quoted at great length by Friend (*Rose,* ed. Lecoy, ll. 8437–9330; trans. Dahlberg, 156–68). The "adversaries" of Chastity referred to here are the ancient and medieval authors who argued against marriage and whose discourses are incorporated into this monologue, most notably Juvenal's *Satires* and Theophrastus's now lost *Golden Book,* as filtered through Saint Jerome, Walter Map, and John of Salisbury.

17. Chastity's complaint seems to be referring to the Jealous Husband's quotation of a passage from Juvenal, but the latter's reference to "sins that dare not be named" (italicized in the following passage) is not itself included in the *Rose:* "Postumus, are you really getting married? Tell me what Tisiphone and what snakes are driving you mad. Can you put up with any woman as your boss with so many ropes available, when those dizzily high windows are wide open, when the Aemilian bridge offers itself to you so conveniently? *Alternatively, if you don't like any of these many ways out, don't you think it would be better to have a boyfriend sleep with you?*" (Juvenal, *Satire 6,* ll. 28–34; *Juvenal and Persius,* trans. Braund, 237. Cf. *Rose,* ed. Lecoy, ll. 8707–14; trans. Dahlberg, 160).

18. Reference to a brief passage in the Old Woman's speech regarding the natural desire (of women, of animals, of all creatures) to be free (*Rose,* ed. Lecoy, ll. 13937–96; trans. Dahlberg, 239–40).

19. "Greek fire" was an incendiary weapon used in warfare during the Middle Ages, most notably in the Byzantine Empire (whence its name). It was especially effective in battles at sea, as its particular formulation allowed it to continue burning on the surface of water.

20. Gerson seems to be thinking of (in order): Venus's speech to Shame just before attacking the castle (*Rose,* ed. Lecoy, ll. 20690–752; trans. Dahlberg, 339–40); either Cupid's speech

and consumed my beautiful houses and dwellings and my sacred temples of human souls; and I am ignobly ejected from them.

"FIFTH ARTICLE. He defames Lady Reason, my good mistress, by attributing utter folly and vulgar blasphemy to her. She actually advises that people speak baldly, without cleaning up their speech, and shamelessly, like the Goliards, about all things, however abominable or ignominious they might be to say or do, even among people who are quite dissolute and enemies of mine.[21] Alas! Even if he didn't wish to spare *me*, what wrong did Reason do to him? But so it is. Without any doubt, he has declared war against all the virtues.

"SIXTH ARTICLE. When he speaks of sacred, divine, and spiritual things, he mixes in here and there dissolute words that provoke all sorts of lewd behavior;[22] nevertheless, lewdness will never enter heaven in the way he describes it.

"SEVENTH ARTICLE. He promises paradise, glory, and rewards to all those men and women who accomplish the work of the flesh, even outside marriage; for in his own person, and according to his own example, he advises men to "try out" all women indiscriminately, and he curses those men and women who don't behave thus[23]—at least all those who welcome me and keep me close to them.

"EIGHTH ARTICLE. In his own person he names the dishonorable parts of the body, as well as filthy and vile sins, with words that are holy

referring to his mother's sexual proclivities (ll. 10719–856; trans. Dahlberg, 190–92) or his speech to Venus before starting the attack (ll. 15808–46; trans. Dahlberg, 268); the entirety of Genius's sermon; and the Lover/Narrator's scarcely veiled description of sexual intercourse through the figure of the pilgrim (ll. 21316–712; trans. Dahlberg, 348–53).

21. Reference to the Lover's discussion with Reason on proper and improper language usage, which is a major point of contention for all the debate participants: ll. 5667–94, 6898–7198; trans. Dahlberg, 115, 133–37 On the reputation of the Goliards, see above, ch. 2, n. 33.

22. Genius's above-mentioned sermon mixes together an allegorical vision of paradise with a blunt discussion of the need for sexual intercourse and procreation, along with a condemnation of all forms of nonreproductive sexual relations, including sodomy. Article 7 also refers to this episode.

23. Gerson here mixes together reference to Genius's sermon (the promise of paradise) and to the Lover/Narrator's later discourse, in which he uses the metaphor of the path to speak of intercourse with women, his point being that one must try all types of paths in order to have proper knowledge: "il fet bon de tout essaier" (l. 21521; it is good to try everything; trans. Dahlberg, 351). In this sentence and at the beginning of the next article, Gerson uses the expression *en sa (propre) persone*, which I have translated in both cases as "in his own person," to refer to passages at the end of the work in which the narrator addresses the reader directly, as opposed to speaking through the discourses of the various allegorical characters.

and sacred, as though such practice were always divine and sacred and to be worshiped, even outside marriage and accomplished by means of fraud and violence. And not content with having spread the above-mentioned offenses orally, he also had them written down and illustrated insofar as he was able, lavishly and with care, in order better to attract all people to look at them, hear them, and embrace them.[24] There is still worse, for in order to deceive people more subtly, he mixed honey with venom,[25] sugar with poison, venomous serpents hidden under the green grass of devotion. And this he does by assembling a variety of materials, which quite often have scarcely anything to do with his argument except for the above-mentioned motive, and so that he would be better believed and of greater authority to the extent that he would seem to have witnessed and studied many things.

"Thus I beg from you, Lady Justice, a quick remedy and provisional sentence for all these wrongs, as well as many others not contained in this brief supplication; but his book provides much more testimony than would be necessary."

After this entreaty submitted by Chastity was read clearly and openly in that place, you could detect from their faces and demeanors that the entire council and all the noble knights seemed truly indignant. Nevertheless, being wise and even-tempered, they said the case would be heard. But since the Foolish Lover who was accused was not present (he had already crossed the great threshold from which no one returns),[26] it was asked whether there were to be found in the court of Christianity any proxies, supporters, or well-wishers whatsoever.

And then you would have seen people young and old, of all sexes and ages, advancing in a great crowd, an innumerable multitude of people, who—in total disorder and in a haphazard, thoughtless manner—expressed their wish: one to excuse the Foolish Lover, another to defend him, still another to praise him. One asked for a pardon because of his youth and folly, alleging that he had repented when he later wrote: "I composed in my youth

24. This is an interesting reference to the manuscript format of the *Rose* text, which was frequently transcribed in lavishly illustrated volumes. Gerson was clearly concerned with visual, as well as verbal, obscenity, though obscene illustrations in these manuscripts are rare. See, however, Sylvia Huot, *The Romance of the Rose and Its Medieval Readers: Interpretation, Reception, Manuscript Transmission* (Cambridge: Cambridge University Press, 1993), 291–301.

25. Cf. Ovid, *Amores*, 1.8.104: "inpia sub dulci melle venena latent" (wicked poisons have for hiding-place sweet honey) (rev. trans. Showerman, 354–55). The association of *fiel* (bile) or venom with honey had a proverbial resonance, as in this line from the *Champion des dames* quoted by di Stefano (*Dictionnaire des locutions*, 545): "Soubz miel ont couvert leur venin" (they covered their venom with honey).

26. Jean de Meun died in Paris in 1305, nearly a century before the debate.

many a poem through vanity."[27] Another defended him because he had been such a noteworthy cleric and an impressive speaker unequaled in French, while still others did so because he had so correctly spoken the truth about all estates, without sparing noble or nonnoble, country or nation, the secular world or religion.

"And what harm is there," said one of the shrewdest among them,[28] "what harm is there if this man of such intelligence, such erudition, and such renown saw fit to write a book made up of fictional characters, in which, with great mastery, he has each one speak according to what is right and proper to him? Doesn't the prophet say in the voice of a fool that God does not exist?[29] And did not the wise Solomon in particular compose all of his book Ecclesiastes in this way, in consideration of which he is excused for hundreds and hundreds of errors written there? If he spoke frivolously, it was the comportment of Venus, Cupid, or a foolish lover that he wanted to represent. And didn't Solomon speak in his Song of Songs in the guise of lovers, using words that could draw people to evil? Still, we read it. If he says in the character of Reason that everything should be called by its name, let his motives be considered: in truth, what evil is there in words, if someone doesn't put it there? Words are words, one just like the other; thus, since the same thing is understood by one word or by another, what should it matter which name one uses to express it? It is certain that there is nothing offensive in nature. Only in sin is there indecency, and yet one speaks of *it* every day by its proper name, as of murder, larceny, fraud, and theft.[30] In the last analysis, if he spoke of paradise and of pious things, why is he being blamed for things for which he ought to be praised? But let us posit that there might be some evil in his book; there is no doubt that there is much more good. Let each person take the good and leave aside the evil! He declares expressly that he

27. Quotation of line 5 of Jean de Meun's *Testament,* in which he seems to be repenting for the *Romance of the Rose,* among other works of his youth. Pierre Col will, however, interpret this line differently in his response to Gerson.

28. Gerson makes the interesting choice of introducing a spokesperson for the Foolish Lover, since he is not able to defend himself. It has frequently been suggested that this discourse might provide an outline of what Jean de Montreuil had written in his lost treatise.

29. Ps 13:1: "Dixit insipiens in corde suo: Non est Deus" (The fool hath said in his heart: There is no God).

30. Gerson is here alluding indirectly to a passage from Cicero's *De officiis* (Of Duties), to which he refers explicitly in his sermon *Considerate lilia* (see above, ch. 2, n. 105) and later in the present treatise. The Cynics and Stoics blame those who hold that "the mere mention of some actions that are not immoral is shameful, while other things that are immoral we call by their real names. Robbery, fraud, and adultery, for example, are immoral in deed, but it is not indecent to name them" (1.35.128, trans. Miller, 129–31).

is reproaching only evil men and women, and that if anyone feels guilty he should make amends for it. But it is also the case that no one is so wise that he does not on occasion commit an error;[31] even the great Homer erred.[32] And what ought to make this wise court of Christianity even more inclined toward pardon and indulgence is the fact that Saint Augustine and nearly all the other teachers of faith erred in some ways, yet are not condemned or accused for this, but rather honored. And truly, one must have a beautiful rose in his chaplet to blame the rose called *The Romance of the Rose!*"

At these words, it indeed seemed to the friends and supporters of the Foolish Lover that his cause was completely won, without any possibility of a response. And they were smiling to each other and glancing back and forth, whispering and making different signs, when Theological Eloquence (the advocate of the Christian court), at the request of both Conscience and her beloved Chastity, and because of her official function, rose to her feet, her countenance beautiful and her manner temperate. With a show of great authority and dignified solemnity, and an air both wise and experienced, after briefly casting down her gaze in the manner of a man given to reflection, she[33] looked up, radiating composure and serenity. She turned her eyes

31. This is a well-known proverb: "Il n'est si saiges qui aucune fois ne foloit" (Morawski, *Proverbes français,* no. 942; Hassell, *Middle French Proverbs,* 223 [S7]). Hicks's edited text omits the *si,* but several of the manuscripts, as listed in his variants, include this more typical version of the proverb.

32. Hicks adduces a line from Horace's *Art of Poetry,* l. 359: "indignor quandoque bonus dormitat Homerus" (and yet I also feel aggrieved wherever good Homer "nods"). *Satires, Epistles, and Ars Poetica,* trans. Fairclough, 481.

33. The Hicks edition and the majority of the manuscripts have the masculine pronoun *il* here, even though the gender of this character, which would normally be dictated by the grammatical gender of the name (as is typical in personification allegory), should be feminine. This could be an error stemming from the text's transmission, perhaps following upon the widespread knowledge that Eloquence was the spokesperson for Gerson in the work. But in fact the gender of the character is never directly at issue in the treatise; the only mention of Eloquence explicitly as a man occurs in the preceding clause, where it is said that the character is immersed in thought "in the manner of a man," which is not equivalent to saying that he or she was a man (rather that, from the perspective of Gerson, women would not normally be thought of as a model of reflection or thoughtfulness). In any event, two of the earliest readers of the work, Pierre Col and Christine de Pizan, both understood the character as gendered female, so I have taken the liberty of using the reading of one of the manuscripts that does in fact make Eloquence a female personification, as did the individual who translated Gerson's French text into Latin (cf. "The Epistles on the Romance of the Rose and Other Documents in the Debate," ed. Charles F. Ward [Dissertation, University of Chicago, 1911], 42). Gerson himself necessarily, because of grammatical agreement, recognizes Eloquence as a female in his letter to Pierre Col, *Talia de me* (no. 28 in this volume). It is quite possible that since a female personification is the spokesperson for Gerson in this treatise, he preferred to avoid excess signs of femininity, such as never using the title "Dame," which he does regularly for other personifications, such as Chastity and Reason.

toward Justice and, surveying her entire barony, opened her mouth; with a voice resonating smoothly and moderately, she began her argumentation and her case as follows:

"Were it pleasing to God—whom you represent here, Lady Justice—I would truly wish the accused author had returned from death to life so that he could be physically present. There would then be no need at all for me to multiply my words or entertain the court with a lengthy accusation, for I maintain in good faith that he would instantly, voluntarily, and with all his heart confess his error, ask for pardon, beg for mercy, and make amends. Indeed, several pieces of evidence induce me to make this presumption, especially the one that some people have alleged: that already while he was alive he repented and thereafter wrote books treating of true faith and holy doctrine. I myself testify to this on his behalf; it was unfortunate that foolish youth or some other evil inclination misled such a cleric to turn, naïvely and in such a fickle manner, his cunning insight, his great and fervent learning, and his gift for speaking in verse and prose toward such a blameworthy frivolity. Would that it had been God's will that he had made better use of them!

"Alas! Fair friend and subtle cleric! Were there not more than enough foolish lovers in the world without your adding yourself to the crowd? Was there not someone to lead them and teach them in their inanities without your offering yourself as their captain, leader, and master? He is a fool who does foolish things, and folly is not good sense. He who brings disrepute upon himself and assumes the role of a scoundrel truly wants to be blamed. To be sure, you were worthy of another sort of mastery and another role. Believe me, vices and sins are learned all too easily: there is no need for any teacher there! Human nature, especially in youth, is very much inclined to stumble, slide, and fall into the filth of all kinds of carnal behavior; there was no need for you to drag them or forcibly shove them into it. What is more readily set ablaze or inflamed by the fire of base pleasures than the human heart? Why then did you fan this fetid conflagration with the winds of the most frivolous words and the authority of your person and example? Even if at that time you did not fear God and his vengeance, why did the punishment inflicted upon Ovid not make you wise and reflective?[34] Would that your honorable condition at least had restrained you from doing these things. You would have been ashamed, I have no doubt, to be found in public and broad daylight in a place where foolish women prostitute them-

34. Ovid (43 BCE–17 CE) was banished from Rome by Augustus, and he himself says that the reason was the scandalous nature of his *Art of Love*. See below, n. 48.

selves, speaking to them in the way that you write. But you do even worse, for you exhort people to worse things: on account of your folly (so vast!) you have condemned to death and either murdered or poisoned thousands and thousands of people with a variety of sins, and you continue to do so day after day with your foolish book. And you certainly are not to be excused because of your method of speaking through personifications, as I will hereinafter prove clearly; but I can scarcely say everything at once.

"O most beneficent and all-powerful God! But if you, Foolish Lover (since it is thus that people insist on calling you), if ever in your life you repented of many writings that you had composed in your youth out of vanity, why did you allow them to survive? Should they not have been burned? Placing poison or some other noxious substance on the table, or fire in the midst of oil and hemp fibers, creates a dangerous mix. If someone has set fires everywhere and not put them out, how can he remain guiltless for the houses that are burned down by them? And what fire is worse and more red-hot than the fire of lasciviousness? What houses are more precious than human souls (as Chastity's entreaty rightly says)? For they must serve as the sacred temple of the Holy Spirit. But what more effectively burns and inflames these souls than dissolute words, or than lascivious writings and painted images? We observe that honorable, holy, and devout words, images, and writings inspire devotion, as Pythagoras was wont to say (this is why sermons and images are found in churches).[35] Much more easily, on the other hand, evil ones lead to debauchery. There is no one who has not experienced this, and many stories illustrate it.

"But, dear friend (I am speaking to you for no particular reason, for you are not here, and this entire matter came to displease you and would continue to displease you, as I have said, if you were present—and even if then you were not aware of it, you have since learned of it, at painful cost and expense to you, at the very least in purgatory if not through penance in this world),[36] you will perhaps say that you did not have the power to get your book back once it was published, or perchance that it was stolen from you without your knowing, or in some other way. This I do not know, but I do

35. Seneca, *Epistulae morales ad Lucilium* (Moral Espistles to Lucilius), epistle 94.42 (trans. Gummere, 6:38–39): "Pythagoras ait alium animum fieri intrantibus templum deorumque simulacra ex vicino cernentibus et alicuius oraculi opperientibus vocem" (Pythagoras declares that our souls experience a change when we enter a temple and behold the images of the gods face to face, and await the utterances of an oracle).

36. Theological Eloquence seems to be positing that even if the Foolish Lover did not start to pay for his sins by repenting while he was still alive, he would at least have done so after death, while in purgatory.

know that when Berengier, long ago a disciple of Peter Abelard—whom you often recall—arrived at the hour of death (at which point the truth regarding who has done good is revealed—and it was the day of the Epiphany of our Lord), he said, heaving a great sigh: "My God, today you will come to me, I hope, for my salvation, because of my repentance; or, as I fear, for my painful condemnation, because those whom I deceived through heretical doctrine I was not able to lead back to the straight path of the truth of your holy sacrament."[37] Perhaps *you* spoke thus. To put it succinctly, this is not a game, for there is no more perilous thing than to sow heretical doctrine in people's hearts, insofar as the torments, especially of those who are damned, increase from day to day; and if they are in purgatory, their liberation is hindered and delayed. Regarding Solomon, who was the wisest man in the world, learned scholars are uncertain whether he was saved. Why? Because, prior to his death, he did not order the destruction of the temples full of idols, which he had built on account of his foolish love for foreign women.[38] Repentance is not sufficient when one does not do everything in one's power to eliminate the possible effects of one's own sins and those of others.

"Nevertheless, whatever the result of your repentance (whether it was accepted by God or not—I hope it was), I am speaking only of the deed in itself and of your book;[39] and since you wisely do not defend it in the slightest, I shall direct all my arguments toward those who cause serious harm to your well-being, honor, and salvation, and defy your own judgment and wishes, by seeking this way and that, indiscriminately, to defend your frivolity[40]—not only defend it, but make it uglier and more excessive! In this they are undermining you when they think they are defending you; they are causing you displeasure and inflicting harm in their wish to please you. They resemble the reckless physician who wishes to heal and ends up killing, or the naïve lawyer who thinks he is helping his client and is actually destroying his case.

37. As Hicks notes (*Le débat*, 211), Gerson confuses Abelard's disciple, Berengier of Poitiers, with Berengier of Tours. The scene of the latter's death is taken from William of Malmesbury's *Chronicle of the Kings of England*.

38. 3 Kings [1 Kings], 11:1–2: "Rex autem Salomon adamavit mulieres alienigenas multas . . . ardentissimo amore" (And king Solomon loved many strange women . . . with a most ardent love).

39. Gerson also states this point in his letter to Pierre Col, *Talia de me* (no. 28 in this volume).

40. The word used here is *vanité*, the primary meaning of which through the Middle Ages was "emptiness, futility, frivolity, trickery." Gerson's point here is that the Foolish Lover (Jean de Meun), having disavowed the *Rose* later in life, would have been opposed to his disciples' attempt to justify what he put in it; and, further, that by doing so they are making matters even worse.

"I, on the contrary, shall render this service to your soul and provide it this gratification, or rather this relief, on account of your scholarship and erudition, for I shall reprove that which you wish to be definitively reproved. What ignorance is this here, fair friends—or rather, what foolish presumptuousness on your part, you whom I see and hear speaking in this place, and who wish to excuse the folly and error of this man who condemns himself, who displays, transcribed on his forehead, the mark of his condemnation! Yes, indeed, of his condemnation! Don't look at me that way. According to your own words, he presents himself as a foolish lover. In all truth, were I to variously defame such an author, I could scarcely make any worse accusation against him than by naming him a foolish lover. This label carries with it the overwhelming weight and heavy burden of every kind of lewdness and a carnality that exterminates all virtues, setting fires wherever it can. This is what Plato, Archytas of Tarentum, Cicero,[41] and others said about it. Who long ago destroyed magnificent Troy with fire and flames? A foolish lover. Who put to death a hundred thousand men, Hector, Achilles, Priam, and others? A foolish lover. Who once upon a time exiled King Tarquin and all his lineage from Rome?[42] A foolish lover. Who deludes honorable girls and saintly nuns with deceit and treacherous false oaths? A foolish lover. Who neglects God and holy men and women, paradise and his own end? A foolish lover. Who considers neither family, friends, nor any virtues whatever? A foolish lover. Whence arise conspiracies among citizens; pillage and theft to provide for reckless prodigality; bastardy or the suffocation of stillborn children; the hatred and death of husbands; and, to state it briefly, every variety of evil and folly? From a foolish lover.

"But I can easily see that with this title and this blame you wish to excuse him his follies, since one need seek nothing other than folly in a foolish man. True enough, dear friends, in the name of God! Nonetheless, one must point out his folly to the foolish man; and all the more so when he is clever and plays the fool; and even more so if what he does is to the grievous detriment of a great country, contributing to the vile destruction of good morals,

41. Cicero mentions both Plato and the latter's contemporary, the Pythagorean philosopher Archytas of Tarentum, in a passage of *De senectute* (On Old Age) (12.41) that decries the noxious effects of carnal lust. *De senectute, De amicitia, De divinatione,* trans. W. A. Falconer (Cambridge: Harvard University Press, 1923), 51.

42. The story of Tarquin and the rape of Lucretia is told by Livy, *Ab urbe condita* (From the Founding of the City), 1.58–60, and adapted by Jean de Meun, ll. 8578–8620. Jean de Meun uses Lucretia as one of the few examples, along with Penelope (both associated by Walter Map, *De nugis*), of virtuous women; Gerson's purpose is, on the contrary, to criticize unbridled passion through Tarquin's son, who raped Lucretia.

of Lady Justice and of all her noble court of Christianity. You see the way Lady Chastity complains. Shame, Fear, and my mistress Lady Reason are distressed, and, to speak bluntly, the entire council and the noble confraternity of the holy virtues are deeply offended; this you can well see from their demeanor. And why not? You will say, because it is not this author who speaks, but rather others who are introduced in thc text. This is too slight a defense for such a great crime. I ask you: if someone proclaimed himself an adversary of the king of France and, using this name and this identity, made war, would this name preserve him from being a traitor and incurring death? You won't answer. If, through the personage of a heretic or a Saracen—indeed even the devil—someone writes down and sows errors against Christianity, will he be excused for it? Once upon a time, a man wanted to do just that, and he was immediately forced by one of the chancellors of the church of Paris to recant and correct himself in a public hearing before a tribunal; and however much he might have been speaking in the company of clerics listening attentively to him when he made the claim 'I am speaking as a Jew,' the chancellor replied, 'and you will recant as a Christian.'[43]

"Suppose someone writes defamatory pamphlets about an individual, whether or not of a modest, or even wretched, condition, and that it is done through a fictional character. The laws judge that such a person be punished and disgraced. But what must the laws then pronounce, as well as you, Lady Justice, when it concerns not a pamphlet but a great book full of all sorts of disgraceful statements, pointed not only at men but at God and all the holy men and women who love virtue? Answer me! Ought one listen to someone who would say to a prince or a noble lord: 'Truly, my lord, I am telling you through the character of a jealous man, or an old lady, or by means of a dream, that your wife is most wicked and is cheating on her marriage: be forever on your guard and don't in any way trust her. And as for your daughters, who are so young and attractive, I advise them without delay to give themselves over to every carnal act and to any man who is willing to pay them a good price.' Tell me, dear friends, are you so brazen and ignorant that you would deem that such a man should suffer no punishment? That he

43. The text seems to mean implicitly that when this Christian man spouted heretical statements and then proclaimed that he was saying things that a Jew would say, the clerics were following him in an interested or even complicitous manner, but that the chancellor reprimanded him in spite of this. At the moment of writing this, Gerson was himself the chancellor of Notre-Dame de Paris, essentially meaning also chancellor of the University of Paris, in which position he succeeded his mentor, Pierre d'Ailly, who had held it since 1389 and who was instrumental in his disciple's promotion. Is Gerson recalling here an event he personally witnessed, involving either himself or his predecessor, or is he simply inventing the anecdote?

should be supported, heard, even excused? And it's even worse if, beyond mere words, he sent around books or illustrations!

"Moreover, what is worse: for a Christian cleric to preach counter to the faith, having adopted the persona of a Saracen, or to bring forward the Saracen himself to speak or write? In any event, the latter outrage would never be allowed; yet the first, that is, the deed of the Christian, is nonetheless worse, so much more harmful is the hidden enemy than the overt one, inasmuch as one receives him, listens to him, and believes him more readily and with a greater sense of familiarity. Suppose I give poison enveloped in honey and someone dies from it. Will I be innocent? Suppose I strike someone while kissing or murder someone while in an embrace: Will I get off scot-free? Suppose I say to a devout person in public: 'In all truth, some people who view you with envy and hate call you a deceitful hypocrite, adding that you are a thief and a murderer, and they are volunteering to prove it.' Shall I be excused for this slander? Suppose a horrible, dissolute man performs and describes the most debauched acts that can be imagined between a man and a woman before an innocent young lady, saying, 'Don't do what you see us doing, and so on and so forth; pay careful attention!' Is such a person to be tolerated? Certainly not, for chastity, reputation, vision,[44] and faith do not admit of games or jokes and are far too easy to damage and corrupt.

"But I can hear clearly what all of you are murmuring together: you are saying, as one of you alleged earlier, that Solomon and David did the same thing.[45] This is too great an outrage, accusing God and his saints and dragging them into the argument, in order to excuse a foolish lover. It cannot be done. I truly wish that the Foolish Lover had not used these characters except as Holy Scripture does, that is, in order to reprove evil, and in such a way that everyone would perceive the reproach of evil and the approval of good—and, what is most important, without an excess of frivolity. But that is not at all what he does. Everything seems to be said in his person;[46]

44. The word used here is *oeul,* literally "eye." Gerson is certainly referring to the last example and the susceptibility of one's sight (especially the viewing of lewd acts) to lead one to sin, as he had previously mentioned was the case with obscene pictures. The use of the word to refer to the sense of vision is rare, but attested elsewhere, including in some of Gerson's other works. See below, ch. 4, n. 19.

45. Gerson here reminds the reader that through Theological Eloquence he is addressing his contemporaries, clerics (and others) who defend the *Romance of the Rose.* In his reference to "one of you," is he perhaps referring to a detail contained in Jean de Montreuil's lost treatise? This could be the case, but Christine's mention of this same argument in the *God of Love's Letter* could simply suggest that this is a cliché of clerical discourse.

46. The expression used here, *en sa persone,* which I have translated as "in his person," is the same as the one used previously (see above, n. 23) in this treatise. The interpretive issue that most

everything seems as true as the Gospel, especially to the naïve, foolish lovers he is addressing. What distresses me most is that everything feeds the flames of lust, especially when he seems to be reproaching it. Even the very chaste, were they to deign to study, read, or listen to the work, would end up the worse for it.

"Scholars say that in ancient times the Canticles of Solomon, however temperate they might indeed be, were not read save by those who were at least thirty years old, so that they would not perceive therein any evils of the flesh whatsoever. What then will naïve and easily swayed youngsters do when faced with such a book—rather, such an inferno, more inflammatory than Greek fire or than a furnace producing glass? 'Fire!' I shout, 'good people, fire!' Put it out, for God's sake, put it out! Flee immediately! Save yourselves and remain wisely on guard, you and your children! That is the solution and there is no better one. He who does not flee the peril will fall headlong into it and be trapped, as are rats when lured by bacon, or wolves by the wolf trap, or the moth by the flame of the candle and its brightness, or foolish men or children by the beauty of glistening swords or fiery coals, unless these perils are actually removed.

"If you say that many good things are to be found therein, I ask you, is it then the case that the evil is eliminated from the text? If it is not, then isn't the fire even more perilous? Does the hook harm fish less if it is covered by bait? A sword, if it is covered with honey, does it not pierce just as deeply? Moreover, have good and pure teachings been unsuccessful elsewhere when not mixed with wickedness? As to whether one must maintain and cherish and praise a good lesson when it has been wrapped up with an evil one, I declare that Mohammed, with his great and clever sinfulness, conflated the truths of our Christian law with his foul errors. Why? To attract Christians more readily to his law and to disguise his outrageous teachings. Moreover, doesn't the devil speak several truths at once, through the possessed, through his spokesmen, the enchanters, and also through heretics? But this is meant only to deceive all the more underhandedly. Evil doc-

---

obsesses Gerson (and, to a lesser extent, Christine de Pizan) is that Jean de Meun is playing a subtle game that consists of expressing his own obscene and subversive opinions, occasionally using his own direct voice as narrator, but most often hiding behind the allegorical characters who in fact enunciate most of the offensive material in the text. By saying that "everything seems to be said in his person," Gerson is expressing the frustration of knowing that Jean de Meun is responsible for every piece of doctrine that is contained in the text but that, for the most part, he could simply claim, as he does in his authorial retraction, that he was only quoting other authors or allegorical personifications. For a more detailed discussion of this issue, see my "Words and Deeds: Jean de Meun's *Romance of the Rose* and the Hermeneutics of Censorship," *New Literary History* 28, no. 2 (1997): 345–66.

trine is made all the worse and more invidious the more good is mixed in with it.

"Believe me—not just me, but the Apostle Saint Paul, Seneca, and common experience—evil words and writings corrupt good morals[47] and lead people to sin shamelessly, banishing all good sense of modesty, which in young people is the main way of preserving the most proper behavior in the face of all sorts of evils. A young person without shame is totally lost. Why was Ovid, a great cleric and a most gifted poet, thrust into a harsh and irremediable exile? He himself asserts that it was on account of his unfortunate *Art of Love,* which he had written at the time of the Emperor Augustus,[48] this notwithstanding the fact that he composed a book in opposition to it, the *Remedies for Love*; Ovid would have been quite capable of speaking through a dream or through personifications if he had expected to be excused by such means.

"O God! O holy men and women! O devout court of Christian religion! O present-day morals! Among the pagans, an unbelieving pagan judge condemns a pagan who published teachings leading to foolish love, while among Christians (and by these same Christians!) a comparable, indeed more objectionable, work [by a Christian] is supported, praised, and defended! In all faith, I couldn't adequately describe the disgracefulness and the error of this thing: I lack the words to reprove it. But that such a work is baser than Ovid's, this I do indeed maintain, for not only is the *Art of Love,* which Ovid wrote, entirely enclosed within the said book [the *Rose*], but many other books, by Ovid as well as by others, are translated, assembled, and, as it were, extracted violently and without apparent purpose—books that are no less immoral and perilous (the writings of Heloïse and Peter Abe-

47. 1 Cor 15:33. Gerson mentions the passages of both Saint Paul and Seneca concerning evil words in his sermon *Considerate lilia* (no. 12 in this volume).

48. In his *Tristia* Ovid laments his exile and entreats Augustus to show him clemency; he also specifically attributes his exile in part to the *Art of Love*: whereas his other books can be displayed proudly on a bookshelf, "tres procul obscura latitantes parte uidebis— / sic quoque, quod nemo nescit, amare docent" (three [books] will strive to hide themselves in a dark place, as you will notice—even so, as everybody knows, they teach how to love) (*Tristia* 1.1.111–12). He states specifically that these three books of the *Art* were themselves banished: "carmina fecerunt, ut me moresque notaret / iam demi iussa Caesar ab Arte mea" (verse caused Caesar to brand me and my ways by commanding that my "Art [of Love]" be forthwith taken away) (*Tristia* 2.1.7–8). Finally, he states that "perdiderint cum me duo crimina, carmen et error" (Though two crimes, a poem and a blunder, have brought me ruin), he must remain silent about the latter; as for the former, "altera pars superest, qua turpi carmine factus / arguor obsceni doctor adulterii" (The other [crime] remains: the charge that by an obscene poem I have taught foul adultery (*Tristia* 2.1.207, 211–12). Trans. A. L. Wheeler, rev. G. P. Goold, 2nd ed. (Cambridge: Harvard University Press, 1988), 11, 57, 71.

lard, Juvenal, and the fables—all fabricated for the same cursed purpose—of Mars, Venus and Vulcan, Pygmalion, Adonis, and others).[49] Ovid expressly declared that it was not his intention to speak about virtuous matrons and married ladies, or about those ladies that it would not be permissible to love.[50] But does your book do the same thing? It admonishes and blames all women; it has contempt for all women, with not a single exception. At the very least, since the author claimed to be a Christian and on occasion spoke of heavenly things, why did he not make an exception for the saintly blessed virgins and innumerable others who maintained chastity in the temple of their heart, to the point of suffering very severe torture and cruel death? Why did he not uphold this reverence for the holiest of all holy women? But no! He was a foolish lover and so did not care about this; he did not wish to exonerate any woman, in order to promote in all women greater boldness in prostituting themselves. And he couldn't accomplish this any better than by making women think they are all this way and that they would be unable to refrain from such behavior.

"Necessity has no law.[51] God! What doctrine—no, not a doctrine, but

49. Consciously or unconsciously, Gerson cites the most famous couplet in the entire *Romance of the Rose,* drawn from Guillaume de Lorris's prologue and often used in the manuscripts to identify the work, either at the beginning or at the end: "ce est li *Romanz de la Rose,* ou l'art d'Amors est tote enclose" (This is the *Romance of the Rose,* where the art of love is completely enclosed) (ed. Lecoy, ll. 37–38; trans. Dahlberg, 31 [altered]). Contrary to what Gerson had said earlier, Jean de Meun does not frequently cite Peter Abelard in the *Rose;* he was probably thinking about the fact that Jean had translated the correspondence between Abelard and Heloïse into French, which, short of having read the translation, he would have known from Jean's mention of that fact in the prologue to his Boethius translation. Abelard's name is mentioned in only one episode, and while his *The Story of My Calamities* is referred to, it is Heloïse who is quoted there. Juvenal's sixth satire, against women, is quoted likewise by the Jealous Husband. The story of Mars and Venus being caught in a trap by Venus's jealous husband Vulcan is told by the Old Woman (ll. 13810–38, 14127–56) but also referred to in a rather different context by Nature (ll. 18031–99). The stories of Pygmalion and Adonis are told directly by the narrator, both from Ovid's *Metamorphoses* (ll. 15633–720 for Adonis and Venus, and ll. 20787–21152 for Pygmalion).

50. *Art of Love* 1.31–34: "Este procul, vittae tenues, insigne pudoris, / Quaeque tegis medios, instita longa, pedes. / Nos venerem tutam concessaque furta canemus, / Inque meo nullum carmine crimen erit" (Keep far away, ye slender fillets, emblems of modesty, and the long skirt that hides the feet in its folds. Of safe love-making do I sing, and permitted secrecy, and in my verse shall be no wrong-doing). *The Art of Love and Other Poems,* trans. J. H. Mozley, rev. G. P. Goold, 2nd ed. (Cambridge: Harvard University Press, 1979), 15.

51. "Necessity has no law" was a well-known proverb (cf. Morawski, *Proverbes français,* no. 237 and the variant in note) meaning something like "when one is in need or under some kind of constraint, one does not observe what either civil or moral law would dictate." Here, Gerson is referring to what he had just said about Jean de Meun's attitude toward women—that by nature they are lascivious—to state the proverbial conclusion to Jean's reasoning, that they will therefore do anything.

rather blasphemy and heresy! He thus endeavors to demonstrate that young people will never be constant and steadfast in their religious devotion, which is a false teaching and contrary to experience. But if one wanted to linger, so as to criticize everything of evil intent that is included in the aforementioned book, the day would reach its end sooner than the debate. But also it is perhaps possible that too great a specificity could do more harm to good morals than benefit to the cause: I could lapse into the vice that I am reproving. Therefore I shall shorten my speech and talk about nothing other than the articles contained in Lady Chastity's supplication and presented by Conscience. As it is, I already feel I have taken care of some of the simpler articles; now it is time to dig down to the graver and more inexcusable ones. The case is weighty, Lady Justice; may your council be intent upon listening with diligence, in order to attend to it urgently.

"Assuredly, with regard to the book in question—if it ought to be called a book—the common proverb is quite applicable: 'At the end lies the venom.'[52] Horace's mocking words regarding the painter who depicted the head of a very beautiful woman but ended up with [the tail of] a fish are also fitting here (something similar is said of the Harpies, who have a virginal face, but a belly and other parts that are most repulsive).[53] Alas! What filth is gathered and placed there! What blasphemous words are pronounced in this book! What diabolical seeds are sown therein! Having just spoken of God and paradise, of the very chaste and tender lamb, of the beautiful fountain, he then, in the person of the author, suddenly recounts without any transition his own highly dissolute life—there is no one so debauched that he would not be ashamed of it!—exhorting all men to act in the same way, to give themselves over to every woman, be she a virgin or not, in order to try out everything![54] But this is the height of evil: he claims such things to

52. This proverb seems to have its origin in the scorpion: "En la queue gist le venin" (the poison resides in the tail) (Morawski, *Proverbes français*, no. 661, with variants that accord with Gerson's version).

53. Horace, *Art of Poetry*, ll. 1–5: "If a painter chose to join a human head to the neck of a horse, and to spread feathers of many a hue over limbs picked up now here now there, so that what at the top is a lovely woman ends below in a black and ugly fish, could you, my friends, if favored with a private view, refrain from laughing?" (*Satires, Epistles, and Ars Poetica*, trans. Fairclough, 451). Virgil, *Aeneid* 3.212, 216–18: "Harpyiaeque . . . virginei volucrum vultus, foedissima ventris / proluvies, uncaeque manus, et pallida semper / ora fame" (Harpies . . . virgin faces have these birds, foulest filth they drop, clawed hands are theirs, and faces ever gaunt with hunger). Virgil, *Eclogues, Georgics, Aeneid 1–6*, trans. Fairclough, 387 (altered).

54. Gerson is here conflating a critique of Genius's sermon, with the allegory of the park and the lamb that represents paradise, and a critique of the lewd taking of the castle recounted by the narrator at the poem's end.

be sanctuaries and sacred objects, worthy of reverence! He would better have called them execrable, damnable, and detested, or—what else could I say here? In truth, it is a great abomination just to think of it: never will my mouth be defiled by saying any more on this subject, nor will your holy ears be tormented and this court befouled by listening to such things.

"I beg you nonetheless that this not be prejudicial to my case; and if what Saint Augustine said is true (as indeed it is!), that 'it is no less evil to despise the sacred words of God than the body of Jesus Christ,'[55] the author of this work was no less irreverent to God by speaking in this way and intermingling vile things with divine and sacred words than if he had thrown the precious body of our Lord at the feet of swine or on a dung heap. Think of what an outrage, what an abomination, what an error this is! He couldn't have done worse if he had thrown the text of the Gospel or the crucifix into a deep, filthy pool of sludge! Aristotle said (and Seneca repeated) that one must never act with so much reverence and morality as when one speaks of God,[56] and this person here, when speaking of God, throws the precious and holy jewel of Christian truth in its entirety into a vile cesspool replete with filth! I argue the case as follows: if he believed what he said about paradise (as I consider it), then, alas, he did not think about what he believed. If he did not believe it, then he was a deceitful and treacherous heretic. This is my reasoning, drawn from his dissolute life, which he exalts and boasts about.

"Furthermore, I would speak—were it not the case that he might still in some way redeem himself[57]—about how, at one moment through the character of Nature, and at another through Genius (along the lines of what Chastity correctly proposed), he exhorts and orders people to indiscrimi-

55. Hicks locates this reference in a sermon perhaps erroneously attributed to Augustine, entitled "How the word of God is to be received" (*PL* 39, col. 2319): "Verbum Dei nil minus quam corpus Christi. Nec indignius percipiendum" (The word of God is no less than the body of Christ. It is not to be received with less reverence . . . Because he who listens to the word of God carelessly is no less guilty than he who would allow the body of Christ to fall to the ground out of negligence).

56. This passage is also referred to in the sermon *Considerate lilia* (no. 12 in this volume).

57. This passage admits of two possibilities. I have translated it according to the Hicks edition: Theological Eloquence is saying that since the Foolish Lover still has an opportunity for redemption, she will not go on detailing his transgressions. She said previously that she hoped he would be pardoned by God and later says that she is criticizing the work and not the person. One might, however, suspect a corrupt text with a missing negation in the second part of this sentence, in which case the translation would be "were it not impossible for him ever to redeem himself in the slightest." According to this reading, the prosecutor would be saying that since the Foolish Lover's guilt was already so proven, there would be no need to further detail his transgressions. It would seem that the former reading, however counterintuitive in the mouth of a prosecutor, is probably the correct one.

nately practice every kind of carnal act and maligns all men and women who will not do so. And never is there a single mention of marriage—which nonetheless is dictated by nature; never is moderation of language maintained, and he promises paradise to all those who perform in this manner. Consequently, anyone is a fool who does not believe him, who does not follow such teachings, who does not sing them out everywhere. It is true that this poetic fiction was inaccurately lifted from the great Alan of Lille, in his book *On the Complaint of Nature*;[58] for it is also the case that a very large part of all that our Foolish Lover does is practically nothing but a translation of others' writings. This I know well: he who willingly deigned to take things from his neighbors was just showing his humility, outfitting himself with so many feathers, as the fables say of the crow—but this is of little interest to me.[59] I come back to Alan and make the point that he never spoke in such a manner, through any personage whatsoever. He would have been reluctant to do so. All he does is condemn and reproach vices contrary to nature. And justifiably so. I do the same. May all those who will not refrain from these vices be cursed and may Justice burn them. But it is not the case that he [Alan] is encouraging just any sinful activity in order to avoid another sin. It would be idiotic for a surgeon to attempt to heal one wound by making another one, or to extinguish fire by means of fire. And if someone wishes to excuse these acts and transgressions by saying Nature is the one speaking, I respond on your behalf, Lady Nature; for never did you advise sin, never did you advise anyone to run afoul of one of the Ten Commandments (which we indeed call your commandments)[60] by carrying out the "commandments

58. As noted above (see ch. 2, n. 18), Alan of Lille's outrageously satirical and phenomenally popular attack on sodomy, written around 1170, was a major influence upon Jean de Meun, providing him with the figures of Nature and Genius, who occupy a large portion of the last quarter of Jean's continuation. Sections of Reason's speech, much earlier in the continuation, were also translated from Alan's Latin original. When Gerson refers to "this poetic fiction," he is certainly referring to these particular episodes, for the latter were themselves inserted into the larger framework provided by Jean's predecessor, Guillaume de Lorris.

59. The classic fable of the crow had the bird bedecking himself with peacock feathers in order to make himself more beautiful; but he is rejected by the peacocks and reproached for his pretensions. A medieval version of the tale made it more of an exemplary tale in having the crow borrow feathers from a number of other birds, an illustration of "the result of pride in acquisitions not really earned" (Helen P. South, "The Upstart Crow," *Modern Philology* 25, no. 1 [1927]: 85). It is clearly the medieval tradition of the fable, which found its way into sermon collections, that Gerson is calling upon: his reference to Jean's humility is thus highly ironic.

60. This passage seems somewhat contradictory, as the speaker has just addressed Nature with the pronoun "you" (*vous*) and then refers to the Ten Commandments of God as "your commandments" (*vos commandemens*). But clearly the commandments of Nature are distinct from those of God, as this very sentence indicates. Theological Eloquence here reconciles the two by affirming that natural law is subservient to the Ten Commandments and must obey the dictates of faith;

of Nature." To say the contrary would be an error of faith (namely, to claim that, according to the law of nature, the "natural" act between a man and a woman outside marriage is not a sin).

"Lady Justice, I have spoken at some length—but though I am fully aware of the length of time, it is still all too brief compared with the enormity of the crime. This, despite the fact that you and your very wise and enlightened council understand all things when stated concisely, you who so despise any kind of vile filth, who know all the laws and legal rights, and who have also for some time heard talk of this case. What has been said—albeit without undue specificity (for I know to whom I am speaking, in front of whom, and for whom)[61]—what has been said could thus be quite sufficient to condemn and ban the book in question, as has happened with others that are harmful to our faith and good morals, just as the apostles did in the case of new converts.[62] The ancients did the same with the books of a poet named Archilochus; even though the books were of great authority, they inflicted more harm on the good morals of young people than they brought profit to their minds, as is precisely the case here.[63]

"I would therefore place my conclusion here, were it not that wise Lady Reason, my good mistress, has made a sign to me to continue speaking—not surprisingly, for her honor greatly depends upon it. She would be perfectly capable of defending herself, that is clear, but since I have begun and she is pleased for me to continue, I will do so gladly and most succinctly—indeed, more briefly than the crime would require.

---

sexual activity between a man and a woman is undeniably natural, as indicated in the following sentence, but it runs counter to God's law if it is performed outside of matrimony. The problem of the reference to "your commandments" can be explained if we recall that Theological Eloquence's entire legal case is being addressed to Lady Canonical Justice, God's representative on earth and dispenser of his justice; Eloquence has briefly diverted her attention to Nature in order to defend her, but then turns back to Lady Justice in this quasi-theatrical shift, but nothing other than the context of the argument allows us to determine this to be the case. However, Lady Justice *is* directly addressed immediately hereafter, at the beginning of the following paragraph.

61. We are reminded that the person speaking is Eloquence, and that decorum—propriety in level of speech with regard to the context, in particular the people being addressed—is a fundamental precept of rhetoric.

62. Acts 19:19: "Multi autem ex eis, qui fuerant curiosa sectati, contulerunt libros, et combusserunt coram omnibus" (And many of them who had followed curious arts, brought together their books, and burnt them before all).

63. Valerius Maximus, *Factorum et dictorum memorabilium* (Of Memorable Deeds and Writings) 6.3, ext.1: "The Lacedaemonians ordered that the works of Archilochus be removed from their community because they thought them immodest and immoral reading. They did not wish their children's minds to be imbued with it, lest it do more harm to their character than good to their intelligence" (ed. and trans. D. R. Shackleton Bailey, 2 vols. [Cambridge: Harvard University Press, 2000], 2:41–43).

"O you who are here in support of the Foolish Lover, if this irrational error that imputes a type of madness to Reason (for is it not madness to declare that one ought to speak irreverently and without concealment or modesty, no matter how indecent the words might be in the opinion of all people, even those lacking a sense of proper conduct or shame?)—I say, if this error had not long ago been denounced by the ancient philosophers, neither this author nor you who defend (or rather accuse!) him would merit so much blame. But it is the truth that even before the coming of Jesus Christ, Cicero in his book *De officiis,* as well as other philosophers (and since then, the holy teachers, as you can still read and learn), reproved this foolishness;[64] but likewise good custom, which prevails over nature,[65] despises, dreads, and shuns it. How, therefore, can giving such a character to Lady Reason be tolerated—as if those who do not act in this way were out of their minds and lacking reason!—even though it was not the wise but rather the besotted and sullied Reason who spoke. In the name of God! This characterization would have been better suited for swine or dogs than for Reason. I am not, however, making up this claim by myself, for some ancients who held the title of 'philosopher' were called dogs on account of this disgraceful doctrine. And was Ham not cursed and made a vile slave for simply having looked at the secret parts of his father, Noah, without covering them?[66] This was also the error of the Turlupins,[67] in maintaining that nakedness was the state of innocence and of the highest perfection on earth. How could one attribute a more irrational thing to Reason? How could one better embolden all irrational people than by having Reason speak thus, especially when she recounts provocative things leading to all sorts of wantonness in her discourse? Give, go ahead, give your daughters and children to such a teacher, and if they are not clever enough, send them to the school of such a Reason! Acquaint them with all evils, if they are not capable of finding enough of them by themselves, and beat them if they do not speak of things in the way Reason commands! In addition, according to the same line of argument,

64. For this statement and what follows in this paragraph, see above, ch. 2, nn. 103–107.

65. The text of this proverbial expression printed by Hicks uses the verb *vault,* which means "is equal to." But the context of the argument and the typical versions of this proverb (which go in both directions), "Nature passe norreture" (Nature surpasses education; Morawski, *Proverbes français,* no. 1328) and "Noureture passe nature" (Education surpasses nature; ibid., no. 1399), suggest that the best reading is the variant *vaint* (defeats, surpasses, prevails over), which I have incorporated into my translation.

66. Gen 9:21–27. The Bible says in fact that Ham's son Chanaan was made the servant of Shem (Gen 9:26).

67. On the sect of the Turlupins, see above, ch. 2, nn. 104 and 107.

one could prove that people ought to walk around naked anywhere and everywhere without being bashful; I believe that given her stance, this is what Reason would maintain. Now, let anyone who likewise espouses this view walk through the streets in order to find out how "Reason" will protect him from being shouted at, jeered, and vilified!

"Still, if Reason had been speaking to a wise cleric who understood the nature of things, or to a great theologian who knew that nothing would bring shame to us had it not been for original sin, he[68] would have had somewhat of an excuse. He could have invoked the nudity of Eve and Adam—even though the issue is not the same for the state of innocence and for our own. The difference is comparable to that between a healthy person and a sick one. Wine that would not harm a healthy man will make one trembling with fever delirious. Thus it is that to hear of, or to see, certain fleshly things without concealment and in their natural state would stir up in sinners extremely base desires, while it would not have been thus in the state of innocence. All of this is evident, for before sin Eve and Adam were naked without shame; then they sinned, and instantly they hid and covered themselves with great embarrassment. And there is no need to ask why one way of speaking is to be blamed more than another when in both cases the same thing is signified. It is not necessary for me to pause at every step to explain something [that is] innate, for experience makes it abundantly clear: fantasy gets stirred up, and fantasy is what generates all desire. It follows that Lady Idleness is the gatekeeper of Foolish Love, for the latter doesn't encounter imagination or fantasy in a person who is busy; still, one way or the other Foolish Love conveys carnal desires to him. Hence, there is no precaution like busying oneself with some interesting task. Because of this, it often happens that a melancholy, sickly person with a frail temperament will be more ardently tempted by fleshly things than someone who is healthy and sanguine, laughing and playful. But everything derives from fantasy. Is it a surprise if one is less quickly burned by a fire covered by ashes than by open flames? It is the same for carnal things said or looked at openly.

68. The pronoun "he" is ambiguous here. It could be referring to the last mentioned masculine noun, either "cleric" or "theologian," but according to the grammatical construction (this clause completes the hypothetical if-clause that opens the sentence) it should be referring back to the main subject of the sentence, which happens to be "Reason," a feminine character. I take it to be an example of the not-uncommon slippage from the female character to the male author of the work. Thus the "he" would be referring to the latter: he (Jean de Meun) would have had somewhat of an excuse (for making Reason speak the way she does) had her interlocutor been a theologian rather than a foolish lover. This becomes clear in the following paragraph, when Theological Eloquence "comes back to her argument" in order to blame both Reason and the author precisely for her having said such things to a foolish lover and not to a "wise . . . cleric."

"But I come back to my argument and insist that it would have been one thing if the character of Reason were speaking to a wise and established cleric. But no! Reason[69] is speaking to a foolish lover. And here the author did not uphold the dictates of my school (the rules of rhetoric), which are to pay attention to the person who is speaking, to the person being addressed, and to the occasion upon which one speaks. And this is not the only shortcoming, for in numerous places he attributes to the person speaking things that shouldn't belong to that person (as he presents Nature speaking of paradise and of the mysteries of our faith, and Venus who swears by the flesh of God).[70] But I am not going to pay attention to this, even though it is a flaw in someone whom some wish to exalt above almost any other person who ever existed. I am too distressed for Lady Reason and Chastity that he made wise Reason say such ribald things to a foolish lover—to whom previously Cupid, who calls himself the god of Love, had forbidden all vile and filthy speech and all blame directed at women—as though Cupid were more chaste and reasonable than Lady Reason and Chastity![71]

"O God! I am mistaken: It was not one and the same author. *This* was rather the author upon whose beginning the one of whom I am speaking constructed his work.[72] Long before, the foundations were laid by the first

69. The pronoun here is masculine, *il*. I take it as referring to the expression *le personnaige de Raison* in the preceding sentence, as a way of bridging the gap between the fictional character and, in the next sentence, the author who is responsible for what the character says.

70. The situation of Nature is slightly more complex, as Jean de Meun has the goddess evoke some of the mysteries of the faith, including the trinitarian nature of God and the virgin birth (ll. 18991–19160), but she also makes it very clear that these matters are beyond her ken and outside her domain: though she is responsible for the physical reproduction of man, the granting of understanding to man is not among her duties ("La ne s'estant pas ma baillie" [l. 19028; "that is not my area of responsibility," trans. Dahlberg, 315]; she admits, further, that she was astonished at the birth of Christ from the Virgin Mary, for she herself is incapable of effecting any birth from a virgin [ll. 19131–32]; Gerson's remark about the limited domain of Nature substantiates the principle that the goddess and her "laws" are subordinate to the rule of faith (see above, n. 60). At the moment of launching the castle siege, Venus swears by "the flesh of God" ["Par la char Dieu!"; l. 20696]).

71. Among the instructions the God of Love gives to the Lover in Guillaume de Lorris's fragment is in fact an injunction not to use dirty words or to speak of vile things (ed. Lecoy, ll. 2097–2100). This produces the later irony of the Lover reproaching Reason for mouthing obscenities, basing himself upon Cupid's lesson.

72. As is the case with modern critics, Gerson was intrigued by the ideological differences between the two authors. In this, he parts company with Christine de Pizan, who considers the entire work to be of one piece. In the middle of the poem, Jean de Meun has the God of Love prophesy the death of Guillaume de Lorris, adding that "more than forty years after" (ed. Lecoy, l. 10560; trans. Dahlberg, 188) Jean de Meun would continue his work. For this important authorial passage see ll. 10496–644; trans. Dahlberg, 187–89. Jean de Montreuil likewise rebukes the lawyer to whom he writes his self-proclaimed invective (no. 6 in this volume) for preferring Guillaume to Jean.

one, using his own hands and subject matter—no begging around here and there, and no mixing in the sort of vile filth and smelly, dirty sewage that is included in the climactic ending of this work. I do not know whether the continuator thought he was honoring him; if he truly believed he was, he was mistaken. For to a beginning that might well be acceptable even among Christians, given its intention, he added a very dirty ending and irrational middle sections contrary to reason. Even the pagans were never able to tolerate or endure in their republic (as I said of Augustus and the philosophers) the sorts of things contained in the conclusion and middle sections of this work. Likewise, the Church Fathers corrected and rectified their works, but this case is not comparable to those.[73]

"Thus I conclude before you and your noble court, Lady Canonical Justice, that measures must be taken to deal with this offense, by a final judgment without any possible appeal or opposition by the defendant. I conclude nothing against the person of the author—may he indeed make his amends to God—but it is of the too great offense that I speak. What do I mean by 'too great offense?' I have already demonstrated, and briefly repeat: too great by reason of its errors, its blasphemous words, its venomous teachings, the numerous ways it reduces poor Christian souls to destruction and despair, its illicit waste of precious time, at the expense of Chastity, its destruction of loyalty both within and without the bonds of matrimony, its banishment of Fear and Shame, its defamation of Reason, the outrageous dishonor it thrusts upon you, Lady Canonical Justice, your laws and rights, and upon this entire religious court representing all Christianity, indeed upon all good people—even upon all wicked people, who are made worse by it!

"May such a book be seized and banished without ever being consulted, especially in the sections where the author sets his sights on disreputable and forbidden characters, such as the damned Old Woman (who ought to be sentenced to the pillory), Venus (which is to say Lust, a mortal sin), and the Foolish Lover, who must not be granted free rein in his wantonness: one could not do him more injury nor be more hateful toward him.

"Accordingly, my request is pleasing to God; it is reasonable to you, Lady Justice; it is acceptable to your court; and to foolish lovers—however much they may at present protest against it—it is profitable and caring; and when they are cured, it will be pleasant and delightful. And in order that

73. The paradox that Gerson seems to be emphasizing in these closing pages is how remarkable it is that the pagans had enough moral indignation to condemn works like Ovid's *Art of Love,* but that a book much more offensive and dangerous, Jean de Meun's *Rose,* is praised by his Christian contemporaries.

no one believe or complain that I am accusing something other than the vices—certainly not any of the people involved!—I make this petition and peroration in the name of Chastity and Conscience against all images, writings, or poems that incite to lechery. Our frailty is itself too favorably inclined toward lechery without inflaming it even more disastrously and pushing it into the depths of vice, far from the virtues and from God—who is our glory, our love, our salvation, joy, and felicity."

Eloquence had drawn to a close, but I did not notice the moment when my heart flew back just as it had flown off; and without hearing any of the sentence, I found myself in my study at dusk, in the year 1402, on the eighteenth of May. There I found many other matters to occupy my heart, so that it would cease to be so flighty. And those matters included the blessed Trinity in its divine and simple unity, then the holy sacrament at the altar,[74] etc.

21. PIERRE COL TO CHRISTINE DE PIZAN (LATE SUMMER 1402)[75]

FRENCH PROSE

The response of Master Pierre Col, a canon of Paris, to the two preceding treatises[76]

After I heard talk of your lofty intelligence, your glistening wit, and your melodious eloquence, I very eagerly wanted to see some of your letters and other such little items. So after taking great pains to make inquiries into it, there came into my hands a certain letter of yours addressed, as I understand, to a lord and distinguished master of mine, my lord the provost of Lille. It begins, "Reverent and respectful greetings, etc.," and by means of it you strive to rebuke that very devout Catholic and most exalted theologian, that very divine orator and poet and highly accomplished philosopher, Master Jean de Meun, in reference to some specific passages of his book of the *Rose,* which I myself dare not open my mouth to praise, no more than I would move my foot forward in order to fall into an abyss. Indeed, following what

74. As Hicks notes, the feast of the Holy Sacrament fell on May 25 in 1402, four days after Trinity Sunday; his sermon *Memoriam* (cf. Louis Mourin, *Jean Gerson, Prédicateur français* [Bruges: De Tempel, 1952], 134–36) seems to correspond to the sermon Gerson intended for that special feast, whereas another sermon, *Videmus,* would likely correspond to the one delivered on Sunday, May 21. In his response to this treatise, Pierre Col refers to a sermon delivered by Gerson on the Trinity at the church of Saint-Jean-en-Grève, which suggests that he heard the very sermon Gerson was preparing as he completed his treatise against the *Rose.*

75. Translated from *Le débat,* ed. Hicks, 89–112.

76. Namely, Christine's letter to Jean de Montreuil (no. 5) and Gerson's treatise (no. 20).

we read about Herod, who did more good to the Innocents out of hatred, in having them killed, than he could have done out of love,[77] it is the same thing with you and others who, like yourself, endeavor to attack this very noble writer, Meun. You praise him more when you think you are blaming him than I could possibly praise him by using every one of my body parts, were they at once all transformed into tongues. This is due to the coarseness of my wit, the denseness of my understanding, my failing memory and poorly developed verbal skills, but truly even more to the unfathomable multiplicity of merits in the book that no man could possibly express, but to which you call attention, all the while thinking you are reprimanding him.

Nonetheless, confident in the truth, I will make an effort, by use of his very own arguments, to respond to yours—arguments that are more refined in their language than your own discourse is graced with reason—rather than to the arguments of those other adversaries of his (which I have seen or heard, but which I am unable to recall).[78] And let it not be ascribed to presumptuousness or arrogance on my part, for this in truth is not what makes me do it: It is rather because I aspire to occupy at least the lowest rank among the other disciples of the aforementioned Meun, and because the arguments that you bring forward in opposition (if they may be called arguments) are such that there is scarcely a need for the fair to middling disciples of the said Meun, not to mention the most advanced ones, to respond to them. I am also confident in the great righteousness I wish to uphold, even though it upholds itself admirably through its own arguments. Rather, I use them as my shield. And do pardon me if I use the familiar form *tu* to speak to you,[79] for I do it in order to show that this response of mine comes from kind affection, that is, it is meant to lead you back to the correct path; it is also used to speak more fittingly, as did our ancient masters.

First, for no apparent reason, you begin with the chapter of Reason and say that she names man's private parts by their proper name. I respond to such a contention by saying that since God created these things, they are good and therefore can be named. Indeed, you claim as follows: "I profess that God truly did create all things pure and clean coming from himself and

77. The slaying of the innocents is recounted in Mt 2:16; nothing is said of the good that ensued.

78. As G. Hasenohr pointed out (review of Hicks, *Le débat,* 131), the syntax of this sentence is corrupt, undoubtedly owing to a lacuna, and needs to be supplemented in order to make clear sense (what I have translated as "rather than to the arguments of" is missing in the Middle French and corresponds to Hasenohr's hypothetical emendation).

79. On the humanist use of the singular form *tu,* see above, ch. 2, n. 122, and the closing lines of no. 19.

that it would not have been an offense to name them in the state of innocence; but by the pollution of sin man became impure . . ." And you provide the example of Lucifer, who at first was beautiful and whose name was beautiful, "but who was later reduced to horrible ugliness by sin; whence the name, albeit beautiful in itself, leads those who hear it into error . . ."[80] You say moreover that "the name does not create the indecency of the thing, but the thing makes the name indecent." Here you resemble the pelican: you kill yourself with your beak.[81] By your faith! If the thing makes the word indecent, what name can you give to that thing that would not be indecent, if the thing does not change as does the name?

But now I turn to where you say that in the state of innocence it was permitted to name the private parts and that God created them in such a state. I ask you: If you were speaking of the private parts of a two- or three-year-old child—for you would not deny that God forms every single one of us—would you dare name them by their proper name? If you say you wouldn't, it is nonetheless the case that the child is in a state of innocence, without defilement in word or deed. And it is useless to invoke as you do original sin, for that came about from disobedience. And if the defilement of our first parents renders the name of the private parts so repugnant that it is not permitted to name them, I claim, calling upon a more compelling argument, that one ought not to pronounce the names of our first parents, for they are the ones who sinned and not their private parts. But if your response is affirmative (that is, that one could name the private parts of a child), I beg you to inform us up to what age it is permissible to name them, and also whether one can call by their proper name the private parts of an aged man who has remained chaste and virginal for his entire life; likewise, tell us whether you would dare name the organs corresponding to the private parts in dumb beasts (for they do not sin at all), so that you might teach Reason and the

80. As stated in the Volume Editor's Introduction, the version of Christine's letter to which Pierre Col had access differed from the version transmitted in the other manuscripts (and thus sanctioned by Christine). Here, the word *erreur* (error), found in Pierre's quotation, is written *horreur* (horror) in the other version of the letter and is therefore translated in that letter (no. 5) as "arouses horror in those who hear it."

81. In medieval bestiaries, which describe the qualities and characteristics of both imaginary and real animals, the pelican is reputed to be struck by its offspring soon after they are born, whereupon the father strikes them back, killing them. Three days later, he opens up his side by pecking with his beak and the blood that flows out revives the dead birds. As with much of bestiary lore, the pelican story was Christianized and interpreted as a figure for Christ's sacrifice on the Cross. Pierre Col is through this example certainly playing with Christine's name, formed as it is from the name of Christ, an onomastic play that Christine had already used in the closing lines of the *Debate of Two Lovers* and that she would use on several occasions later in her career.

disciples of the aforementioned Meun how one ought to speak. In truth, the Lover, in the chapter on Reason, makes more arguments—and more convincing ones by half—than you do. And Reason answers them! You, however, do not respond to *her* arguments, which you ought to have done before criticizing her. So there is no further need to respond to you on this point.

Be that as it may, I have seen a text written as a sort of legal case in the holy court of Christianity, in which Canonical Justice was seated as judge and the Virtues around her as her council, of which the principal one, acting as chancellor, was Penetrating Judgment, joined in close company with Lady Reason, Prudence, and Knowledge, with the others serving as secretaries, and Theological Eloquence as advocate for the court; the promoter of lawsuits was Conscience, who was made to stand up and present a request on behalf of Chastity couched in the following form: "To Justice, defender of the law, who occupies the place of God on earth, and to her entire court, devout and very Christian. Chastity, your faithful subject, submits the following plaint and begs humbly that measures be taken, that a succinct provisional sentence be pronounced against the intolerable crimes that someone who calls himself the Foolish Lover has committed, and does not stop committing, against me." Thereafter she appended eight or nine articles.

Now, in truth, I believe I know the person who put together this legal case, and (may this not displease him!) I am afraid that he speaks of a Foolish Lover as a cleric speaks of warfare.[82] For, by my faith, I contend that just as he himself, while preaching in the [church of Saint-Jean-en-] Grève on Trinity Sunday,[83] stated that we see and come to know this Trinity as a reflection and as though through a mirror, thus it is that he sees, understands, and speaks of a foolish lover.[84] Indeed I believe not only that he never was one

82. "Parler comme un clerc d'armes" (to speak as a cleric does of arms/warfare) was a common late medieval proverb meaning "to speak out of ignorance." Cf. di Stefano, *Dictionnaire des locutions,* 173; Hassell, *Middle French Proverbs,* 191 (P47).

83. Pierre Col makes it abundantly clear that he knew Gerson was the author of the treatise against the *Rose,* as well he should have. Gerson had been the chancellor of Notre-Dame since 1395; Pierre Col had been a canon there since 1389. His mention of the preaching on the Holy Trinity at the Church of Saint-Jean-en-Grève corresponds to Gerson's activities there and the fact that he mentions in the treatise that he was working on the Holy Trinity in May 1402. See above, n. 74.

84. Pierre here refers to one of the passages of the Bible most discussed by medieval commentators, for inasmuch as it deals with the incomplete or obscure way in which the secrets of God are detected by most mortals, it served as a foundation for the allegorical understanding of things found in the world: "videmus nunc per speculum in enigmate tunc autem facie ad faciem nunc cognosco ex parte tunc autem cognoscam sicut et cognitus sum" (For now we see through a glass, darkly; but then face to face: now I know in part; but then shall I know even as also I am known). Indeed, the sermon Gerson prepared for that Trinity Sunday took as its title the first

but that the thought never crossed his mind. I would even dare to affirm that he provided a better account of the Trinity, having thought more about it, than he did of the Foolish Lover. This is why I would have considerable justification in saying that there is no need to respond to any of this legal case, for the entire speech made at the hearing is based upon a foolish lover, but the author doesn't know what a foolish lover is. And it is pointless to contend that even though he is not a foolish lover, still he understands perhaps better than someone who is or has been one; this cannot be,[85] but I dare to assert that even if the author had been a foolish lover but were no longer one at present, he would understand better by half than he does now, for direct experience has so much more—what can I say?—power than even the effect of speech produced by a living voice. In any event, truth and righteousness are so clearly in favor of the person he calls the Foolish Lover that it will not trouble me at all to respond to the specific charges that Lady Theological Eloquence puts forth, as she is alleged to have done. For as I will explain hereinafter, never, by my faith, was the good lady concerned with this matter—even assuming that the aforementioned Meun might have been a foolish lover for a certain time.

So at the outset Lady Theological Eloquence says that Master Jean de Meun bears inscribed on his forehead the mark of his condemnation with the name "Foolish Lover" when she declares: "Who long ago destroyed Troy the Magnificent with fire and flames? A foolish lover. Who back then caused the death of more than a hundred thousand men, Hector, Achilles, and others? A foolish lover. Who exiled King Tarquin from Rome? A foolish lover . . ." and other similar comparisons. I ask Lady Eloquence whether this argument is intended to blame someone for being a foolish lover, or to blame the book of the *Rose* for having been composed by someone who was a foolish lover. If it is intended to blame foolish lovers, I have nothing to respond, for I admit that to be one is irrational and an act of folly. Furthermore, it would be pointless to try to blame a foolish lover more than the book of the *Rose* does. Let him who reads it consider carefully: Does he not say about

---

verse from 1 Cor 13 cited here (cf. Mourin, *Six sermons français inédits de Jean Gerson: Étude doctrinale et littéraire suivie de l'édition critique et de remarques linguistiques*, Études de Théologie et d'Histoire de la Spiritualité, 8 [Paris: Vrin, 1946], 151; and *Jean Gerson, prédicateur français*, 133–35). Gerson objects to this remark in his sharp Latin rejoinder to Pierre Col (no. 28)—perhaps, among other things, feeling his sermon was being mocked by the canon of Notre-Dame.

85. I follow here G. Hasenohr's (review of Hicks, *Le débat*, 131) suggested emendation to Hicks's text. Whereas the latter reads "this can be," Hasenohr argues, correctly to my mind, that the reasoning is flawed unless the clause is made negative.

the god of Love: "He is the god who turns them all from their road?"[86] And later: "But I want them to keep themselves from that foolish love which inflames hearts and makes them burn . . ."[87] And again: "that is what is making your skin waste away . . ."[88] And again: "these . . . have kept their hearts set on the love of woman. As a result, many have lost body and soul . . ."[89] Again: "It is Love who fans and inflames the coals that he has put in your heart."[90] Again: "Whoever accords with Reason will never love *par amour.*"[91] Again: "the more they frequent it [the path of Give-Too-Much, guarded by Wealth, who is speaking], the more they repent in the end."[92] And again and again in more than a hundred other places that I omit for the sake of brevity, except one couplet, which suffices very well for all of them: "many, I dare say, lose [in that love where you are caught] their sense, their time, possessions, body, soul, and reputation."[93] Now let those who wish to blame the Foolish Lover more than Master Jean de Meun already does boldly analyze *his* supposed reputation,[94] and I believe that they will find nothing there to

86. *Rose,* ed. Lecoy, l. 4312; trans. Dahlberg, 95.

87. *Rose,* ed. Lecoy, ll. 4563–64; trans. Dahlberg, 99.

88. *Rose,* ed. Lecoy, l. 4576; trans. Dahlberg, 99.

89. *Rose,* ed. Lecoy, ll. 13903–904; trans. Dahlberg, 239. The quotation of Pierre Col differs from that of the editions of Ernest Langlois and Lecoy in that it puts the first clause in the singular ("he has kept his heart"). Since this does not fit into the context of the passage, where many men are being spoken of, I have retained Dahlberg's translation.

90. *Rose,* ed. Lecoy, ll. 6369–70; trans. Dahlberg, 125. Once again, Pierre Col's quotation does not correspond to the editions, as they have Love personified, whereas Col quotes it as a common noun, "l'amour." But this does not fit the context (Reason is speaking), as she refers in the two preceding lines to "the god who put you here, your good master, your good friend." I therefore retain Dahlberg's translation.

91. *Rose,* ed. Lecoy, 6854–55; Dahlberg, 132.

92. *Rose,* ed. Lecoy, ll. 10095–96; trans. Dahlberg, 181. Pierre Col reverses the two clauses in his quotation, but this does not alter the sense of the passage. The Lover has taken Friend's advice to follow the path of Give-Too-Much, which was founded by Foolish Generosity, in order to penetrate the castle. He encounters Wealth, who informs him that she guards the entrance to the path but that, after Foolish Generosity has exacted a heavy price from them, Poverty leads them back.

93. *Rose,* ed. Lecoy, ll. 4597–98; trans. Dahlberg, 99 (altered).

94. The last word in the quotation Col has just provided, translated by Dahlberg as "reputation," is Old French *los,* which has a range of meanings extending from "advice," to "praise," to "[good] reputation." In the quotation from the *Rose,* Jean de Meun's Reason is referring to the loss of reputation following upon the sort of love that has taken hold of the Lover/protagonist. Pierre Col's taking up of the term in the following sentence, since it is being used to relate to the detractors of Jean de Meun, would seem to be referring more specifically to Jean's dubious reputation as a foolish lover. But could there also be a semantic slippage here, by which this repetition of the term preceded by the demonstrative "this" (*ce*) is referring to the supposed praise

add to their list. And when Master Jean de Meun calls the private parts of women "sanctuaries" or "relics,"[95] he does so in order to show the immense folly to be found in the Foolish Lover: For a foolish lover thinks of nothing other than this rosebud; it is his god and he adores it as his god. But also in this passage he was fabricating in a poetic way, and, as Horace says, license has always been granted equally to poets and to painters to fabricate all things.[96] Furthermore, it is not such a poor choice of words as one might claim, to call these private parts sanctuaries, for the doors and walls of a city, according to the laws, are called sacred because if someone submits them to force or passes through them without permission, he receives punishment. Thus it is with the private parts of a woman: he receives punishment who either commits rape or who, without using force, improperly transgresses upon them.[97] The Bible also says that people used to sanctify the private parts of women.[98]

But if the argument is intended to blame the book of the *Rose* for having been composed by someone who was a foolish lover,[99] I wonder how it is

---

Jean gives throughout of foolish love? This, after all, is Col's central point: whereas Jean is criticized for portraying, and supposedly praising, foolish love, he actually is criticizing foolish love even more forcefully than his detractors. It is in any event the case that Christine, in her response to Col, took it simply as a reference to the word as it occurs in the quotation (which however has little to do with the context of Col's remark).

95. The words used by Pierre Col here, *saintuaires* and *reliques*, are indeed both used by Jean de Meun to refer to women's "private parts," specifically in the conclusion of the romance (e.g., ed. Lecoy, ll. 21570, 21572; trans. Dahlberg, 351). The translation of *saintuaire* is somewhat tricky, as it could be rendered as "reliquary" or as "sanctuary" (with the meaning of "a specially holy place in a temple or church"). Jean's use of it, as is the case for the general figurative texture of the conclusion, is somewhat fluid: When he refers to its being covered with a precious cloth (ed. Lecoy, ll. 20777–78; trans. Dahlberg, 340) it would seem to be a concrete object, a reliquary, but later, he refers to the relics as being covered with a curtain and the sanctuary as being somehow separate, a place before which he will get down on his knees and pray (ed. Lecoy, ll. 21562–72; trans. Dahlberg, 351). Because of the uncertainty of the referent, I have preferred the less concrete word "sanctuary" (as above) to the more concrete "reliquary."

96. *Art of Poetry* 9–10: "pictoribus atque poetis / quidlibet audendi semper fuit aequa potestas" (Painters and poets have always had an equal right in hazarding anything) (*Satires, Epistles and Ars Poetica*, trans. Fairclough, 451).

97. Col here repeats the same words or phrases in the two cases in order to make the parallel perfectly clear: "commet force" for the city, "fait force" for the woman, "les trespasse sans congié" for the city, "induement les trespasse" for the woman. Since the expression *faire force* is such a common one for "to rape," I felt in the latter case that it would be infelicitous to translate it in a more literal way, even though Col does want us to see the explicit connection between literal and figurative here, which he has of course borrowed from Jean de Meun.

98. Gerson counters this in his response. Hicks suggests that it might be a reference to ritual purifications mentioned in the Old Testament, citing Lev 15:29–30.

99. Here Pierre Col returns to his initial question addressed to Theological Eloquence.

that Lady Eloquence does not first direct her conclusions against Solomon, David, and other foolish lovers who lived quite a long time before Meun—men whose books are mixed in with Holy Scripture and whose words are incorporated into the holy mystery of the Mass. Who had Uriah, the good knight, killed by treachery in order to commit adultery with his wife?[100] A foolish lover. Who had temples with idols built for the love of foreign women?[101] A foolish lover. And so many others that I pass over. It is against these ones here that Lady Eloquence should first have been speaking, if she were formally presenting her argumentation. But in fact, not at all! Do we not read that Saint Peter and Saint Paul, after having sinned, were more firm in their faith, and likewise many others?[102] I claim that Master Jean de Meun, after having been a foolish lover, adhered firmly to reason: for the better he understood the folly to be found in foolish love through experience, the more he disparaged it and praised Reason. And when he wrote this book of the *Rose* he was no longer a foolish lover, but rather repented for having been one, as is apparent from his ability to speak so well of Reason. If he had not known, loved, and understood Reason, he would have been incapable of speaking of her as he did. Indeed, by all accounts, it is true that a foolish lover neither knows nor loves nor understands her. Thus he says in the chapter of Nature, when he speaks of paradise, that the things of the orchard of Delight are but trifles;[103] and of the fountain of Narcissus, he says: "What a good and pleasing fountain, where the well become sick . . . ,"[104] adding that it intoxicates the living with death.[105] How better could he have shown that he was not a foolish lover and that he loved Reason than by casting blame on the orchard of Delight and the things found there, and by praising Reason and creating another park (another park or orchard), in which he depicts symbolically, and in so remarkable a way, the Trinity and the Incarnation by means of the carbuncle and the olive tree that derives its spurt of growth

100. David's killing of Uriah in order to possess Bathsheba is recounted in 2 Kings (2 Sam) 11:2–17.

101. Solomon's deeds are recounted in 3 Kings (1 Kings) 11:1–8. Gerson had referred to this same story (see above, n. 38) in order to stress the insufficiency of repentance if some action is not taken along with it: Since Solomon did not destroy the idols, it is unsure whether he was saved. For Pierre, these great figures of the Old Testament are comparable to Jean de Meun (in spite of Gerson's argument) and provide proof of his standing and not of his failure.

102. The sins of Peter and Paul are not related to sexual ones.

103. *Rose,* ed. Lecoy, l. 20322; trans. Dahlberg, 333. These and the following three passages are actually contained in Genius's sermon, but perhaps Pierre considers that the "chapter" of Nature includes the speech of her emissary.

104. *Rose,* ed. Lecoy, ll. 20391–92; trans. Dahlberg, 334.

105. *Rose,* ed. Lecoy, l. 20595; trans. Dahlberg, 337.

from the dew of the fountain, etc.?[106] As soon as he started to write, he embraced reason. And God knows to what extent he holds firm: he can hardly extricate himself from reason (while the first author had scarcely adhered to it).[107] And I don't think that when he said in his *Testament*: "In my youth I wrote many a poem out of vanity,"[108] he was referring to the book of the *Rose*; for truly, as I will explain later,[109] he was referring to some ballads, rondeaux, and virelays that we do not have in written form—at least I do not.

But let us turn to what relates to your[110] discussion. Lady Eloquence, addressing her remarks to those who support this Foolish Lover, says as follows: "Is it not madness, she says, to declare that one ought to speak crudely, lasciviously, and without shame, no matter how indecent the words might be in the opinion of all people, etc." Ha! Lady Eloquence! You are here made to articulate poorly your main point, upon which you base all of your following arguments. But do not be displeased with the person who did this, for I truly maintain that he did not do it knowingly.[111] To be sure, he got little pleasure

106. *Rose*, ed. Lecoy, l. 20498 (carbuncle), l. 20465 (olive tree); trans. Dahlberg, 336. The comparison of the Park with the Lamb, a vision of paradise, with the garden of Delight as introduced in Guillaume de Lorris's fragment is developed at length by Genius (Lecoy, ll. 19901–20596; Dahlberg, 328–37); he does not, however, praise or even mention the goddess Reason.

107. Reason comes to the narrator/Lover in the first part of the *Rose* in order to get him to quit the folly of love but is rejected by him (ed. Lecoy, ll. 2955–3082; trans. Dahlberg, 73–75). Pierre does not mention, however, that the narrator at the end of Jean de Meun's continuation, after the taking of the castle, thanks Amor and Venus for his success but specifies his disregard for Reason: "Mes de Reson ne me souvint, / qui tant en moi gasta de peine" (But I did not remember Reason who wasted so much time on me) (Lecoy, ll. 21730–31; Dahlberg, 354 [altered]).

108. *Testament*, l. 5. On the later, devout works attributed (rightly or wrongly) to Jean de Meun, see above, ch. 2, n. 112; for the works and translations he himself claims to have written in the prologue to his translation of Boethius, see below, n. 197. The *Testament* circulated widely, as it has survived in over one hundred manuscript copies, and was frequently copied in MSS with the *Romance of the Rose*. Jean famously opens it with this disavowal of his works of youth, thereby suggesting that in his old age he exchanged irreverence for piety.

109. Hicks (*Le débat*, 95) adds a negation to this clause, since, as he reasons, Pierre Col does not in fact come back to this question of Jean de Meun's "lost" poems later in his letter. But the negated clause makes little sense ("for truly, as I will not demonstrate further"). I maintain the clause as written and simply assume that while Col might have intended to return to this issue, he failed to do so.

110. Col here turns back to his direct address to Christine de Pizan, reverting to the familiar second person singular, *ton*. He is revisiting the topic of obscene language that he had already critiqued in Christine's letter to Jean de Montreuil. This back-and-forth movement between Lady Eloquence and Christine is criticized by Gerson in his response to Col (no. 28 in this volume), which he calls a "confused order" (*confuso ordine*).

111. As Gerson had accused Jean de Meun of incorrectly portraying the character of Reason (by having her, for instance, use dirty words), Pierre Col applies the same criticism to him, suggesting that he has done a disservice to his own personification.

out of this very noble book of the *Rose,* as a result of which he looked at little or nothing of it—or rather, as I'd believe more easily, because he did not look at much of it, displeasure resulted. I haven't the slightest doubt that if he had looked at it and reread it many times over, retaining it in memory—so much does his intelligence surpass that of so many others, indeed any I know of—he would all the more have praised, valued, loved, and honored it. Look here, look here at the words spoken by Reason: "Fair friend, I can very well, without creating a bad reputation for myself, name openly and by its own name a thing which is nothing if not good. In truth, I can safely speak properly of evil, etc."[112] He does not say that one has to speak of it; he says that one can speak of it. To have to and to be able to are not the same thing. I admit that seeking out opportunities to speak of the work of nature out of which arises that defilement that some people so abominate and using one's cleverness to speak of it in varied ways for the excessive pleasure one might get from it, these would be bad things to do. And it is thus that Cicero understands it in his book *De officiis* (On Duties),[113] along with the other philosophers who spoke of it in a similar fashion. But when one is speaking of a variety of different topics and, without being drawn to it by some particular ardent desire, one gets down to the private parts, one may speak properly about them. And that's the way that Master Jean de Meun spoke of them in the chapter devoted to Reason. For God's sake! One must speak of them at least on one occasion, when they were first given a name. They were not named in the beginning in order to speak of them only at that time and never again. And if it is permissible to speak of them by their proper names on one occasion, it is permissible to speak of them in the manner that Reason does. In addition, Holy Scripture names them with their proper name, as do likewise (and most explicitly) legal writings in many places. Moreover, the private parts are necessary, useful, beneficial, beautiful, and good; the Bible even forbids men who have had them cut off from entering the church, and there it names them quite literally.[114] Also, I do not believe that any of Jesus

112. *Rose,* ed. Lecoy, ll. 6915–20; trans. Dahlberg, 133.

113. Pierre Col here refers to Cicero's argument, which is rather different: "To perform these functions [the needs of Nature]—if only it be done in private—is nothing immoral; but to speak of them is indecent" (*De officiis* [Of Duties] 1.35.127; trans. Miller, 129). See above, ch. 2, n. 105, and, in this chapter, n. 30, for other references to this same text.

114. Lev 22:24: "Omne animal, quod vel contritis, vel tusis, vel sectis ablatisque testiculis est, non offeretis Domino, et in terra vestra hoc omnino ne faciatis" (You shall not offer to the Lord any beast that hath the testicles bruised, or crushed, or cut and taken away: neither shall you do any such thing in your land); Deut 23:1: "Non intrabit eunuchus, attritis vel amputatis testiculis et abscisso veretro, ecclesiam Domini" (An eunuch, whose testicles are broken or cut away, or yard cut off, shall not enter into the church of the Lord).

Christ's body parts could not be named decently. You, as well as your associates, speak of them by means of a nickname, but these nicknames were invented in order to specify more precisely these things, inasmuch as the proper names have become common to a diversity of things.[115] And Reason does not speak of the act in which there is defilement but rather names the members assigned to this and other functions.

Nonetheless, however much these names might displease certain people, they do not displease everyone (I say this because Lady Eloquence says the following: "inasmuch as the words are indecent in the judgment of all people"); hence, one must never say that "good custom" forbids people from speaking literally of them. As to whether the custom is good or evil, I remain silent. But in saying that women are not accustomed to speak of them in such a straightforward way, Lady Eloquence will not be rewarded for her originality.[116] For in the chapter of Reason it is said: "If women in France do not name them, it is nothing but their lack of custom."[117] And it is noteworthy that she says "in France," since the book is written in French, and it could indeed be the case that elsewhere than in France women name them literally. Still, I am astonished by this custom, for women certainly name their own private parts with their proper name, but they don't want to name those of men:[118] yet I don't see why theirs would be more decent than those of men.

True enough, but, as Lady Eloquence says, he [the author of the *Rose*] adhered poorly to the rules of rhetoric: for he should have been attentive to the person Reason was addressing. If she had been speaking to a cleric or to a theologian, "that would have been one thing"; but she was speaking to a

115. I have translated the Middle French word *seurnon,* which indicates a word used to substitute for another, by "nickname," inasmuch as "surname" has a different application in English and "euphemism" is semantically more specific. This sentence is somewhat unclear, but the idea (however questionable) seems to be that even though Christine and her colleagues avoid use of the proper names for indecent objects such as the sexual organs (and thus verbal obscenity), their substitute terms are in fact more specific in their denotation than the proper terms, which have acquired a wider semantic range over time.

116. The idiomatic expression used here by Col, *avoir les gants,* typically means "to receive a reward" or "to be the first one to come up with an idea" (see di Stefano, *Dictionnaire des Locutions,* 394). The context of the remark is that Theological Eloquence's statement repeats one already made by Reason, hence my translation.

117. *Rose,* ed. Lecoy, ll. 7101–2; trans. Dahlberg, 135.

118. What we have translated as "they," referring to "women," is found as *ilz,* normally the masculine plural pronoun, in the text. As Christiane Marchello-Nizia (*La langue française aux XIVe et XVe siècles,* rev. ed. [Paris: Nathan, 1997], 224) points out, however, whereas the singular *il* for the feminine is rare during this period, the plural is frequently used without gender distinction (cf. English *they*). Marchello-Nizia cites this and another example in Pierre Col's letter.

foolish lover, whose carnal desire could be aroused by such words—which would not be the case for a great cleric or theologian. It would seem from this statement that being a cleric, a philosopher, or a theologian does not admit of being at the same time a foolish lover; rather the two states are incompatible. Alas, in fact the situation is, has been, and will continue to be quite different—which is unfortunate—as was the case with David, Solomon, and others (some learned men even say that Solomon composed his Canticles for love of the Pharaoh's daughter;[119] nonetheless, he was considered to be the wisest among all who came before him and among those of his time). In short, one could adduce more than a thousand examples of men who were both clerics and foolish lovers, for they go together as well as being at once a learned man and a knight, as were Pompey, Julius Caesar, Scipio, Cicero, and others. But I believe that it is because the man who compiled this lawsuit is a cleric, a philosopher, and a theologian, without being a foolish lover, that he believes the same to be true for others. And is it not possible that he himself, in times to come, might be a foolish lover? Yes it is, by God! Yet he would be no less a cleric, at least at the outset of his foolish love. Moreover, a man does not bestir himself to love foolishly on account of someone's naming two or three private parts—for God's sake!—when it is necessary to name them in that way. At the moment Reason names them, she is preaching to the Foolish Lover that he should extricate himself from foolish love, and while speaking of diverse matters, it suited her argument to speak of the private parts. Indeed, if he had always been captivated in this way, Idleness would never have opened the door of the orchard to him;[120] furthermore, in spite of the fact that he was already a foolish lover, Reason managed to stir him to extricate himself from it, as the god of Love reproaches him for doing.[121]

119. As Hicks notes (*Le débat,* 218), this statement reports an opinion of Theodore of Mopsuestia that was condemned in 553.

120. This statement is somewhat unclear. Pierre seems to have mixed together his two major points: that it is easy for people to fall in and out of love, no matter how wise (examples of David, Solomon, even the possibility of Gerson becoming a foolish lover); and that dirty words alone will not turn someone into a foolish lover. The protagonist was not a foolish lover before entering the garden (otherwise Idleness would not have let him in), but afterward Reason manages to remove him from that state (as indicated at the close of this long sentence), in spite of her naming the private parts in the normal course of her argument.

121. The pronoun *luy* is here grammatically ambiguous, referring potentially to the Foolish Lover (reproached him) or to Reason (reproached her). However, the scene being referred to, in which the God of Love revisits the Lover in the middle of the *Rose* in order to have him reiterate his oath of homage, does include a mild reproach of the Lover for having wavered in his loyalty: "The other day you wanted to leave me. You were just a little short of robbing me of the homage due me, and you made a sorrowful complaint about Idleness and me. Moreover, you said of Hope that she was not certain in her knowledge, and you even considered yourself

And as for the assertion[122] that Master Jean de Meun in the chapter on Reason stooped to speak of the private parts not on account of any excitement that he might have gotten by speaking of them in an unglossed and licentious way, but rather because it suited the argument and also served to point out to people their foolishness when they say that in no instance is it permissible to speak of them by their proper names: this point becomes clear when elsewhere, where he speaks of the works of Nature, he does not call them by their proper name (as in the chapter devoted to Friend and the one involving the Old Woman, in which he speaks of the "game of love," the "duty of love," and "this intrigue"). Thus it must not be said that he adhered poorly to the rules of rhetoric, for he demonstrates clearly that he possessed them both naturally and through his study. I dare say that whoever reads and understands him will agree with Master Jean de Meun that one must not speak otherwise than the way he spoke. And when Lady Eloquence claims that he portrays Nature speaking of God, I reply that Nature can and ought to do it, and that the chambermaid certainly can speak to her master. Likewise Saint Augustine, in his book the *Soliloquies,* where he has the devout soul ask the earth and the other elements whether they are her god: they answer no and direct her to search higher, after which Augustine says that the responses of things are the attestation of God.[123] Thus Meun wanted to show that he was being both natural and Christian in speaking of Nature, but he was also a poet, as I have said, by virtue of which he was allowed to speak of everything through fictions.

True enough, but, says Lady Eloquence, this Foolish Lover has Reason say things that previously Cupid forbade. And then Lady Eloquence makes a show of correcting herself: "Wait," she says, "it was not one and the same author, but rather the author upon whose beginning Meun constructed his

---

a fool for coming into my service, and you agreed with Reason" (*Rose,* ed. Lecoy, ll. 10299–307; trans. Dahlberg, 184). It is worth noting that the passage being referred to by the God of Love is located in the opening lines of Jean de Meun's continuation, between the Lover's first encounter with Reason in Guillaume de Lorris's part and the second encounter being discussed here by Pierre Col.

122. See above in the text: "But when one is speaking of a variety of different topics and, without being drawn to it by some particular ardent desire, one gets down to the private parts, one may speak properly about them."

123. Saint Augustine, *Soliloquiorum animae ad Deum* (Soliloquies of the Soul to God), chap. 31 (*PL* 40, col. 888): "Interrogavi terram si esset Deus meus, et dixit mihi quod non; et omnia quae in ea sunt, hoc idem confessa sunt. Interrogavi mare et abyssos, et reptilia quae in eis sunt; et responderunt: Non sumus Deus tuus; quaere super nos eum" (I asked the earth if it was my God, and it said "no" to me; and all the things that are in it confessed the same thing. I asked the sea and abysses, as well as the crawling beasts that are in them; and they responded: "We are not your God; look for him above us.").

work." The foundations were solid and untarnished, and the latter placed on top of it a heap of muddy filth. This is very well said indeed! To what end, I ask her, does Cupid give the rosebud (in other words, allowing him to succeed in his foolish amorous enterprise)? Certainly, this is an incredible contradiction: he[124] blames Reason, who castigates the Lover for being a foolish lover, and praises Cupid, who teaches how one can accomplish one's goal.

But you[125] cannot remain silent, so you say, regarding Reason's statement that "in the war of love, it is better to deceive than to be deceived," arguing that "it follows from this that both are good, which cannot be." By my oath, it would have been to your benefit if you had refrained from writing this argument. It is not something to put formally into writing. No, it is for schoolchildren who are at a loss and lacking any other arguments, when several of them are assembled to debate one same proposition. Did not Jesus Christ say it would have been better for Judas if he had never existed than to have betrayed his master?[126] It would follow, according to your argument, that both are good. One must not take words literally in this way, but according to the preceding words and the intention of the author. The verse immediately preceding these four that you invoked is: "But such people are less deceived than the others."[127] I do not believe that this amounts to saying that it is good to deceive. Furthermore, I maintain that it would be better for me—which is to say that it would harm me less—to pretend that I love you in order to take carnal pleasure in your body than if, to achieve this same goal, I became a foolish lover because of it, as a result of which I would abandon my learning, "sense, time, possessions, body, soul, and reputation" (as has been said). For all the evils that follow from the first case follow from the second, but all those that follow from the second do not follow from the first. In any event, I consider that these four verses ("For it is always better, dear master, etc.") and some others have been interpolated: those who do such a thing are as a result committing a great error, for I do not see that one can add anything to the text or take anything away without spoiling it.

124. The transition from the feminine character Eloquence to the masculine pronoun used here (*il*) suggests that, as elsewhere, Pierre Col goes back and forth between speaking of the fictional character and attributing what she says to the putative author, Jean Gerson.

125. Once again, Pierre Col returns to the informal *tu*, switching his direct address back to Christine.

126. Mt 26:24: "Filius quidem hominis vadit, sicut scriptum est de illo: væ autem homini illi, per quem Filius hominis tradetur! bonum erat ei, si natus non fuisset homo ille" (The Son of man indeed goeth, as it is written of him: but woe to that man by whom the Son of man shall be betrayed: it were better for him, if that man had not been born).

127. *Rose*, ed. Lecoy, l. 4368; trans. Dahlberg, 96.

Now let us move forward: "What indecency there is (so speaks Lady Eloquence, and you as well)[128] in this chapter about the Old Woman! What can one find there except total filth?" And similarly in the chapter on Jealousy. And you would really like to have found someone capable of explaining to you—in a way that your judgment might be appeased—"what profit can be derived from so many indecent words that are in this book . . ." However, you affirm, "I do not condemn the author in all parts of the said book . . . ," as though you wished to say that you condemn him for what you reproach him for, fashioning yourself as a judge—this after having spoken based upon opinion or reckless presumption. Oh, what very foolish arrogance! Oh, what a speech issuing forth too rashly and thoughtlessly from the mouth of a woman, which condemns a man of such lofty intellect, of such devoted scholarship, who with such great effort and mature reflection made a book of such great nobility as that of the *Rose,* which indeed surpasses all others that have ever used the language in which he wrote his book. When you have read it a hundred times, if you understand the better part of it, you will never have better used your time or your intellect. Truly, the person who compiled the lawsuit of Lady Eloquence was more prudent and more gracious than you were, for he said at the end of his legal appeal that he did not hear any judgment being rendered. But after all! According to what Terence said ("Obsequiousness makes friends, the truth makes you unpopular"),[129] I suspect that because he said the truth you wish to bite him. But I advise you to watch out for your teeth.

I respond to Lady Eloquence and to you with one and the same answer, and state that Master Jean de Meun presented personages in his book, and makes each personage speak according to what pertains to him—which is to say, the Jealous Man like a jealous person, the Old Woman like an old woman, and likewise for the others. And it is quite mistaken to say that the author considers the defects that the Jealous Man describes, in acting out his personage, to be actually found in women. He certainly does not, but rather reports what a jealous man says every day about all women, and he does so in order to illustrate and to correct the very great irrationality and the disordered passion that are to be found in a jealous man. And the reason why a jealous man says (that is, the reason that impels him to say) so many nasty things about all women, and not solely about his own wife, is

128. This is in fact a passage quoted from Christine's letter (no. 5) and is considerably shortened.

129. *Andria* 1.68: "obsequium amicos, veritas odium parit" (obsequiousness makes friends, the truth makes you unpopular). This same passage is alluded to by Jean de Montreuil in one of his Latin letters (no. 7).

that as a general rule, it seems to me, every married man, before becoming jealous, believes he has the best wife, or at least as good a one as exists. And this belief originates in part, as I see it, from the love that he has for her—and a beloved object is not easily mistrusted! This love arises because the wife belongs to him, and our own possessions seem better and more beautiful than those of others; also, in part, because the woman behaves as impeccably and as demurely as she can in the presence of her husband—even assuming that in his absence she acts wantonly. This is why, as Saint Jerome says in one of his epistles, "every man is typically the last to know the misfortunes of his own household."[130] I do believe there are a lot of other reasons, but nonetheless, whatever reason there might be, experience demonstrates what I said previously, namely, that a man, before becoming jealous, believes his wife to be the best or as good as there is, especially with regard to chastity. And it is a good thing to think this way in marriage, according to the moderation promoted by Terence (namely, "nothing in excess"),[131] for otherwise there would be no peace between spouses. This was the way Aspasia created harmony between Xenophon and his wife, as Cicero recounts in his *De inventione.*[132] This is why, when jealousy comes upon a husband, and he suspects some misbehavior in the woman that he previously considered so good that there was no cause for distress—assuming that she is not guilty, as often happens—he, in a sudden burst of anger, engulfed in this rage and disordered passion known as jealousy, which is rightly termed a ruthless illness, says that all women are like that. This is what Aristotle says in his *Rhetoric:* that whoever has a noxious neighbor believes that all the others are the same.[133] If, in a given kingdom, a knight has the reputation of being the strongest, the most adroit, the boldest and sharpest in the exercise of arms

130. Jerome, Letter 147 (*Ad Sabinianum lapsum* [To the fallen Sabinianum]), *PL* 22, col. 1203: "Solemus mala domus nostrae scire novissimi, ac liberorum et conjugum vitia, vicinis canentibus, ignorare" (We are accustomed to be the last to know the ills of our home, and to ignore the vices of our spouses and children, while the neighbors sing them out). Hicks (*Le débat,* 219) notes that this passage is also cited by Abelard in his *Historia calamitatum* (Story of My Calamities).

131. *Andria* 1.61: "ne quid nimis."

132. *De inventione* (On Invention) 1.31, 51–53.

133. *Rhetoric,* book 2, chap. 21 (1395b): "The maxim, as has already been said, is a general statement, and people love to hear stated in general terms what they already believe in some particular connection: e.g. if a man happens to have bad neighbors or bad children, he will agree with anyone who tells him, 'Nothing is more annoying than having neighbors,' or 'Nothing is more foolish than to be the parent of children'" (*The Complete Works of Aristotle: The Revised Oxford Translation,* ed. Jonathan Barnes, 2 vols., Bollingen Series, 71 [Princeton: Princeton University Press, 1984], 2:2223).

and everyone considers him to be so, and a foreign knight were to come along who defeated him in chivalric combat, people would consider that there was no other knight in that kingdom that the foreigner would not have defeated. Similarly a jealous man brings judgment upon all women when he considers his own to be fallen, especially those men who, before jealousy overcame them, believed most deeply in their wives and considered them to be good and chaste.

Now for the comparisons made by Lady Eloquence. "If someone proclaims himself an adversary of the king of France (so says Lady Eloquence) and under this name wages war against him . . . ; if through the personage of a Saracen . . . someone sows errors of faith, will he be excused for it?" And she makes other similar ones, which are scarcely relevant. I ask her: For that matter, if Sallust recounts the conspiracy of Catiline against the republic of Rome, is he guilty of conspiracy on account of this?[134] For that matter, if Aristotle rehearses the opinions of ancient philosophers containing philosophical errors, is he sowing errors in doing so? Likewise, if Holy Scripture tells of the abominable sins of Sodom and Gomorrah, is it exhorting people to imitate them?[135] When you go to a sermon, do you not hear preachers attack the vices that men and women commit every day, in order that they follow the right path? In good faith, young lady, the answer is yes: one must be reminded of the foot on which one is limping in order to walk straighter![136]

Ha! Lady Chastity! Is this the reward you wish to confer upon Master Jean de Meun, who so esteemed you and all the other virtues, while blaming all the vices that human understanding can conceive? Truly, that human understanding can conceive. Don't smile at this! I maintain that whoever reads this book carefully and often, in order to understand it better, will find instruction for fleeing all vices and pursuing all virtues. Indeed, does he not say in the chapter of the Jealous Man that "no one who lives a chaste life

134. Jean de Meun quotes a passage from Sallust in the midst of his authorial apology (*Rose*, ed. Lecoy, ll. 15147–62; trans. Dahlberg, 258). Pierre Col's evocation of Sallust here is obliquely but not necessarily directly related to or inspired by Jean's. Whereas Pierre is talking about one's ability to report stories (or in the following example of Aristotle, to describe philosophical doctrine) from an external perspective without being guilty for what they represent, Jean's quotation of Sallust has to do with the need to use the words required by the subject matter ("the words must be neighbor to the deed" [l. 15161]). What unites the two is their attempt to defend speech against adverse criticism.

135. Gen 18:20–33 and 19:1–28.

136. Here, Pierre Col switches back to address Christine. The image of the limping person is drawn from the concluding passages of Christine's letter, thus pointing out the strong parallels between her discourse and that of Gerson.

can come to damnation")?[137] And in the chapter of Reason: "Do you know what they do who go seeking delight? They give themselves up, like serfs or foolish wretches, to the prince of all vices"?[138] And that "[to seek delight] is the root of all evil, as Tully [Cicero][139] concludes . . . Youth pushes men into folly, debauchery, ribaldry, lechery, excesses"? And to blame the vices further he says that "the wicked are not men."[140] And in the chapter of the Jealous Man he says that all the vices made Poverty leap out of hell to populate the world;[141] and of Shame he says that she restrains and disciplines.[142] He speaks out even more against men than against women: Does he not in the chapter of Nature reprove twenty-six vices with which men are blemished?[143] And in so many other places that I will skip over them, for they are innumerable (in the chapter of Nature, [he says] that clerics given over to vices ought to be more severely punished than lay people and plain folk;[144] and that nobility lies in the virtues, among which virtues he includes honoring ladies and maidens).[145] By God! This does not amount to blaming the entire female sex! (I say this to counter your excuse placed in the closing words of your letter.)[146] Saint Ambrose, in one of his sermons, blames the female sex more; for he says that it is a sex accustomed to deceiving.[147] In

137. *Rose*, ed. Lecoy, ll. 8981–82; trans. Dahlberg, 163. Jean de Meun has the Jealous Husband point out, l. 8979, that this statement is quoted (rather, adapted) from Virgil's *Aeneid* 6.563: "nulli fas casto sceleratum insistere limen" (no pure soul may tread the accursed threshold).

138. *Rose*, ed. Lecoy, ll. 4395–98; trans. Dahlberg, 96.

139. *Rose*, ed. Lecoy, ll. 4399–4400, 4433–35; trans. Dahlberg, 96–97. As Reason points out, these thoughts are taken from Cicero's *De senectute* (On Old Age).

140. *Rose*, ed. Lecoy, l. 6292; trans. Dahlberg, 124.

141. *Rose*, ed. Lecoy, ll. 9496–9508; trans. Dahlberg, 171.

142. *Rose*, ed. Lecoy, ll. 14077–78; trans. Dahlberg, 241.

143. *Rose*, ed. Lecoy, ll. 19195–204 and 19840; trans. Dahlberg, 317, 327. In order to counter charges of Jean de Meun's misogyny, Pierre Col slyly transforms Nature's enumeration of man's (meaning "mankind's") sins into those of men, as though she were drawing a gender distinction between men and women, which she is not.

144. *Rose*, ed. Lecoy, ll. 18633–36; trans. Dahlberg, 309.

145. *Rose*, ed. Lecoy, ll. 18659; trans. Dahlberg, 309.

146. Christine had in the closing lines of her letter to Jean de Montreuil (no. 5) justified her attack upon Jean de Meun by providing the excuse that he, one single man, had defamed an entire sex.

147. Hicks (*Le débat*, 220) adduces the following passage from Ambrose's *Hexameron* that Augustine quotes in the fourth book of his *On Christian Doctrine* (4.21.50), a text to which Pierre Col refers later in this letter: "Pictus es ergo, o homo, et pictus a Domino Deo tuo. Bonum habes artificem atque pictorem. Noli bonam delere picturam, non fuco sed veritate fulgentem, non cera expressam sed gratia. Deles picturam, mulier, si vultum tuum materiali candore oblinas, si

fact, you do the same thing. You are not solely blaming Meun when you say that if one read the book of the *Rose* before queens, princesses, and other distinguished ladies, they would be obliged to cover their faces, blushing with shame. After all, why would they blush? It seems that they would feel guilty of the vices of women that the Jealous Man enumerates.

Nor does he criticize religion, as Lady Eloquence accuses him of doing. It is quite true that he says that Hypocrisy "has betrayed many a region with his religious habit."[148] He does not say "with religion" but "with his religious habit." For, as he says, "if you were to put the fleece of Dame Belin, instead of a sable mantle, on Sir Isengrin, etc."[149] And this is what both you and Lady Eloquence have stated in other words, namely, the idea of mixing "honey with venom"[150] in order to cause more harm. And as for Lady Eloquence's claim that he says that young people are not at all stable in their religious faith, I maintain that when a young man enters religion out of youthful whim and not out of devotion, he will not be resolute in that devotion. Indeed, this is what Jean de Meun says in the chapter of the Old Woman,

---

acquisito rubore perfundas. Illa pictura vitii, non decoris est: illa pictura fraudis, non simplicitatis est: illa pictura temporalis est, aut pluvia, aut sudore tergitur: illa pictura fallit et decipit; ut neque illi placeas, cui placere desideras, qui intelligit non tuum, sed alienum esse quod placeas; et tuo displiceas auctori, qui videt opus suum esse deletum." (Therefore you have been adorned, O man, and adorned by the Lord your God. Consider the artisan and the painter to be good. Do not scratch out this good painting, resplendent not with a purplish hue but with the truth, represented not with makeup but with grace. You disfigure the painting, woman, if you smear your face with material luster, or cover it with artificial rouge. That is a painting of vice, not beauty; it is of fraud, not innocence. That painting is ephemeral; it is erased either by rain or by sweat. That painting misleads and deceives: May you not strive to please the one you want to please, lest he understand what pleases not to be yours but someone else's and lest you displease your creator who sees that his work has been disfigured) (6.8.47 [*PL* 14, col. 260c–d]).

148. *Rose,* ed. Lecoy, ll. 10443–44; trans. Dahlberg, 186.

149. *Rose,* ed. Lecoy, ll. 11093–95; trans. Dahlberg, 195). In this quotation of the words of False Seeming, the figure who represents religious hypocrisy and who, somewhat paradoxically, reveals the "truth" of hypocrites, he states that what matters is how people are inside and not what they wear. Lay people can be as devout as (or more devout than) those who have taken religious vows. Likewise, the wolf Isengrin, one of the protagonists of the well-known beast fable the *Roman de Renart,* would devour ewes even if he were clothed in the fleece of Lady Belin, the sheep.

150. The accusation of mixing honey with venom is in fact contained in the eighth article of Chastity's supplication. Lady Theological Eloquence will speak of coating a sword with honey. Christine does not use this image but does make the same point: the inclusion of good lessons in the *Rose* makes the work even more dangerous, because bad teachings are made credible when mixed together with the good. Thus, according to Pierre Col's argument, Jean de Meun makes precisely the same point as his two critics when he reveals the potential deception of those wearing religious garb (but having on the inside harmful, not pious, thoughts).

and you can see here the words themselves: "It is the same, I tell you, with the man who goes into a religious order and comes to repent of it afterward. He needs only a little more grief to hang himself."[151] Thus, clearly, the presupposition is that he is speaking of a man who is repentant about having entered a religious order—as often happens. Then he says afterward that "he will never have shoes or hood or cowl so large that Nature will not remain hidden in his heart, etc.").[152] And a bit after that he says: "By my soul, fair son, it is thus with every man and every woman as far as natural appetite goes, etc."[153] It is certain that man's natural appetite does not incline him to force himself never to eat meat, or to remain chaste or poor his entire life, or to be forever faithful to one woman; or, likewise for a woman, to be forever faithful to one man. As Lady Eloquence herself suggests, our frailty is inclined to vices. Does she thereby wish to praise these vices? Not at all! Likewise, if Master Jean de Meun claims that our natural appetite turns not to religion but to its contrary, he does not thereby wish to criticize religion and praise its contrary.

But on this point you will reply to me that I am quoting the good words and not the evil ones, which incite to lechery and teach how to take the castle of Jealousy; and Lady Eloquence claims that he wishes to drive Chastity out of all women. I respond by telling you that in all forms of war it is a greater advantage to be a defender than an assailant, provided that one is warned beforehand. Thus, let us assume that Jealousy had a strongly fortified castle built, that she posted competent guards to protect it, and that this castle was taken by means of a certain type of attack. If Jean de Meun wrote about the manner in which it was taken, does he not provide a greater advantage to the guards of the castle, by having taught them through which point of entry it was taken (so as to protect themselves henceforth by blocking the opening through which it happened or by posting better guards there), than he does to those who would wish to attack it? By God, yes indeed, taking as a given what I said previously—that it is an advantage to be a defender. And especially since he describes the way of taking it in a language that is common to men and to women, young and old, namely, in French.

Ovid, when he wrote the *Art of Love,* wrote in Latin, which women do

151. *Rose,* ed. Lecoy, ll. 13937–40; trans. Dahlberg, 239.

152. *Rose,* ed. Lecoy, ll. 13979–82; trans. Dahlberg, 240. I have altered Dahlberg's translation which states the opposite of what is given in the old French ("so large that Nature may be hidden in his heart"). The idea is that Nature remains lodged in one's heart, no matter what clothing one puts on.

153. *Rose,* ed. Lecoy, ll. 14057–59; trans. Dahlberg, 241.

not understand.[154] So he gave it only to the assailants in order to teach them to attack the castle. That was the goal of his book, and without speaking through personages (but he [Jean de Meun], like Ovid, gave all his teachings). Because of this, and by means of the most exceptional jealousy of Roman husbands, he was exiled—what am I saying, "by means of"!—certainly it *was* the beginning, middle and end explaining why he was exiled—yes it was, the very great and cruel jealousy of Roman husbands![155] As I have heard tell from people who have been to many countries, the wife of the least jealous man in the countries of Italy and of Greece[156] is reined in more closely than the wife of the most jealous man in France. And this is why, if Ovid was exiled, it was because of jealousy. When a man, even after having written against the faith, recants, he will never be exiled, but his book will be burned. Yet the book for which Ovid was exiled endures, will endure, and has endured for all of Christianity, even though Ovid also recanted when he wrote the book called the *Remedia amoris*.[157] I truly do not understand how this exile can be reasonably justified. I say that if a book is the motive for exiling

154. One can only imagine that Pierre Col is facetiously suggesting that Roman women did not understand Latin, perhaps as a way of calling into question Christine's knowledge of Latin and therefore weakening her credentials.

155. Pierre Col makes here an untranslatable pun on the preposition *moyennant* (by means of, on account of) and the word from which it is derived, *moyen* (< Lat. *medianus*), which means literally "something in the middle" (hence, "beginning, middle, and end") but also "means" (from the word's extended meaning of "intermediary").

156. The word used here by Pierre Col is "Rommenie" and, further down in this paragraph, "Ronmain." This place name seems to have had various applications, referring for instance to the Byzantine Empire in the twelfth century. After the capture of Constantinople in 1204, the Latin Empire established there was referred to by that name, *Imperium Romaniae*. By the time of the debate, it would appear that the name was generally used to refer to Greece, as by this anonymous writer in 1395: "ung estroit passage en mer par ou les vaisseaux vont en Rommenie que l'en souloit appeller Grecce" (a narrow passage on the sea where ships go to *Rommenie*, which used to be called Greece). Perhaps it had a less specific association for Pierre Col, but nonetheless undoubtedly referred to a Greek-speaking Christian empire in Asia Minor. It makes little sense to translate these two names as referring to Italy and Rome (cf. Baird/Kane, *La querelle de la Rose*, 108; Greene, *Le débat*, 212), as though the two were entirely separate entities. The adjectival form *ronmain* does, however, seem to be ambiguous, as it is used to refer to Roman husbands in the context of Ovid, but undoubtedly to Greek men, when juxtaposed with the nominalized adjective "Italian" later in this paragraph.

157. As Hicks points out (*Le débat*, 220), Ovid does not actually recant in the *Remedia amoris* (Remedies for Love) 7–12; *Art of Love and Other Poems*, trans. Mozley, 178–79: "ego semper amavi, / Et si, quid faciam, nunc quoque, quaeris, amo. / Quin etiam docui, qua posses arte parari, / Et quod nunc ratio est, impetus ante fuit. / Nec te, blande puer, nec nostras prodimus artes, / Nec nova praeteritum Musa retexit opus." (I have ever been a lover, and if thou askest what I am doing, I am a lover still. Nay too, I have taught by what skill thou mightest be gained, and what was impulse then is science now. Neither thee do I betray, O winsome boy, nor mine own craft, nor does the new Muse unravel the old work.)

its author, then the book should first be exiled. However, regarding what Lady Theological Eloquence said, namely, that "wine that will not harm a healthy man will make one trembling with fever delirious," likewise I maintain that a glance given by the wife[158] of a Greek or an Italian will, as I have heard say, provide the husband grounds to poison her and thus to murder her mercilessly, whereas in France a kiss would not provide grounds to pick a quarrel with one's wife or so much as strike her. Also, it makes no sense to claim [by way of criticism] that Jean de Meun incorporated into his book not only Ovid's *Art of Love* but also works by many other authors, for the more he details different methods of attack, the more he provides counsel to the guards of the castle so that they may defend themselves from it. And it was to this end that he wrote it. In truth, I know a man—a foolish lover—who, in order to extricate himself from foolish love, borrowed the *Romance of the Rose* from me: and I heard him swear under oath that it was the thing that most helped him to free himself from it. (I say this because you query, "How many have become hermits or entered religion on account of it?" adding that he went to great pains for nothing).[159]

158. Hicks (*Le débat,* 105) provides "la fournie ou la fame"; I have not been able to find the word *fourni(e)* elsewhere, other than as the past participle of the verb *fournir* or as an adjective derived from it, meaning "(well) equipped." Baird/Kane (*La querelle de la Rose,* 108) translate the passage "the sister or wife," whereas Greene (*Le débat,* 212) has "la maîtresse ou la femme," but such a reading is purely hypothetical. It could be explained as an assimilation between the past participle (feminine) of the verb *fournir* (meaning "to hand over or provide," hence "a woman who has been granted" or a prostitute) and the idiomatic expression *emprunter (prendre) son pain sur la fournee,* which means literally "to take one's bread from the batch fresh out of the oven" (*fournee,* from *four* [oven], means "the amount of bread that can be baked at the same time in an oven"), but referred to a man having sexual relations with his girlfriend prior to marriage. However, scrutiny of the manuscript provides another possibility. The manuscript has an *f* followed by what looks like an *o,* then six minims, then an *e.* Now, in this scribe's hand, the minim could stand, singly, for an *i* or an *r* or, in combination, for a *u* or an *n* (two minims) or an *m* (three minims). But also, typically, the scribe uses a fine, elongated superscript line to demarcate an *i;* there is no such line highlighting this word, indicating that *fournie* is a less likely reading of this word. Indeed, Ward ("Epistles on the Romance of the Rose," 70) had transcribed the word as *fourme,* which, however, makes as little sense as *fournie.* One other issue of note: whereas the scribe typically differentiates *o* and *e,* with the former formed by a complete circle and the latter showing a distinct space between the upper curve and the lower one, there are several examples of an *e* that is closed, very nearly like an *o.* I would hypothesize that the word is actually to be read as *femme* and that what we have here is simply an example of dittography, undoubtedly committed in the model of our scribe (I might add that the second occurrence of the word is written as *fae* with a nasalization line above it—a very common shorthand for this scribe, hence Hicks's transcription *fame*). This hypothesis actually accords better with the context, for in the rest of the sentence it is a question only of husbands and wives, and not men and their lovers in a general sense.

159. Here, once again, Pierre's use of the singular *tu* denotes a switch from Lady Eloquence's argument (about Jean de Meun's borrowings from several authors) to Christine's statement, the

What is more, the Old Woman, whom you and Lady Eloquence blame so much, formally declares, before preaching to Fair Welcoming: "I must tell you at the outset that I don't want to put you in the way of love, but if you want to get involved with it, I will gladly show you the roads and the paths by which I should have traveled, etc."[160] And afterward she states explicitly to Fair Welcoming that the reason why she is preaching to him is so that he will not be deceived in this affair: "he is a great fool, so help me God, who believes in the oaths of lovers."[161] And if there are passages that seem excessively bawdy, or overly defamatory of the female sex, he is quoting the authors who have said these things, for, as he puts it, in those passages he does "nothing but retell."[162] Thus it seems to me that one ought first to blame the authors rather than those who quote them, as I have already said. But you will reply to me: "Why did he quote them?" I claim that he did it in order to teach the gatekeepers more effectively how better to protect the castle; and also because these passages are relevant to his discussion. For his intention was to continue the subject matter undertaken and treated by Guillaume de Lorris and, in so doing, to speak of all things according to their station for the benefit of humankind, as much for the soul as for the body. It is for this reason that he speaks of paradise and of the virtues—in order for people to pursue them (and of the vices, in order for people to flee them). And the more he speaks of vices and virtues, of hell and paradise, the one next to the other, the better he shows the beauty of the one and the ugliness of the other. And what he says in the chapters of Jealousy and of the Old Woman, as well as in other places, concerning the act of love, was done in the course of continuing the work initiated by Guillaume de Lorris.

Nor does Genius promise paradise to foolish lovers, as Lady Eloquence accuses him of doing. For he is speaking of those who virtuously carry out the works of Nature, and it is not the same thing to carry out the works of Nature virtuously and to be a foolish lover. Neither Nature nor Genius urges that one be a foolish lover, but both exhort the pursuit of the works

latter part of which seems not to be a direct quotation but rather a paraphrase of what I have translated above as "great effort was made—just without any profit" (no. 5). This passage, by the way, is not found in the version of Christine's letter contained in the "rhodophile" manuscript. This same idea is also expressed toward the beginning of Christine's letter, but with a general, not specific, thrust: "anything lacking value, however great the labor and effort with which it may have been conceived, composed, and brought to completion, can be called idle."

160. *Rose*, ed. Lecoy, ll. 12940–45; trans. Dahlberg, 225 (altered).

161. *Rose*, ed. Lecoy, ll. 13109–10; trans. Dahlberg, 227. The first line of Pierre Col's quotation differs from the one printed in Lecoy's edition.

162. *Rose*, ed. Lecoy, l. 15204; trans. Dahlberg, 259.

of Nature, which are permissible for the purposes they specify in urging their performance, namely, in order to continue the human species and to refrain from the act that is contrary to Nature, about which, abominable as it is, no more is to be said. And although I neither dare nor wish to say that to perform the work of Nature for the two above-mentioned goals outside wedlock is not a sin, nonetheless I dare say that it is permitted to perform it for these two purposes within the bounds of marriage. And this is what Jean de Meun says in the chapter of the Old Woman: "For this reason men made marriages, through the counsel of wise men . . . in order to prevent dissolute conduct, contention, and murders and to help in the rearing of children, who are their joint responsibility."[163] By God! To say that marriage was decreed by wise men is not to blame it! I will, however, tell you what Saint Augustine says about it in his book of *Confessions*: "It is a good thing for a man not to touch a woman"; and "He who is without a wife in marriage thinks of matters concerning God in order to please him; but he who is joined in marriage thinks of worldly matters in order to please his wife."[164] I remind you of this, you and those who, without reason, endeavor through their words to instruct and correct an author who is renowned and who has never previously been reproached—even though it might be that he[165] is even more knowledgeable than the person calling it [Augustine's statement] to mind. But there is no person so hopelessly deaf as he who does not want to hear.[166]

163. *Rose*, ed. Lecoy, ll. 13885–86; trans. Dahlberg, 238 (altered). Pierre Col has essentially rewritten Jean de Meun's text here, altering the text of line 13885 (changing the original "before men made marriages" to "for this reason men made marriages") and joining these two lines with a passage drawn from a different, previous sentence (ll. 13,861–64). The context of these passages in the *Rose* is not only different from its presentation here but actually nearly the opposite. The Old Woman is speaking of women's natural desire to be free, *in spite of* the social needs for marriage bonds. Marriage is thus at odds with nature rather than in accord with it, as Pierre Col would have it.

164. Augustine is actually quoting/paraphrasing here Saint Paul (1 Cor 7:1 [for the first quotation] and 7:32–33 [for the second one]): *"Bonum est homini mulierem non tangere;* et, *Qui sine uxore est, cogitat ea quae sunt Dei, quomodo placeat Deo: qui autem matrimonio junctus est, cogitat ea quae sunt mundi, quomodo placeat uxori"* (*Confessions* 2.2 [*PL* 32, col. 676]).

165. In a slippage not atypical for Pierre Col, after having spoken of Christine, whom he is addressing, and of unmentioned critics of Jean de Meun in the plural, he continues with a singular masculine pronoun. The only other singular used in this passage is the word "author," but it would make no sense for this to refer to Jean de Meun (the person). Pierre Col certainly has in mind Gerson, author of the treatise featuring Lady Eloquence, and the only person to whom he is likely to defer regarding familiarity with the text of Saint Augustine or the latter's views on marriage. This also forms a continuity with the last sentence of the paragraph: Gerson is clearly the person who does not want to hear.

166. This is a well-known proverb: see Morawski, *Proverbes français*, no. 940.

It thus seems that if the work of Nature is permissible in some cases, it is not bad in itself, but rather because of some incidental factor. If Genius encourages people to accomplish the works of Nature specifically for the two goals that I have mentioned (adding that it is permissible to perform them, at least in marriage, and promising paradise to those who pursue them well "providing that they guard themselves well against the vices"—these are his very words),[167] I do not see any wrong in it. And since not everyone has read the book of the *Rose*, I will here quote Genius's own words. May I be excused, however, if I go on quoting the book's very words at too great a length, here and elsewhere. Two reasons compel me to do it. One is so that people not think that I am saying something that is not in the book, since there are many who have never read it, as I have said; the other reason is that I could not express an idea in prose as concisely as Jean de Meun does it with his rich rhymes. Here, therefore, are the words of Genius: "[Let him] who struggles to love well, without any base thought, but with lawful labor, go off to paradise decked with flowers; as long as he makes a good confession, I will take on me all his deeds with such power as I can bring to them."[168] And, in order to recapitulate his sermon, he says: "Think how to do honor to Nature; serve her well by working well. If you get anything from someone else, give it back, if you know how, and if you cannot give back the good things that are spent or played away, have the good will to do so when you have benefits in plenty. Avoid killing; keep both hands and mouth clean. Be loyal and compassionate, and then you will go by the delectable fields, following the path of the lamb, etc."[169] This is in brief the recapitulation of Genius's entire sermon and his understanding of the things he stated previously. Since this is his stated intention, and given that you, as well as those who reproach him, have read it[170] in full, why do you not pay heed to it?

167. *Rose*, ed. Lecoy, l. 19360; trans. Dahlberg, 319. I have emended Dahlberg's translation, as he mistakenly translates the locution *mes que* as "But" instead of "providing that." These are in fact the words of Nature and not of Genius, as Pierre Col claims.

168. *Rose*, ed. Lecoy, ll. 19505–11; trans. Dahlberg, 322.

169. *Rose*, ed. Lecoy, ll. 20607–19; trans. Dahlberg, 337–38.

170. "It" could conceivably be referring to the "recapitulation" or to the "entire sermon," but since the past participle *leu* does not accord with the feminine noun *recapitulacion*, it is without any doubt referring to the entire sermon. Up to this point, when Pierre Col has used the second-person pronoun, it has most often been the singular form, *tu*, referring unambiguously to Christine, to whom the letter is addressed. However, here and for the rest of the letter, he uses both forms, wishing to address both Christine individually and a collective that includes (perhaps along with Gerson, or perhaps not) the other unnamed opponents of the *Rose* who are vaguely alluded to from the beginning of the letter (in the first paragraph, Pierre refers to

I really cannot sufficiently express my astonishment at how anyone dares blame this author—and I am speaking not only about him but also about those who esteem and love his book of the *Rose*. As for myself, in honest truth I would rather be among those who are blamed and reproached for esteeming and loving the book of the *Rose* than one of its clever accusers and critics. Moreover, let all those who reproach it know that there still remain seven thousand at the ready to defend it, who would not bend their knees before Baal.[171] If he were to have lived at the same time as the group of you who blame him, I would posit that you had an express hatred for him personally; but you have never seen him. So I cannot imagine where it comes from, unless it is on account of the very lofty grandeur of the book, all the more susceptible of being buffeted by the winds of envy.[172] For ignorance is not the cause of it in any among you, unless, however, it were to have come from having read little of the book of the *Rose*; or it is perhaps that you are only pretending to blame the book in question for the purpose of exalting it by stimulating those hearing your words to read it, for you know well that whoever reads it will find the opposite of what you have written about it and consider all the teachings to be most remarkable. And in this case the accusers ought to be considered completely pardoned, for their goal and their intention would be good, whatever means might have been used.

So I beg you, woman of great ingenuity, to preserve the honor you have acquired for the breadth of your intellect and your finely tuned linguistic skills. For if people have praised you for having shot a little cannonball over the towers of Notre-Dame, do not on account of this put yourself to the test of trying to hit the moon with a heavy, massive arrow. Beware, lest you resemble the crow, who, because people praised his song, began to sing louder than was his custom and let his mouthful drop.[173] And for a final

"you and others who, like yourself, endeavor to attack this very noble writer, Meun"). Even prior to Gerson's intervention, Gontier Col had referred, in no. 13, to "those who have denounced this work."

171. 3 Kings [1 Kings] 19:18: "et derelinquam mihi in Israël septem millia virorum, quorum genua non sunt incurvata ante Baal, et omne os quod non adoravit eum osculans manum" (And I will leave me seven thousand men in Israel, whose knees have not been bowed before Baal, and every mouth that hath not worshipped him kissing the hands).

172. Quotation from Ovid's *Remedia amoris* (Remedies for Love) 369 (trans. Mozley, 202–3): "Summa petit livor; perflant altissima venti" (What is highest is Envy's mark; winds sweep the summits). The Latin is quoted directly by Peter Abelard in his *Historia calamitatum* (Story of My Calamities) (*La vie et les epistres Pierres Abaelart et Heloys sa fame*, ed. Hicks, 6).

173. Beast fables, such as those going back to Aesop, were widely circulated in collections known as "Isopets." The fable of the fox and the crow, best known to us from La Fontaine's ver-

resolution, I entreat all men and women who wish to reprimand or blame it[174] in whatever part to read it first at least four times, taking their time in order to understand it better; and I trust their thoughtful reading will provide a conclusive explanation.[175] But if they don't wish to do any of this, let them consider his purpose in writing the book, let them read his apology without being predisposed against it, and I have no doubt that they will consider him to be pardoned, for no apology or response is necessary other than the one he places directly prior to the beginning of the attack. For there and there alone does he speak as the author, and there, as author, he declares: "No one should despise a woman unless he has the worst heart among all the wicked ones."[176] He then makes a solemn declaration that it is not his intention "to speak against any living man who follows holy religion or who spends his life in good works, no matter what robe he covers himself with . . ."[177] and that if there are words either too bawdy or too foolish, "my subject matter demanded these things; it draws me to such words by its own properties,"[178] and that in the book he does "nothing but retell."[179] And, generally, he affirms that he never said anything that was not "for our

---

sion, would have been quite accessible at this time. Cf. *Recueil général des Isopets,* ed. Julia Bastin, SATF (Paris: Champion, 1929), 1:83–84, 146–48.

174. The article *le* could here apply either to the author or to the book (or to both simultaneously, the one being coextensive with the other). Since the ambiguity can't be maintained in English, I have chosen it to refer to the book, which was the most recent object of reproach mentioned by Col, in the concluding lines of the preceding paragraph.

175. A significant translation difficulty in this passage comes from Pierre Col's use of the word *solucion* twice. The word could mean in the Middle Ages "solution, resolution, explanation, elucidation, response, conclusion," as suggested by modern English and French usage, but also "absolution, pardon (for an offense or a sin), or payment, acquittal (of a debt)." Baird and Kane clearly understood the second usage of the word in the latter way, translating the final clause as "I will accept such a thorough reading for their absolution" (*La querelle de la Rose,* 113). But this sentiment does not seem to cohere with the passage, where Pierre is trying, however archly, to invite Jean de Meun's critics to read his work with good will and close attention so that they will understand its qualities and, as he says in the following sentence, pardon Jean. Insisting upon a pardon or absolution of the critics themselves seems incompatible with this endeavor and also does not really follow from his previous statements aimed at Christine. I have thus translated the first use of the word, in the otherwise unattested expression *pour toutes solucions,* as "for a final resolution" and the second as "I trust their thoughtful reading will provide a conclusive explanation."

176. *Rose,* ed. Lecoy, ll. 15179–80; trans. Dahlberg, 259.

177. *Rose,* ed. Lecoy, ll. 15222–26; trans. Dahlberg, 259.

178. *Rose,* ed. Lecoy, ll. 15143–45; trans. Dahlberg, 258. I have slightly altered Dahlberg's translation, as he writes "such things" rather than what is more literally "such words" for *tex paroles.*

179. *Rose,* ed. Lecoy, l. 15204; trans. Dahlberg, 259.

instruction,"[180] namely, so that each and every person have knowledge of himself and of others; and, finally, that if there is any "utterance that Holy Church may consider foolish,"[181] he is prepared to rectify it.

So I am absolutely dumbfounded to see how he[182] placed in the mouth of Lady Theological Eloquence and of all those of the court of Holy Christianity the recommendation to examine whether there was anything in his book with which to take issue—this book which they had allowed thus to lie dormant for a period of a hundred years or more, with the result that it is now published everywhere in the Christian world and, what is more, translated into foreign languages. But I believe that they were waiting for you, you and the others who endeavor to reproach him, for I know in truth that no one before now has been inclined to reproach him. Yet the four mendicant orders[183] have been around for some time, among whom there have been very illustrious clerics who had no little influence upon the pope and the temporal princes and princesses, and whom he did not exactly flatter. Now, consider what sort of promoter this Conscience is, who allows a lawsuit to lie dormant for a period of a hundred years! By the body of God! One does not show any respect for that entire holy court of Christianity by accusing it of such negligence; and especially not for Lady Theological Eloquence, when one presents her principal argumentation poorly and undertakes a flawed legal dispute by having her argue and speak in the manner that the teachers of rhetoric provided in their books, something that is not appropriate for Lady Theological Eloquence, as Saint Augustine says in the fourth book of *On Christian Doctrine.*[184] I say it in good faith, Lady Eloquence

180. *Rose,* ed. Lecoy, l. 15173; trans. Dahlberg: 258.

181. *Rose,* ed. Lecoy, ll. 15269–70; trans. Dahlberg, 260.

182. The context tells us that this pronoun refers to the author of the *Treatise against the Roman de la Rose,* i.e., Jean Gerson.

183. The four mendicant orders referred to by Pierre Col, all founded in the thirteenth century, are the Franciscans, the Carmelites, the Dominicans, and the Augustinians.

184. *De doctrina christiana* 4.1.2 (*PL* 34, col. 89): "Primo itaque exspectationem legentium, qui forte me putant rhetorica daturum esse praecepta quae in scholis saecularibus et didici et docui, ista praelocutione cohibeo, atque ut a me non exspectentur, admoneo; non quod nihil habeant utilitatis; sed quod, si quid habent, seorsum discendum est, si cui fortassis bono viro etiam haec vacat discere, non autem a me vel in hoc opere, vel in aliquo alio requirendum" (But first in these preliminary remarks I must thwart the expectation of those readers who think that I shall give the rules of rhetoric here which I learned and taught in the secular schools. And I admonish them not to expect such rules from me, not that they have no utility, but because, if they have any, it should be sought elsewhere if perhaps some good man has the opportunity to learn them. But he should not expect these rules from me, either in this work, or in any other) (trans. D. W. Robertson Jr. [Indianapolis: Bobbs-Merrill, 1958], 118).

was made to undertake a very difficult duty, and so she needed all the help she could get. But I know well their response: they will say that this never occurred to them.[185]

Nonetheless, I beg that entire blessed court to pardon this man who imposed this upon them,[186] for I know in all certainty that he is heading toward a positive goal, namely, the very same toward which Master Jean de Meun is heading. It is true that I could not entirely excuse him, as though there were not an error in attributing to them such negligence, or wanting to make them undertake a flawed legal dispute—only it was not on account of some evil intent (for I consider that there is none in him, or as little as is to be found in any living man), but rather for the sole reason that he had looked little at the illustrious book of the *Rose* (for what he did look at was done skillfully). Therefore, please pardon him, you, Lady Canonical Justice, Reason, Eloquence, Conscience, and the other barons of the holy court of Christianity, and order him as penance for this crime to read in all its depth and breadth, in a leisurely fashion, this very noble book of the *Rose* three times, in honor of that blessed Trinity in its unity. May that Trinity grant to all of us a fleece so white that we may, with the aforementioned Meun, graze in the grass that is in the park with the gamboling little lamb.

Amen.

185. The use of pronouns in this paragraph is quite difficult because of numerous ambiguities, due either to Pierre Col's intention or to a flawed transmission of the text. At the beginning of the paragraph, as noted above, a distinction is made between the agency of Lady Eloquence and that of Gerson, the author of the *Treatise*. The author has, in short, betrayed the characters he has portrayed. In the middle of the paragraph, though, the pronoun is switched from *il* (he) to *on* (one), even though it seems to be applying to the same author; by means of this, Pierre Col coyly attenuates the accusation he is making by depersonalizing it. This presents syntactic problems, as what I have translated above as "when one presents her principal argumentation poorly" could, as a relative clause, also be referred to Lady Eloquence: "Lady Theological Eloquence, who presents her principal argumentation poorly." It is only in the next clause, with the expression "by having her argue and speak," that it becomes more likely that the relative clause is referring to "one" and not to "Lady Eloquence." The penultimate sentence continues the use of *on*, which I have translated as a passive. Finally, in the last sentence, Pierre uses the plural possessive (*leur*) and subject (*ilz*) pronouns, presumably transitioning unconsciously from a singular assailant (Gerson) to a plurality, as he did earlier in the letter.

186. "This man" is obviously Gerson, whom Pierre Col accuses of having negligently betrayed the Holy Court of Christianity through his treatise against the *Rose*. He thus, and rather extravagantly, turns the tables on the chancellor of the University of Paris and puts him on trial for his "crime" against Theological Eloquence and the entire Court. One can detect early in the letter that Pierre had this conclusion in mind when he states that Theological Eloquence is "alleged to" have made these remarks and that, in fact, "never . . . was the good lady concerned with this matter."

22. CHRISTINE DE PIZAN TO PIERRE COL (OCTOBER 2, 1402)[187]

FRENCH PROSE

To Master Pierre Col, secretary of the king our lord

Because human understanding cannot be elevated to the height of transparent knowledge that comprehends the entire truth of hidden things (owing to the gross, terrestrial obscurity that encumbers it and removes true clarity), it is necessary to use opinion rather than hard science in order to ascertain the plausibility of things conceived in the mind. It is for this reason that various disputes are set into motion by opposing opinions, even among the most insightful of people. Each one strives through brilliant argumentation to demonstrate his opinion to be the correct one. That this is manifest through experience is patently obvious, as we can ourselves discern in the present situation. This is why I declare, in responding to you, O shrewd cleric—you whose keen perception and linguistic skill in expounding the opinions you have formed are not diminished by any lack of instruction—that I want to assure you that however much your arguments, in opposition to my own opinion, might lead convincingly to your intended goal, these arguments, in spite of their pleasing eloquence, do not in the slightest shake my innermost convictions, nor do they cloud my thoughts or turn them to the opposite of what I have previously written on the subject. In this regard, you have recently seen fit to goad me and take up once again the pointed incitations that had already been launched at me in the writings of other prominent individuals on this matter. Accordingly, you have sent me your new essay dealing with a certain debate stirred up some time ago over the compilation known as the *Romance of the Rose.* And although I am occupied with other things[188] and had no intention of speaking any more about this, still I will respond to you bluntly and plainly, as is my habit, with the unmitigated truth. Moreover, since I would be incapable of matching your beautiful style, please make allowance for my faults and lack of skill.

You write me in your opening words that since you wished to see some

187. Translated from *Le débat,* ed. Hicks, 115–50.

188. At the end of this letter to Pierre Col Christine provides the date October 2, 1402. In the prologue to her *Chemin de longue étude* (Long Road of Learning), she dates the opening scene to October 5 of the same year. Christine was also undoubtedly in the process of writing *La mutacion de Fortune* (Fortune's Transformation) at this time, as it was begun in 1400 and only completed in November 1403.

of my writings, there came into your hands a certain letter of mine addressed to my lord the provost of Lille, which begins, "Reverent and respectful greetings, etc." Then you say right afterward that I strive to rebuke this "very eminent Catholic, divine orator, etc.," Master Jean de Meun, in the book of the *Rose* with regard to some specific passages—a man whom you would not dare open your mouth to praise, any more than you would move your foot forward in order to fall into an abyss. Mother of God! Let us linger here a bit! Is he thus comparable to Jesus Christ or to the Virgin Mary, greater than Saint Paul or the doctors of Holy Church, for you to say that you could not adequately praise him by using every one of your body parts, even if they had all become tongues? In any event, it is true (with all due respect) that too extreme and excessive praise given to a mortal being merits reproach and leads to blame. And since the pure truth obliges me to provide you a response when I would rather remain silent (because the subject matter is not to my taste), I will do so, in my unpolished style. However, just as you write to me asking me to pardon you if you speak to me using *tu,* I entreat you to do likewise, as it appears to be the most appropriate according to our ancients—as you yourself affirm.[189]

First, you declare that I blame without reason what is said in the aforementioned *Romance of the Rose* in the chapter of Reason, where she names men's private parts by their proper name: and you recount what I once replied elsewhere, that "truly God created all things as good . . . but by the pollution of the sin of our first parents man became impure": and I gave the example of Lucifer, whose name is beautiful but whose person is horrible, and I said in concluding that " the name does not create the indecency of the thing, but the thing makes the name indecent." And because I said that, you claim that I resemble the pelican, who killed himself with his beak. You then make your conclusion, asking afterward, "if the thing makes the word indecent," what name can I give to that thing which would not be indecent?

I will reply to this directly, without making any detours, for I am not a master in logic, and, to tell the whole truth, such tortuous argumentation is not at all necessary. Without a doubt, I admit openly that I could in no

189. One can detect a sharpness of tone in this remark, for Christine clearly wants to turn back upon Pierre Col a potentially demeaning use of the familiar form of address. Be that as it may, Christine famously refers to her use of the familiar form in a verse letter, dated February 10, 1404, to her contemporary, Eustache Deschamps, whom she calls her "master and friend," with no sense of irony: "Te suppliant que a desplaisance / Ne te tourt se adès plaisance / Ay qu'em singulier nom je parle / A toy, car je l'ay apris par le / Stille clergial de quoy ceulx usent / Qui en science leurs temps usent" (Begging you not to be displeased if I now take pleasure in speaking to you in the singular voice, for I learned it from the clerical style, used by those who devote their lives to learning) (*Une epistre a Eustace Mourel,* ll. 17–22, *Oeuvres poëtiques,* ed. Roy, 2:296).

way speak of something indecent, of immoral desire or its goal (whatever name I might give it, whether it concerned the private parts or some other indecent thing), without the word being indecent. However if in the specific case of an illness or some other urgent situation it were necessary to speak openly either of those body parts or of whatever it might be, and I did speak of it in a manner so as to be understood, but without naming it by its proper name, I would not at all be speaking indecently. This is because the reason for which I would be speaking of them would not be indecent. But if I named them to you by their proper name, even if it were for a good reason, I would nonetheless be speaking indecently, for the initial signification of the thing has already made the word indecent. From which it follows that my first statement is true, "that the thing makes the name indecent, and not at all the name the thing."

And as for the question you ask me, "if I were speaking of the private parts of a small child," who is innocent, would I dare name them, since he is without the defilement of sin? Before I answer you, I ask that you tell me whether a small child is restored to a comparable innocence, a prior state more or less identical to that of Adam when God created him. If you say yes, this is incorrect, for the small child dies in torment before having sinned;[190] this would not have been the case for Adam in the state of Innocence, for death itself came about as a result of his sin.[191] If you say no to me, then I affirm to you that my statement is true: that this modesty is engendered in us on account of the defilement of our first parents. And as for your saying that "it is useless to invoke original sin, for it came from disobedience," I admit to you that it did indeed come from this. But you go on to tell me, if the defilement of our first parents makes the name of the private parts indecent, then, you say, "it is all the more the case that one should not pronounce the names of our first parents, for they are the ones who sinned and not their private parts." As a response to this, I will now propose to you a difficult problem, and I would like you to resolve it for me satisfactorily. Why was

190. Gerson will later, in his response in Latin to Pierre Col's letter, specify this theological error as the Pelagian heresy. See below, ch. 4, n. 65.

191. Gen 2:17: "de ligno autem scientiæ boni et mali ne comedas: in quocumque enim die comederis ex eo, morte morieris" (But of the tree of knowledge of good and evil, thou shalt not eat. For in what day soever thou shalt eat of it, thou shalt die the death). As Hicks notes (*Le débat*, 222), Christine is probably thinking of Rom 5:12: "Propterea sicut per unum hominem peccatum in hunc mundum intravit, et per peccatum mors, et ita in omnes homines mors pertransiit, in quo omnes peccaverunt" (Wherefore as by one man sin entered into this world, and by sin death; and so death passed upon all men, in whom all have sinned), which is also cited in the passage of Saint Augustine referred to by Gerson in his letter to Pierre Col (*De nuptiis*, 2.3.8 [*PL* 44, col. 440]; see below, ch. 4, n. 65).

it that as soon as our first parents sinned and had the knowledge of good and evil, they instantly covered their private parts and blushed with shame, even though they had not yet used them?[192] I ask you why they did not cover their eyes or their mouths, with which they had sinned, instead of the private parts? It seems to me that from that moment reasonable shame was born, which you and your associates, as well as your master's Reason, wish to negate and to extirpate. So it appears to me that I didn't at all kill myself with my beak, as you accuse me of, etc.

Since I am not alone in holding this very true, just, and reasonable opinion that runs counter to the compilation of the said *Rose* (on account of the very contemptible exhortations that are found there, notwithstanding such good as there might be in it), it is to be confirmed that from among the other good people agreeing with my aforementioned opinion, there came along to take a stand against it, after I had written my letter (which you say you have seen), a very prominent scholar and master in theology—eminent, admirable, praiseworthy, a celebrated cleric, distinguished among the most excellent. Driven by the desire to promote virtue and destroy vice, with which the said poem of the *Rose* might have poisoned many people's hearts, he compiled a brief work, brilliantly informed by impeccable theology. You refer to it in your treatise, writing that you have "seen a sort of legal case in the holy court of Christianity, in which Canonical Justice was seated as judge and the Virtues around her as her council, of which the principal one, acting as chancellor, was Penetrating Judgment, joined in close company with Lady Reason, Prudence, Knowledge, and others serving as secretaries, with Theological Eloquence as advocate for the court; and the promoter of lawsuits was Conscience, who was made to stand up and present a request on behalf of Chastity, couched in the following form: 'To Justice, defender of the law, who occupies the place of God on earth, and to her entire devout court, representative of the Christian religion. Chastity, your faithful subject, submits the following plaint and begs humbly that measures be taken, that a succinct provisional sentence be pronounced against the intolerable crimes that someone who calls himself the Foolish Lover has committed, and does not stop committing, against me.' Thereafter she included eight or nine articles."[193]

192. Gen 2:25 and 3:7: "Erat autem uterque nudus, Adam scilicet et uxor ejus, et non erubescebant . . . Et aperti sunt oculi amborum; cumque cognovissent se esse nudos, consuerunt folia ficus, et fecerunt sibi perizomata" (And they were both naked: to wit, Adam and his wife: and were not ashamed . . . And the eyes of them both were opened: and when they perceived themselves to be naked, they sewed together fig leaves, and made themselves aprons).

193. This entire paragraph is syntactically one sentence in the original, containing numerous subordinated clauses and an anacoluthon. I have broken it up into three distinct syntactic units in order to make it somewhat easier to understand.

And in spite of the fact that you address the opening prefatory material of your aforementioned composition to me alone (I am now convinced that, confident as you are in your good sense and your cleverness, you presume that it will be easy for you to refute my arguments on account of my inexperience), you dare to include your criticisms, such as you care to express them, of the statements of so noteworthy a person as the one mentioned above, contained in a work as well conceived as is his, because this work contradicts the opinion to which you adhere. Now, consider—yes, do consider—whether I might not reasonably call to your attention the disgraceful things that you say to me in some parts of your letter, in the following manner: "Oh, reckless presumptuousness! Oh, what very foolish audacity! etc." Yet it is not at all my intention to take it upon myself to argue against you in every detail the issues raised by the above-mentioned Lady Eloquence (for they scarcely touch upon the topics contained in my first letter), except in some parts where they do touch upon the subject matter for which you rebuke me. For I will leave that to the person who composed the legal case in question, who will be more capable of arguing it in a few words than I ever could if I spent my entire life examining his righteous claims. But I certainly can say this much, that you endeavor to charge him with ignorance, you who think you understand it better than he, a man full of wisdom and profound learning. You do indeed say, in order to speak more courteously of such an eminent person, that if he had attentively studied the said book, he would have all the more praise and esteem for it, insofar as his intellect surpasses that of all other people. In this way—praise be to God!—you yourself admit that he is an illustrious person. How good it is for you then to believe, indeed to assume, that such a man would have publicly attacked a work that he had not first examined and understood well!

I can also easily provide a response to your charge that he speaks of a foolish lover as a cleric would speak of arms (just like someone who had never had any feelings of that sort): namely, that it is not at all necessary to have had the experience of something in order to speak fittingly about it.[194] Indeed, many examples of this could be provided to you. You yourself know that the effects of love are open to the understanding of an astute man of learning; after all, many more subtle matters, ones beyond natural perception, have been aptly described. You yourself likewise admit that it is not necessary to have had the experience, and yet you conclude that if he

194. It is to be noted that Christine had stated rather the opposite about her own experience as a woman in her letter to Jean de Montreuil (no. 5): "But insofar as I am in fact a woman, I am better suited to attest to these matters than he who, not having had this experience, speaks instead through conjecture and in a haphazard manner."

had the experience of a foolish lover, he would have spoken other than the way he did.

At this point I pass over some of the articles of the above-mentioned lawsuit of Lady Eloquence because it is not up to me to furnish a response. This is especially true regarding what you say Master Jean de Meun named "sanctuaries," since I never debated this point,[195] for it is more decent to remain silent about it. Nonetheless, when you justify it and claim that they [women's private parts] can legitimately be named this way and that this serves to demonstrate the folly of the Foolish Lover, I must beg your pardon, for it is undeniable that what you say is other than what you think. You know very well that he never said it as an assertion that the thing can be called holy, but rather as a more alluring type of mockery, or to cause greater excitement in the lecherous. (At the very least, whatever intention he might have had, I know well that it sounds evil to those who do not take delight in such carnality).

I do not wish to overlook your statement that I must not at all believe that he [Jean de Meun] was referring to the book of the *Rose* when he said in his *Testament*: "In my youth I wrote many a poem through vanity." And as though you were certain of it, you affirm that he never repented of it and that he did not make the statement for this reason. Yet in no way did he make an exception of it. Nonetheless, you claim that he meant ballads, rondeaux, and virelays that we do not possess. Where, then, are these other vain and foolish works he composed? It is astonishing that, being by such a supreme poet, they were not reverently preserved, for there is a lot of talk about other works that do not compare to his, yet there is no one alive who has ever heard of these specific ones of his. And truly, I myself have frequently wondered how such a great author could have come to a halt with so little work—this notwithstanding the fact that many who are favorable toward him wish to attribute to him even works by Saint Augustine.[196] But in any event, if you mean that he was silent about these works in order to avoid vainglory and that he truly did compose a number of them, take a look at the prologue of the Boethius that he translated, where he enumerates the

195. The word in the original text, "debatis," is a form of the past tense and not the future, as Baird/Kane translate it ("nor will I discuss your remark" [*La querelle de la Rose,* 120]). It would indeed seem that she is referring to what she is planning to do, but the past tense, as I translate it, is referring backward, to the fact that she did not speak about this topic in her previous letter. Aside from the grammatical issue, the future is contradictory, for she does go on to speak of it in the following lines. Christine's argument of course requires her not to provide the literal word for what Jean de Meun names "sanctuaries," that is, women's genitalia.

196. As Hicks notes (*Le débat,* 222), there is no such attribution in any known text.

translations and writings that he composed: I do indeed believe that he did not leave out anything.[197] This I say on account of those who want to attribute other writings to him, even though it makes no difference to me. But as for our discussion, I truly believe and maintain that he said what is stated in his *Testament* solely on account of this romance, for it is manifest in his words and we do not have any knowledge to the contrary.

You then come to my argument and say that Lady Eloquence queried: "Is it not madness," she says, "to declare that one ought to speak without restraint, lasciviously and shamelessly, no matter how indecent the words might be in the opinion of all people?" Then you tell Lady Eloquence that she has been made to poorly articulate her main point, upon which she bases all her following arguments, but afterward you pardon her author[198] by accusing him of ignorance, and you state what I previously quoted here: that it is, as you maintain, on account of a failure to look at the work and because he studied it but little.

In responding to Lady Eloquence you quote the words that Reason used in the aforementioned romance, which are essentially as follows: that she can certainly name with their proper name things that are nothing if not good; and you claim that he[199] did not say that one must speak of them, but that one can speak of them. So I will answer you briefly on behalf of Lady El-

197. "Je Jehan de Meun qui jadis ou Rommant de la Rose, puis que Jalousie ot mis en prison Bel Acueil, enseignai la maniere du chastel prendre et de la rose cueillir et translatay de latin en françois le livre Vegece de Chevalerie et le livre des Merveilles de Hyrlande et la Vie et les Epistres Pierres Abaelart et Heloys sa fame et le livre Aered de Esperituelle Amitié" (I Jean de Meun, who previously in the *Romance of the Rose*, after Jealousy had imprisoned Bel Accueil, taught how to take the castle and pluck the rose, and translated from Latin into French the book of Vegetius on Chivalry and the book of the Marvels of Ireland [*Topographica Hibernica* of Giraud de Barri] and the Life and Epistles of Peter Abelard and his wife Heloïse and the book of Aelred on Spiritual Friendship [*De Amicitia Spirituali* of Aelred de Rievaulx]) ("Boethius' *De Consolatione* by Jean de Meun," ed. V. L. Dedeck-Héry. *Mediaeval Studies* 14 (1952): 168 [preface, ll. 2–7]). Boethius was one of Christine's favorite authors, and we now know that the French translation with which she was familiar is the anonymous one in verse and prose recently edited by Glynnis Cropp (*Le Livre de Boece de Consolacion*, Textes Littéraires Français, 580 [Geneva: Droz, 2006]), to which the preface of Jean de Meun's own prose translation was affixed (see also Cropp, "Boèce et Christine de Pizan," *Le Moyen Âge* 87, nos. 3–4 [1981]: 387–417).

198. The "author" of Lady Eloquence is of course Gerson.

199. The pronoun used here is masculine, *il*, and Hicks (*Le débat*, 122) provides no variants from the other MSS. Christine, rather than referring to Reason, seems to be slipping from the female personification to the author ("he" in this case designating Jean de Meun) as ultimate agent, something not uncommon in the present context, as we have seen abundantly in Pierre Col's letter (no. 21), where he alternately attributes statements in the *Treatise against the Romance of the Rose* to the female personification, Theological Eloquence, and to the male author. As noted above (n. 118), at this period the masculine singular pronoun is rarely used for the feminine.

oquence, albeit without much finesse: I know very well, in truth, that having to do something is a matter of constraint and that to be able to do something is a matter of free will, but nonetheless, as regards the manner of speaking that one uses in such a case, one cannot speak of these things blatantly or immoderately without committing a wrong (as was proven previously here and will again be proven later). But you maintain along with Jean's Reason that she did speak literally[200] of those things or that she can do so without committing a wrong, and you allege that holy writings and the Bible name them by their proper name where it is expedient. But I reply to you, fair sweet friend: if the Bible or holy writings name them, it is not in the same way or for the same purpose: rather, the subject matter is very far from enticement of the flesh. Moreover, the Bible is not about a female character who calls herself the daughter of God, nor does she speak to a Foolish Lover whose inner flames she might stir up.

Furthermore, you state that even if the word displeases some people, it doesn't at all displease everyone: I do believe you very well on this point! For not everyone is displeased by something that is maliciously done or said. You add that you make this statement because Lady Eloquence said: "inasmuch as the words are indecent in the view of all people." Well, right here you have twisted yourself up in the rope with which you thought you had snared me (when you said that one must not at all take words so literally), for you know well that the majority is taken to refer to the whole, and, in all truth, it would displease the majority of people to hear something indecent being named in public.

You state that one must never say that "good custom" forbids people from speaking literally of them, but, you add, you remain silent "on whether the custom is good or evil." Yet I don't understand why you remain silent if you know there is something good in it; however, if you think the opposite, your opinion is foolish, for women have never had the habit of speaking thus. This is what Lady Eloquence said, as you admit: she spoke the truth, and it would be a pity if it were otherwise and if in other countries so great a reproach could be directed at the women of this kingdom. For it is said in a common proverb: "By one's manner of speaking one's inclinations are

200. The word used here is *proprement,* which, both in Jean de Meun's work and the debate discussions, straddles the ground been "properly" in a moral or social sense and "properly" in a linguistic sense, meaning "literally." In order to avoid the inherent ambiguity of the English adverb "properly" here and in other contexts, I have chosen to translate it as "literally" (for Christine is referring to Reason's use of proper names for the private parts, as the rest of the sentence makes clear).

known."[201] That Reason to whom you grant so much authority said that in France "it is for no other reason than being out of the habit." It is not at all a matter of being out of the habit, for they never did have the habit. And how does it happen that they do not have the habit? It comes from reasonable shame, which—thank God!—has not at all been banished from their thoughts.

You go on to say that it is possible that women in other countries speak of them literally, but I don't know why you make such an inference when you know nothing about it. Indeed, there is no evidence that anywhere in the world women or even men speak of them candidly and in public. But you are astonished, this you say, by this custom, for "women certainly name their own private parts with their proper name, but don't want to name those of men." To this I reply that with all due respect, certainly honorable women do not do it in public; and if some women more readily name things that are very familiar, indeed intimate, than those with which they are less familiar, you should not be surprised. You, however, who argue so strenuously, and with so many objections, that they must be named candidly by their name, and that Jean de Meun's Reason spoke well, I ask you earnestly—you who are his very prized disciple, as you say—why do you not name them candidly in your writing without beating around the bush? It seems to me that you are not a good student, for you don't follow your master's doctrine very well.[202] Who has induced you to act this way? If you say it is not the custom, that means you are afraid to be reproached for it. What does this custom matter to you? Do you wish to live according to the opinion of other people? Follow good doctrine and demonstrate to others how they should act; for all things must be begun at some point, and even if you are blamed at first, afterward you will be praised when people find this habit to be good and attractive. Aha! By God! It doesn't work that way, and you can't deny it! Where indeed is Jean de Meun's Reason? She has little power since Shame has routed her.[203] Blessed be such Shame that routs this sort of Reason. And

201. This is a proverbial phrase, of which Morawski provides a variant version (*Proverbes français*, no. 51): "A la parole cognoit on l'omme" (one knows the man by his speech).

202. Gerson picks up this point from Christine's letter in his response to Pierre Col (no. 28).

203. Christine astutely suggests that Pierre Col's inherent modesty (he avoids using the obscene words of Reason) has in point of fact negated the linguistic behavior argued for by Jean de Meun's Reason. Whereas Hicks in his edition does not capitalize the word for shame, I have chosen to do so, as the concept is clearly being personified by Christine. This point is especially clever in that the allegorical "genealogy" provided by Guillaume de Lorris in the first part of the *Rose* (ed. Lecoy, ll. 2821–28; trans. Dahlberg, 70) makes Shame the daughter of Reason, conceived by the mere sight of Misdeed.

if I hated you, I would say, "Would that it had pleased God for you to act thus!" However, I am well disposed toward you for your good sense and the positive things people say of you (even though I don't know you). Thus I would not wish dishonor on you. For decent speech that propagates the virtues is most fitting in the mouth of a praiseworthy person.

I have the impression that you are reproaching Lady Eloquence's way of speaking when she said that Meun adhered poorly to the rules of rhetoric (for he should have paid attention to the person Reason was addressing, namely, a Foolish Lover who could have been more aroused by it: "which would not be the case for a great cleric expert in theology, etc"). And you say that apparently he means that a great cleric, a philosopher or a theologian, cannot be in love. But yes he can, as you state, providing the examples of David, Solomon, and others. Yet you amaze me, you who wish to correct someone else for the same fault that you regularly fall into: you advocate wherever it pleases you what for others you set out to demolish. It is good to find out that when that estimable man of virtue[204] spoke of the Foolish Lover, he assumed that the latter was devoid of any learning once he succumbed to Foolish Love, assuming that he did possess great learning; but when he spoke of a great cleric expert in theology, he assumed that the passion of Foolish Love was totally absent from him—for it is necessary that his penetrating intellect, which never goes astray, should comprehend it thus or even more subtly! But then you claim that a man will never be roused to loving foolishly on account of such words. Yet you were told that he has already been roused up because he is a Foolish Lover and that the heat of his passion could easily increase because of it. You say that when Reason named them she was preaching to the Lover that he should totally withdraw from that state. Response: If the situation is as you understand it and accords with what Jean de Meun described as the goal of love (which is a point that could be debated, for it is not a general rule for people to tend so energetically toward that goal), Reason acted upon the Lover just as I would if I were speaking to a pregnant woman or to a sick man, and I made them think of tart apples, fresh pears, or some other fruit, which might be quite tempting to them yet noxious, and told them that if

204. Christine here refers to Gerson. So the following lines are her report of what she alleges Pierre Col was saying about the theologian. She had already surreptitiously switched her focus from Lady Eloquence to Gerson when she used the masculine pronoun a few lines before: "you say that apparently *he* means." It is slightly unclear what her point is here, but she seems to be pointing out Pierre's inconsistencies—arguing at different points that the protagonist is and is not a Foolish Lover, stating that being a Foolish Lover and a scholar are two incompatible states, but also saying that a cleric could be a Foolish Lover—and the fact that he attributes this inconsistency to Gerson at the same time.

they ate any of them it would cause great harm. I sincerely maintain that the memory of these things, once named, would be more powerful and would have more influence on their craving than the order not to eat them, and this serves to illustrate the point I made previously—and which you so criticize—that one need not point out to human nature which foot it is limping on.

You argue that master Jean de Meun, "in the chapter on Reason stooped to speak of the private parts not on account of any excitement that he might have gotten by speaking of them," but "to point out the foolishness of people who say that it is not permissible to speak of them." But if this is the reason why he did it, he unquestionably failed in his project, when he thought to suppress a very wise principle by doing something so very ridiculous. Yet you say it is obvious that he did not do it at all for the sake of sensual gratification, for the simple reason that "elsewhere, where he speaks of the work of Nature, he calls it 'the game of love.'" Come on now! Ha! Dear God! You say some astonishing things! You could just as well claim that at the end of his book he doesn't ever designate the indecent things that are found there by their literal names! And indeed he does not! But what does that matter? He names them with readily intelligible figurative language—six times more enticing, more piercing, and more enrapturing for those inclined to such things than if he had named them by their literal names.[205]

You go on to say that whoever reads and understands the romance in question "will understand that Jean de Meun should not have spoken otherwise than the way he spoke."[206] Your statement is quite correct, provided that one understands the book as you do. Do you know what reading it is like? It is just like the books of the alchemists: some people read them and understand them in one way, while others who read them understand them in the opposite way.[207] And each of them believes he understands all too

205. The expression, used twice in this passage, that I have translated as "literal names" is *noms propres*. See above, n. 200.

206. Christine's quotation differs from Pierre Col's text (as was the case with the quotation about people's foolishness in the previous paragraph), and therefore my translation does not correspond exactly to the one I gave previously: "will agree with Master Jean de Meun that one must not speak otherwise than the way he spoke." Specifically, Christine replaces Pierre's *avec* (with) with *que* (that) and changes an infinitive, *devoir* (which denotes an unspecified subject for this verb, "ought to") with a conjugated verb in a relative clause, *devoit*, which can only refer back to Jean de Meun ("he should not have spoken" as opposed to "one must not speak").

207. Christine has her character Opinion disparagingly describe the work of the alchemist in *Le livre de l'advision Christine* (Christine's Vision), part 2, chap. 18 (ed. Reno and Dulac, 82–84). Interestingly enough, it is Opinion who, only three chapters later, claims responsibility for the debate over the *Romance of the Rose* (see no. 32 in this volume). As a result of Jean de Meun's brief discussion of alchemy contained in Nature's speech (*Rose*, ed. Lecoy, ll. 16035–118; trans.

well. Thereupon they put themselves to work and prepare furnaces, alembics, and crucibles, and they operate their bellows at full strength: And when there appear small amounts of distillation or condensation, which they find extraordinary, they believe they have achieved a miracle. Then, when they have done this and done that and wasted their time, they know as much as they did before. But what cost and expense in this process of distillation and this production of a few useless condensations! It's the same thing with you and me and a number of others: you perceive it and understand it in one way, and I in entirely the opposite way. You declaim, I reply. And when we've done this and done that, it's all worthless, for the subject matter of our discussion is most revolting, just as is the case for some alchemists who think they are making gold out of dung. It would have been good to remain silent over it, and I would prefer not to be an alchemist in this dispute, but a defensive position is fitting for me since I have been assaulted.

As for what you argue[208] afterward, in opposition to the testimony of Lady Eloquence before Justice, for which the aforementioned master is responsible, I will leave it to him to handle it. For he will certainly be capable of responding to you on this matter, and he will provide his defense when he wishes.

You recall something I said some time ago: that I cannot remain silent, nor can I be sufficiently astonished, over the fact that Reason asserted that even in the game of love "it is better to deceive than to be deceived." You add that I argue that it would thus follow that both are good, which cannot be. And then you affirm by your oath that if I had refrained from writing this argument it would have been to my benefit, and that it is the kind of proposition schoolchildren make when they argue. Nevertheless, I promise you wholeheartedly that I do not intend to retract it, whatever you might think about it. But regarding the fact that you think you can demolish my argument by saying, "Jesus Christ said that 'it would have been better for Judas if he had never existed than to have betrayed his master,'" I reply that, in truth, it was good that Jesus Christ died and it was good that Judas was born. However, it would have been better *for him* if he had never been born, on account of the misery of his despair and the punishment of his betrayal. But you yourself don't keep to the rule in all of your explanations and arguments, by which you attempt to criticize me, and you interpret in an astonishing way

Dahlberg, 272–73), he maintained a reputation as a dabbler in that science into the sixteenth century, as Lecoy notes (2:298).

208. The proximity of the verb *arguer* (used here and two paragraphs before) to Christine's particular form of the word for alchemist, *arguemiste,* accentuates what was for her the intimate connection between the specious material manipulations of the latter and the verbal sophistry of writers like Jean de Meun and Pierre Col.

what is said clearly and literally ("it is much better, dear master, to deceive than to be deceived") when you claim that it is the same as saying that it would harm you less to pretend that you love me in order to satisfy your carnal needs with my body than if that love caused you to abandon your "learning, sense, time, soul, body, and reputation." That's a very extreme thing to say! Therefore it seems that one must either deceive or else abandon "sense, time, soul, etc."! Without a doubt, the bias that you have in this affair makes you go to great lengths in order to find this extreme justification (whatever the case may be, he[209] does not put together these two extreme ideas). But still I say to you once again that according to the law of Jesus Christ and his doctrine, it is more forbidden to deceive one's neighbor than to be deceived (and this refers to fraudulent deceit, for as a manner of speaking one can call something deceit that is not a great vice at all). But before I forget, I will say something about which I am content, namely, that you express the opinion that Jean de Meun never wrote this in his book, and that it is an interpolation. I beg your pardon, but it certainly does seem that you are speaking capriciously, for does the passage not correspond to the work's own language, and is it not of the same style and versification? Nonetheless, you would prefer that he had never said it! You can indeed say confidently that such a statement was never uttered by Reason, the daughter of God.

Ha! Fraudulent Deception! Mother of Treason! Who is the person that dares bring you up at any opportunity? But since we have entered into this matter, by God, let me linger a bit upon it, however verbose it might be (for many things cannot be adequately understood in few words). By your faith, consider a bit, you who are well read in history, which is the vice that has played the greatest role, and continues to do so, in supporting and accomplishing the grossest perversities? You will find it to be Deceit. Think about it, didn't Deceit at the beginning bestow death upon us?[210] Read the Trojan histories: you will discover how, according to Ovid and others, Lady Discord sowed the seeds of war but would not have reaped her harvest had Lady Deceit not come on the scene, causing the fortified city of Troy to be betrayed and captured.[211] The story is so full of her deeds that it would be

209. The "he" Christine refers to here must be Jean de Meun. The two extremes that Pierre Col brings together are not even to be found in Jean's text!

210. Gen 3:13: "et dixit Dominus Deus ad mulierem: Quare hoc fecisti? Quae respondit: Serpens decepit me, et comedi" (And the Lord God said to the woman: Why hast thou done this? And she answered: The serpent deceived me, and I did eat).

211. As Hicks notes (*Le débat,* 223), Christine is referring to the "Apple of Discord" myth, which she could have read in the widely circulated thirteenth-century prose compilation, the *Histoire ancienne jusqu'à César* (Ancient History up to Caesar), or in the early fourteenth-century translation of, and commentary on, Ovid's *Metamorphoses,* the *Ovide Moralisé* (Moralized Ovid).

too long to recount. Ha! God! How every noble heart must be on its guard against the appearance within it of such a reprehensible vice, which surpasses all others in its pernicious effects! What distinction do you make between Treachery and Deceit? I don't know of any, except that the one sounds worse than the other. And if you say that it is therefore better for one to avail oneself of it over and against someone else than the reverse (someone else availing himself of it against oneself), I tell you once again that it is not: for according to God's justice someone who injures another is punished more harshly than the one who is injured (and let us add that this applies in particular to the case of love, [which I say] because Master Jean de Meun's Reason said that "It is better, etc."). I will candidly declare my opinion on this, and I do not care who will consider me a fool for doing so, so much do I hate Deceit. I have only one son[212]—may God consent that I not lose him—but I would like for him to fall totally in love with a well-bred and wise woman who treasures her honor, using the good sense that reasonable men possess and with which I hope God will provide him. Then let happen to him whatever might happen. But I would much prefer this to his making every effort to be a deceiver of all, or even of many, women. For I would imagine that by deceiving many women he might more quickly lose "sense, time, soul, body, and reputation" than by loving only one woman well.

And do you think in good faith that I believe that the worst mishap that can befall a young man is to be in love? To the contrary, provided that it be in a suitable place where there is honor and good sense, for he who would love a shepherdess had better want to look after sheep. And I say this not at all because of the social status but in order to show that the loving heart always desires to conform to the situation of the one it loves. This is why I believe that those who wish to love must choose carefully where they will direct their attentions, for that is, I believe, where the peril lies. Do you also think I believe that all those who have been or who are truly in love find all their happiness in striving to go to bed with their ladies? You can be sure that I don't believe this at all, for I believe that there are many men who have

212. At the time that Christine was left a widow, in 1390, she had three children, one daughter and two sons. As she tells us in *Christine's Vision,* her elder son, Jean de Castel, was sent to England to stay with the earl of Salisbury and remained there for three years, returning to France undoubtedly some time in the first half of 1402. Also in the *Vision,* Christine mentions her joy at her son's return, since Death had left him her only son. However, when she tells of his departure, which probably took place in late 1398 or early 1399, she states simply that she reluctantly let "the eldest" of her sons go; this suggests strongly that the younger son died some time between 1399 and 1402. She does not appear to have spoken elsewhere about that event, however. Either before (1399) or after (1402) her son's stay in England, Christine dedicated to him a book, *Moral Teachings* (see no. 2 in this volume), intended for his instruction.

loved loyally and impeccably without ever going to bed with them. Never did they deceive nor were they deceived, for their principal intention was that their morals be improved through this experience. Indeed, on account of this love they became valiant and truly renowned, so much so that in their old age they praised God that they had been lovers. Thus I have heard it said that this was particularly the case for the good constable Messire Bertrand du Guesclin,[213] Messire Maurice de Trésiguidi,[214] and many other chivalrous men. So these men did not on account of it lose their "sense, time, body, soul, and reputation." I have spoken at such length about this sort of "reputation" because you wrote to me that I should carefully dissect it: Now I have dissected it for you.

But here you will provide me several responses. You will say for instance that Master Jean de Meun meant to speak of those who are utterly love-crazed. I reply to you that all things, even good ones, can be used badly; but since he wished to speak of love in its entirety, he should not so exclusively have oriented it toward a single goal, indeed a goal treated so indecently. You will tell me that I am disagreeing with Lady Eloquence (who speaks of the Foolish Lover Meun describes), but I maintain that to be truly in love it is not necessary to be foolish or to lose from it one's "sense, time, etc." You will further say to me that I am encouraging young people to be lovers: I say to you that I do not advise[215] them to be such, for all earthly love is but vanity. However, if one of the two is necessary, it is worse to deceive than to be in love virtuously, and worse things can result from it. But since Master Jean de Meun, who fully described many things, never described the essence of the deceiver, I shall speak about it a bit in a blunt manner in order to whet the appetites of those who take pleasure in such things.[216] The nature of the deceiver is to be a liar, a perjurer, a hypocrite, a flatterer, a traitor; he is misleading, malicious, spying, underhanded, and an infinite number of other evil things. And in the end, when he can do nothing else, what remains is derision, slander, envy, and suspicion. These are his deeds. But inasmuch as

213. Bertrand du Guesclin (1320–80), high constable of the king of France, was one of the most illustrious knights in the Hundred Years' War. Christine mentions him in the *Debate of Two Lovers* (*Oeuvres poétiques*, ed. Roy, vol. 2, ll. 1569–85) as one of the contemporary men who "wanted to devote their heart to perfect love" (l. 1565), adding that he specifically "first took arms for [the God of] Love and, he said, in order to be loved" (ll. 1578–79).

214. Hicks notes (*Le débat*, 224–25) that Maurice de Trésiguidi was a Breton squire who participated in the "Combat of the Thirty" against the English (1351) and later entered the service of Charles V as a knight.

215. To Hicks's text, *lay* (allow), I prefer the variant he lists from the B MSS, *lo* (advise).

216. Hicks's text omits what I have translated as "in such things." I have used the variant from the B MSS, *s'i*.

I have spoken of those who love honorably, I can affirm that just as you have declared that the person who composed the above-mentioned legal case never felt what it was like to be a foolish lover, so do I believe that Master Jean de Meun never felt what it was like to be an honorable lover.

Afterward, you recall what Lady Eloquence and I, out of our great astonishment, say about the great lewdness to be found in the chapter of the Old Woman, when we ask: "Who will find anything there but filth and vile teachings?" But we say much more than you mention, and the same thing goes for the chapter of Jealousy.[217] But then you leap all the way forward to what I said at the end of my aforementioned letter (I beg your pardon, but your evocation of this passage is not very coherent),[218] when you claim that I said that I don't condemn the author or authors in all parts of the book in question, as if, you assert, "I wanted to say that I condemn him for what I reproach him for," and that I assume a position as judge based solely upon the opinion I express. I reply to you that in truth you have, with all due respect, clumsily gathered the flowers of my essay and made of them an ill-formed and poorly arranged garland. For I said, not by opinion but by certain knowledge, that in many parts he spoke in a very filthy and indecent fashion and provided very wicked exhortations. Indeed, this judgment is easy to make, for it is proven by the work itself. So I, or anyone who understands French, can condemn him on this point. But it is because he does not treat this kind of immorality in all parts of the work that I say I do not condemn him throughout.

Then you reply most correctly that I would like to find someone, as I said, who would be able to provide me a satisfactory explanation of what could possibly be the good of so much indecency. And yet, instead of providing me any solution, you go on to another topic without responding to this query. Then, like a madman, without any reason, you make a disgraceful retort such as what follows: "Such reckless presumption! Oh, what very foolish arrogance! Oh, what a speech issuing forth too rashly and thoughtlessly from the mouth of a woman, which condemns a man of such lofty intellect, of such devoted scholarship, who with such great effort and mature reflection made a book of such great nobility as that of the *Rose*, which indeed

217. By which she means the Jealous Husband.

218. Indeed, the version of Christine's letter that Pierre Col had in his possession was certainly similar to the one included in the "rhodophile" manuscript, which places this passage, found toward the end of the letter as Christine published it, in the very center. This version of the letter, marred by mistakes introduced in its scribal transmission, shortens it by a little over ten percent (in Hicks's edition it occupies 317 lines of prose, whereas Christine's comes to 357). Some of the omissions are due to scribal error, while others seem to have been done by design.

surpasses all others that have ever used the language in which he wrote his book: When you have read it a hundred times, if you understand the better part of it, you will never have better used your time or your intellect." My reply: O man deceived by obstinate opinion! I could certainly reply to you insultingly, but I do not wish to do so—notwithstanding the fact that you dismiss me with ugly reproaches, having little justification and no reason to do so. O obscured understanding! O perverted knowledge, blinded by your own will, you who judge painful venom to be a remedy for death, perverse doctrine to be a salutary example, bitter gall to be sweet honey, horrible ugliness to be consoling beauty! You whose error can be criticized by a simple little woman, in accord with the doctrine of Holy Church! Flee and bring to an end this perverse doctrine that could lead you to damnation—a doctrine that, when God has enlightened you with true understanding, will fill you with horror when you turn back and look at the path you traveled on the way to disaster.

In order to rebuke me, you say, "Obsequiousness makes friends, the truth makes you unpopular" (so says Terence).[219] And because of this you fear that I might want to bite him, and you advise me to watch out for my teeth. But, with all due respect, you should know for a certainty that your imagination is lacking. Indeed, because of the deceitful lies and the lack of truth in this work, I wouldn't just want to bite it but indeed rip out the very great, fallacious lies that are found there.

You respond to Lady Eloquence and to me that Master Jean de Meun introduced personages into his book and had each one speak according to what pertained to him. But in truth I must honestly confess to you that while one must have the tools appropriate to the game one wants to play, it is the will of the player that prepares them for use according to his needs. Nonetheless, begging your pardon, he certainly failed to present his personages adequately when he attributed to some of them things lying outside their proper function. This is the case with his priest whom he calls Genius, who so insistently orders men to bed women and to continue performing their duty without stop, but then declares that one ought to flee women more than anything else and says more evil and degrading things about them than anyone else in the book. I simply cannot understand how such remarks might pertain to his function or to those of many other personages who speak about this matter. You say that it is the function of the Jealous Man to do so. I say to you that, to some extent in all the personages, he [Jean de Meun] can scarcely refrain from insulting women who, thank God, are

219. See above, n. 129.

not harmed in any way by this. But I have already spoken extensively in my other letter about this topic, with regard to which you have scarcely offered me a response, so I do not intend to burden myself with it here.

Since this book of the *Rose* is so necessary and beneficial for the teaching of how to live virtuously as well as usefully, I beg you to tell me how this assemblage of the dissolute sayings of the Old Woman could bring profit to the common good. For if you mean that it is so that one may protect oneself, I really do not think that most people have ever had anything to do with the sort of terrible acts she describes, nor do they even know that they might exist. Thus such evil could not bring profit to the common good, for most people are not concerned with such things. And I would like to know if you yourself, after having read these things, retained the good lesson of being on your guard and living chastely, or instead held in memory the licentiousness of the words. This is indeed a rather surprising interpretation that you and the rest of his allies make, turning such horrible wickedness into such a great virtue. But also, with regard to the Jealous Man, who, you claim, speaks as would a jealous man, I say to you, what was the great need of wasting so many ungracious words for the good and for the teaching of common virtue? I thus give you the same reply as I did regarding the Old Woman.

What you say further, about what makes the Jealous Man, in your opinion, say so many evil things about women, is scarcely relevant to my argument, and so I pass over it.[220]

Later on, you ask Lady Eloquence and me, using comparisons, whether, if someone relates what someone else has said (as does Sallust who recounts the conspiracy of Catiline against the Roman republic, or Aristotle, who enumerates the opinions of ancient philosophers), he is responsible for the same crime he reports. When "Holy Scripture tells of the abominable sins of Sodom and Gomorrah, is it exhorting people to imitate them in doing so?" You seem to think that you make a good point, and a relevant one. But in the case of these authors or others, or even of Holy Scripture, I ask you whether, when they speak of these things, there are characters or other discourses, either before or after, that use indulgent and seductive words to encourage and embolden people to commit treason or to be heretics, and likewise with other evils—you know very well that this is not the case. For in whatever place such evils or others are similarly recounted in books, it is done in or-

220. Christine is certainly referring to the passage in which Pierre Col declares that a man's jealousy comes from his extreme love for his wife, which makes him believe that she is better than all others. When she misbehaves, he therefore declares that since she is superior, all others must be subject to the same faults (or worse). Obviously, Christine does not countenance men's love (rather than hatred) as a source of their mistreatment of women.

der to rebuke the thing, in such a way that when it is read out it makes an unpleasant impression upon those who hear it. And as for that preacher you wrote me about, saying that in his sermon he did indeed call to mind the foot on which one is limping (this you said because I declared that [human] nature did not need to be reminded of it in order to walk straighter), how did he call it to mind? How did he put it? "My children, play, have a good time, take it easy, for that is the path God created to paradise!"?[221] My Lord, he certainly did not! Rather he called this foot to mind in such a way as to horrify those listening to him. Someone could likewise say to you "May God give you a good day" in a way that sounds unpleasant and angry.

And then you make a kind of complaint against Chastity and say: "Ha! My lady! Is this the reward you wish to confer upon Master Jean de Meun, who so esteemed you and all the other virtues, while blaming all the vices that [human] understanding can conceive?" Truly, you repeat, "that human understanding can conceive." And then afterward you say that I should not smile at this. Ha! Indeed, you knew very well that I would laugh at this fine speech! For when I think of the exemplary teachings on chastity and the virtuous speeches that are in the book, truly I have reason to burst into laughter at what you are saying. Then after that, you declare, "whoever reads this book carefully will find instruction for fleeing all vices and pursuing all virtues"; then you recite some of the teachings that you say are found there. But I tell you in all honesty that you will have to say the same thing about the law of Mohammed. If you read the Koran, you will find therein some very good and very pious points according with our faith, and it would please you greatly. But it is completely worthy of scorn; taken as a whole, it is without value. The result is a total waste, for everything is measured by the conclusion. Do you not know that even in council, whatever might have been proposed beforehand, people stand by the final decision? And if Master Jean de Meun, I dare say, had spoken throughout his book of many things toward which human nature is inclined and which come to pass, but then returned to his argument and based his conclusion upon the morals and customs of a good life, you would have had greater reason to say that he did it for a good purpose. For you know that if a writer wishes to use the rules of rhetoric, he formulates his premises based on the topic he wishes to treat, and then goes from argument to argument, speaking of several things if he wishes, then

221. The context of these remarks, though unstated, is certainly Genius's speech in the *Romance of the Rose.* The personification, dressed as a religious figure, delivers a sermon in which he incites the listeners to sexual activity with the goal of procreation and states that this is the way to attain paradise. In Christine's mind, the preacher mentioned by Pierre Col suggests the preacher function of Genius.

comes back in his conclusion to speak of the reason why he composed his account.[222] But truly in this case the author did not at all fail in the aforementioned book, for ignorance had no part in it. But you will tell me that this was the work of Lorris.[223] Response: I consider it all to be one same edifice. And this will suffice as a response to this portion of your letter, even though you have said in it many things in support of your argument that I pass over, for everything must come to an end. But you can continue to dissect it as much as you see fit.

You said earlier that he does not reproach women but rather says good things about them. I am waiting for the truth of that statement to be proven. And you say that Saint Ambrose blamed the female sex more than he does, for he said that it is a sex accustomed to deceiving. I shall respond to you on this point. You know well that when the Church Fathers, and even Jesus Christ in his sermons, spoke, it was with a double meaning. It is therefore important to know that Saint Ambrose never said this about women themselves. For I believe that the good man would not have wanted to reproach anything except vice. He certainly knew that there have been many holy women, but he wanted to say that it is a sex concerning which men frequently deceive their souls. It is the same idea as when Solomon said: "The misdeed of a man is preferable to a woman's good deed."[224] We know that it would be erroneous to take this literally, and so instead we can use his very experience as an example. The misdeed of a man [committed against Solomon] would have been better for him, whatever might have been the circumstance, than any good quality that he could observe in the woman he loved so much that he worshiped idols because of her.[225] He might also have said it in the framework of God's plan,[226] for the misdeed of Judas is worth

222. The word used here is *narracion*, which is typically used with the meaning "story" but can also mean the telling of something, be it a fictional or real tale, or the formulation of an argument, which is clearly the sense it has here.

223. Christine seems to be thinking that a possible refutation would be not that Guillaume de Lorris wrote the conclusion but that he conceived the entire framework, or maybe simply that the image of the castle, source of the objectionable final sequence, was indeed the invention of Guillaume. Thus, the defense of Jean de Meun she anticipates from Pierre is that the continuator of the *Rose* would be guiltless because he simply carried out the intention of the first author.

224. Ecclesiasticus (Sirach) 42:14: "melior est enim iniquitas viri quam mulier benefaciens."

225. 3 Kings [1 Kings] 11:1–8 (text also referred to by Gerson [no. 20]).

226. The text reads *par prophetie* which, translated literally, "by (or through) prophecy," makes little sense. The use of the term "prophecy" in medieval theology meant something more than the common meaning of predicting something to come; it has to do with the fact that all events, both in the Bible and in history, have a purpose in God's larger, unknowable scheme; more specifically, the Old Testament frequently prophesies events in the New Testament. Hence, my

more than the good deed of Judith who killed Holofernes, or that of some other woman.

But afterward you say some incredible things, for you affirm unequivocally that I reproach women more than he does when I claim that if one read the book of the *Rose* before queens and princesses, they would be obliged to cover their faces, blushing with shame. And then you explain as follows: "Why would they blush? It would seem that they would consider themselves guilty of the vices that the Jealous Man recounts of women." Ha! God! How poorly stated this is, and how improperly reported! You do yourself no honor when you recount something of which the opposite could be proven; it is ill thought out. When I said that women would be obliged to cover their faces, blushing with shame, it was not at all on account of the words of the Jealous Man. I was referring instead to their hearing the horrible things included in the ending: most abominable! This is why I said: "What good can there be in such a book, which cannot be read in their presence with decency?" And in saying that they would blush because of it, I am not in the slightest reproaching them, but rather praising them for having the chaste virtue of modesty.

You then respond to Lady Eloquence, because there is included in her complaint mention of the defamatory and vituperative statements that Jean de Meun makes about religion: you claim that he did not criticize it at all. Well, I reply to you sincerely and with all due respect that since he was a public defamer, he defames it excessively and without any exception. And that good Catholic of very devout will is certainly capable of understanding this and knows how to admonish the writer's wrongdoing; so I will leave this to him, for it does not pertain to the discussion in my first letter.[227] But as you yourself concede that I might say to you (and there you speak the truth), you quote the good words and go along gathering them as you please and as it suits your argument, while leaving out the evil ones.[228]

As for the exhortation that Lady Eloquence bemoans (regarding the instructions for taking Jealousy's castle, with which she claims he wanted to

translation. What Christine means is that the events are understood after the fact to have a different meaning in God's plan, so that what seems reprehensible at first glance might take on a different meaning later. For a medieval Christian, Judas's betrayal is much more important and crucial than Judith's defiance of Holofernes.

227. The "good Catholic" who will answer this point is, of course, Jean Gerson. This is another example of Christine's slippage from the statement of the character Lady Eloquence to that of the author.

228. Christine is referring specifically to Pierre Col's statement: "But on this point you will reply to me that I am quoting the good words and not the evil ones."

drive chastity out of all women), you make an incredible rejoinder when you say that it is meant to advise the guards to "block more effectively the places through which it might be captured or to post better guards there." And then you say that in all types of wars those who are attacked are at an advantage, provided that they are forewarned. Now, let's talk a little bit about wars, perchance between you and me. I tell you that there is one type of war in which the assailants have the advantage. And do you know what that is? It is when the captain or leader is more malicious and better trained in war, and he is dealing with a weak and innocent opponent unaccustomed to war. There is still another factor that often harms the defenders, even assuming they are strong: it is the betrayal and perfidious flattery of those very people they trusted (this is how the fortified castle of Ilion was taken long ago). Furthermore, with regard to a castle under siege, neither you nor anyone else would be capable of giving advice on how the crevices of betrayal could be plugged up, for they are too well concealed. Master Jean de Meun teaches how Jealousy's castle will be attacked and captured. He does not at all do it so that the defenders may plug up the crevices, for in no way is he speaking to them nor is he on their side. Rather he sustains and encourages the assailants in every type of assault, just as if I were to advise you on how to defeat your enemy, it would not at all be so that he might protect himself from you. If you wish to claim that he does not teach this but simply recounts how the castle was taken, I say to you that whoever were to recount a malicious way of making counterfeit money or how someone actually might have done it, he would indeed be teaching it. This is why I say with certainty that he did it for no other purpose than to instruct the assailants.[229]

Afterward, if you were willing to give it some thought, you say something that catches you in your own trap when you bring Ovid's *Art of Love* into your discussion. Then you provide further proof of this, for which I am grateful, when you say that he was wrongly exiled because of it. You contend that when Ovid wrote it, it was in Latin, which women did not understand, and that he gave it only to the assailants to teach them how to attack the castle. That was the purpose of his book. However, the excessive jealousy of Roman men drove him into exile on account of it without any

229. The verb used here is *introduire,* which, as in modern French, can mean "to introduce, to lead [someone] into a place." However, it frequently has the meaning "to instruct," and Christine de Pizan uses it unambiguously with that meaning in several other works. It is tempting to see here the first, more concrete meaning, as do Baird and Kane in their translation, "to admit the assailants" (*La querelle de la Rose,* 134), but normally in that case the place would be specified. It is, however, quite possible that Christine used this particular word for "to instruct" here precisely because of its ambiguity in the context of a castle siege.

reason, so you say. There is no doubt in my mind that if you had given it careful consideration you would not have introduced Ovid's *Art of Love* into the argument in order to excuse your master. But you are justified in doing so insofar as it is the absolute foundation and principle for this book of the *Rose,* which is a mirror, indeed a model for the good and chaste life, just as Jean derived it from the aforementioned Ovid, who speaks of nothing other than chastity! Ah! Good God! How obvious it is that your sheer willfulness has blinded your good sense when you say that he was exiled without cause, indeed, that the Romans, who at that time ruled all their affairs with impeccably organized government, banished him wrongly, so you say, because of jealousy. How can this be? Then you say that Meun incorporated not only the *Art of Love* by Ovid in his book but works by many other authors as well. Thus, by your very reasoning, it is proven that Meun speaks to the assailants, as did Ovid, whom he adapts. But you claim that "to the extent that he recounts different methods of attack, in the same measure he provides counsel to the guards of the castle so as to defend themselves." Indeed, he is doing this in the same way that someone who would attack you with a mind to killing you (may God protect you from this!) would actually be teaching you how you ought to defend yourself! He would be doing you a great favor! You should thank him for it! At the very least you cannot deny that he does not teach how to harm the assailants, however weak or strong the defenders might be.

I do not yet wish to remain silent on your statement that Ovid was exiled out of jealousy and without reason. When the wise Romans saw and took note of the perverse doctrine, the perilous venom prepared in order to inject into the hearts of young people an attraction to dissolution and sloth, and the traps set out to deceive, to capture, and to seduce their daughters and wives, indeed to deprive them of their virginity and chastity, they exiled the author of such doctrine. They grieved over its dissemination with good reason, and thus inflicted a punishment that was, truth be told, more merciful than sufficient. And there is no doubt that they burned his book wherever they could find it, but the root of a noxious plant always remains.[230] Ah! What a poorly named book, *The Art of Love!* For it is not at all about love! It can well be called the art of delusive and malicious efforts to deceive women. What a beautiful doctrine this is! Is it the be-all and end-all to deceive women? Who are women? Who are they? Are they serpents, wolves, lions, dragons, vipers, or rapacious, devouring beasts and enemies of human-

230. Hicks's manuscript (*Le débat,* 138) omits the word "always" (*toudis*), which I reinstate from the B manuscripts.

ity, so that it is necessary to devise an art of deceiving and capturing them? Then read this *Art*: learn how to invent ruses! Take them forcefully! Deceive them! Insult them! Attack this castle! Men, take care that none of them be released among you and that everything be given over to shame! But by God, they are nonetheless your mothers, your sisters, your daughters, your wives, and your girlfriends; they are you yourselves and you yourselves are they. Now deceive them a great deal, for "it is much better, dear master, to deceive,"[231] etc.

It makes me laugh when you say that you loaned your book of the *Rose* to a man who was a foolish lover in order for him to free himself from his foolish love, and that it worked so well you heard him swear by his faith that it was the thing that most helped him to rid himself of it. And you claim that you said this because I said at the end of my letter, "How many have become hermits because of it?" Response: Well, I promise you that if you had loaned your friend a devotional book of Saint Bernard or some good legend leading to salvation and aiming to demonstrate that there is only one good love—to which one must fasten one's heart and one's devotion, in the way that Philosophy demonstrates it to Boethius—or some other similar thing, you would have acted more to his benefit. But make sure that you have not given him the means to remove himself from the sun's heat only to throw himself into a blazing furnace. Let me give you another example without lying, since we are on the miracles of the *Romance of the Rose*. Not long ago, I heard one of those companions you have in your office, and whom you know well, a man of authority, talk about a married man he knows, who has as much faith in the *Romance of the Rose* as he does in the Gospel. He is exceptionally jealous, and when his passion takes hold of him most violently he goes to fetch his book, reads it before his wife, and then he strikes her and beats her up, saying: "Foul woman, just like the one he speaks of, truly you are playing the same kind of trick on me. That good and wise man Master Jean de Meun knew well what women are capable of doing!" And at each word that he finds applicable to him he strikes a blow or two with his foot or the palm of his hand. So it seems to me whenever someone swears by that book, a poor wife such as she pays dearly for it.

I find such great prolixity of language tiresome;[232] since it is tiresome to

231. Hicks's manuscript (*Le débat*, 139) omits "to deceive," which I reinstate from two of the B manuscripts.

232. The words used here, the noun *ennuy/anuy* and the verb *anuye(r)*, typically refer in the Middle Ages to notions of annoyance, unpleasantness, or even suffering, but could also have the modern French meaning of "boredom." Both semantic fields are possible here, but since Christine is referring to the prolixity of her argument, I have chosen the latter as a translation.

me, then I suppose that it could be so for the readers. However, since I must reply to the arguments that have been advanced (otherwise, it would not be understandable), I must because of that lengthen my own matter. May I thus be excused by anyone who considers it boring.

You still cannot stop talking about the Old Woman, and say that when she speaks to Fair Welcoming, she says to him at the outset: "I don't want to put you in the way of love, but if you want to get involved with it, I will gladly show you, etc."; and then she claims that she is preaching to him so that he will not be deceived. Response: Good God! What a malicious way of deceiving this is, to show that what one is doing and saying, however evil it might be, is aimed at a good purpose and for a good reason! For there is no one so naïve that he will not be on his guard against deceit, if he is made aware of it: one must therefore hide it with trickery, and the ruse typical of the malicious deceiver is to begin his discourse with a pleasing introduction in order better to accomplish his wickedness. So what you have proposed is no justification in this section.

You say that if there is anything evil said about the female sex and that defames it, these things are only being quoted by him from other authors. Response: I know well that he is not the first person to have said evil things, but he makes it worse when he repeats it.

You say that all this was meant to better teach those being attacked how to protect the castle. Response: When someone is being encouraged and advised to perform evil acts, there is no reason to infer that it is done so that he will avoid them.

You say that he did it also in order to follow up the subject matter of Master Guillaume de Lorris. Response: He who follows someone who has strayed from his path does not deserve to be excused if he himself goes astray.

You say that, in so doing, he speaks of all things according to their station for the benefit of humankind, as much for the soul as for the body. Response: We do not hear him[233] speak of all things openly according to their station; moreover, he speaks of many things in ways that do not accord with their station and to the detriment of body and soul, as has already been proved.

You say that "it is for this reason that he speaks of paradise and of the virtues: in order for people to pursue them (and of the vices, in order for

233. Hicks's edition (*Le débat,* 141) gives the reading "il ne lait" from his manuscript, which does not seem to make sense in the context, for it would yield a reading such as "he does not neglect to speak." Hicks does not indicate variant readings for this line in the other manuscripts. I have used the reading from Ward's edition, "on ne l'oit" ("Epistles on the Romance of the Rose," 104), which provides a perfectly acceptable reading.

people to flee them)." Response: True enough, but he claims vices to be virtues when he has his characters advise people to do evil, as has been said; and he turns virtues into vice when he attributes so many shameful and wretched misfortunes to the state of marriage, which is sacred and sanctioned, and likewise to other fine estates which he globally defames. And he speaks ill of paradise when he says (however much it might be in somewhat veiled terms—though it comes down to the same thing) that lascivious people will go there. And this he has Genius say, Genius who excommunicates by his power (which is nil) those who refuse to perform the work of Nature. It is the vices that he teaches more adequately than the virtues.

You say that "the more he speaks of vices and virtues, of hell and paradise, the one next to the other, the better he shows the blessedness[234] of certain ones and the ugliness of the others." Response: He does not at all show the blessedness of paradise when he says that malefactors will go there. He mixes paradise in with the filthy acts of which he speaks for the following reason: in order to lend more credence to his book. But if you wish to hear a better description of paradise and hell using more subtle terminology, expressed more majestically from a theological perspective, more profitably, more poetically, and with greater efficaciousness, read the book attributed to Dante or have it explained to you since it is brilliantly written in the Florentine language.[235] There you will hear another discourse, more wisely conceived and with a better foundation, and, may it not displease you, where you can find more profit than in your *Romance of the Rose*—and a hundred times better written. Do not be angered by this, but there is no comparison.

You claim that Genius does not in the slightest promise paradise to foolish lovers. Response: The devil makes him promise it since it is not his to give. But you state that Lady Eloquence accuses him of it, whereas he is speaking, so you say, of those who will virtuously carry out the works of Nature. Response: Now you come to my bailiwick, thank God! In truth he [Genius] places there [in paradise] quite plainly (specifying neither "virtuously" nor "wickedly") those who will carry out the above-mentioned works.

234. Christine's quote uses the word *beatitude,* whereas Pierre Col's text has *beauté;* this could be due either to a misreading on her part or to one that occurred in the transmission of the text (either Pierre's or Christine's).

235. As Hicks notes (*Le débat,* 226–27), this is an early, but not the earliest, reference to Dante in the context of French letters. One should remember as well that Christine's Italian heritage would have disposed her to the Florentine poet as a counterbalance to the massive reputation that Jean de Meun had acquired. It is likewise interesting to note that what is generally considered to be the first French work inspired in part by the *Divine Comedy* is Christine's *Long Road of Learning,* the beginning of which is dated only three days after this letter.

And you say that doing this [the works of Nature] virtuously is not the same thing as being a foolish lover. Response: In this passage he never spoke about doing it virtuously. But I can tell you that it is worse to be lecherous in several places, as he wishes to teach, than to be a foolish lover in one single place.

You say that Nature and Genius do not urge people to be foolish lovers, but rather to pursue the above-mentioned works, which are permissible for the goals [that Nature and Genius urge, namely, in order to continue the human species].[236] Response: Then you mean to say that since Nature does not urge it, being a foolish lover is contrary to nature, which, I beg your pardon, is not at all the case; but since he [Genius] says these works are permissible for these goals, it would be important to know in what manner one ought to accomplish them.

You say it is to continue the human species and to relinquish the wicked sin that one must not name. Response: There is no reason to debate this issue at such length for, thanks be to God, the human species is not at all coming to an end: It is a foolish enterprise, a waste of time, to encourage water to flow downhill! And the other sin he alludes to has no notoriety in France, God be praised! There is no need to put such advice in anyone's mouth.

You say that although you neither dare nor wish to say that to perform

236. The passage in Christine's letter is here corrupt (it says only *aux fins* [to the ends, for the goals], without specifying which ones) and must be completed by Pierre Col's original statement in his letter, which I have put in brackets. The passage from the manuscript Ward edited ("Epistles on the Romance of the Rose," 105) gives "aux fins amoureux" (which Hicks's note [*Le débat,* 142] indicates is found solely in the British Library MS Harley 4431), obviously a scribal error (the word following *fins* in Pierre's text starts likewise with an *a*); Baird and Kane (*La querelle de la Rose,* 138) translate this most puzzlingly as "courtly lovers," which makes no sense in the context of this argument. Furthermore, in two spots (the last sentence of the previous paragraph and the sentence following this note) the manuscript tradition transmits *fort amoureux* (for *fol amoureux*), which Baird and Kane (ibid.) translate as "deeply in love," but once again there is never any question in this argument of people deeply in love. For instance, the following line is translated by Baird and Kane as "Do you then mean to say, since Nature does not preach it, that it is against nature to be deeply in love?" But Christine is clearly referring to the first line of this paragraph, where it is a matter of Nature and Genius not urging people to be "foolish lovers." It might seem surprising for Christine to be defending foolish lovers by saying that their actions are not "contrary to nature," but the latter expression, *contre nature,* is a coded one referring to sexual relations considered perverse, such as sodomy, bestiality, and incest. It would be normal to insist that heterosexual relations, even excessive ones, are indeed within the realm of nature. It is in fact to such unnatural sexual activity that Christine refers in the following paragraph with the phrase "the wicked sin that one must not name." Furthermore, this remark fits into Christine's global argument against Pierre, who suggested that having as much sex as you want, as long as it is for the purpose of procreation, is preferable to being a foolish lover. As Christine just stated in the last line of the preceding paragraph, the faithfulness of a foolish lover to one person is, in fact, preferable to the promiscuity she sees in Genius's doctrine.

the work in question "outside wedlock is not a sin . . ." Response, without going any further:[237] True, but God only knows what you—and other disciples like you, who might have dared to say it—think about it; however, it is best to remain silent on that score, and for good reason. Nonetheless, so you say, it is permitted in marriage. Response: God be praised for this! This we know well! Yet the book of the *Rose* never expresses it in this manner anywhere; rather, it says clearly and literally: "All women for all men and all men for all women."[238] But you try to argue that this is the way Master Jean de Meun understood it when he delivered the following speech in the chapter of the Old Woman: "For this reason men made marriages, through the counsel of wise men, in order to prevent dissolute conduct . . ."[239] Response: You have gone to some length to find this quotation for me and introduce into the argument something that was said in another context. The Old Woman was not preaching to Fair Welcoming about marriage. She took great pains not to do so, and there is not a thing she says that is directed toward a good purpose. And so I believe that Master Jean de Meun did not at all have her deliver this speech to praise marriage, for this was never her role. And you should remember that you said elsewhere that it was not Meun who was speaking anyway; rather each of the characters was speaking according to his role. Yet it was *he* who delivered this praiseworthy speech, while he was not the one speaking in the chapter of the Jealous Husband! In this way you state something and then deny it, and this is quite far from Genius's argument, of which we were speaking, for the good man never gave a thought to marriage![240] And whatever you say, God help me, this is not at all your opinion either [that Genius was speaking of marriage]. Still, since you are so intent upon exonerating Meun, you strive to add a gloss, saying that this is what he meant: "that one can perform the work in question licitly at least in marriage." Yet it is quite nonsensical to say that in the state of marriage one is supposed to perform the act with such application and diligence, when he so adamantly and excessively criticizes what he claims to be found in married life, stating that there are so many quarrels and shameful, unpleasant incidents that there is no one who, however much he might wish to en-

237. Christine is aware of not having finished the previous sentence and cuts it off knowingly, as though to display rhetorically the urgency of her correction.

238. *Rose,* ed. Lecoy, 1. 13856; trans. Dahlberg, 238 (altered).

239. On Pierre Col's use of this quotation, see above, n. 163.

240. This is a sharp retort to Pierre Col's way of playing fast and loose with the intentions of allegorical characters, as he had said about Theological Eloquence (using identical terms): "never . . . was the good lady concerned with this matter" (no. 23).

ter marriage, should not recoil from doing so (if one were to believe him). As a result, these works would be inadequately carried out. He should have praised the state in which one is supposed to perform these works [marriage] in order to make people eager to enter into it. But he does the exact opposite and so it is quite nonsensical. Nor does it appear that he understands it in this way; you yourself, in order to bolster your effort, say next (about praising marriage, in order to confirm that this is why he said it) that Saint Augustine said: "He who is without a wife in marriage thinks of matters concerning God in order to please him," but as for the man who is "joined in marriage, he thinks of worldly matters in order to please his wife." Regarding which you claim afterward that you said this for those who, without reason, wish to verbally reproach an author without regard to his quality, though he is noteworthy and has never previously been reproached. You have indeed proved very well that Master Jean de Meun, in speaking so much about performing the work of Nature, meant it to be in wedlock! God, how well this is proved! Indeed, as the well-known proverb says about the glosses of Orléans: they destroy the text.[241]

You still are not capable of remaining silent and take off on another long speech, in your continued effort to excuse your good master. But I have no intention of repeating the whole thing word for word, for I would find it too boring, and it is already boring me to speak at such length about this topic—furthermore, everything ultimately comes to an end.

You say that "since not everyone has read the book of the *Rose*," you will quote Genius's own words, as they are found in the book. So you do indeed quote many of the things he says, but you skip over many others, and you go along gathering here and there the ones you find most pleasing; and you have no desire to place the good he says back along with the evil. You do not neglect to mention that he said that one should give back what belongs to others, if one has it, and that one should be compassionate and merciful, and other such things.[242] And indeed, that one should do the works of God for God's sake and one will go to paradise. I believe that he wanted to follow

241. Hicks (*Le débat,* 227) suggests that it was proverbial to refer to the glosses of Orléans as destroying the text. The schools of Orléans, going back to the twelfth century, were known for the study of the classics and their extensive commentary tradition. Hasenohr (review of *Le débat,* 131) posits instead that it is a reference to juridical practice there, inasmuch as it had become a center of the teaching of law as of the mid-thirteenth century (although she does not specify what aspect of this practice would turn it into a proverbial expression).

242. Christine is here alluding to the closing words of Genius, quoted by Pierre Col (*Rose,* ed. Lecoy, ll. 20607–17; trans. Dahlberg, 337).

the order and the sect of the Turlupins,[243] and thus mixed venom with honey, and sweet liquor with bile.[244] Behold the good to be found there.

I don't know why we are debating these questions at such length, for I believe that neither you nor I have any desire to alter our opinions: you say he is good; I say he is bad. Go ahead, convince me that he is good, and when you and your other accomplices have debated a great deal, using all your clever arguments, and you have managed to turn the bad into the good, I will then believe that the *Romance of the Rose* is good! But I know well that it is fit for those who want to live a wicked life and who want to protect themselves from others more than they want others to protect themselves from them. However, for those who wish to live a good and simple life, without getting too wrapped up in the sensual pleasures of the world, not wishing to deceive other people or to be deceived by them, the book is useless. In truth, I would rather be on the side of its opponents than of its accomplices, for I am of the opinion that the wolf should have the smaller portion. And as the good and worthy man who composed the above-mentioned legal case said: "Would that God had not allowed such a *Rose* to have ever been planted in the garden of Christianity!"—[I say this] even though you claim to be one of his disciples. And since you want to be one, so be it. As for me, I renounce his teaching, for I am drawn to another that I consider more profitable and that is more pleasing to me. Moreover, I am not alone in this opinion; I do not know why you, his disciples, go after me more than the others. There is absolutely no honor in attacking the weakest adversary. There is such a great mass of wise and learned men, worthy of belief and full of knowledge, and in truth there are also among the great princes of this realm knights, nobles, and many others who are of the same opinion as I and consider this to be a useless and dishonorable work. Why do you not all proceed to tear apart the great trunk of the tree and do all you can to uproot it and eradicate it, so that the root, out of which can spring and rise up the sap and juices, would be totally destroyed, instead of going after the little branches on top that have neither strength nor vigor? You believe you are extirpating the whole thing when you attack me, I who am but the voice of a little cricket who beats his tiny wings and makes a lot of noise, all of which is absolutely nothing compared with the noble and delightful song of the gracious birds.

But you say that you cannot sufficiently express your "astonishment at how anyone dares blame him—not only him, but those who esteem and love

243. On the heretical sect known as the Turlupins, see Gerson's *Considerate lilia* (see above, ch. 2, nn. 104 and 107).

244. Images comparable to these are used in Gerson's treatise (no. 20).

his book of the *Rose*." Response: I *can* sufficiently express my astonishment at how someone dares undertake to praise this book, in which are included many topics that are enough to lead a human soul into damnable error.[245]

You say that, as for yourself, you prefer to be "blamed for esteeming and loving his book rather than being one of its extremely clever accusers." You resemble Heloïse of the Paraclete, who said that she would prefer to be called the *meretrix* of Master Peter Abelard than be crowned queen.[246] It would seem that wishes that are most preferred are not all reasonable.

You say that everyone should know that "there still remain seven thousand . . . who are at the ready to defend it." Response: It is a general rule that an evil sect multiplies without any urging, like a weed,[247] but in many situations the greatest number does not warrant that something be presumed better. And, God willing, never will such a large gathering take place, for this is not an article of faith. Let each person maintain what he wishes.

You say that if he were to have lived at the same time as the group of us who blame him, you would posit that we had an express hatred for him personally; but we have never seen him, so you cannot imagine where it comes from. Response: Since we have never seen him and he has never done us any harm, that gives you all the better reason to think that we are motivated by the pure and simple, legitimate truth. For a person moved by hatred is not to be given any credence. You go on to say, "unless it is on account of the grandeur of the book, all the more susceptible of being buffeted by the winds of envy. For ignorance is not the cause of it in anyone," so you say, "unless it is because of having read little of the book." Response: You can be certain that

245. Unlike the B manuscripts, that used by Hicks does not repeat the negation contained in the reference to Pierre Col's text ("I cannot sufficiently express . . ."). Clearly, as throughout this passage, Christine's response mimics Pierre Col in order to belittle his argument. Here, either with or without negation, it provides an acceptable text, but it seems to me that to remove the negation is a clever way for Christine to show that she is indeed capable of being sufficiently astonished that people might praise the *Rose.*

246. Christine is here paraphrasing a statement made by Heloïse in her response to Abelard's *Story of My Calamities.* Her point is that freely given love is preferable to the chains of wedlock: "If Augustus, Emperor of the whole world, thought fit to honor me with marriage and conferred all the earth on me to possess for ever, it would be dearer and more honorable to me to be called not his Empress but your whore." (*Letters of Abelard and Heloise,* trans. Radice, 114). The passage is adapted by Jean de Meun in the *Rose,* which is undoubtedly where Christine got it, since both contain the detail of the crowning: "I still would rather . . . be called your whore than be crowned empress" (ed. Lecoy, ll. 8791–94; trans. Dahlberg, 161). Christine uses the Latin term for "whore," which I have maintained.

247. Christine is playing with one version of a well-known proverbial expression: "male herbe croist volentiers" (a bad weed grows readily) (Morawski, *Proverbes français,* no. 1164, and variants).

the good and wise man who rebukes him[248] (regarding whom you are willing to admit that it is not out of ignorance) has no feelings of envy toward that book; for I believe the dignity of his very exalted life would not allow him to envy even something more worthy. As for myself, in spite of my ignorance, I promise you that I feel no envy with regard to it. And why would I? It leaves me neither hot nor cold, nor does it give or take away good or evil [from me]. Nor does it speak of any situation in which I find myself and which could give me cause for indignation, for I am not married, nor do I wish to be, nor am I a nun: Nothing he says applies to me. I am not Fair Welcoming, I am not afraid of the Old Woman, and I have no rosebuds to protect. Yet I promise you that I love beautiful, insightful, and well-written[249] books and that I look around for them, seek them out, and read them with pleasure, however rudimentary my understanding of them might be. And if I do not at all like the book of the *Rose*, it is simply and entirely because it is an exhortation to evil and an indecent thing to read, inspiring more evil than good in people's hearts. Moreover, in my judgment, it can be the cause of damnation and deterioration of the lives of those who hear it and delight in it, drawing them to lewd behavior. So I swear to you on my soul and by my faith that I am motivated by no other cause. And what you say afterward, that it is possibly the case that we criticize it in order to make people more eager to read it, and that our opinion would therefore be good, you can be certain that this is not our motivation![250]

After all this, you attribute greater merit to me than I in fact have—I thank you for that—and claim that you are begging me to preserve "the honor" that I have to look after . . . ; and that if people have praised me "for having shot a little cannonball over the towers of Notre-Dame," that I should not attempt "to hit the moon with a heavy, massive arrow"; that I should beware lest I "resemble the crow, who, because people praised his song, began to sing louder and let his mouthful drop." Response: In truth, I could not answer for any topic as fittingly as I can for my own situation. Thus I can at this point bear witness to the truth out of reliable knowledge. You charge, or rather accuse, me as though I were guilty of self-importance. But I swear to you by my faith that I never had the presumption to claim that I had shot as high as the towers of Notre-Dame and do not know

248. Christine once again refers here to Gerson.

249. I have preferred the text of the B manuscripts, *bien traittiez,* to that of Hicks's manuscript (*Le débat,* 147), *biaux traittiés,* which is doubtless due to a scribal error.

250. Gerson takes much greater exception to this implication in his response to Pierre Col, seeing his entire professional status and probity called into question (see no. 28).

how I might attempt anything higher; never will the presumption of singing louder make me drop a mouthful. For I reckon my status and knowledge to be things of no greatness. There is nothing else to it whatsoever except that I love study and the solitary life, this I can claim truthfully. It is quite possible that by frequenting the solitary life of study I have gathered some of the low-lying little flowers of the delightful garden, rather than climbing into the tall trees in order to gather the beautiful, sweet-smelling, and tasty fruit (not at all that the appetite and the will to do so were not great, but that the weakness of my understanding did not allow it). But on account of the fragrance of even the little flowers, out of which I had made slender garlands,[251] those who wanted to obtain them (to whom I would not have dared or had the capacity to refuse them) were astounded by my labor, not for any greatness to be found there, but because of its novelty, which is out of the ordinary. So they did not keep quiet about it—even though it had been concealed for a long time, and I promise you that it was not made public at my request. And if you are suggesting that I might have composed some things in consideration of certain individuals, this happened after it was already common knowledge (I do not say this to make any excuses, for there is no need for any, but in order to dispel any opinion that I was assuming some kind of authority through my actions).[252]

Also, I beg you and those who share your opinion not to be displeased with me on account of my writings and the present debate over the book of the *Rose*. For the beginning of it happened by accident and not by a preconceived intention, whatever opinion I might have had on the question, as you

251. Christine uses elsewhere the gathering of flowers to speak of her confection of her books, as in the following passage from *Christine's Vision*, part 3, chap. 25 (ed. Reno and Dulac, 136): "et les fleurs d'icelui [livre de Boece] je ay cueillies et appliquees yci a ton propos pour faire d'une sorte ung graciex chapel avec les ditz des sains docteurs pour ton livre a la fin comme victorieux couronner" (and I have gathered the flowers of the book of Boethius and applied them to your situation in order to make a gracious chaplet of sorts with the sayings of the Church Fathers, as a way of crowning your book victoriously at the end). Here Lady Philosophy explains her exposition of Boethius and others as a service to Christine's book.

252. Pierre's suggestion of Christine's presumption in her professional endeavors leads her to defend herself for her enterprising solicitation of the protection of various noble patrons (consider for instance her dedicatory letters to the queen of France and Guillaume de Tignonville [nos. 16 and 17 above]). One recalls that Christine's *Debate of Two Lovers* (no. 3 above), written at least a year or two earlier, was dedicated to the duke of Orléans and that her first great success, *Othea's Letter*, certainly completed by the time of this letter, has survived with dedications to four different noble patrons. Christine's defense is, quite simply, that her fame was not initially of her making, that she had in fact tried to keep her work a secret, and that it was only after people actively sought out her writings that she dedicated copies to them. What I have translated as "in consideration of" corresponds to the Middle French expression *au nom de*, which in this context certainly means something like "in order to seek the protection or patronage of."

can see in a small pamphlet where I laid out the initial cause and the last term of our debate. And it would be very distressing to me to be subject to such a lack of freedom that I would not dare respond to others with the truth according to my conscience on a topic that cannot cause any harm; rather, it might provide advice to someone wiser than myself, inducing him to reflect further on something that he has not considered at sufficient length, for, as a common proverb says: "Occasionally a fool advises a wise man."[253]

And it is nonsense when you say the Holy Church, in which there have been so many worthy men since it [the book of the *Rose*] was written, tolerated it for a long time without rebuke (it was waiting for myself and the others to come along to reproach it!). For you know that all things are set in motion at a certain time, and that nothing is long when compared to the expanse of years. And it often happens that a great swelling can be cured by a tiny lancet. How did Holy Church allow the opinion concerning the conception of Our Lady, which is a more important issue, to persist for such a long time without reproaching anyone for it? But not long ago something that had never been debated came forth with a great outburst, and yet it is not an article of the faith any more than this is.[254] So let each person believe what he wants to the best of his ability. As for me, I do not intend to write any more on this topic, no matter who writes to me about it, for I have not undertaken to drink the entire Seine. What I have written is written. It is not at all for fear of making a mistake relating to opinion that I will remain silent, even though a lack of wit and of knowledge deprives me of a pleasing style, but that I would rather tackle some other material more to my taste.

So I beg all those who come across my modest writings to have the good will to make allowances for the deficiency of my knowledge out of consideration for the person in question, and to attribute everything to an

253. See for example Morawski, *Proverbes français,* no. 2450: "Ung foul conseille bien ung saige" (A fool indeed provides counsel to a wise man). The exact verb used by Christine, *avise,* is found in Morawski's variants.

254. This is an oblique reference to the Juan de Monzon Affair (1387–89), in which the latter, a Dominican and student at the University of Paris, voiced a series of propositions in a public lecture required of all doctoral candidates. Among these propositions was a statement previously supported by medieval theologians, to the effect that the Virgin Mary's birth was not immaculate, but to which many ardent worshipers of the fourteenth century were opposed, including Pierre d'Ailly, who was at the time chancellor of the University of Paris. Juan de Monzon was officially condemned and excommunicated, largely owing to the case pled by Pierre d'Ailly before the pope, and the Immaculate Conception became a part of Church orthodoxy. See Hicks, *Le débat,* 228; and Guenée, *Between Church and State,* 159–68. Interestingly enough, Jean Gerson's earliest extant work was a treatise against Juan de Monzon written in 1389–90 (on which see G. Ouy, "La plus ancienne œuvre retrouvée de Jean Gerson: *Le brouillon inachevé d'un traité contre Juan de Monzon (1389–90),*" *Romania* 83 [1962]: 433–92).

honest intention in view of a beneficial goal—without which I would not want to publish anything. Thus I will draw to a close my essay devoted to this debate, devoid of acrimony, that was begun, elaborated, and ended in a spirit of cheerful entertainment, disrespectful to no one. So I pray to the blessed Trinity, perfect and complete wisdom, that it might wish to illuminate you and all those in particular who love knowledge and the nobility of good morals with such true light that they may be led to celestial joy.

Amen.

Written and completed by me, Christine de Pizan, the second day of October, in the year 1402.

Your well-wisher, a friend in knowledge,
Christine de Pizan

23. PIERRE COL TO CHRISTINE DE PIZAN (FRAGMENT, NOVEMBER 1402)[255]

FRENCH PROSE

To a woman of lofty understanding, demoiselle Christine de Pizan

In spite of the fact that you, a wise and reflective woman who knows and recognizes that it is human to sin but that persistence is the work of the devil, have proposed to write no more words of censure or blame against the compilation of the *Romance of the Rose,* you will nevertheless not keep my pen from writing back to you. For after so many rebukes and retorts[256] that have been advanced and written down by you against so prominent a writer, both the cause of justice and good custom grant me the right of a reply, I who as a disciple of the writer in question have written only one response—though it is scarcely necessary, since, to the extent that my meager intellect can comprehend it, the reading of your evasive arguments alone is enough of an answer. Moreover, your extravagantly specious statements and rhetorical ornaments do not in the slightest obscure the truth that I uphold, nor do they inflict any stain on the brilliant renown of Master Jean de Meun. And I believe that this is why the provost of Lille did not bother to respond to you. For the same reason, I myself was for some time inclined not to respond to you, as well as

255. Translated from *Le débat,* ed. Hicks, 153–54.

256. The word used here is *duplicacion,* a somewhat rare term used in a legal context to refer to an objection raised to a first objection, or even the turning of an objection on an adversary.

because I had much to deal with elsewhere. Nonetheless, as an entertaining way of learning and practicing my skills, I will respond to some specific details and evasive arguments contained in your letter replying to me, which was delivered on the thirtieth of October. I ask you to consider as reiterated the justifications included in my other response.

Even though you say a bit before the end of your last reply that there is no honor in taking you on, you being the weakest adversary, and that one ought to "tear apart the great trunk" and not limit oneself to the little branches, given that there are many "wise and learned men . . . great princes of this realm and knights . . ." who are of the same opinion as you, I have never heard of anyone who blamed it [the *Rose*] either before or after you, except the person who composed the court case of Lady Eloquence. And yet you reproach me when you say that I dared to criticize the work of such a prominent cleric, which sounds like a contradiction. Don't be upset, but here and elsewhere you fall into the pit that you had prepared for me, namely, that of affirmations and retractions, when you say that the others ought to have been attacked, and you reproach me for not having seen to it.

When I think of the tiny little branch, I remember the familiar proverb that goes: "This blame amounts to great praise for you." O sweet, glorious God! How many people there are who never demean their reputation, or who blame themselves somewhat only to glorify themselves! Here you are calling yourself a tiny little branch and yet . . .[257]

257. The cause of the fragmentation of this letter in the sole manuscript containing it, as well as Pierre Col's initial letter, is not material. The scribe simply stops writing in the middle of the page, leaving the rest blank, suggesting that his model was not itself complete.

IV
AFTERMATH

24. FROM JEAN GERSON, SERMONS OF THE *POENITEMINI*[1] SERIES (DECEMBER 1402)[2]

FRENCH PROSE

Against Lust (Poenitemini Sermon 3, December 17, 1402)[3]

[In the opening of this sermon delivered on the third Sunday of Advent, Gerson discusses the Gospel for that Sunday, on the mission of Saint John the Baptist as messenger announcing the coming of Christ. It is possible that these texts represent notes for the sermons,[4] which would explain their fragmentary, and occasionally incoherent, quality.]

. . .

Let us turn to morality according to the topic we have undertaken,[5] and let us say that filthy and dissolute Lust causes in any human creature that lodges

1. Latin for "repent." Since Gerson periodically uses brief Latin quotations or expressions in these sermons written in French, I maintain the Latin in order to replicate the effect.

2. These texts are translated from Jean Gerson, *Œuvres complètes,* vol. 7* (part 2), 822–51.

3. This and the following sermon devoted to "lust" in the *Poenitemini* series were preached in the church of Saint-Jean-en-Grève in Paris, just off the Place de Grève (currently the Place de l'Hôtel de Ville). See above, ch. 3, n. 74.

4. See Badel, *Le Roman de la Rose au XIVe siècle,* 449.

5. The so-called *Poenitemini* series of sermons, the first of which was delivered on the first Sunday of Advent, 1402, was intended to focus on the seven deadly sins. Gerson had announced that the topic of the first sermons would be gluttony and lust: Gluttony was the topic of the first sermon, and lust (and its converse, chastity) of the three following ones, indicating Gerson's relative interest in these two topics. In the first of the latter three, Gerson laid out his program: first, to enumerate the six "ugly and hideous daughters" of Lust (fornication, adultery, sacrilege, rape, corruption of lineage, and unnamable abominations); second, to speak of the signs of these sins; and third, to answer the complaints of those who oppose chastity.

and receives her all the troubles and sicknesses that are represented in our Gospel, and those with respect to the soul always following upon those of the body.[6] And there are twelve ills: lust blinds, it makes one lame, it gives leprosy, it deafens, it kills, it obstructs good teaching, it provides a moral lapse contrary to Jesus Christ, it provokes instability, it does away with abstinence and wisdom, it does the work of the devil, it dirties the path to God. Lust simultaneously blinds the eyes of the soul and of the body; this is why the poets pretend that Cupid, whom they call the god of love, is a foolish child who sees nothing and strikes haphazardly. And Ovid says, *quid deceat non videt ullus amans:*[7] no lover sees what is good and fitting; and *supercecidit ignis et non videant solem:*[8] when the fire of lust rains down, it blinds the soul so that it will not see the sun of justice. There are stories about this without number: about the two treacherous old men who accused Susannah,[9] and about Samson who, literally, on account of this lost the eyes from his body.[10]

Lust makes one limp and stumble on the path of the virtues, for her left foot, which passes on top of carnal affections, is too large, and her right foot too short. I leave aside the appearance of Jacob and how by the effects of gout, becoming lame,[11] etc.

But, moreover, what can make a person as leprous and as sick in body and in soul as lust? There are no things so good that its thought does not blemish.

What makes a person more deaf in hearing and believing the good advice of his parents and friends than lust? Look at it in a foolish lover or a foolish woman in love.

It is also certain that lust kills the soul through sin, and often also the body, in languorous torment, making it gout-stricken, consumptive, or enraged. Note that lust shortens one's life; it is evident in horses, etc. Note that if a person died not having felt lust, he would be a martyr; example of virgins.

6. Throughout this passage, "lust" is alternately personified and used as an abstract noun. In the former case, the noun is capitalized and referred to with feminine pronouns; in the latter case, it is not capitalized and neuter pronouns are used.

7. *Heroides,* 4.154: "quid deceat, non videt ullus amans" (Of what befits, no one who loves takes thought).

8. Ps 57:9: "fire hath fallen on them, and they shall not see the sun."

9. The story of Susanna and the Elders is often referred to as Daniel 13, but it does not appear in the canonical book of Daniel, which ends with chapter 12. Chapters 13 and 14 are sometimes included in Daniel (as in the Douay Rheims Bible) but also sometimes separately in editions of the Bible that include Deutero-canonical books along with the canonical scriptures.

10. Judges 16:21: "Quem cum apprehendissent Philisthiim, statim eruerunt oculos ejus" (Then the Philistines seized upon him, and forthwith pulled out his eyes).

11. On Jacob's limp, see Gen 32: 24–32.

In the last analysis, there is no vice that hinders one more from believing the pure spiritual teaching of the Gospel and of salvation than Lust, to whom it all seems to be a lie and a joke when she hears talk of hell and paradise; and she swears by her good gods that she would not want already to be in paradise, adding that at the risk of being damned, she will love. And by this you can see that a lascivious person is plunged into confusion and totally muddled in his understanding of Jesus Christ and his deeds. And how do you know that Jesus Christ ordered purity in word and in deed? He commanded virginity in himself and in his mother; he taught people to endure cold and heat, to perform penitence, and to be indifferent to scorn in this world. Alas! Indeed, what things can best confuse and muddle Lust more [than these]? She seeks quite the contrary: defloration, joy, delight, honors, dissolute and earthly pleasures. She prevents people from believing sermons: *vinum et mulieres apostatare, etc.*;[12] *voluptas furata est et intellectum ipsius sapientis Aristotelis,* etc.[13] Note about those who speak against the faith on account of this.

But in addition, what makes an unstable person bend like a reed to all winds, swearing, promising, and then breaking his word without sticking to anything? This is what lust does. *Mulier linguata.*[14] The conditions of oaths are instantly voided. And it also makes people seek out soft and exotic garments, for three ends: either to achieve singularity and shame, or for pleasure, or to please someone else. It takes away the gift of prophecy, even from those who had it previously, for according to scholars a prophet cannot prophesy during the time he is accomplishing the carnal act, even with his wife. And you know that Solomon, who was very much wiser than the others, lost his wits because of it;[15] the prophet David lost the Holy Spirit on account of it until his repentance brought it back to him.[16] Saint Augustine says that there is

12. Ecclesiasticus (Sirach) 19:2: "Vinum et mulieres apostatare faciunt sapientes, et arguent sensatos" (Wine and women make wise men fall off, and shall rebuke the prudent).

13. "Sensual pleasure even swayed the intelligence of wise Aristotle himself." Is it possible that Gerson was thinking of Henri d'Andeli's well-known, fabliau-like *Lai d'Aristote* (Lay of Aristotle), in which the famous philosopher, his passions aroused by a seductive young lady, gets down on all fours and allows her to ride him like a horse? After being discovered by Alexander in this shameful position, Aristotle confesses, "ne puis contre amor rendre estal . . . Quant que j'ai apris et léu / M'a desfait nature en .j. eure / Qui tote science deveure / Pus qu'ele s'en veut entremetre" (ll. 560, 563–66; I cannot take a stand against Love . . . Everything I have learned and read has been undone in one hour by Nature, who annihilates all wisdom once she takes pains to do so).

14. Ecclesiasticus (Sirach) 25:27: "ascensus arenosus in pedibus veterani, sic mulier linguata homini quieto" (As the climbing of a sandy way is to the feet of the aged, so is a wife full of tongue to a quiet man).

15. 3 Kings [1 Kings] 11:1–10.

16. 2 Kings [2 Sam]11–12.

nothing that so hinders the learning of true wisdom as the work of carnality, even in marriage, but more so outside it. Regarding which Cicero said when he was asked why he was not getting remarried: "because," he said, "I could not be intent both upon a wife and upon philosophy." This is how it happens that so few people are contemplative or see God vividly. *Beati mundo,*[17] etc.

Such maladies, such misfortunes, such ills are what lust brings to the person who plunges into it. But you, dearest savior Jesus, in order to bring us a remedy you consented to come to us as much by the Incarnation, according to what is said, as by preaching and redemption, even though you very nearly failed to come because of lust. But your goodness cannot be overcome by our sinfulness, nor has it yet been so; you, Lord, have accomplished this through this joyous season of Advent, by means of totally beautiful and pure Chastity.

. . .

Lust is remedied by repentance, for many foolish lovers, men and women, have come to the light from the state of blindness; from being powerless and deformed they have been made strong enough to walk with ease; from filthy leprosy, they have come to purity; from deafness to hearing clearly; from death to life; from ignorance to knowledge; from horror of you to love of you; from inconstancy to stability; from self-indulgent clothes to hair shirts and harsh treatments; from carnal knowledge to prophecy and, higher than prophecy, to the point of seeing your divinity; from the office of devil to that of angel; and from an ugly path to a beautiful and clean one. And it is Lady Repentance, who is symbolized by Saint John the Baptist in the wilderness, who makes us see the path to receiving all these benefits.

I thus begin again my cry and shout out to you with a ringing tone: *poenitemini.* Repent: which is to say, lament all your past sins and protect yourself from those to come, *quos Christus vix distulit.*[18] It is true that it is difficult or impossible to repent adequately for lust when one does not know what it is, and when the deeds have already been accomplished. Everyone knows well enough that it is deadly and to be reproved and confessed, as I said in my other sermon. But when Lust lies in hiding, kept secret, under cover, either simply in the heart or through obscure outward signs and an unconscious scheming for sport and amusement, it is not easy to truly detect and to eval-

17. Mt 5:8: "Beati mundo corde: quoniam ipsi Deum videbunt" (Blessed are the clean of heart: for they shall see God).

18. "which Christ had scarcely spread around."

uate her wickedness. So I will reveal her, the filthy beast and the venomous serpent, which hides in the green grass of worldly pleasures; and I will ask some questions; and I will speak of the six senses, five outside and one inside, which is the heart, that are given to us to govern, like six pupils. First the heart asks reason, etc. heart, mouth, eye, touch, smell, hearing.[19] About the heart: he who protects his heart protects his soul.

Lust means abusing or wishing to abuse the shameful members designed for procreation.

Is every carnal thought a sin, as when a man thinks of a woman, or a woman of a man, with some pleasure? I respond that the thought can come about in four ways: first, from an initial temptation and a first glance, or what the theologians call a first movement; and here there frequently is not sin, or it is venial. Secondly, one retains for a certain time the thought in question, up to the moment when Reason reflects upon it, deliberates, and judges; then she rejects it to the best of her ability. And here it is a venial sin as far as the first part is concerned, but the resistance put up by Reason in rejecting it is highly meritorious and a work of virtue. Even supposing that the person cannot control himself for one day, suppose even that the body is so possessed that defilement follows (my presupposition here is that Reason would still be putting up a fight and refusing all filthy pleasure). It is something to take into consideration when confronted with those in a troubled state as well as those who are tempted, and especially with regard to some types of defilement that happen as though without pleasure and, more than anything else, because of a weakness and sickness; nonetheless, it is good to be on one's guard against it to the extent that one can.

19. I have translated the terms used by Gerson literally, although it is clear that he understands the two organs, mouth and eye, as metonyms for the senses—respectively, taste and vision. But it would be a mistake to translate them schematically and reductively in this way, as Hicks does. For Gerson, the organs in question are conduits (mostly for sinful temptations), but they are not equivalent to the senses. Throughout this sermon, the various sensual temptations are indiscriminately associated with different senses. Dancing, for instance, is dangerous because of touching, because of the thoughts it arouses, and because of the seductive sound of the music. Hicks somewhat misrepresents the sermon more generally when he states that Gerson follows the order of the senses in the following exposition and that the questions that are asked in the rest of this sermon are being voiced by the personified senses ("It is a question asked by Vision that brings about the first allusion to the *Romance of the Rose*" [*Le débat,* 179]). In fact, the questions asked throughout this sermon are not attributed to anyone but the speaker (a line or two before this, Gerson simply says "I will ask some questions"). It is only in the next sermon that *Bouche* directly asks questions of her teacher, Reason. In this context, Hicks translates *Bouche* somewhat clumsily as "Taste" (*Le débat,* 181), when in fact "Mouth" represents different senses for Gerson: speech, singing, touch (kissing), and never in fact is there any mention of taste, which is for him the least likely activity related to that organ that will lead to sin.

Third, when the thought stays in the soul with the explicit consent of Reason, and it takes delight and rubs itself, and savors this carnal thought as though embracing it, and kissing it, even though it would in no way want to perform the lascivious act on the outside. And here the most difficult to decide is whether this thought and pleasure are taking place based only on a condition, such as saying: "if God did not forbid me this and that, I would do it and would take pleasure in doing it." I believe that it is a sin of curiosity; if the flesh is inflamed and so intensely and immoderately heated up, and Reason truly notices it and nonetheless it continues, it seems to me that Reason is in peril of providing an evil consent. And the Wise Man says: "he who loves peril will perish in it," *qui amat,* etc.[20] But if Reason strives to reject it, she begins to have merit, and especially to the extent that she judges correctly that since God forbids such filth, she will obey. I would say the same thing about those who hear confession or who preach about this vice.

If the pleasant thought concerns something that is not at all in itself a mortal sin for the person, I consider that it is not a mortal sin, as long as Reason consents to it, if by doing this it does not keep the person from other things that need to be done or thought at that time; if, for instance, a woman thinks of her husband and desires him and his company, but not at all that of another man.

If the dirty, carefully considered thought concerns things forbidden to the person, as if a married woman thinks about the sins of others or a young girl about the acts of married people, I would say that the most sound advice would be for this person to make her confession as she would for a mortal sin.

Fourth, the thought comes from consent to the carnal act on the outside, which is forbidden, as if a woman wanted and desired the company of another if she could have it, or put her effort into it through various signs and proceedings; with regard to this thought, there is absolutely no doubt that it is a mortal sin, for the will counts as a deed, as I will say forthwith . . .

If the person desires the company of another in exceptional cases, as if the cousin desires his female cousin, is this truly a case remitted to the confessional? I say not; but I also say that it is too dangerous if the thought were as strong and ardent and evil as it would be in the deed; and also many

20. Ecclesiasticus (Sirach) 3:27: "Cor durum habebit male in novissimo, et qui amat periculum in illo peribit" (A hard heart shall fear evil at the last: and he that loveth danger shall perish in it).

types of harm would result from the act, for which it would be necessary[21] to atone, and which do not result from will alone. Nevertheless, one must confess oneself and state the degrees of kinship of the person one was thinking of when desiring.

What to do about certain thoughts of heinous and execrable blasphemy that arise counter to both the heart and the will of the person? I reply that one cannot prevail over them better than by not taking account of them but rather laughing about them in one's heart, and saying to the devil who sends them: "may your blasphemy fall on you." And one must never confess it, unless it is to a wise and experienced confessor in order to ask for advice and about any possible consequences, and also for greater self-assurance—but one time and no more, for the more you were to think about it and the more effort you were to make, the worse it would be for you, and you would also bring shame to your innocent confessor. But if you consent to such abominations, you must confess to someone such as I have described . . .

If a woman judges with certainty that her parish priest will do a poor job in taking her confession and will be moved to desire her foolishly if she confesses to him all the deliberate carnal thoughts she has had, and perhaps even with regard to the priest himself, what will she do? Will she give her confession? I respond that she must request leave to confess elsewhere: but if the priest does not wish to give it to her, she must go there. In any event, a person must use discretion in making such certain judgments. I would say the same in many cases on the topic of confession.

Is it necessary that the person confess all his evil thoughts, and the number of times he had them? I respond that if the thoughts that are mortal sins could be described and numbered, the safest thing would be to describe them; nonetheless, it is sufficient to declare one's guilt in an honest generality and humility, as by saying: I have sinned so many times in this way that I don't know the number. And in such a way that the confessor will understand what is meant, without telling a long tale that is not to the point. As for the ones that are not mortal sins and that sometimes incite people to evil as well as to good, there is no need to confess them in their particulars; rather it is sometimes better to keep quiet about them.

Can a person lose her virginity simply by her thoughts? I respond "yes" with regard to the virginity of the soul and toward God; and this is accomplished by evil consent to the carnal act. But as for the body, one can lose one's virginity by oneself alone. In the first case, repentance brings back

21. Glorieux's text reads *commandroit,* which is not recognizable; I emend to *couvandroit.*

the state of virginity, but not in the second case if the body has been violated . . .

. . . What the eye does not see does not bring suffering to the heart.[22] *Oculus meus depredatus est,* etc.[23]

Looking at a beautiful person and getting pleasure out of it, is that a mortal sin? I say that it is often a dangerous curiosity; it is often the cause of harmful suspicion on the part of one's husband or mother. It is often something that causes the person one is looking at to fall into the sin of pride or lust, even assuming that one does not care about or desire that person at all.

And according to these consequences, good or bad, judge what is the nature of the sin; also according to the source of your thought and the harm that you do to others. I know a person who hundreds and hundreds of times keeps from looking at others for certain of the above-mentioned reasons more than for fear of his own sin. Note the good people who must be on their guard, etc., and about the basilisk.[24]

Is looking at oneself naked (for either a man or a woman) or taking pleasure in gazing at oneself a sin? In response I ask you to consider the end result that comes from it and the intention you have; and according to this, judge the case . . .

Looking at things outside oneself that are indecent, in animals or in paintings or elsewhere, is that a sin? I respond as before.[25]

Above all, it is particularly incredible that reading books that incite to lust is not a mortal sin. Moreover, those who hold onto them should be compelled by their confessors to burn them or rip them up, so that they themselves or others might henceforth not commit sin with them; books such as Ovid, or I don't know what [passages of] Matheolus[26] or a given part of the

22. This is a well-known proverb (Morawski, *Proverbes français,* no. 1766, and a variant version, no. 1767: Qe oyl ne voyt quer ne desyre [What the eyes does not see, the heart does not desire]). With this and the following quotation, Gerson makes a transition from thoughts to vision.

23. Lam 3:51: "Oculus meus deprædatus est animam meam in cunctis filiabus urbis meæ" (My eye hath wasted my soul because of all the daughters of my city).

24. A reptile reputed by the ancients to be able to kill just by looking at someone.

25. Gerson is here undoubtedly referring to what he said in the previous paragraph, that the sinful nature of looking at things indecent or not is judged by one's intention and by what ensues. This also explains why he says in the following paragraph that, in spite of what he feels about books that incite to lust, reading them is not in itself a mortal sin.

26. Gerson is here referring to the *Lamentations of Matheolus,* one of the most well-known antimatrimonial and misogynistic texts of the latter Middle Ages. The original *Book of Lamentations,* composed probably by 1290, and thus a decade or so after Jean de Meun's continuation of the *Rose,* is attributed to a cleric named Matheolus and is a collection of traditional clerical arguments and anecdotes against marriage. It undoubtedly had a decent circulation and was trans-

Romance of the Rose, or rondeaux or ballads, or songs that are too licentious. Judge what penance those who compose and publish them must perform; on this I have already written clearly. Likewise speak about filthy and indecent paintings.

Looking at or showing oneself at the baths or in hot tubs before the children of one's family, is this a sin? I respond that it is a thing to keep from doing regularly once the children are more than two years old, for even if those of four or six years of age don't think any evil about it then, nonetheless afterward, when they come of age, the memory comes back and they are powerfully tempted. Even more, I say that married people or others should not say or do the slightest indecent thing either in the sight of or in the hearing of small children, no more than they would do it in the presence of an angel . . .

Looking at dances, is that a sin? I say that if a person is wickedly roused by it, then or afterward, and he indeed recognizes it (for he is bound to recognize it), or if by his glance or his presence it seems to give him boldness and approval for some licentious act, it is a peril and a sin, and to be refrained from, as prelates, priests, and all religious must do . . .

Listening to secular songs, dances, and musicians, is that a sin? You can take your response from what is said about looking at people: it's the same thing when one listens to the secrets of married people or others. And consider also that beyond the peril of lust, there is harmful curiosity, and one does to others what one would not want done to oneself, namely, listening to others' secrets . . .

Are kisses always sins? I respond that kisses given between spouses in which decency is maintained, such as the kiss of peace at church, or publicly, are without sin. But they could be given with such unseemly behavior that it would be a very abominable mortal sin. I say no more about that. If kisses are exchanged between strangers and in public, and in accordance with the custom of the country, and through familial affection, without lewd thoughts, there is no sin. But the will can be such, and such evil might come of it, that it would be better to have a child with one's first cousin. And especially if this occurs among those of religion and among those of the same family or sex, and in a hidden place, and over a long period. I refer each person to his conscience. Note about Dido, whom Virgil makes fall in love with Aeneas

---

lated into French verse around 1380–87 by a certain Jean Le Fèvre, a procurator for the Parlement of Paris who also had a significant literary career as poet and, especially, as translator. As Badel (*Le Roman de la Rose au XIVe siècle,* 178–200) has shown, Le Fèvre was much beholden to the *Rose* and solidified the latter text's reputation as one of the great works opposing women and marriage.

by kissing his son Ascanius. Lust has neither faith nor loyalty, reason nor law. Note about the man who did not want to touch the hand of his mother. In some, spiritual love easily slides into the carnal.

Conversations that take place at dances through singing, and between foolish lovers by promising and going back on one's word, and by pimps and procuresses as they deceive others, are these sins? I respond that you can know this by what is said, and by studying the evil that comes from it: attracting and inciting others to evil is the office reserved for the devil.

Are the oaths made by foolish lovers to be kept? I say, "some yes and some no," according to the good or the evil that would come of it. If the oath is decent and permissible, it should be kept.

Is a person obliged to lead someone he has deceived by his deeds or his words back on the right path? I respond "yes," with all his power; and he must be obliged to do this as penance. And this is applicable to everyone. Note how here one will speak against the *Romance of the Rose* which, through the character of Reason, tries to make people speak in a ribald manner. Such words stimulate people to lust, and this is why these words are to be forbidden. Note Seneca; *turpia,* etc.[27] Aristotle, the seventh book of the *Politics.*[28] Noah and Ham. Cicero. Saint Augustine. Note the peril of the *Romance* and similar works, etc., and the ugliness of the ending, etc., *videatur finis.*[29] Note about the child who certainly retained the evil of the *Romance.* Note that he is damned if he did not repent. Note that his suffering increases the secondary and aleatory punishment.[30]

27. "Indecent things." For the full quotation of this passage, see Gerson's sermon *Considerate lilia* (see above, ch. 2, n. 106). Most of these examples are in fact found both in that sermon and in Gerson's treatise against the *Rose.*

28. Glorieux's edition contains the reading "Aristote. V° Politice," whereas Hicks's (*Le débat,* 180) has "Aristote (7° *Politice*)," which I follow for the translation. Gerson is indeed referring to the seventh book of Aristotle's *Politics,* as he does below, in the sermon he delivered on December 24. At the end of book 7, Aristotle speaks of the ways in which the legislator must be highly attentive to the upbringing of children: "there is nothing which the legislator should be more careful to drive away than indecency of speech; for the light utterance of shameful words leads soon to shameful actions . . . And since we do not allow improper language, clearly we should also banish pictures or speeches from the stage which are indecent." *Politics,* book 7, chap. 17 (1336b); *Complete Works of Aristotle,* trans. Jonathan Barnes, 2:2120.

29. "Let the ending be scrutinized." As Hicks suggests, this is undoubtedly part or all of a proverbial expression, comparable to Morawski, *Proverbes français,* no. 2496 ("Voy en quanque feras la fin a qu'en venras" [In all that you do, look toward the end you will be coming to]) or no. 510, which has roughly the same meaning ("De la chose que tu feras garde a quel fin tu en venras").

30. This rather elliptical statement is undoubtedly a version of what Gerson says more clearly below in the following sermon about Jean de Meun, namely, that "those who do read it in its wickedness increase his torment if he is damned or in purgatory."

Is smelling good odors or some other pleasant thing a sin? I say that here one must consider the goal and the intention, decent or indecent, and the evil that can or does come from it.

Finally let us speak about touch in different ways.

Is it a sin for a man to write letters of love to a woman, or a woman to a man? I reply that you should look at the goal and the intention; and here I do not know what to say (if it is better that a woman know how to write and read or not), on account of the good things that can come from it on the one hand, and the bad ones that can result on the other.

Is dancing always a sin? I judge not, in many cases, when it is done for itself. But the weakness of people is such that they have difficulty doing it without sinning in diverse ways. It is certainly so for the person who neglects doing what he is supposed to do in order to dance; or in knowingly making someone else sin, he is sinning greatly; or when the dances are openly licentious and lacking reasonable moderation; or when pregnant women lose their fetus because of it, as happens. Note all the sins when dancing at the dance, etc.

Is touching children on the face and elsewhere a sin? I say that it is better to refrain from it; moreover, a greater sin can happen from it than having ten children with one's own first cousin. And since children also touch, would that it pleased God that it was the custom in France for children to sleep by themselves in small beds, whether they be brothers or sister or others, as is the custom in Flanders.

Can a woman make herself up and show her hair openly in public? Here I respond that a greater moderation in dress or in such embellishments would be better and safer. Consider briefly the goal and the intention and what comes from it. Nonetheless I do not condemn any woman who maintains herself and adorns herself lavishly according to her status and that of her husband, and according to the custom of the country, and in order to take some measure of solace, for the Romans long ago gave such clothing to their wives for this purpose, in order to honor them and allow them to put up with the difficulties they endure in their marriage by bearing children. And, to tell the truth, it is not possible for a woman to conduct herself in such a way that she can prevent some foolish and harmful people from inflicting harm upon her [if they wish to do so]; and sometimes [this can result] more readily from the sight of the most plainly dressed woman than from that of the most elaborately made up one, as Ovid said of Lucretia in the sight of Tarquin.[31]

31. Ovid's version of the rape of Lucretia, based upon Livy's well-known account, is in *Fasti,* 2.721–852.

However, there are some comportments that cannot be excused from sin; and some clothes are worn so tight that the fetus is either harmed or dies.

Do small children who do not know that what people make them do is a sin have to confess it afterward, when they realize the evil that was done at that time, as happens often? I advise "yes" . . .

Must one confess for the illusions or the dirty dreams that come while one is asleep? I advise "yes," because one does not know from what cause this moral weakness and defilement arise, either from gluttony or from wicked thoughts, or from the temptation of the devil, or from lying down in a dissolute manner, or from having fasted too long and being very weak. But if, after the fact, you feel joy for the pleasure you took in it, you are beginning to sin.

Must a confessor make someone he has absolved promise that he will never have a relapse? If the sin is very immoderate and contrary to all decency, a priest can on occasion make the guilty person promise that he will never relapse into it, in order better to show him his licentiousness and the duty that henceforth obliges him, namely, God's commandment. And here it is not, properly speaking, a vow, for every person who confesses himself must have a firm and explicit intention not to have a relapse. It is true, if the sins are common, or if one thinks that in spite of such an oath the person will never refrain from it, one must not ask for such oaths. And because it is difficult to know such circumstances, it is safest, in the common run of things, to refrain from making or requesting such oaths.

Here we will end . . .

Against Lust (Poenitemini Sermon 4, December 24, 1402)

. . . If on the past three Sundays, I have exhorted you to repentance for gluttony and lust, during which I have spoken of the three advents, today more especially, on this [Christmas] eve, I must tell you to get to work, to accomplish in deed the good intentions that I am confident you have had in your heart.[32] Devout people, repent, for you will thus be carrying out the mission of Saint John the Baptist, who was sent in advance of Our Lord in order to exhort people to prepare and purify the paths in preparation for his coming.[33] These are the paths of good works. And you know how gluttony and

32. The word translated by "heart" here is *voulanté,* literally, "will."

33. The expression is *devant sa face,* which means literally "before his face" but can also have a spiritual meaning akin to encountering God, hence my translation "in preparation for his coming."

lust are in particular dirty and muddy, and how they pollute all clean proceedings, of both the body and the soul . . .

. . .

In thinking about the coming of the birth of God, many questions have arisen, etc. But I leave these for tomorrow in order to come to the topic of which I must speak, against Lust. And, to tell the truth, certain of her daughters seemed to me so hideous that Saint Augustine said that God very nearly didn't come to us because of them.[34] I spoke of this a short time before; and of other types of behavior, and I still must speak of them. But before that, while thinking of this, there came to my attention—I heard rather indistinctly—that there were several complaints being made by foolish lovers, men and women, very feebly and frivolously, as they are in fact feeble and frivolous. One complaint was why God (this they said) forbad lust from us, in particular simple fornication. The other complaint was that, to put it bluntly, they were not capable of living chastely. The third complaint was that they truly wanted to live chastely, but not so soon; [they claimed that] it was necessary for youth to pass and that this was the least grievous sin there was.

What might I say here? Will I respond to these foolish complaints? Yes, indeed; for according to the example of the apostle[35] I owe satisfaction to the foolish as I do to the wise, by saying as much as is possible. Open your ears, I beg you, you who make this first complaint: Chase out, at least for a bit of time, foolish love, which obstructs them and closes them up, and hear what evils would follow if God did what you ask, surrendering every unmarried woman to every man as per your foolish request . . . Afterward, understand that marriage would cease to exist and no one would pay attention to it. And what then? Following this, pregnant women would have a difficult time, for they would not have a man of their own to help them; and since, as you know, the carnal work of a man and a woman was not established for any other reason than to have a lineage and succession, this purpose would be greatly hindered, for women become barren and sterile when they have excessive commerce with men. Also, finding themselves poor, and lacking aid and consolation, women might murder their children at birth or before. Hear what a horror this is! Moreover, consider yourselves, and take some-

34. On the "daughters" of Lust, see above, n. 5.

35. Rom 1:14: "Graecis ac barbaris, sapientibus, et insipientibus debitor sum" (To the Greeks and to the barbarians, to the wise and to the unwise, I am a debtor).

one else's heart as though it were yours. I ask you, if you have daughters, sisters, or unmarried cousins, would you like them to be given over to all men, and your children to all women, or your own mother, if she were widowed? What would you say about that? I am certain that in your judgment you would not for anything want to allow such shameful filth among your relatives. Thus why would you want others to do it?

This is what Reason imposes—even assuming that God had not already decreed his opposition [to fornication]—but this is not the way things are, for God can do with his creation and impose moral obligations upon it as he pleases. And that is the only necessary condition; I am pleased that it is thus.[36] It is as if a knight asked why one doesn't give him the honor without the battle, etc. Can he [God] not retain any sign of his authority over his creation? Can he not maintain that the souls that are his daughters keep themselves pure, as a king or a prince of this world wishes it for his own daughters? It would be stupid to ask a prince: "Why do you not allow your daughters to be able to give themselves over without sin to any unmarried man?" For truly God has given humankind an advantage in forbidding this, as much for the sake of children, who would not be nurtured or taught, as for the sake of women, who would have all the hardship, and as for the sake of men who would be so given over to carnal works that they would forget God and their salvation, and would fall into thousands and thousands of languorous sicknesses, cutting short their lives as a result. Example of the Saracens, who abuse more than others and to this end . . .

Now I come to the second complaint: I could not live chastely, say some. I ask you who speak thus, what do you mean when you say: "I could not live chastely"? Do you want to say that God has ordered you to do something that you cannot accomplish? This is an error of faith and counter to good morals, for no one sins with regard to what is beyond his power. And also you know from the lives of saints, both men and women, how many people kept their chastity up to the end. If you say that you cannot, it means that you are unwilling, and is not an excuse. If you mean that it is difficult and laborious, I grant you that and am with you. In truth it is a harsh suffering and the temptation is powerful; but it is necessary to put up with it in order to have something better, to save oneself, and to gain paradise by obeying God. Think well, think what troubles, what sorrows, and what an-

36. This passage is somewhat unclear, but Gerson seems to be saying that even if it is reasonable for people not to fornicate indiscriminately, the only important consideration is that it is God's dictum. Reason is fundamentally subservient to Theology.

guish the servants of a lord put up with in order to earn a bit of money—what dangers, what injuries, and sometimes what beatings . . .

The third complaint leads people to perdition all the more because it is more common. I will repent, you say, when I want. Indeed, my friend. If you will repent when you want, wish therefore to do it right now, and sooner rather than later, for often he who does not want to do something when he can, cannot do it when he would like. "Certainly not!" you will say to me. "I want first to get past my youth." O sovereign judge of the world! How many of them do we see who propose this in their youth and do not in any way make amends in their old age, but rather stumble or slide ever lower and lower; and even if the body is failing, the will and the wicked heart are still young and flightier than those of children, even near death. Tell me, I pray, who gave you the assurance that you would improve yourself tomorrow or later—not just improve yourself, but go on living? If you do not want now to abandon your evil carnality, how will God give you grace afterward, without which grace you cannot prevail over this temptation? You propose to do the worst you can to God, yet you give yourself the hope that then he will do better to you than now when you have angered him purely out of willfulness. It seems that you do not know very well that this is a bad habit, how ponderous it is and how it follows a person all the way to hell, in the manner of a weighty millstone, however much the person might wish or make an effort to climb back up. Accept it as a certainty that if today you are not able or willing to abstain from it, you will be even less so tomorrow; and less the day after tomorrow. *qui non est hodie, cras minus aptus erit.*[37] So commence immediately and today, if you believe me.

Is this the "least grievous" sin, one that makes people break the faith of marriage, etc., bastards inherit, bodies get stolen, etc., [people get] imprisoned, commit suicide, die out of despair, [commit] murders of children? Note Archytas Tarantinus.[38] What causes sacraments to be broken or sullied, what makes a person act like a beast, what makes him go out of his mind and sometimes die? *Nota de prima.*[39] What makes God and his judgments be forgotten and people plunge into hell through bad habit? The *Romance of the Rose* says it [lust] is the least grievous sin that blemishes a woman's body,

37. "He who is not equipped today will be less so tomorrow."

38. Archytas of Tarentum is mentioned in Gerson's treatise against the *Rose*. See above, ch. 3, n. 41.

39. "Note about the first." Hicks (*Le débat,* 232) suggests that this is a reference to the first sermon in the *Poenitemini* series.

etc., the cause for her to devote herself to all the other evils.[40] Note against those who turn women toward errors in order to deceive them and make them heretics. *Cape penitentiam.* Rush to do penance while there is time. Take the sure, etc. Repent, etc.

Last time, I began to show how Reason, the good mistress, taught these six pupils[41] to be on their guard against lust which is furtively hidden under a number of games and amusements, and I spoke of the heart, the eye, and hearing. Here I will speak of the nose, of the mouth, and of touch.[42]

Reason tells her pupil Smell not to be an emissary, not to provide assistance for other things by smelling something that might lead to gluttony or lust. And Smell asks whether it is a sin to smell good odors. She replies, "Yes, if the end is wicked"; and it is sometimes too great a curiosity and a cause for lust, as the Scripture says: *halitus eius prunas cadere facit.*[43] This is why it is forbidden for people to look at each other or smell each other during confession. Because smell is of much less importance for us than it is for dogs, we scarcely think of it. Note about the man who up to his death did not want to smell the scent of a woman.

Reason teaches the Mouth to have good control of herself, praising her because she is what makes man different from other beasts through speech. It is through her that we praise God, it is through her that we carry out all the trash from our school (for God enters when the basket of sin is outside), provided that deadly shame not keep her closed during confession. "So you must watch out," says Reason, "for kisses and debauchery, etc." The Mouth asks if all kisses are sins. Kisses can be given by custom, as among nobles of a family; for virtuous enjoyment, as between spouses and in the church; for natural love, as with my child; and for dissolute concupiscence. In these first three cases, kisses can be given with decency and free of evil circumstances;

40. *Rose*, ed. Lecoy, ll. 9112–18; trans. Dahlberg, 165 (altered).: "Mes forment vos en reconforte / Juvenaus, qui dit du metier / que l'en apele rafetier / que c'est li mandres des pechiez / don queur de fame est entechiez / car leur nature leur conmande / que chascunne a pis fere entande" (But Juvenal gives one great comfort for this situation when he says, of the need to fornicate, that it is the least of the sins by which the heart of a woman is stained, for their nature commands each of them to give her attention to doing worse).

41. The "six pupils" are the six senses mentioned above in the previous sermon. See above, n. 19.

42. Gerson's ordering of his discussion does not completely follow his practice in these two sermons, as he also spoke of kisses, touching, and smell in the previous one. This explains some of the repetitions, such as those regarding kisses in Reason's discussion with Mouth below. See above, n. 19.

43. Job 41:12: "Halitus ejus prunas ardere facit, et flamma de ore ejus egreditur" (His breath kindleth coals, and a flame cometh forth out of his mouth).

but not in the fourth case. And one must be aware that the devil lays there his traps, snares, and glue, under the appearance of good, so much so that the results of it are worse than they would be if one ate meat on Good Friday . . . I say moreover that one must no less refrain from kissing male infants or holding them naked, especially in their private parts, than doing so with women or girls. And I say that a child must refuse to be held or kissed; and if he has done otherwise, he must confess it, whatever the result. Moreover, I say that they can be interrogated during confession as to their will. Even assuming that they did not have any evil thoughts in doing so and that the other was abusing them, they can still have the guilt and torment . . . And he who does not actively confess himself will only with great difficulty have peace with his conscience; so it is good in one's youth, etc. I have seen children cry over the wicked acts they had been taught and from which they were incapable of abstaining.

And if you ask what I call a decent kiss, I say that it is the sort given in public or in church. Note that it would be good to sleep alone. Note about the son who had a child at nine years of age, according to Saint Jerome. Note in the miracles of Our Lady, regarding the mother who had a child with her son and killed it. But repentance protected her. Therefore repent, etc. Your prelate can absolve you of it.

Mouth asks if songs are permissible. Reason makes the distinction: either they are decent both in time and in place, or filthy and licentious, or false and heretical, or done in an inappropriate time and place and harmful of others, as in church. The three last examples are sins and are forbidden. Note that the voice of women is like the sirens, which Ulysses got past by plugging up his ears.

Mouth asks whether speaking literally about the shameful body parts and about all this sin [that concerns them] is an unreasonable thing. And she maintains the opinion that it is not: first, on the authority of the *Romance of the Rose*; second, because of the reasons that are given in that book, for words are not by themselves foul, and if the things are foul, it is because of sin; and sin is likewise found in murder and robbery, which people freely talk about. Reason[44] responds to this that speaking literally about things can

44. Throughout this sermon, Gerson makes Reason an authority who teaches her "six pupils," but here there is a slight ambiguity, as Reason was also the character of Jean de Meun (as mentioned later) who sanctioned lascivious language. Which of the two is this? I think that since Reason is simply listing the ways in which literal language is used to speak of unspeakable things (without herself making a judgment), she represents Gerson's Reason and not the objectionable one of Jean de Meun. This would be Gerson's way of displacing Jean de Meun, by setting aright the allegorical character.

be done, first, out of ribaldry; or it comes about as a result of having roused oneself to lust, or through a fictional character, or through theoretical speculation among wise and learned people who are seeking nothing other than the truth of things. The first of these [ribaldry] must not be done; and to say the contrary is an error, as it would be to say that one ought to walk around naked, or pardon Ham for not covering up his father. It is the error of the philosophers who were on account of this called dogs. Aristotle forbids it in the seventh book of his *Politics*. Seneca says *turpia non dixeris*.[45] Dirty speech leads to dirty actions. Saint Augustine says that it is an error to take leave of oneself. Cicero, in *De officiis* (On Duties): they call it dirty and besmirched language. Saint Paul says that many things that are done in private are not even to be named;[46] they corrupt good morals,[47] etc. As for those who say the opposite, I'd just like to see them instruct their daughters this way, according to Reason.[48]

The second reason and behavior [being roused to lust] cannot be excused: even between married people respectability must be maintained. As for the third [through fictional characters], it must not be done in public for the above-mentioned reasons; indeed, truth and decency must be maintained likewise in fictional characters. The fourth manner [theoretical speculation] is permissible as is the fifth [walking around naked] in certain cases, as a sick man will present himself totally naked to a doctor in order to be cured. And if Master Jean de Meun understood it thus, he was correct. But he was in error when he had Reason speak like a foolish lover; secondly, when he exhorted women and others to speak openly; third, when he made his book available to young people who made use of it with wicked intent; fourth, when his arguments demonstrated also that one should go around in the nude. So I say by way of response that the words are ugly because of the evil that comes from them and that is perceived in them; as also are glances at naked women, on account of the evil desire that follows from

45. "You will not say indecent things." On all these passages, which are associated by Gerson when he comes to this topic, see above, n. 27, and ch. 2, nn. 103–107.

46. Eph 5:12: "Quae enim in occulto fiunt ab ipsis, turpe est et dicere" (For the things that are done by them in secret, it is a shame even to speak of).

47. 1 Cor 15:33: "Nolite seduci: corrumpunt mores bonos conloquia mala" (Be not seduced: Evil communications corrupt good manners).

48. There would appear to be a slippage here from Gerson's Reason, who is in principle providing these lessons, to the Reason of Jean de Meun and her advocating dirty language. It is the preacher saying that even if people go along with Jean's teachings about language use, they would never, out of decency, want to hear their own daughters speak that way. This is an allegation that Christine de Pizan makes regarding Pierre Col's avoidance of dirty words (ch. 3, nn. 202 and 203), which is in turn taken up by Gerson in his own Latin letter to Col (no. 28).

them. Note Saint Augustine, *De nuptiis et concupiscentia* (On Marriage and Concupiscence);[49] and the common proverb: there is no evil when one is not intent upon it. Good people, take away these books from your daughters and children, for they will take in the evil from them and leave aside the good. Example of the child, etc. Note what is the end. Note the poetry of Ovid who was exiled because of it. Note that stupid Matheolus.

I make three assertions: the first, that if I had a *Romance of the Rose* that was a unique exemplar and it were worth a thousand pounds, I would burn it sooner than I would sell it, lest it be circulated such as it is. Secondly, if I knew that he had not repented for it, I would no more pray for him than for Judas; and those who do read it in its wickedness increase his torment if he is damned or in purgatory. Thirdly, if I were confessing someone who had made evil and excessive use of it, I would order him to erase several things, or to throw the whole thing away. The same goes for dirty pictures that excite people, or that are made for foolish lovers, male and female, etc.

Mouth asks about someone who cannot speak. Reason says he must confess using sign language. And the most difficult case involves people who are born mute and deaf . . .

Here would arise the question of whether minstrels are in a state of salvation. I consider that they are if they behave modestly, etc.

. . .

I pass on to hands and other forms of touching. As far as dress and makeup are concerned, one should refer to what was said about kisses and, before, how one should behave with regard to them. Any touching of hands or other things that is done in order to stir oneself so much as to bring carnal pleasure to a climax is forbidden outside marriage; and within marriage, respectability must be maintained.

Touch asks about nocturnal defilement, whether one should make of it a matter of conscience, since one cannot resist it. Reason says that it results either from having eaten too much, or from previous thoughts, or from moral weakness, or from the temptation of the devil. And it is sinful according to the nature of the consent, be it before or after; and thus one must confess it whatever the result and according to one's condition. And note that if its accomplishment occurred while awake, and the pleasure is because of na-

49. This reference is undoubtedly related to Gerson's use of it in his letter to Pierre Col, in which he accuses him of believing the Pelagian heresy regarding original sin. See below, n. 65.

ture's having been purged, etc. Reason provides remedies: the first, sobriety with regard to garlic, spices, and strong wines. Note, with regard to married women, whether they can repent without the permission of the husband, or with regard to girls engaged to be married. Reason says that everywhere there must be moderation and that the body is not at all to be destroyed by it. Note whether one can use medicine. I say "yes." And whether one can cut off one of one's members, by disfiguring oneself, or by castration, as did Origen. One must make the distinction among types of disfiguration, and whether it is due to divine inspiration, as the nun who sent her eyes, etc.[50]

The second remedy is to flee opportunities, letters, sweet talk, and gentle touches, etc. Note about the man who threw roses into the toilet. And what will a young person do if someone wants to touch her playfully? She must refuse it and will be praised for it afterward; if she does not have control, she must scream. And what if she fears death if she screams? Be that as it may, she must not kill herself, as one woman did long ago, Lucretia: the retribution for such an act does not go away. Note about Saint Lucy.[51] And note whether the confessor must forbid all killings, and how, and which kind. And whether he must make the person taking confession promise anything. And let there here be made a distinction; and to consider carefully the way of promising, and what, before it is done, it obliges and what it is worth. Note that in the first place the confessor must know what kind of intimacies the person confessing has had.

The third remedy is to sin as little as possible and to do every day the most good possible. Note that it should be kept secret, [be done] neither on feast days nor in a holy place, and to unrelated persons. Note that people always plan to repent. To do this is not to sin against the Holy Spirit; it is rather when one thinks that one will be saved without repentance . . .

In the final analysis, let us repent frequently, asking for God's kingdom to come. O Lord, our good father, may there not be such confusion in your spiritual kingdom as there is in us, lest you be kept outside and the devil be made the master, lest reason be trampled under the feet of sensuality, who is like our she-ass; and, according to the example of the woman who requested chastity in honor of the Nativity and the childhood of Our Lady, etc.

50. The legend of a woman gouging out her eyes and sending them to a suitor so that he will stop asking for her is told notably of Saint Lucy.

51. Having refused marriage, Lucy is ordered to be raped in a brothel but is saved by divine intervention. They attempt to kill her on a pyre, and when that is not successful, a sword is thrust into her neck. See also the preceding note.

On Chastity (Poenitemini sermon 5, December 31, 1402)

. . . I consider that chastity occupies three lodgings according to three states, and according to its having three names. It lodges in the state of virginity, that is, virginal chastity; [in the state] of marriage; [and in the state] of widowhood.

Chastity is an integrity of body and thought that never consents to experience or try out the sort of carnal pleasure that follows from touching the shameful member intended for procreation. Chastity of marriage is abstinence from the carnal act except insofar as the terms of marriage allow it or require it. Example of the man who fasts but who might nonetheless eat dinner. Chastity of widowhood in general is an abstinence that remains in the heart and body after the person has been married, like Our Lady, or after the person has experienced carnal pleasure, either in or out of marriage; in this way, priests who live chastely after their defilement can be said to possess chastity of widowhood. And these three lodgings accompany three types of life: one contemplative, one active, and the other a mixture of the two, first one then the other, as coequals. The contemplative life belongs to virginity, the active to marriage, the mixed to widowhood and to prelates. Beautiful and pure chastity is like a golden clasp in the state of virginity, a silver clasp in the state of marriage, and a clasp of yellow copper or brass, which is a mixture of gold and silver, in the state of widowhood. The infant Jesus was of the state of virginity alone, Joseph of the two, and Mary and Anne, of the three.

. . .

But I am obliged to respond to Earthly Carnality, silly and flighty, and who speaks against you, Virginity, and who also wishes to create a disagreement among these three states, as the poets tell the fable of Envy which thrust itself among Juno, Pallas, and Venus through a quarrel over their beauty. Earthly Carnality says that if everyone were a virgin, the world would come to an end. First, this consequence is not to be feared. And even if it did happen, the world would be coming to an end as is destined to happen, I don't know when. Secondly, the necessity of a condition [sexual intercourse as a precondition for the survival of humanity] does not argue in favor of its excellence over the others. This is clear in professions; and in the body of man, in the eye, etc. Thirdly, one would provide for it by a public ordinance.

Carnality says afterward that marriage is better for the good of the children and the republic. I do not wish here or on another occasion to blame marriage; but I do say that in the balance the state of virginity, as far as concerns oneself and virginity, and for the present time, in the balance, is more perfect. I say "as far as concerns oneself" because a person can on occasion better save his soul than in marriage, either through his own condition or through some other great good that comes of it [virginity].[52] I say "for the present time" because in the ancient law it was otherwise, in order to increase the population of the Jews, but at present we can increase the size of Christianity with all people. Note the statement of Saint Augustine about Abraham and Saint John the Baptist. And it says here that the deeds of the good virgins are often better and more meritorious. Note that marriage provides children only with their body. Note that virginity engenders spiritual sons in oneself as well as through prayer. Note that preaching increases the number of sons of God. So here there must not be a disagreement among the various conditions, for the virtues of each are not always the same, as a married woman will [on occasion] suffer death for the sake of God sooner than a virgin . . .

Earthly Carnality says in the third place that the state of virginity is too difficult and perilous and nearly impossible, either in religion or outside it. I respond that it is hard with respect to the beginning, and if it is not governed; but later it is easier than marriage, as much with respect to maintaining chastity as to the other opportunities to sin, such as avarice, wrath, quarrels, jealousy, and the others that rule over marriage if one is not on his guard against them.

And to this [to why a female virgin can more easily maintain chastity and the other virtues than a married person] I assign four reasons: protection that comes to her and not to the married woman; spiritual consolation; shame which provides help; and good habits, which make this disposition go elsewhere . . .

I conclude that parents or others who would hinder the state of virginity through wickedness would be committing a sin. With good reasons one can advise one's friend, male or female, to aim at what is best for his or her salvation, for different people are redeemed in different ways. And by this one can understand when it is a sin to prevent someone from entering re-

52. This text is hopelessly muddled, because of shortcomings either in Glorieux's edition or in the manuscript transmission of the text. In particular the text as edited reads "a person can better save his soul in marriage," which is in direct contradiction with what precedes. I propose adding a *que* before *en mariage*, which results in the translation I have given.

ligion or from maintaining a state of perfection (for instance by impeding someone's studies in theology or obstructing their undertaking the prelacy) and when it is not.

Finally Carnality in its filth goes on to say against these things that it is a contradiction [to say] that the state of virginity is easier [to maintain] and at the same time more perfect, *quia virtus est circa difficile.*[53] Make the distinction: either the difficulty comes from the work itself which is more arduous, or it is a result of either the innate weakness of the person and his temperament, his bad company, or the wicked inclination of his practices. The first and second difficulties contribute to moral worth, weighing all things; the third not, when one can or must reject it, nor the fourth. . . .

On Chastity (December 31, 1402)[54]

. . . Devout people, as I was thinking the other day about this subject matter, I felt a discussion arise in the inner reaches of my heart, namely, which form of chastity is more recommendable, virginity or marriage or widowhood? But before all other things I assumed that each of these daughters of Chastity[55] was good and to be praised, for I know that some heretics have wanted to condemn the state of virginity, others the state of marriage, and still others paid no attention to any chastity whatsoever; rather, they praised lust and said that it was in accord with nature, insofar as the *Romance of the Rose* has Genius, who claims to be the god of nature, say it; and then the author in person says it again, in a more filthy manner, at the end.

And after this assumption, I made the following one: that virginity is more to be praised in our times with respect to the individual, and then widowhood, and then marriage. The other conclusion is that each of these forms of chastity ought to praise and honor the other without pride, for certain people in marriage save their souls better than some others of the other two states. Would you like me to expand a bit upon the arguments that heretics were accustomed to making, and that some still make, against these three states and against the assumption that I have proposed? I believe you would indeed like to hear it; and I will do it as comprehensibly as I can, and quite briefly: one reason against each state.

What good is virginity, some people have said, since the world would

53. "because virtue stays around with difficulty."

54. Undoubtedly an alternate version of the preceding sermon.

55. Glorieux's manuscript omits *de chasteté*; corrected by Hicks's edition of this passage (*Le débat,* 184). The other version of this sermon does not refer to the three states of chastity as her daughters, whereas earlier in this one it is stated: "[Saint Anne] lodged these three types of chastity, which are like her three beautiful and pleasant daughters."

come to an end if everyone was a virgin? I respond that this thing is beyond doubt were everyone to maintain a state of virginity; and if it were the case that God wanted it, then it really would be the end of the world, for some day this end must come. Moreover, I claim that one must not [say], if marriage is necessary, that virginity is lesser or even blameworthy. What thing is more necessary than certain professions, such as shepherds or tailors or bakers? Nonetheless, if a person chooses to be a cleric or a bourgeois, one must not say that he is doing something bad or that he is not doing what is best; it is the same with our statement. Thirdly, I say that for this time of grace and for this Law to which all other people can be led through baptism, marriage is not as necessary as it was at the beginning of the world or during the Old Law which comprised only the Jews.

The heretics argued against marriage, especially the Manicheans, saying that procreation could not be accomplished without mortal sin and damnation, since the child thereby incurs original sin. I respond that the faith and beauty of the sacrament of marriage pardons this sinful deed, as much for the goal of having a lineage that will serve God as [for the couple] to maintain their mutual faith and loyalty during their life together. And if you say that all who get married do not have this intention, I say that they must have it. This is one reason why, among others, I consider that there are so many miseries and unfortunate events between some married couples, because, if their intention was perverse and corrupt at the beginning, what surprise is it if a worse middle and a very painful ending follow upon it, forever worse and worse? Note the examples of Tobias and Sarah.[56]

Certain people argue against widowhood and, generally, against all chastity outside marriage, for it seems to them that nature wishes and assents to the companionship of a man and a woman and that God commands it; and that, secondly, it is also not to be believed that chastity may be maintained, whatever some unmarried people say, claiming they are chaste, but [in fact] they do worse, so say these critics. What will I say here, devout people? Will I deny that nature and God assent to the companionship of man and woman? To be sure, I will never deny that; I do say that in all things that are sanctioned there must be moderation and order, or otherwise one foolishly abuses them. The examples are without number in our body and elsewhere, with hands, feet, etc. In the same way it is necessary that the companionship of man and woman be accomplished through marriage for the reasons given previously. As for what they [these critics] add, the incapacity to live chastely, they lie and insult the saints, male and female,

56. Tob 7–8.

[as well as those] who have maintained this ecclesiastical state, also outside marriage, in a saintly and pure manner; and I previously argued against this error in my last sermon. . . .

25. CHRISTINE DE PIZAN, BALLADE (REDOUBTEE, EXCELLENT) ADDRESSED TO THE QUEEN OF FRANCE (JANUARY 1, 1403)[57]

FRENCH VERSE

[According to lines 12–13, this ballad accompanied a book that Christine was offering as a New Year's gift to the queen of France, Isabeau de Bavière. Even though the calendar in France started the New Year at Easter (see above, ch. 2, n. 129), the custom of giving gifts (estraines) *on January 1, which went back to Roman custom, was maintained. Since it is stated that the book contained elements of a dispute, it is assumed that the book in question was a collection of the Debate documents. But since the first version of that debate had already been dedicated to Isabeau de Bavière on February 1, 1402, and, in addition, this ballad was not included in Christine's manuscript of her collected works completed in June 1402, it is further assumed that this is the augmented version of the volume, including Christine's response to Pierre Col (no. 22), and that it was presented to the queen on January 1, 1403. It is considered likely that the following rondeau was also composed on that date and that the lord to whom it is addressed might be the same Guillaume de Tignonville to whom she had sent the first version of the documents (no. 17).]*

Revered, excellent, very wise, and exalted,
noble, distinguished, possessed of great honor,
celebrated and most gracious queen,
the highest of those ladies who are held in esteem.
I pray to God, who has mastery over all,
that he send you on this New Year's day
such a good reward that there be kindled in you at once
every earthly joy without end.

My revered lady, to whom the entire world bows down,
because I know that you, well educated as you are,
love books, I, your unworthy maidservant,
am sending you this one, in which is included
material that I have acquired from a very high place.
May you, very noble and full of wisdom, accept it with pleasure:

57. Translated from *Le débat,* ed. Hicks, 157.

May there forever remain in you, without ever being dislodged,
every earthly joy without end.

And if it pleases you, very powerful, just, and pure,
that your great Highness might read a little
of my work, and your wisdom settle
the dispute of which the terms are there laid out,
my venture will by all accounts gain in value;
so do pronounce judgment over it, most lofty princess,
and may God, in all manner of ways, favor you with
every earthly joy without end.

Eminent and powerful lady, full of noble spirit,
very humbly I recommend myself
to your genuine merit, you in whom may there be found and secured
every earthly joy without end.

26. CHRISTINE DE PIZAN, RONDEAU (MON CHIER SEIGNEUR) ADDRESSED TO A LORD (GUILLAUME DE TIGNONVILLE?; JANUARY 1, 1403?)[58]

FRENCH VERSE

[*As indicated in the previous item, this rondeau requesting support in the debate might have been sent out at the same time as the ballad to the queen, January 1, 1403, though nothing is said either of gift giving or of an accompanying document. The possibility that it might have been addressed to Guillaume de Tignonville is supported by the terms it uses and the way it describes her situation, which are all quite similar to those contained in the letter Christine sent to him with the first set of documents (no. 17).*]

My dear lord, be on my side!
In a great war that has broken out, I have been assaulted
by the allies of the *Romance of the Rose,*
because I have not been converted to them.

They have mounted such a cruel battle against me
that they truly think they have already nearly contained me:
My dear lord, be on my side!

58. Translated from *Le débat,* ed. Hicks, 158.

I will not be held back on account of their attacks
from pursuing my argument, but it is commonly held
that people attack those who dare defend a just cause;
but if I am poorly assisted by my wits,
my dear lord, be on my side!

27. CHRISTINE DE PIZAN, BALLADE (JADIS AVOIT), TO AN UNKNOWN ADDRESSEE (JANUARY 1, 1403?)[59]

FRENCH VERSE

Once there was in the city of Athens
a blossoming of instruction coming from the highest clerical learning.
But in spite of the authoritative pronouncements
of their great intelligence, one quite unfortunate error
deceived them, for it was many diverse gods
that they worshiped, regarding which some for their betterment
preached to them that they ought to know
that there is only one God; but it turned out badly for them:
One is often beaten down for speaking the truth.

Aristotle the very wise, adept at the lofty
corpus of human knowledge, was a runaway
from that city entirely devoted to such an error; many troubles
he suffered because of it; Socrates, who was a fountain
of understanding, was chased from that place;
many others were killed by the envious
for speaking the truth. And this all
can recognize, that everywhere under the heavens
one is often beaten down for speaking the truth.

Whether this is the way it goes with pronouncements of this world,[60]
that is why I announce that many have picked a quarrel
with me because I dared to censure very wanton
and indecent pronouncements, and unreliable defamation,
in young people and old,

59. Translated from *Le débat,* ed. Hicks, 158-9.

60. The topic of the first two stanzas was religious belief, whereas in Christine's context it is a matter of predominantly secular ideas.

as well as the *Romance*, pleasing to the inquisitive,
of the Rose—which ought to be burned!
But many will jump all over me for this remark:
One is often beaten down for speaking the truth.

Prince, certainly speaking the truth is disagreeable
to liars, who wish to deceive;
this is why we see the son lie to the father:
One is often beaten down for speaking the truth.

28. JEAN GERSON TO PIERRE COL (WINTER 1402–3)[61]

LATIN PROSE

You, a learned man and a most cherished brother in the love of Christ, have written the sort of things about me to which I cannot lay claim for myself, for I do not consider myself worthy of such an honor. Rather, I am horrified at this praise being expressed when it is mixed together with frivolous things, or even worse—forgive me, brother, for telling the truth—with extravagant lies. It happens that, albeit in the midst of other affairs, I could not put off responding to you, my zeal finding it necessary to return your affection and show you my good will—you who, rather than pretending to care for me (far from you such a feint!), display it sincerely. But it is at the same time my confident hope that you will not repudiate your trust in the person whom you have praised so highly. But also, finally, it is because my profession of faith requires that I fight as strenuously as I can against errors and vices—this same profession that some time ago made me publish in the French language, under a certain fictional covering, a speech for the prosecution, lasting a single day, not against the Foolish Lover but against writings, words, and pictures seducing, stimulating, and urging people to illicit forms of love more dreadful than death.[62]

However, I am not about to repeat myself, or translate into Latin those

61. Translated from *Le débat*, ed. Hicks, 162–74. The unique MS containing this letter labels it as a *Responsio ad Scripta Cuiusdam* (Response to the Writings of a Certain Person).

62. Gerson is obviously referring to the *Treatise against the Romance of the Rose*, explicitly claiming his authorship of it. The reference to the "single day" follows the treatise, which starts in the morning and ends at vespers. He uses the technical term *involucrum* (literally "veil," but which I have translated as "fictional covering") in order to speak of the allegorical "covering" of the work, suggesting likewise that Theological Eloquence is indeed a thinly veiled disguise for himself.

issues that were debated in the same place and that you have read; I consider that I have sufficiently argued therein that writings, words, and pictures that provoke libidinous and lascivious thoughts are to be condemned and banned from the republic of the Christian religion—and this, in truth, is valid for every mind that has been illuminated by the Catholic faith and not at all corrupted by a vicious passion. But what sort of speech can be expected to persuade those others who, in truth, do not want to be persuaded; who take pleasure in their error, whom the malice of those who are devoted to a "reprobate mind"[63] have blinded, who turn away their eyes lest they see the end of things, those who, finally, succumb to the most serious kind of curse, namely, being charmed by bad habits or being seduced and tricked by their own iniquity? Among whom, of course, I must not count you, very dear brother; and, falling to my knees, I pray that I never will have to do so.

I have, however, set as a goal to pick out certain of those items contained in a text of yours that was shown to me yesterday evening that need to be corrected or eliminated.[64] What am I saying, "certain," when nearly all things (I am speaking to you as a brother) are to be reproached in one way or another! On account of this, as soon as you have received this letter—if there is a bit of wisdom in me—either a roaring flame will consume that other one, or it will proceed into eternal oblivion having been torn up into the smallest of pieces. However, I particularly would want for you and those like you to be warned lest such a great, hyperbolic admiration of this author [Jean de Meun], who is scarcely to be numbered even among the mediocre, should limit you to an ignorance of wiser authors, for many are superior to him as the great British whale is to dolphins or a grove of cypresses to bushes. Indeed, now pay heed to what sort of precipice your attempted examination of theological material has prepared for you.

Thus you claim that a child of two or three years of age is in a state of innocence. This is the Pelagian heresy, and someone who tenaciously defends it is to be declared a heretic. These things, along with many others, which you have set in motion in order to dismantle irrefutable reason, wrap themselves around you more and more with the knots of that same heresy,

63. Rom 1:28: "Et sicut non probaverunt Deum habere in notitia, tradidit illos Deus in reprobum sensum, ut faciant quæ non conveniunt" (And as they liked not to have God in their knowledge, God delivered them up to a reprobate sense, to do those things which are not appropriate [translation altered]). Interestingly, the context of this biblical passage involves abuses of a sexual nature, including homosexuality.

64. Gerson is of course referring here and below ("that other one") to Pierre Col's letter, in French, addressed to Christine but critiquing both her letter to Jean de Montreuil (no. 5) and Gerson's treatise (no. 20).

following the example of birds caught in a net or in a glue trap fluttering around every which way—so troubling and harmful it is to fight against the truth. It is not I who should be read but Saint Augustine in his *De nuptiis et concupiscentia* (On Marriage and Concupiscence), especially the second book;[65] what I am saying will be found there. You thought, however, as I judge, what you should not have thought: that the child is in a state of innocence for this reason, either because he is ignorant or because he is not yet guilty of an intentional sin. But your mind should have turned its attention to the original corruption of immoral concupiscence, your mind that is lost because of it, as they all are.[66]

You say something about which I wonder whether you are not ashamed or repentant: only a foolish lover, you say, can adequately judge a vicious or rather a delirious passion of this sort. Someone removed from it (of which sort you say I am, but I myself do not say so) does not know it unless it is "through a glass darkly"—as though, in other words, it were necessary for all those who rightly and without corruption are to pass judgment on vices to have themselves beforehand been corrupted by vice. It is very much otherwise: no one pronounces a more twisted judgment on vicious acts than those very people who, by the feverish sickness or mortal passion of such acts, "have been corrupted and made abominable in their desires."[67] The examples due to sensuality are legion. "Every corrupt judge examines the truth inadequately,"[68] as Horace says.

But as far as your adding that the private parts of women were long ago

65. *De nuptiis* 2.3.9 (*PL* 44, col. 441): "Catholici dicunt humanam naturam a creatore Deo bono conditam bonam, sed peccato vitiatam medico Christo indigere . . . Pelagiani et Coelestiani dicunt humanam naturam a bono Deo conditam bonam, sed ita esse in nascentibus parvulis sanam, ut Christi non habeant necessariam in illa aetate medicinam." (Catholics say that human nature was created good by God the good creator, but that, having been corrupted by sin, it has need of Christ's healing . . . The Pelagians and Celestians say that human nature was created good by the good God, but [unlike Catholics] that little ones are healthy when they are born, in such a way that they do not need the medicine of Christ at that age.)

66. Hasenohr (review of *Le débat,* 132) suggests that Hicks's text needs to be emended, the relative pronoun *que,* feminine, necessarily referring back to the feminine word "mind," but that it makes more sense for the antecedent to be the child, and so the relative pronoun should be changed to a subordinating conjunction, *quod,* giving a reading such as "for it [the child] is lost because of it, the same as the rest of us." If, however, we understand the cunning tactic of Gerson, which involves calling into question Pierre Col's power of reasoning because of this flaw, the manuscript reading is acceptable.

67. Ps 13:1: "In finem. Psalmus David. Dixit insipiens in corde suo: Non est Deus. Corrupti sunt, et abominabiles facti sunt in studiis suis." (Unto the end, a psalm for David. The fool hath said in his heart: There is no God. They are corrupt, and are become abominable in their ways.)

68. Horace, *Satires* 2.2.8–9: "Male verum examinat omnis / corruptus iudex" (Every judge who has been bribed weighs badly) (*Satires, Epistles and Ars Poetica,* trans. Fairclough, 137).

sanctified by custom, I do not know what sort of Bible taught you this, unless by chance you have another one than ours in your possession. Or unless this passage from Luke has influenced and seduced you: "Every male opening the vulva will be called consecrated to the Lord."[69] What, I pray, "will be called consecrated to the Lord"? If you remain silent, I respond: "the first-born."

Moreover, your author (and very nearly your God!) wrote many good things, you claim—yes, many that are beyond the common intelligence of all learned men, and the reading of which is not understood unless it is repeated ten times. Yet what if he mixed together an excess of evil things, indeed, many more of them that are contrary to the good ones? What is there left to say except that like a foolish lover he went mad, became unstable, and wallowed in contradictions, and, along the lines of what Terence said, he wanted to "go mad with reason."[70] This is why that work is rightly called a formless chaos, a Babylonian confusion, a type of German broth, and a Proteus changing itself into all forms, a work precisely of the sort to which one can apply that which is recited to children: "He who is in disagreement with himself will not be in accord with anyone."[71]

Without a doubt, what is claimed about theologians, whom you say sometimes fall into foolish love (something of which you menace even me—may the true God of love and not the false Cupid turn me away from that evil!), has been put forward, it seems to me, more for the defamation of the theologians than for its pertinence to the topic, and perhaps so that these theologians, under the shadow of their own greater guilt, would either attenuate or hide or approve of his crimes. For if Cicero, when he describes the eloquent man, calls him a good man with a talent for speaking,[72] I have all the more reason in invoking the name of the Theologian to qualify him as a good man, learned in sacred Scriptures.

69. Lk 2:23; this passage refers back to the Old Testament, Ex 13:2 and 12 and Num 8:16. In both cases, it refers to God's blessing of the firstborn male.

70. Terence, *The Eunuch*, ll. 61–63: "incerta haec si tu postules / ratione certa facere, nihilo plus agas / quam si des operam ut cum ratione insanias" (If you try to impose certainty on uncertainty by reason, you'd achieve no more than if you set about going insane by reason) (*Terence*, trans. Barsby, 1:321). As with the topic of the foolish lover, it is a question of the lover's confusion (with regard to his beloved's inconsistent behavior) at the opening of the play.

71. *Distichs of Cato*, ed. and trans. Wayland Chase, 1.4: "Sperne repugnando tibi tu contrarius esse: / Conveniet nulli, qui secum dissidet ipse" (Ne'er with thyself perversely disagree; Who's out with self in peace with none will be).

72. Hicks suggests (*Le débat*, 230) that the quotation seems rather to come from Quintilian, who in turn attributes it to Cato: "Sit ergo nobis orator quem constituimus, is, qui a M. Catone finitur, *vir bonus dicendi peritus*" (Let the Orator we are putting together be the one that M. Cato describes as a good man with a talent for speaking) (*Institutio oratoria* 12.1.1; my translation).

Come on once again, if your author did not speak shamefully because of his personal disposition, explain what compelled him to introduce those things about which Reason spoke in such obscene and filthy language.

Moreover, your author is guilty, not because he introduced Nature speaking about God, but because of the way in which she speaks of those mysteries that only supernatural revelation, given freely by the grace of God, provides.

And because, in your assault against my short work, you associated me with an exceptional woman, I ask you whether that manly woman to whom your speech is directed—although in such a confused order that it rapidly changes places, at one moment from her to Theological Eloquence, and then the reverse at another—whether that manly woman, I say, who called attention to this erroneous position expressed as a proverb, "It is better to deceive than be deceived," did not successfully refute it. The reflection you provide as a way of getting out of it, so worried and contrived, shows the woman brought you down with a great sting of reason when you took refuge by saying that in that part the book had been disfigured by a spurious interpolation—but you never state the reason for your being able to know this, nor do I see it.

Immediately thereafter, this woman cleverly announced that queens would blush upon reading your author—as would blush all minds exercised in good morals and provided with innocent modesty. Your writings demonstrate moreover that your mind is of the same cast, whether you like it or not: for your good natural disposition was not capable of saying anything obscene there. But it certainly does not follow that those people who act in this way show themselves to be suspect of crimes on account of this. Rather, in truth, if they blush, it is more of a good sign, as an expression of Terence says.[73]

It is not possible for me to touch upon everything. Otherwise, almost any line would find itself being taken out—such as when you say that it is not the natural desire of a man to be joined in matrimony, a single man with a single wife and a single woman with a single man. For this is false and it is in disaccord with one of your writings when you defend Genius, the god of nature, because, you say, he spoke only of the bonds of marriage.

Likewise that you should have thought to hide the disgracefulness of the author by means of this portrayal, namely, that he taught evil so that, once recognized, it would be avoided, or that on account of this a man

73. Terence, *Adelpoe* (The Brothers), l. 643: "erubuit. salva res est." (He's blushing! All's well!) *Terence*, trans. Barsby, 2:325.

known to you, captivated by love, prepared a remedy for himself from this poisonous honey as one would prepare theriac[74] from venom. All such things are indeed without merit.

It is also not very Catholic to have advanced that certain men have said the Song of Songs was composed for the purpose of praising the daughter of the Pharaoh, for whoever said this lied impiously.

It truly appears more perfidious when, by arguing, you wish to convince people that it is necessary to return to the book: "The book," you say, "does not contain in all things what the attack on it claims." I do not wish to dispute this; I prefer to give up my vanquished arms, I prefer to surrender, rather than to submit once again to such a dishonest and polluted reading.

Further on, the end of your text notes that those by whom this despised book is vilified "bent their knees before Baal." I would like to say honestly what I think: either the introduction of this remark corrupts the meaning of the text and is faulty; or, if it was said seriously, insofar as it is scandalous, injurious, mendacious, and tasting of heretical teaching against faith and morals, it is in the final analysis to be eradicated.

You never were able to glorify my modest standing so much with your panegyrics as you disparage it when what may be called the liberty you take in speaking with me claims falsely that I said the things I said so that a more intense flame might engulf men, who we know gravitate toward what is forbidden,[75] and incite them to repeat the reading of this book—as though, in other words, I would have transformed my profession into a sham, and it were my function to act deceptively in the teaching of morals and be in disaccord with my very self (or rather, with the Christian religion!), speaking both sincerely and insincerely,[76] in the manner of your author. I would sooner die than ever be found cloaked in deception of this kind. Instead, consider whether this accusation of fraud might not have tainted your au-

74. Theriac is an antidote to poison, typically to the bites of venomous snakes.

75. Ovid, *Amores* 3.4.17: "nitimur in vetitum semper cupimusque negata" (we gravitate toward what is forbidden and always desire things denied us) (*Heroides and Amores,* trans. Showerman, 461 [altered]). This line immediately precedes the one referred to by Christine at the end of her letter to Jean de Montreuil (no. 5).

76. The text here is literally "speaking beyond/outside the heart/soul [*corde insuper*] and according to the heart/soul [*corde*]"—hence my translation, "speaking both sincerely and insincerely." Hicks's translation, "saying the opposite of what I think" (*Le débat,* 171) is a good alternative, but corresponds somewhat less to Gerson's point, inasmuch as he repeatedly emphasizes that the great danger of Jean de Meun's text is the undetectable mixture of the good and the evil, which leaves the reader in a state of total confusion as far as proper doctrine is concerned. Were Jean de Meun to say only things that were condemnable, the reader's (and the critic's) task would be much easier.

thor. For when he introduces criticisms of carnal love—of which he more often sings the praises—why will he not, as per your idea, actually have been endeavoring to make impressionable individuals even more inclined to that love?

What might I say about your author's protestation, which, as a type of covering, he tried to add on top of his repulsive work?[77] I did not, he says, put anything into it of my own. He thereby declares himself to be not an author but someone who quotes others. Thus you, his admirers, if he indeed spoke brilliantly, must not attribute praise to him, just as he does not want his calumnies to be turned to his shame, if he translated certain objectionable things. For this reason, do not burst out with hatred against us or speak out against us with such bombastic words and your cheeks puffed out, if this book is critiqued on its own terms. For it is not people we discredit but writings, whoever made them, unless it is indeed esteemed that a person who serves up a poisoned drink, even prepared by someone else, is not to be, because of that, judged exempt from guilt.[78] Again, what is this, great God, to declare one thing and in the very same context to contradict one's own protestation?[79] This certainly is not to justify oneself but to act in such a way that it might be said: "I judge you by your own mouth, worthless servant."[80]

77. The "protestation" is the famous authorial defense, indeed exculpation, placed just before the God of Love's major attack on the castle, abetted by Venus, and the lengthy episode devoted to Nature and Genius (*Rose*, ed. Lecoy, ll. 15105–272; trans. Dahlberg, 257–60).

78. The logic of this sentence is not totally clear. Gerson seems to be saying that he is only condemning whatever is written down, whoever wrote it. But then he asks, even if it is only a matter of the content, shouldn't we consider a poisoner complicitous in his crime, even if someone else prepared the poison? In other words, Gerson is in some way contradicting his previous point by saying "yes, the person who serves the poison, the person who repeats the scandalous words of others, *is* guilty." This is the way Hicks understands it in his translation (*Le débat*, 171). Alternately, the latter statement could be understood ironically: "unless we think that the person who serves the drink is guilty (which we don't)." I tend to agree with Hicks and see in this sentence an indication of Gerson's profound ambivalence, illustrated likewise in his treatise: His principle that words and not people are being condemned is in conflict with his profound disgust with Jean de Meun's writerly tactics (indicated by his quotation from Luke at the end of the paragraph).

79. Here again, a difficulty arises as to whether Gerson is speaking about Jean de Meun or about his supporters, among them Pierre Col, the addressee of this letter. The contradiction he is criticizing is inherent in Jean de Meun's text but is also a flaw in the argument of his supporters, who at the same time praise him for his brilliant poetry and unequaled erudition but declare him innocent of anything reprehensible he might have said, because he was only quoting other authors. It is possible that Gerson is speaking of both.

80. Lk 19:22: "De ore tuo te judico, serve nequam."

Finally, I have never offended you, O Christian court, in thought or in word. I confess that you cannot correct all misdeeds. Otherwise what would be left for divine justice in the future? In many cases a conviction through laws and common edicts suffices. But particularly where no public accuser is found, just as it is against simony, theft, homicide, and adultery, so it is against that most contagious unrestrained liberty in speaking or writing in a wicked manner. Because of this, I do not propose pardoning those numerous men of the Church you have in mind on the subject of the many books of Ovid, or on the subject of magical fantasies, or specifically on the subject of this book and others that have been preserved, leading to the ruin of many people; I do excuse those whom no official position constrains to condemn and who, for their part, rebuke such things, verbally or in writing, generally or specifically, as I do now and many have before.

Nor do I think that what is written in the Acts of the Apostles is to be passed over, that all new converts to the faith who had avidly sought out cultic secrets burned their books with a value of fifty-thousand silver coins.[81] Here, I swear in the presence of God that I am not lying, and—I affirm it, assuming that there is something in me that you deem worthy of trust—if there were only one copy of your author's book and it belonged to me, worth a thousand pounds and even more, I would sooner throw it into roaring flames to be burned than sell it and, in that way, allow it to be made public. See how much I am moved (or rather, in truth, I am not moved) to reread it, not, to be sure, out of ignorance as you imagine—although there is much of it in me—but on account of my conscience and that of others. Thus I remember having some time ago, already from my adolescence, drunk from all those fountains, or nearly all, from which the works of your author, or rather certain poorly translated tiny streams, came forth: Boethius, Ovid, Terence, Juvenal, Alan of Lille, Guillaume de Saint-Amour, Abelard along with his Heloïse, Martianus Capella, and perhaps others.[82] Know, moreover, that there is a small volume whose title is *The Journey of the Soul toward God*, by Master Bonaventure, which I read in its entirety in one day, and which I would not hesitate to oppose, as regards the profundity of its learning, to

81. Acts 19:19: "Multi autem ex eis, qui fuerant curiosa sectati, contulerunt libros, et combusserunt coram omnibus: et computatis pretiis illorum, invenerunt pecuniam denariorum quinquaginta millium" (And many of them who had followed curious arts, brought together their books, and burnt them before all; and counting the price of them, they found the money to be fifty thousand pieces of silver).

82. This is a very good summary of the most important influences upon, and texts incorporated into, the *Rose*, but Terence and Martianus Capella do not happen to be among them.

your entire book—or rather it along with ten comparable ones. And you judge that we are too thick and obtuse to understand this book!

However, in view of your recommendation that I reread it and thus understand it, I give as a response the alternative: read, my brother, and read once again the fourth book of *On Christian Doctrine.* For it offers somewhat more difficulty than your book that is written in the vernacular. You will notice, believe me, that no cruel damage has been done to Eloquence if we have associated her with theology.[83] You will perhaps be ashamed of your impudence in referring to things that you have not fully looked at. Augustine clearly cries out against you, both with very precise words found there (in the fourth book of *On Christian Doctrine,* at the very opening of the work),[84] and then with the fact of his own works, carefully crafted with the great force of his eloquence. Moreover, if you pay attention, I spoke with tempered moderation when I introduced Theological Eloquence as speaking with a middle style, vigilantly keeping at a distance any preciosity I might now be criticized for.

Finally, let the banter come to an end, excellent brother, you who deserve to defend a better cause. For the moment, may the desire either to vanquish or to continue talking silence itself. Let us come to the serious religious issue. I assure you, if I had known that my brother had composed and made public such a book, and that moreover he had finally refused to repent, having been forewarned about this and sufficiently reprimanded, I would no more offer prayers for him to Our Lord Jesus Christ, after he died in this impenitence, than I would for someone who had been condemned. I bid you farewell in him (Our Lord), as you henceforth take yourself to more salubrious and chaste pursuits and no longer provide an opportunity for scandal to innocents. And if something that was said perhaps too harshly has

83. Here Gerson makes Theological Eloquence a female personification—necessarily, because the noun in Latin, which requires grammatical agreement, is feminine (see above, ch. 3, n. 33).

84. *PL* 34, cols. 89–90; trans. Robertson, 117–69, esp. 118–20. Pierre Col had criticized the character named Theological Eloquence by suggesting that Augustine opposed the alliance of rhetoric and religious instruction. Indeed, Augustine says in the first few lines of the fourth book of *On Christian Doctrine* that he is not going to "give the rules of rhetoric here which I learned and taught in the secular schools" (Robertson, 118). But he says soon thereafter that since the art of rhetoric can be used to urge either truth or falsehood, why should it "not be obtained for the uses of the good in the service of truth" (Robertson, 118–119)? To be taught is one thing, but to be moved is another: the goal of the preacher is therefore served by "entreaties and reproofs, exhortations and rebukes, and whatever other devices are necessary to move minds" (Robertson, 121).

offended, give indulgence to my good faith, which has presumed much of you because it has much affection for you. In sum, consider that it is attributable, first to my zealous love of the Catholic truth, and then to my wish for your salvation.

Let us then pray mutually for our salvation.

29. JEAN DE MONTREUIL TO A HIGH-RANKING PRELATE (1403–4)[85]

LATIN PROSE

Since those trifles of mine in metrical form in the vernacular are not worthy, reverend father, to be submitted for your examination, it came to my mind to try some unrhymed pieces. Here therefore, my teacher, I am sending two letters that were produced quite a while ago with no less enthusiasm than the trifles of the other type: one is a eulogy of the brilliantly flowering[86] work of the *Rose,* the other on the same topic, having the form of a satire aimed at the man who has likewise attacked you, albeit for another reason.[87] I certainly hope, request, and implore that they not be considered so base and lowly that they might not be worth alternating for a brief time with the important things you have to do; rather I would be pleased for the aforementioned insipid and empty writings, in their passage through the court of your wisdom, to be, as they say, reaffirmed or even improved, and not come back, like our *Proverbs,* bemoaning a disdainful reception.[88] Socrates, the most learned of all men according to the response of Apollo, "did not blush at playing with children." Scipio Africanus and Cato the Censor

85. Translated from *Le débat,* ed. Hicks, 40–42.

86. The word here is *florentissimi,* which is a superlative of a word meaning literally "being in flower" and, by extension, "flourishing, excellent, brilliant." Since Jean is consciously using the floral metaphor to speak of the "rose," I felt it necessary to maintain it in translation.

87. Hicks and Ornato ("Jean de Montreuil et le débat sur le *Roman de la Rose,*" 200–202 and the table on 219) tacitly consider these two works to be Montreuil's letter to the "great poet" (no. 19 in this volume) and his invective to the lawyer (no. 6), presumably because Montreuil refers to them as "letters." However, no. 19 is not really a eulogy of the *Rose,* but rather a call for assistance. Montreuil does not indeed call his now-lost treatise a letter, but Christine de Pizan does (no. 18). I believe that this eulogy must be his initial treatise on the *Rose.* Since the addressee of this letter, a prelate, has clearly not seen any of these works, he is not to be confused with the addressee of nos. 7 and 9.

88. It appears, according to Hicks (*Le débat,* xl), that Jean de Montreuil had previously sent to this correspondent a now lost volume of proverbs in verse that was not well received (the "trifles of mine in metrical form" that he mentions in the first sentence of this letter).

experienced great joy in counting the pebbles in the sand.[89] And you will really disdain to the point of disgust the exercises of your disciple, whom you ought to inspire in his studies in your role as teacher, and you will lead him into despair over his progress! This would be far from your humanity, far from your paternal affection and your unique benevolence! These are the manners of barbarians, not yours. Up to now, as far as I have heard, you have not acted in this way toward anyone. But Jean will be the first to be struck with your rod? He will be the first to be subjected to this punishment? And so the person I trusted as my master and instructor, I might receive as my most ardent critic? I would not believe this, my father, even if Cicero himself were to make the case for it, nor could I imagine it. No, I will more reasonably wait for the approval and guidance of your good will, coming from the inborn kindness of your affection. May it look upon me with such an eye of benevolence that I will not be forced to retreat to a new asylum, but instead may the provost of Lille obtain the indulgence he has always sought with his dutiful prayers. "And if we have done anything wrong, we'll make amends to your satisfaction," this according to the advice of Terence.[90]

89. Ornato (Jean de Montreuil, *Opera,* 1:219) suggests that this mention of Socrates, Scipio, and Cato is a conflation of two passages, one from Seneca, *De tranquilitate animi* (On Tranquility of the Mind) 17.4: "Cum puerulis Socrates ludere non erubescebat, et Cato vino laxabat animum curis publicis fatigatum, et Scipio triumphale illud ac militare corpus movebat ad numeros" (Socrates did not blush to play with little children, and Cato, when he was wearied by the cares of state, would relax his mind with wine, and Scipio would disport his triumphal and soldierly person to the sound of music), and the other from Cicero, *De oratore* 2.6.22: "Non audeo dicere de talibus viris, sed tamen ita solet narrare Scaevola, conchas eos et umbilicos ad Caietam et ad Laurentum legere consuesse" (I am afraid to say it of personages so august, but Scaevola is fond of relating how at Caieta and Laurentum it was their wont to collect mussels and top-shells) (trans. E. W. Sutton [Cambridge: Harvard University Press, 1948], 213), neither of which contains all the information in this passage. Was Jean reconstructing from memory or is there an unknown other source?

90. *Hecyra* (The Mother-in-Law), ll. 253–55: "si quid est peccatum a nobis, profer: / aut ea refellendo aut purgando vobis corrigemus / te iudice ipso." (If we have done anything wrong, bring it out into the open. We'll either disprove the allegation or apologize, and we'll make amends to your satisfaction.) *Terence,* ed. and trans. Barsby, 2:170–71.

V
CHRISTINE'S LATER MENTIONS OF THE *ROMANCE OF THE ROSE*

30. FROM CHRISTINE DE PIZAN, *BOOK OF FORTUNE'S TRANSFORMATION* (*LIVRE DE LA MUTACION DE FORTUNE*, NOVEMBER 1403)[1]

FRENCH VERSE (RHYMING OCTOSYLLABIC COUPLETS)

[The Book of Fortune's Transformation *is a vast work begun in 1400 but not completed until late in 1403; Christine undoubtedly worked intermittently on it during the period she was involved in the debate over the* Rose. *In the first part, Christine provides an intriguing autobiographical account, in which she speaks of her becoming head of household after her husband's death and her need to work for a living as a writer in terms of Fortune's transformation of her from a woman to a man; the balance of the work centers on the figure of Fortune and her castle, during which Christine describes paintings on the castle wall, whose subjects extend from various moral and philosophical themes to a panorama of the history of the world from the Creation, passing through the Old Testament and ancient world into the present. In this, the third book, she describes the "seats and conditions" of all those lodged in Fortune's castle, extending from the rulers of the world, secular and religious, all the way down the social scale to the bourgeois and common people. In this passage, she speaks of the hypocrisy of courtiers, counselors to princes, likening them to the character of False Seeming, the personification of the religious hypocrite in Jean de Meun's* Rose.]

I believe that I saw here many heinous people, even though they were completely covered in furs, but God knows their innermost intentions. But I truly believe that in finding ways to obtain money, they must have had consid-

1. Translated from the edition of Suzanne Solente (4 vols. [Paris: Picard, 1959–66]), 2:44–46 (ll. 5537–5601).

erable cleverness and depravity: Wherever it came from didn't matter, provided that they could get their hands on it.

In the authentic and true historical accounts of Rome, we find that the counselors of that city, where there were brave knights, were commonly poor, for they never took anyone else's belongings from him; the common good sufficed for them, while private goods were never coveted. As long as the Romans acted in this way, they conquered empires and kingdoms, but as soon as they went after private possessions, their greatest honors dried up. Many evil counselors did not anticipate this, may they be burned at the stake! Likewise I saw there deceitful people held in great honor, more conscientious in acquiring profits for themselves than in pursuing the common profit, yet putting on a semblance of virtue. I saw them to be neither outrageous in their actions nor obstinate, but rather gentle and calm in appearance. Ah! What great blows these men gave, by means of their underhanded and perfidious exteriors, folded up with great defects; what a peril motivated by ambition is that of the malicious and crafty man, who knows how to simulate, speak well, color over and represent things with skill! If great evil abounds there, it is meant to pervert an entire world, both kingdoms and people, in short order. No matter how wise one might be, who would be able to protect himself from such a seducer? None, I believe, when it's examined properly, for there is too much subtle scheming in these scoundrels, as well as sharp ingenuity. One must never portray false appearances, more deceitful than a thieving robber, under the guise of Mendicants or Jacobins and brothers wearing cowls, as did Meun, some time ago, in the *Romance of the Rose,* when he spoke of a lover.[2] For here [among the counselors in Fortune's castle] the false appearance was more perfect, in word and in deed, and much more perilous, without any doubt, than among those who have no dealings with temporal authorities—rather, one would not be doing much for them [by exposing them to temporal authorities]. But the ones I am talking about were involved in the actions of government, where they cooked up, through their very misleading concealments, false contracts and great wrongs; however, in their infinite wickedness, by which many a person has been ravaged and defiled, they knew how to cover up their deeds, for they pretended that they were doing everything for the best and that they hated all wicked contracts.

2. Christine here refers to one of the most satirically outrageous (and provocative) episodes of the *Romance of the Rose,* that of Faux Semblant (False Seeming), the personification of religious hypocrisy, who is portrayed as a friar of one of the mendicant orders that were so visible in thirteenth-century Paris. Here Christine turns the proper name of Jean de Meun's hypocrite back into a common noun, which I have translated as "false appearance(s)."

31. FROM CHRISTINE DE PIZAN, *BOOK OF THE CITY OF LADIES* (*LIVRE DE LA CITÉ DES DAMES,* 1405)[3]

FRENCH PROSE

Book I

I. *Here begins the Book of the City of Ladies, the first chapter of which speaks of why the said book was composed and what instigated it.*

I was sitting in my study one day surrounded by numerous volumes on diverse topics, pursuing an activity that has become my habit, and to which my life's work has been devoted, namely, keeping company with the study of letters. My brain having become at that point somewhat overburdened by absorbing the weightiness of the pronouncements of the different authors I had been studying for quite some time, I lifted my face up from the book and thought I'd put aside subtle arguments that day and entertain myself by looking at some cheerful bits among the works of the poets. With that idea in mind, as I was looking around for some small booklet, a book that I did not recognize—not one of my own but one among several other volumes that had been entrusted to me—found itself by chance in my hands. So I opened it and saw by the title inscribed on it that it was called *Matheolus.*[4] I then thought to myself, smiling, that I would take a look at it as a pleasing pastime, since I had never seen this book before and had heard many times that, compared with other books, this one spoke with true respect for women. But I had not had much time to look at it when I was called by my dear mother, who came to summon me to the dinner table, as the hour had already come; for this reason, planning to look at it the next day, I left it at that point.

The following morning, seated once again in my study, as I am accustomed to doing, I did not forget to follow through with the plan I had

3. Translated from *La città delle dame,* ed. E. J. Richards (Milan: Luni, 1997), 40–50, 64–68, 280–82, and 370–78. English translations of the complete work are found in *The Book of the City of Ladies,* trans. Earl Jeffrey Richards, rev. ed. (New York: Persea Books, 1998); and *The City of Ladies,* trans. Rosalind Brown-Grant (New York: Penguin Books, 1999).

4. On the *Lamentations of Matheolus,* see above, ch. 4, n. 26. The fact that Christine first mentions this work here in the *Cité des dames* but not during the debate or previous to it could suggest that her reading of it was recent and that it was perhaps, as her fiction suggests, the incitement for this, her crowning work in defense of women; she therefore appends it to the works she had been criticizing in her writings for several years, Ovid's *Art of Love* and the *Romance of the Rose.*

formed to examine the book of *Matheolus*. I thus began to read it and progressed somewhat into it. But since the subject matter did not seem to me very pleasant for people who do not delight in calumny, or of any profit for the teaching of virtue or morals, given the disreputable words and topics it touches upon, I took a peek here and there and, having looked at the end, set it aside to apply myself to more dignified and more useful studies. But the perusal of that book, even though it is of no authority, engendered in me a new line of thought that brought about great astonishment in my heart, as I wondered what might be the cause, where it might come from, that so many different men, clerics and others, have been and continue to be so inclined to say in public, as well as in their treatises and writings, so many terrible and vituperative things about women and their various conditions. And it is not only one or two or just this *Matheolus*, which has no status among books and deals with its topic in a style full of mockery, but somewhat generally in all treatises—by philosophers, poets, preachers, whose names it would take a long time to list—to such an extent that it seems they all speak with a single mouth and agree on a similar conclusion, having determined that female morals are inclined to, and replete with, every vice.

As I reflected upon these things deep inside myself, I began to examine my own case and my behavior as someone born a woman. I likewise considered the other women I have frequented, princesses and great ladies as well as a great number of women of modest or low-born condition, who had graciously shared with me their secrets and closely guarded thoughts, in order to ascertain, judging in my conscience and without bias, whether what so many men of all sorts assert about them could be true. But for all my scrutiny, however long I pondered and dissected the question, I could neither recognize nor admit the truth of such pronouncements made against the natural comportment and the various conditions of women. In spite of this, I vigorously cast blame against women, saying that it would be too hard to imagine that so many renowned men—celebrated clerics of such lofty and immense learning, as insightful in all matters as these seemed to be—would have spoken about them so mendaciously and in so many places that I could scarcely find a work of moral instruction by whatever author in which, by the time I reached the end, I did not find certain chapters or passages reproaching them. This reason alone, short and simple, made me conclude that this truly had to be the case, even though my understanding, in its naïveté and ignorance, was incapable of recognizing the great faults in myself and, similarly, in other women. In this way I deferred more to the judgments of others than I relied upon what I myself felt and knew about women.

I remained so immersed in this thought and stuck on it for such a long time that I began to feel as though I were comatose. A great crowd of authors paraded before me on this topic, authors who came to my mind one after the other, just like a fountain gushing forth. In the final analysis, I concluded that when God formed woman he created something abject, and I remained mystified how it could be that such an exalted worker ever deigned make such an abominable work that is, in the words of those men, a vessel containing all evils and all vices—indeed, their retreat and dwelling. Then, as I was deep in thought, great distress and heartfelt sadness arose in me, as I despised myself and the entire female sex as though it were a monster of nature. I spoke the following words as I lamented:

"Ah! God, how can this be? For if I do not err in my faith, I must not consider that your infinite wisdom and most perfect goodness might have made anything that is not completely good. Did you not yourself form woman in her every particular and thence give her such inclinations that you wanted her to have? How could it be that in so doing you failed in any way? Nonetheless, here we have so many accusations, indeed, pronouncements, against them that have already been decided and brought to a conclusion. I cannot understand this contradiction. But if this is the case, dear Lord God, if it is true that abomination is so abundant in the female sex, as many attest, and you yourself declare that the testimony of many of them deserves to be believed (because of which I must not doubt that it is true), alas! dear God, why did you not have me be born into the world in the male sex, so that my inclinations would be entirely to serve you better, so that I would not err in any matter and would be of such great perfection as men claim to be? But since it is the case that your good grace did not extend itself so far toward me, have mercy on my negligence in your service, dear Lord God, and let it not displease you, for the servant who receives fewer rewards from his master is under less of an obligation to serve him." Such words and many more did I address to God, sadly and at great length, in my lamentation—I who, urged on by my folly, considered myself highly disfavored because God had brought me into the world in the body of a woman.

II. *Here Christine tells how three ladies appeared to her and how the one who was in front of the others spoke to her first and consoled her on her distress.*

Just as I was suffering under these sorrowful thoughts, my head bowed like a disgraced person, eyes full of tears, holding my hand under my cheek with my elbow leaning on the knob of my chair, suddenly I saw a ray of light, just like the sun, shine down on my lap; I jumped up, for I was in a dark place where, at that hour, the sun could not cast light.[5] Then, as though I were just awakened from a sound sleep, I lifted up my head to see where the light was coming from and saw before me, standing, three crowned women of majestic stature. The shining light radiating from their bright faces lit me up along with the entire room. No one need ask whether I was at that moment astonished, having taken note that the door was closed with me inside and yet the ladies had entered. Fearing that it was some kind of vision meant to tempt me, I made the sign of the cross on my forehead, filled with great trepidation.

Then she who was the first of the three began to speak to me, smiling: "Dear daughter, don't be frightened, for we have not come to do you harm, or to create any difficulty, but rather to console you, for we are moved to pity by your perturbation, and to lead you out of ignorance, which has so blinded your very knowledge that you have cast away from yourself what you know[6] with certainty, while you lend credence to what you neither know, nor see, nor recognize in any other way than through a multitude of opinions of others. You resemble the fool who, as the joke tells, was dressed in women's clothes while sleeping in a mill, and when he woke up, because men who were making fun of him assured him that he was a woman, he believed their deceptive words rather than the certain knowledge of his own being. How is this, dear daughter? What happened to your good sense? Have you thus forgotten that pure gold is tempered in the furnace and that its qualities do not change or become altered, but rather it becomes more refined the more it is hammered and worked over in various ways? Don't you know that the most precious things are the ones most debated and most argued over? If you wish to aim especially at the highest things, called "ideas," which is to say things celestial, consider whether the very greatest philosophers who ever existed, whose opinions you use to reproach your own sex, ever in the slightest determined what is false and, contrariwise, what is true in this regard and whether they don't criticize and reproach each other, as you yourself have seen in the book of *Metaphysics,* in the place where Aristotle refutes and admonishes their opinions, speaking similarly about Plato and

5. Jacqueline Cerquiglini-Toulet, *The Color of Melancholy: The Uses of Books in the Fourteenth Century,* trans. Lydia G. Cochrane (Baltimore: Johns Hopkins University Press, 1997), 72–73, notes that this position of the hand would be a traditional symbolic rendering of melancholy, whereas this scene in general imitates that of the Annunciation, the light on the lap symbolizing the Virgin's future motherhood. Christine, "playing with the sacred," as Cerquiglini says, puts herself in the position of Mary.

6. I emend Richards's text here, which negates this verb, obviously in error.

others.[7] Note moreover whether Saint Augustine and other Church Fathers did not reproach in some measure even Aristotle in certain parts, though he be called the Prince of Philosophers and the man in whom natural and moral philosophy reached their highest point. But it seems that you believe all the words of the philosophers to be an article of faith and that they cannot err. Moreover, regarding the poets you speak of, do you not know that they spoke on many topics using the method of fabulous narrative and that sometimes they want to be understood as saying the opposite of what their works present literally? One can thus understand them by a rule of grammar called *antiphrasis,* by which is understood, as you know, that, for example, if someone were to say that something was bad, he would be saying in other words that it was good, and vice versa. So I advise you to turn their writings to your advantage and understand it in this way—whatever their intention might have been—in the places where they blame women. Perhaps even that man who called himself Matheolus in his book understood it thus: for there are many things in it that would be pure heresy if someone wanted to take them literally. Moreover, as for the vituperation he expresses—not only he but others, and especially the *Romance of the Rose,* which is considered more trustworthy because of the authority of the author—about the order of marriage, which is a sacred and worthy state, ordained by God, it is clearly proven by experience that the opposite is true regarding the sufferings that they propose and claim to be found in that state, charging women with the fault for it. For where did one ever find a husband who allowed his wife to wield such power that she would have license to say to him the sorts of degrading and injurious things that these authors claim women say? I believe that although you have seen some of these things in writing, you never saw any of it with your own eyes, and it amounts to nothing but viciously colored lies. So I say to you in conclusion, dear friend, that it is naïveté that led you to the present opinion. Now come back to yourself, recover your good sense, and stop troubling yourself over such trifles. Indeed, know for

7. The reference in the *Metaphysics* is to book 1, 983b–992a. When Lady Reason says to Christine "as you yourself have seen," she is undoubtedly referring to the brief discussion of Aristotle and philosophy in *The Book of the Deeds and Good Morals of Wise King Charles V* (*Le livre des fais et bonnes meurs du sage roy Charles V,* ed. S. Solente, 2 vols. [Paris: Honoré Champion, 1936–40], 2:169–75 [part 3, chap. 67]), largely based upon Aquinas's Latin commentary on Aristotle's *Metaphysics,* although there Christine's point is less to impugn the standing of philosophy than to call poetry into question. *The Book of the Deeds* was completed just before the end of 1404, at which time she began writing the *City of Ladies.* Christine comes back to the topic in question the following year, in *Christine's Vision* (*Le Livre de l'Advision Christine,* part 2, chaps. 8–11 (ed. Reno and Dulac, 64–72), where she does cover in some detail Aristotle's criticisms of the ancient philosophers, again basing herself on and translating Aquinas's commentary.

a fact that any evil said so indiscriminately about women harms those who say it and not women themselves."

. . .

[*The lady continues her consolation of Christine and presents the task that she and her two companions have come to assign to Christine: the construction of the City of Ladies, where virtuous women of the past and present will have a place of refuge and be able to defend themselves. She ends her speech, revealing that she is Lady Reason. The other two ladies, Rectitude and Justice, each speak briefly with Christine. Christine accepts the task assigned to her.*]

VIII. *Here Christine tells how, upon the command of Reason and with her help, she began to till the soil in order to place the foundations.*

Then Lady Reason replied and said, "Get up then, daughter, without any more delay: Let us go to the field of Letters. There the City of Ladies will be founded upon level and fertile land, a place where an abundance of fruits and sweet rivers are found and where the land abounds in good things. Take the pickax of your understanding and till vigorously; make a great ditch everywhere you see the lines I have traced, and I will help you to carry away the soil with my own shoulders."

Then, in order to obey their commandment, I stood up unreservedly, feeling stronger and lighter than I had been previously, owing to their virtue. She went first and I followed; we came to the field in question, and I began to dig the ditch and break up the soil according to her directions with the pickax of inquiry. And the first part of my work was as follows: "My lady, I indeed seem to remember that you told me earlier, when you came to the statement that many men are so critical of women and blame their behavior, that 'the longer gold remains in the furnace, the more refined it becomes' (by which is meant that the more they are wrongly blamed, the more the recompense for their honor grows). But I beg you, tell me why this is, and what is the cause that explains that so many different authors have spoken against women in their books—since I already sense from you that it is done wrongly—whether it is Nature that inclines them toward it, or if they do it out of hatred, or where it comes from."

Then she replied as follows: "Daughter, in order to provide you a way of entering more deeply into this matter, I will carry out this first basketful.[8] Know that this does not in any way come from Nature; it is in fact quite

8. Reason is of course referring to the metaphor of Christine's digging the ditch.

the contrary, for there is no stronger bond in the world than the great love that Nature, with the will of God, placed between a man and a woman. But the reasons that have motivated and still do motivate many men to criticize women are diverse and multifaceted, especially among authors in their books, as you have noted. For certain of them have done it with a good intention, namely, to pull men who have gone off the right path away from the frequentation of certain corrupt and dissolute women over whom they can be besotted, or to keep them from becoming besotted. So, in order to make every man flee a lascivious and lustful life, they blamed women indiscriminately in order to inculcate in men a repugnance for all women."

"Lady, I said, pardon me then if I interrupt your discussion. They have thereby done a good thing, since a good intention has motivated them; for it is by his intention, they say, that a man is judged."

"This is an incorrect formulation, fair daughter," she said, "for gross ignorance is not to be pardoned. If someone killed you with a good intention but out of a foolish calculation, would this therefore be a praiseworthy deed? Rather, they acted unrighteously in so doing, whoever it may have been, for there is no justice when one inflicts misfortune and damage upon one person, thinking one is coming to the rescue of another. To blame all female behavior counter to the truth (as I will demonstrate to you through common experience), even if we assume that it was done with the intention of deterring the foolish from folly, is the same as to blame fire, which is itself very good, indeed, necessary, because some people burn themselves, or to blame water because some people drown in it. And the same could be said about all good things that can be used either correctly or improperly: one must nonetheless not blame these things even if fools abuse them. Moreover, you yourself have touched upon this point quite well elsewhere in your writings. But those people who have spoken in this way at such great length, whatever their intention might have been, applied their arguments quite liberally with the sole intention of arriving at their goal, in the same way as someone who has a long and wide robe cut for him using liberally a large piece of cloth that costs him nothing and that no one refuses to him, so he takes and appropriates what is by right someone else's for his own use. But as you yourself have said quite well before, if these men had looked for the paths and the ways to pull men back from folly and prevent them from getting themselves entangled in it by blaming the life and the morals of those women who prove themselves to be corrupt and dissolute—since there is nothing in this world more to be shunned, to tell the pure truth, than the licentious and perverse woman who, just like a monster in nature, is a deformed being far removed from her proper, natural condition, which ought to be innocent, gentle, and virtuous—I fully admit that they would have constructed a good and proper work exceptionally well. But when they blame all women, I promise you that this never came from me and that they very greatly failed in this undertaking, given that there are so many excellent women among them; all those who imitate them are making a mistake as well. So eject these dirty, gnarled, and blackened stones from your work; for they will never be placed in the beautiful edifice of your city."

. . .

Book II

XXV. *Christine speaks to Lady Rectitude against those who say that women don't know how to hide anything, and the response given to her is about Portia, daughter of Cato.*

"Lady, I know now with certainty—and I have noticed it before—that the love and confidence that many women have experienced and continue to experience with respect to their husbands are great. And this is why I wonder at a discourse that circulates quite commonly among men—and especially Master Jean de Meun affirms it very forcefully in his *Romance of the Rose,* and others do it also—that a man must not say to his wife anything that he wants to keep secret, and that women can't remain quiet."

Response: "Dear friend, you must know that not all women are wise, and it is the same for men. On account of this, if a man has some intelligence, he must in truth carefully evaluate what sort of wits and good will his wife has before he tells her the slightest thing that he wants to keep secret, for there could be some danger in it. But when a man feels that he has a good, wise, and discreet wife, there is no creature in the world more trustworthy or more apt to console him. As for the idea that women might be so little worthy of trust as these men profess, and once again concerning women who love their husbands, noble Brutus, husband of Portia, never held this opinion long ago in Rome . . ."

. . .

LIII. *After Lady Rectitude spoke about loyal ladies, Christine asked her why so many valiant ladies did not in the past contradict the books and the men who slandered them; and the responses that Rectitude gives her.*

When Lady Rectitude had told me all these stories, and many others that I leave aside for the sake of brevity (such as about Leontion, a Greek woman, who did not want to denounce publicly two men with whom she was intimate, no matter how much she was tortured, so instead she cut her tongue off with her teeth in front of the judge so that he would lose all hope of getting her to talk by virtue of torture;[9] she also told me about a number of other ladies as well who were of steadfast temperament, to an extent that they preferred drinking poison and dying to yielding and thereby betraying righteousness and truth), after these things, I said to her:

"Lady, you have shown me the great steadfastness in the hearts of women, along with all other virtues; so much so that in truth one could not say any better for any man. So I am truly astonished at how so many valiant ladies—ones who were so wise, so lettered, and who possessed beautiful style in conceiving and composing books—put up with so many horrible things being asserted against them by diverse men, for such a long time and without talking back, when they knew very well that it was quite wrong."

Response: "Dear friend, this question is fairly easy to answer. You can understand from what was said to you previously how women (whose great virtues I have described to you above) devote their attentions to different works, each distinct from the other, and not all to one same thing. This work was reserved for you to put together and not for them; for by virtue of their works these women were praised by people of good judgment and true reflection, but they didn't write anything else. And as for the question of the length of time that passed without their accusers and slanderers having been refuted, I say to you that all things come about fittingly and at their appointed time with respect to the expanse of earthly existence. For how did God tolerate heresies contradicting his holy law to exist in the world for a long period—heresies that were extirpated from it with great difficulty? But they would still subsist if someone hadn't opposed and vanquished them! This is the way it is with many other things that are permitted for a long time, but then debated and proven wrong."

Once again, I, Christine, said to her: "Lady, you speak very well, but I feel certain that many quarrels will arise among the slanderers concerning this present work, for they will say that, even assuming it to be true that there have existed or do exist some good women, nonetheless all women are not good, not even the majority of them."

Response: "It is wrong [to say] that the majority of them are not good; this is clear from what I said to you previously about experience, for we can witness every day their pious deeds, their charitable good works, and their

9. This is actually the story of a Greek prostitute named Leena, to be found in Boccaccio's *De mulieribus claris* (On Famous Women), chap. 50.

virtues, and it is also proven that they are not responsible for the great horrors and evils that occur continuously in the world. But that all of them might not be good, what a surprise! In the entire city of Nineveh, which was so great and so populated, there was not a single good man to be found when Jonah the prophet went there under the aegis of Our Lord for the purpose of overthrowing it, had it not been converted.[10] There were even fewer of them in the city of Sodom, as it became clear when Lot abandoned it and the fire from the heavens consumed it.[11] What's more, note that there were only twelve men in the company of Jesus Christ and one of them was very evil. And men have the nerve to say that all women should be good, while those who are not should be subjected to stoning. But I beg them to look within themselves, and let him alone who is without sin throw the first stone. What about men, what should they be? I say with certainty that when they are perfect, women will imitate them."

LIIII. *Christine asks Rectitude if what many men say, that there are so few women who are loyal in their amorous life, is true; and the response of Rectitude.*

Going further, I, Christine, said once again, as follows: "Lady, let us now go beyond these questions; taking our leave of the terms that have defined our discussion up to now, I would gladly ask you a few questions, if I knew that you would not find the subject matter of my discussion troublesome, since even though it is founded on natural law,[12] it lies somewhat outside the temperance of reason."

She replied to me: "My friend, say what you please, for the disciple who asks questions of the master in order to learn must not be scolded if he inquires about all things."

"Lady, in the world there circulates a natural law governing men's relation toward women and women's relation toward men—a law founded not by human ordinance but by carnal inclination—according to which they love each other with a very great, overpowering passion steeped in unbridled pleasure; yet they do not know what the cause is, why this mutual love penetrates them. Regarding this love that is quite common and to which one applies the expression "amorous life," men often say that women, whatever

10. Jonah's preaching in Nineveh is recounted in Jonah 3–4.

11. Genesis 18:20–19:29.

12. The expression is *loy de nature,* which could be understood either as I have translated it or as a personification, "the law of Nature," in which case one would perhaps also want to personify "reason" at the end of the sentence.

they promise, are not very much affected by love and seldom tarry in one place:[13] they are false and deceitful, and all of this comes from the flightiness of their disposition. Among the authors who accuse them of this, Ovid, in his book the *Art of Love,* lays on them a huge accusation. After having blamed women fully on this score, Ovid, just like the others, says that what these men write down in their books, as much with regard to women's deceitful behavior as to their evil inclinations, is done for the general, public good, in order to make men aware of their tricks so that they can better escape from them, as one would from a serpent hidden in the grass. If you please, dear lady, teach me the truth about this."

Response: "Dear friend, as far as their saying that women are so deceitful is concerned, I don't know what more I could tell you, for you yourself have already quite adequately treated this subject, refuting Ovid as well as the others, in your *God of Love's Letter* and in the *Letters on the Romance of the Rose.* But on the point you touched upon in your question to me (that they say they have done it for the common good), I will show you that it was not at all for that. Here is the reason: nothing is of public or common good in a city or a country or a community of people unless it is a general profit or good in which everyone, men as well as women, participates or has a share. But something that would be done for the purpose of profiting some people but not others would be called a private or personal good, and not at all a public one; and it would be even less so when the good is taken away from some and given to others. Such a thing must be called not only a personal or private good but an absolute extortion from someone else to the advantage of another's interest, taken at his expense in order to sustain the other. For they[14] in no wise speak to women, advising them to watch out for the traps set by men. Nonetheless, it is undeniable that men repeatedly deceive women with ruses and false appearances. Moreover, there is no doubt that women figure among God's people and the human species just as well as do men; they are not of another species or of dissimilar progeny, such that they should be excluded from moral teachings. Thus I conclude that for the common good (that is to say, both sides) they ought to have told women to watch out for men's traps as well as telling men to be wary of women. But to leave aside these questions and come back to my other point, namely, to refute the claim that women are not very much affected by love when their heart is submitted to it, and to argue that they are more constant in it than they say, it will suffice for me to prove it by an example, producing as testimony some

13. See above, ch. 1, n. 15.

14. This "they" is referring back to the authors about whom Christine asked her question.

of those women who persevered in their love until death. First I will tell you of Dido, the queen of Carthage, whose great valor was discussed earlier, even though you yourself have previously spoken of her in your works."

32. FROM CHRISTINE DE PIZAN, *CHRISTINE'S VISION* (*L'ADVISION CHRISTINE,* 1405)[15]

FRENCH PROSE

[*In book 2, Christine meets, in a dream vision, a shade, who tells her about the many exploits she has accomplished in the world.*]

Book II, Chapter 21

The Shade continues to Speak.

"What do you say? Is this sufficient? Have I told you enough about the effects of my many powers, about which, as I have previously told you, you could never in your life hear all the examples, so many and diverse they are? Do you know yet who I am?"

I said to her: "Lady, I would have thought I recognized you, but the contradictory stories you have told me make me hesitate in my recognition. For if I have understood correctly, right at the beginning you told me that where the truth has been proven, there you cannot stay; and yet I know well and am certain that on many topics you have made the pure truth clear to me right here. So I don't understand how it can be that a being full of doubt can attest to the pure truth."

She responded to me: "My daughter, open up the good sense of your intelligence, listen and take note. For I promise you that although previously in many instances I might have lied to you, in this one here I have told you the truth if you understand it well. Don't contradict me on this point if you recall what I have told you, namely, that I am the cause by which true things can be attained, through study and understanding. But it certainly is true that as soon as they are attained I take my leave and tarry there no longer. Moreover, you yourself have experienced that this is true, for although I have spoken to you about these things, it is not I who have made you certain

15. Translated from *Le livre de l'advision Christine,* ed. Reno and Dulac, 86–90. English translations of the entire work are found in *Christine's Vision,* trans. Glenda K. McLeod, Garland Library of Medieval Literature, series B, vol. 68 (New York & London, 1993); and *The Vision of Christine de Pizan,* trans. Glenda McLeod and Charity Cannon Willard (Cambridge: D. S. Brewer, 2005).

of them, it is rather your senses that have done so, by means of your study, which has delivered it [the knowledge of these things] to your understanding, which is by virtue of reason certain that these things are so. This is why at this juncture I will take my leave of you, and in my place certain knowledge will remain with you.

"But to use a better example, do you not remember me and your acquaintance with me by the diverse situations that I made you put into words and speak out upon on many occasions? Was I not the person who set up the debate between the clerics, disciples of Jean de Meun—as they call themselves—and you regarding the compilation known as the *Romance of the Rose,* on which topic you wrote back and forth to each other in opposition, each side supporting its cause, as is manifest in the little book that was made about it?"[16]

Book II, Chapter 22

Christine responds to the Shadow.

Then, when my mind realized the obvious and recognized who this woman who had spoken to me at such length was, I said as follows: "Ah! Lady Opinion, powerful and strong, I certainly must recognize you, for since my childhood I have been acquainted with you. To be sure, I know and confess that your authority is of great vigor and power. Moreover, although you are often reproached, anyone who makes good use of you cannot go wrong, while things can go poorly for others upon whom you do not look favorably. But since it pleased you, by your generosity, to honor me so much as to manifest yourself to me so frankly, describing to me all your great properties, I still ask you that it not displease you to elucidate some of my queries."

And she replied to me: "My daughter, say what you wish."

"Lady, since it is the case that people's initial ideas about human works, whether good or bad, rudimentary or subtle—according to the inclination of their minds—come from you, as you have said, would you kindly assure me whether, among the things that I have begotten[17] on account of you and

16. This is of course a discreet reference to Christine's collection of the documents that she sent to the queen of France and others.

17. This is the past participle of the verb *engendrer,* meaning literally "to engender, to give birth, to beget." Christine frequently uses the birth metaphor to speak of her production of texts, sometimes in the most literal of ways, as she does later in *Christine's Vision,* when the goddess Nature indicates to the future poetess her literary vocation: "At the time that you were carrying children in your womb, you felt great pain when it came to giving birth. Now I want new volumes to be born from you." (ed. Reno and Dulac, 110).

that are expounded upon in my writings and volumes (which things I produced to the extent I was capable, making use of my studies and the knowledge and understanding I possess), I have erred in any details, given that no one is so wise that he does not occasionally make a mistake. For if this did happen, I would rather correct them later than never."

She replied to me: "Dear friend, don't worry. Indeed, I affirm to you that in spite of the fact that I blamed you for having granted preeminence in honor to Fortune while you forgot me, though I am the primary cause, as I told you before, there is no error in your works, even though many people debate about them in diverse ways because of me. For some people say that they are confected for you by clerics or religious men, since they could not come from a female sensibility. But those who say this are ignorant, for they are not familiar with the writings that make mention of so many worthy women—wiser than you, learned, and even possessing the gift of prophecy—who lived in times past; moreover, since Nature is not at all diminished in her powers, there might still be more of these [worthy women to come]. Others say that your style is too obscure and that it is incomprehensible, so there is no pleasure in it. Thus, in its diversity, you make some people praise it and others disparage it, since it is impossible for anything whatsoever to be pleasing to all. But I will tell you this much, that truth, as experience bears witness, does not allow blame to have an effect upon one's reputation. So I advise you to continue your work, given that it is just, and do not fear committing faults with regard to me. For as long as I remain established within you on issues of law, reason, and true feeling, you will not err in the foundations of your works on matters in the realm of probability, notwithstanding the diverse judgments of many people, some motivated simply by me, others by Envy. For I assure you that when she and I are together, very false judgments are made and there is no one so excellent as to be spared by them. Thus, I am deadly when Envy has power over me, for when a person has both of us in him we blind him to things produced by others and to his own deeds. In this way we gnaw at his heart, without allowing him to rest, and we make him want to do many evil things that are sometimes actually carried out. Whoever falls into our hands is poorly governed, however good or powerful he might be.

"Did we not long ago forbid the gates of Rome to the brave Julius Caesar, who was returning to it so victoriously, and ultimately pursue him until he was killed? We have done many such things, and there is no one so wise that he can protect himself from it. I have recounted enough of my adventures to you, so let that suffice. Indeed, because I make one person believe that something is good and well made or that it is true, and make another one believe the exact opposite—from which battles and many debates arise—the prolixity of the telling of my tales could tend to bore your readers. Accordingly, I prophesy to you that the experience of reading this work will be varyingly appreciated by most people. Diverse pronouncements will be made on the means of expression:[18] some will say that it is not especially elegant, and others that the association and arrangement of topics are odd. But those who understand it will speak well of it. In the future it will be more spoken of than during your lifetime. I will just say to you furthermore that you came along at an unfortunate time. Knowledge is in the present day not held in esteem but rather considered something out of fashion. As a proof that this is true, you see few people who are for this reason honored in Fortune's house. But after your death, a prince full of merit and wisdom will come who, through contact with your books, will wish that you had lived in his time, and out of great desire he will wish to have encountered you. Well, I have described myself to you; now give a clear definition of how I appear to you."

I to her: "Lady, since your own description of yourself has provided me the definition, I say that since I now know you perfectly, you are truly the daughter of Ignorance, adhesion to one side of an argument with a constant doubt about the other side. In this regard, I am reminded of what Aristotle said about you in the first book of the *Posterior Analytics,* that someone who possesses you is forever in doubt that what he thinks might be otherwise, given that you are uncertain. Saint Bernard also said in the fifth chapter of his *Consideration* that you are ambiguous and that you can be misleading.[19] So I conclude by saying that you are an adhesion to one side of an argument, an adhesion caused by the appearance of a demonstrable proof, whether the

18. The word used by Christine is *langaige,* which of course means "language" but also "discourse" and "the way in which one expresses one's thoughts." Given that the first example of these pronouncements is stylistic while the second (*composicion,* which I have translated as "association and arrangement" since it potentially encompasses both these aspects) is related to organization of the subject matter, "means of expression" seems more properly general in the context.

19. As Reno and Dulac suggest (175), Christine might have gotten the references to both Aristotle and Saint Bernard in the article entitled "Opinion" in the medieval dictionary to the Bible known as the *Catholicon,* though Aristotle's *Posterior Analytics* is also referred to by Aquinas (though on another topic) in the commentary on the *Metaphysics,* with which Christine was quite familiar and which was an important source for this book of *Christine's Vision.* They add that Christine might have had direct knowledge of Saint Bernard, as he is one of the few authors she specifically recommends to her son in the *Moral Teachings.*

person expressing his opinion has doubts about the other side or not. As for your power, I say that on account of the ignorance found in men, the world is governed more by you than it is by knowledge."

33. FROM CHRISTINE DE PIZAN, *BOOK OF DEEDS OF ARMS AND OF CHIVALRY* (*LIVRE DES FAIS D'ARMES ET DE CHEVALERIE,* 1410)[20]

FRENCH PROSE

[*Christine compiled this technical treatise on warfare, divided into four books, in 1410, incorporating material from celebrated works on the subject such as Vegetius's* De re militari (On Military Institutions) *(which Jean de Meun had himself translated more than a century before), Frontinus's* Strategemata (Stratagems), *and a French work by Christine's contemporary, Honoré Bovet,* L'arbre des batailles (The Tree of Battles). *After discussing strategic and technical aspects in the first two books, Christine turns to legal issues surrounding the topic in book 3. In the opening chapter, a sort of prologue, she recounts a dream apparition, a visit by Study personified.*]

As I was preparing to embark upon this third part of the present book, my mind had become fatigued by the weightiness of the subject matter after toiling over the preceding parts. At that point, I was taken by surprise during my sleep and there appeared before me, as I slumbered in bed, a being that by all appearances had the form of a very solemn man, with the clothing, countenance, and demeanor of a respected judge, grave, wise, and advanced in age. He spoke to me thus:

"Christine, my dear friend, there is never a moment when your labor comes to a halt in the practice of your studies, either in your deeds or in your thoughts. This, along with my observation of the love you have for what learning can teach, especially when it urges people on to noble actions and virtuous behavior, explains why I have come here to provide you assistance in the work you are accomplishing right now on this book of chivalry and arms, with which you have busied yourself so diligently, motivated by a noble will. This is why I am encouraging your laudable desire to provide

20. Translated from *Le livre des fais d'armes et de chevalerie,* in Christine Moneera Laennec, "Christine *antygrafe:* Authorship and Self in the Prose Works of Christine de Pizan with an Edition of B.N. MS 603 'Le livre des fais d'armes et de chevallerie,'" 2 vols. (Ph.D. diss., Yale University, 1988), 2:184–85. English translation of the entire work is found in Christine de Pizan, *The Book of Deeds of Arms and of Chivalry,* trans. Sumner Willard (University Park: Pennsylvania State University Press, 1999).

material to the knights and noble men who have the opportunity to hear it, so that they can apply themselves and enhance their skills in the deeds that nobility requires, namely, in the aforementioned practice of armed combat, regarding both the exertion of their bodies and the legitimate protocols made necessary by law. In this, it is good for you to pick certain fruits from the *Tree of Battles* that is in my garden and make use of them, for it will make your vigor and strength increase so that you may be able to bring your work to completion, weighty as it is. And in order for you to build an edifice suitable to the texts of Vegetius and the others to which you have hitherto helped yourself, you must cut off the branches of this tree, take the best of them, and build upon this timber a part of your said edifice, which I will help you to complete, I as master and you as disciple."

After having heard these things, it seemed to me that I answered him thus:

"O worthy master, I realize that you are that Study which I love and have loved so much that I no longer recall anything else. As a result of your virtues and my frequentation of you, I have already, by the grace of God, finished many fine ventures. But seeing that it must not displease the master if the disciple, anxious to learn, submits questions to him, I beg you to tell me if my work might be reproached for making use of the said fruit, as you have advised me to do."

"Dear friend, I respond to you on this point that the more a work is attested by many people, the more it is authoritative. On account of this, if some people grumble about it, as is the habit of slanderers, saying that you beg around from elsewhere, I respond to them that it is common practice among my disciples to give to each other and distribute the flowers that they gather in different ways in my gardens. And not all those who help themselves to these flowers were the first to pick them. After all, didn't Jean de Meun help himself to the poetry of Guillaume de Lorris, and similarly to that of many others, in his book of the *Rose*? And so no reproach is fitting in this case but rather praise, when [these borrowings] are applied well and appropriately. Therein resides mastery, for it is a sign of having seen an abundance of things and having inspected many books. But where one might make things taken from elsewhere serve inappropriately, that is where the fault would be. So do it boldly and do not fear, for your work is good. Furthermore, I assure you, it will be praised by many a wise man to come."

SERIES EDITORS' BIBLIOGRAPHY

PRIMARY SOURCES

Agnesi, Maria Gaetana, Giuseppa Eleonora Barbapiccola, Diamante Medaglia Faini, Aretafila Savini de' Rossi, and the Accademia de' Ricovrati. *The Contest for Knowledge*. Ed. and trans. Rebecca Messbarger and Paula Findlen. The Other Voice in Early Modern Europe. Chicago: University of Chicago Press, 2005.

Agrippa, Henricus Cornelius. *Declamation on the Nobility and Preeminence of the Female Sex*. Ed. and trans. Albert Rabil Jr. The Other Voice in Early Modern Europe. Chicago: University of Chicago Press, 1996.

Alberti, Leon Battista. *The Family in Renaissance Florence*. Trans. Renée Neu Watkins. Columbia, SC: University of South Carolina Press, 1969.

Aragona, Tullia d'. *Dialogue on the Infinity of Love*. Ed. and trans. Rinaldina Russell and Bruce Merry. The Other Voice in Early Modern Europe. Chicago: University of Chicago Press, 1997.

Arenal, Electa, and Stacey Schlau, eds. *Untold Sisters: Hispanic Nuns in Their Own Works*. Trans. Amanda Powell. Albuquerque: University of New Mexico Press, 1989.

Astell, Mary (1666–1731). *The First English Feminist: Reflections on Marriage and Other Writings*. Ed. Bridget Hill. New York: St. Martin's Press, 1986.

Astell, Mary, and John Norris. *Letters concerning the Love of God*. Ed. E. Derek Taylor and Melvyn New. The Early Modern Englishwoman, 1500–1750: Contemporary Editions. Aldershot: Ashgate, 2005.

Atherton, Margaret, ed. *Women Philosophers of the Early Modern Period*. Indianapolis, IN: Hackett, 1994.

Aughterson, Kate, ed. *Renaissance Woman: Constructions of Femininity in England: A Source Book*. London: Routledge, 1995.

Barbaro, Francesco. *On Wifely Duties*. Trans. Benjamin Kohl. In *The Earthly Republic*, ed. Kohl and R. G. Witt, 179–228. Philadelphia: University of Pennsylvania Press, 1978.

Battiferra degli Ammannati, Laura. *Laura Battiferra and her Literary Circle*. Ed. and trans. Victoria Kirkham. The Other Voice in Early Modern Europe. Chicago: University of Chicago Press, 2006.

Behn, Aphra. *The Works of Aphra Behn*. Ed. Janet Todd. 7 vols. Columbus: Ohio State University Press, 1992–96.

Bigolina, Giulia. *Urania: A Romance.* Ed. and trans. Valeria Finucci. The Other Voice in Early Modern Europe. Chicago: University of Chicago Press, 2005.

Bisha, Robin, Jehanne M. Gheith, Christine Holden, and William G. Wagner, eds. *Russian Women, 1698–1917: Experience* and *Expression: An Anthology of Sources*. Bloomington: Indiana University Press, 2002.

Blamires, Alcuin, ed. *Woman Defamed and Woman Defended: An Anthology of Medieval Texts.* Oxford: Clarendon Press, 1992.

Boccaccio, Giovanni. *Corbaccio or the Labyrinth of Love.* Trans. Anthony K. Cassell. 2nd rev. ed. Binghamton, NY: Medieval and Renaissance Texts and Studies, 1993.

———. *Famous Women.* Ed. and trans. Virginia Brown. I Tatti Renaissance Library. Cambridge: Harvard University Press, 2001.

Booy, David, ed. *Autobiographical Writings by Early Quaker Women.* Aldershot: Ashgate, 2004.

Brown, Judith. *Immodest Acts: The Life of a Lesbian Nun in Renaissance Italy.* New York: Oxford University Press, 1986.

Brown, Sylvia, ed. *Women's Writing in Stuart England: The Mother's Legacies of Dorothy Leigh, Elizabeth Joscelin and Elizabeth Richardson.* Thrupp, Stroud, Gloucester: Sutton, 1999.

Bruni, Leonardo. "On the Study of Literature (1405) to Lady Battista Malatesta of Moltefeltro." In *The Humanism of Leonardo Bruni: Selected Texts,* trans. and intro. by Gordon Griffiths, James Hankins, and David Thompson, 240–51. Binghamton, NY: Medieval and Renaissance Studies and Texts, 1987.

Caminer Turra, Elisabetta. *Selected Writings of an Eighteenth-Century Venetian Woman of Letters.* Ed. and trans. Catherine M. Sama. The Other Voice in Early Modern Europe. Chicago: University of Chicago Press, 2003.

Campiglia, Maddalena. *Flori: A Pastoral Drama: A Bilingual Edition.* Ed., intro., and notes by Virginia Cox and Lisa Sampson. Trans. Virginia Cox. The Other Voice in Early Modern Europe. Chicago: University of Chicago Press, 2004.

Castiglione, Baldassare. *The Book of the Courtier.* Trans. George Bull. New York: Penguin, 1967.

———. *The Book of the Courtier.* Ed. Daniel Javitch. New York: W. W. Norton, 2002.

Cereta, Laura. *Collected Letters of a Renaissance Feminist.* Ed. and trans. Diana Robin. The Other Voice in Early Modern Europe. Chicago: University of Chicago Press, 1997.

Christine de Pizan. *The Book of the City of Ladies.* Trans. Earl Jeffrey Richards. Foreword by Marina Warner. New York: Persea Books, 1982.

———. *Epistre au dieu d'Amours.* Ed. and trans. Thelma S. Fenster. In *Poems of Cupid, God of Love,* ed. Thelma S. Fenster and Mary Carpenter Erler. Leiden: E. J. Brill, 1990.

———. *A Medieval Woman's Mirror of Honor: The Treasury of the City of Ladies.* Trans. Charity Cannon Willard. Ed. Madeleine P. Cosman. New York: Persea Books, 1989.

———. *The Treasure of the City of Ladies.* Trans. Sarah Lawson. New York: Viking Penguin, 1985.

Clarke, Danielle, ed. *Isabella Whitney, Mary Sidney, and Aemilia Lanyer: Renaissance Women Poets.* New York: Penguin Books, 2000.

Coignard, Gabrielle de. *Spiritual Sonnets: A Bilingual Edition.* Ed. and trans. Melanie E. Gregg. The Other Voice in Early Modern Europe. Chicago: University of Chicago Press, 2004.

Colonna, Vittoria. *Sonnets for Michelangelo: A Bilingual Edition.* Ed. and trans. Abigail Brundin. The Other Voice in Early Modern Europe. Chicago: University of Chicago Press, 2005.

Couchman, Jane, and Ann Crabb, eds. *Women's Letters across Europe, 1400–1700.* Aldershot: Ashgate, 2005.

Crawford, Patricia, and Laura Gowing, eds. *Women's Worlds in Seventeenth-Century England: A Source Book.* London: Routledge, 2000.

Daybell, James, ed. *Early Modern Women's Letter Writing, 1450–1700.* Houndmills, England: Palgrave, 2001.

Dentière, Marie. *Epistle to Marguerite de Navarre and Preface to a Sermon by John Calvin.* Ed. and trans. Mary B. McKinley. The Other Voice in Early Modern Europe. Chicago: University of Chicago Press, 2004.

Elisabeth of Bohemia, Princess, and René Descartes. *The Correspondence between Princess Elisabeth of Bohemia and René Descartes.* Ed. and trans. Lisa Shapiro. The Other Voice in Early Modern Europe. Chicago: University of Chicago Press, 2007.

Elizabeth I. *Elizabeth I: Collected Works.* Ed. Leah S. Marcus, Janel Mueller, and Mary Beth Rose. Chicago: University of Chicago Press, 2000.

Elyot, Thomas. *Defence of Good Women: The Feminist Controversy of the Renaissance.* Ed. Diane Bornstein. New York: Delmar, 1980.

Erasmus, Desiderius. *Erasmus on Women.* Ed. Erika Rummel. Toronto: University of Toronto Press, 1996.

Erauso, Catalina de. *Lieutenant Nun: Memoir of a Basque Transvestite in the New World.* Trans. Michele Stepto and Gabriel Stepto. Foreword by Marjorie Garber. Boston: Beacon Press, 1995.

Fedele, Cassandra. *Letters and Orations.* Ed. and trans. Diana Robin. The Other Voice in Early Modern Europe. Chicago: University of Chicago Press, 2000.

Ferguson, Moira, ed. *First Feminists: British Women Writers, 1578–1799.* Bloomington: Indiana University Press, 1985.

Ferrazzi, Cecilia. *Autobiography of an Aspiring Saint.* Ed. and trans. Anne Jacobson Schutte. The Other Voice in Early Modern Europe. Chicago: University of Chicago Press, 1996.

The Fifteen Joys of Marriage. Trans. Elizabeth Abbott. New York: Orion Press, 1959.

Folger Collective on Early Women Critics. *Women Critics, 1660–1820: An Anthology.* Bloomington: Indiana University Press, 1995.

Fonte, Moderata (Modesta Pozzo). *Floridoro: A Chivalric Romance.* Ed. and intro. by Valeria Finucci. Trans. Julia Kisacky. The Other Voice in Early Modern Europe. Chicago: University of Chicago Press, 2006.

———. *The Worth of Women.* Ed. and trans. Virginia Cox. The Other Voice in Early Modern Europe. Chicago: University of Chicago Press, 1997.

Francisca de los Apóstoles. *The Inquisition of Francisca: A Sixteenth-Century Visionary on Trial.* Ed. and trans. Gillian T. W. Ahlgren. The Other Voice in Early Modern Europe. Chicago: University of Chicago Press, 2005.

Franco, Veronica. *Poems and Selected Letters.* Ed. and trans. Ann Rosalind Jones and Margaret F. Rosenthal. The Other Voice in Early Modern Europe. Chicago: University of Chicago Press, 1998.

Galilei, Maria Celeste. *Galileo's Daughter: A Historical Memoir of Science, Faith, and Love.* Trans. Dava Sobel. New York: Penguin Books, 1999.

———. *Sister Maria Celeste's Letters to Her Father, Galileo*. Ed. and trans. Rinaldina Russell. Lincoln, NE: Writers Club Press of Universe.com, 2000.

———. *To Father: The Letters of Sister Maria Celeste to Galileo, 1623–1633*. Trans. Dava Sobel. London: Fourth Estate, 2001.

Gethner, Perry, ed. *The Lunatic Lover and Other Plays by French Women of the Seventeenth and Eighteenth Centuries*. Portsmouth, NH: Heinemann, 1994.

Glückel of Hameln. *The Memoirs of Glückel of Hameln*. Trans. Marvin Lowenthal. New intro.by Robert Rosen. New York: Schocken Books, 1977.

Gournay, Marie le Jars de. *Apology for the Woman Writing and Other Works*. Ed. and trans. Richard Hillman and Colette Quesnel. The Other Voice in Early Modern Europe. Chicago: University of Chicago Press, 2002.

Grimmelshausen, Johann. *The Life of Courage: The Notorious Thief, Whore and Vagabond*. Trans. and intro. Mike Mitchell. Gardena, CA: SCB Distributors, 2001.

Grumbach, Argula von. *Argula von Grumbach: A Woman's Voice in the Reformation*. Ed. and trans. Peter Matheson. Edinburgh: T. & T. Clark, 1995.

Guasco, Annibal. *Discourse to Lady Lavinia His Daughter*. Ed. and trans. Peggy Osborn. The Other Voice in Early Modern Europe. Chicago: University of Chicago Press, 2003.

Guevara, María de. *Warnings to the Kings and Advice on Restoring Spain: A Bilingual Edition*. Ed. and trans. Nieves Romero-Díaz. The Other Voice in Early Modern Europe. Chicago: University of Chicago Press, 2007.

Harline, Craig, ed. *The Burdens of Sister Margaret: Inside a Seventeenth-Century Convent*. Abridged ed. New Haven: Yale University Press, 2000.

Haselkorn, Anne M., and Betty S. Travitsky, eds. *The Renaissance Englishwoman in Print: Counterbalancing the Canon*. Amherst: University of Massachusetts Press, 1990.

Henderson, Katherine Usher, and Barbara F. McManus, eds. *Half Humankind: Contexts and Texts of the Controversy about Women in England, 1540–1640*. Urbana: University of Illinois Press, 1985.

Hill, Bridget, ed. *Eighteenth-Century Women: An Anthology*. London: George Allen and Unwin, 1984.

Hobbins, Daniel, trans. *The Trial of Joan of Arc*. Cambridge: Harvard University Press, 2005.

Hoby, Margaret. *The Private Life of an Elizabethan Lady: The Diary of Lady Margaret Hoby, 1599–1605*. Thrupp, Stroud, Gloucestershire: Sutton, 1998.

Houlbrooke, Ralph, ed. *Family Life in Early Modern England: An Anthology of Contemporary Accounts, 1576–1716*. London: Blackwells, 1988.

Joscelin, Elizabeth. *The Mothers Legacy to Her Unborn Childe*. Ed. Jean leDrew Metcalfe. Toronto: University of Toronto Press, 2000.

Julian of Norwich. *Revelations of Divine Love*. Trans. Elizabeth Spearing. Introduction and notes by A. C. Spearing. New York: Penguin Books, 1998.

Jussie, Jeanne de. *The Short Chronicle*. Ed. and trans. Carrie F. Klaus. The Other Voice in Early Modern Europe. Chicago: University of Chicago Press, 2006.

Kallendorf, Craig W., ed. and trans. *Humanist Educational Treatises*. I Tatti Renaissance Library. Cambridge: Harvard University Press, 2002.

Kaminsky, Amy Katz, ed. *Water Lilies, Flores del agua: An Anthology of Spanish Women Writers from the Fifteenth through the Nineteenth Century*. Minneapolis: University of Minnesota Press, 1996.

Kempe, Margery. *The Book of Margery Kempe*. Trans. John Skinner. New York: Doubleday, 1998.

———. *The Book of Margery Kempe*. Ed. and trans. Lynn Staley. Norton Critical Edition. New York: W. W. Norton, 2001.

———. *The Book of Margery Kempe*. Trans. B. A. Windeatt. New York: Penguin Books, 1985.

King, Margaret L., and Albert Rabil Jr., eds. *Her Immaculate Hand: Selected Works by and about the Women Humanists of Quattrocento Italy*. Binghamton, NY: Medieval and Renaissance Texts and Studies, 1983; second revised paperback edition, 1991.

Klein, Joan Larsen, ed. *Daughters, Wives, and Widows: Writings by Men about Women and Marriage in England, 1500–1640*. Urbana: University of Illinois Press, 1992.

Knox, John. *The Political Writings of John Knox: The First Blast of the Trumpet against the Monstrous Regiment of Women and Other Selected Works*. Ed. Marvin A. Breslow. Washington, DC: Folger Shakespeare Library, 1985.

Kors, Alan C., and Edward Peters, eds. *Witchcraft in Europe, 400–1700: A Documentary History*. Philadelphia: University of Pennsylvania Press, 2000.

———. *Witchcraft in Europe, 1100–1700: A Documentary History*. Philadelphia: University of Pennsylvania Press, 1972.

Kottanner, Helene. *The Memoirs of Helene Kottanner, 1439–1440*. Trans. Maya B. Williamson. Library of Medieval Women. Rochester, NY: Boydell & Brewer, 1998.

Krämer, Heinrich, and Jacob Sprenger. *Malleus Maleficarum*. Trans. Montague Summers. London: Pushkin Press, 1928; reprint, New York: Dover, 1971.

Labé, Louise. *Complete Poetry and Prose: A Bilingual Edition*. Ed. and intro. by Deborah Lesko Baker. Trans. Annie Finch. The Other Voice in Early Modern Europe. Chicago: University of Chicago Press, 2006.

Lafayette, Marie-Madeleine Pioche de La Vergne, Comtesse de. *Zayde: A Spanish Romance*. Ed. and trans. Nicholas D. Paige. The Other Voice in Early Modern Europe. Chicago: University of Chicago Press, 2006.

Larsen, Anne R., and Colette H. Winn, eds. *Writings by Pre-Revolutionary French Women: From Marie de France to Elizabeth Vigée-Le Brun*. New York: Garland, 2000.

L'Aubespine, Madeleine de. *Selected Poems and Translations: A Bilingual Edition*. Ed. and trans. Anna Kłosowska. The Other Voice in Early Modern Europe. Chicago: University of Chicago Press, 2007.

Lock, Anne Vaughan. *The Collected Works of Anne Vaughan Lock*. Ed. Susan M. Felch. Medieval and Renaissance Texts and Studies, 185; English Text Society, 21. Tempe: Arizona Center for Medieval and Renaissance Studies, 1999.

Lorris, William de, and Jean de Meun. *The Romance of the Rose*. Trans. Charles Dahlbert. Princeton: Princeton University Press, 1971; reprint, University Press of New England, 1983.

Mahl, Mary R., and Helene Koon, eds. *The Female Spectator: English Women Writers before 1800*. Bloomington: Indiana University Press, 1977; Old Westbury, NY: Feminist Press, 1977.

Maintenon, Madame de. *Dialogues and Addresses*. Ed. and trans. John J. Conley, SJ. The Other Voice in Early Modern Europe. Chicago: University of Chicago Press, 2004.

Marguerite d'Angoulême, Queen of Navarre. *The Heptameron*. Trans. P. A. Chilton. New York: Viking Penguin, 1984.

Marinella, Lucrezia. *The Nobility and Excellence of Women and the Defects and Vices of Men*. Ed. and trans. Anne Dunhill. Introduction by Letizia Panizza. The Other Voice in Early Modern Europe. Chicago: University of Chicago Press, 1999.

Mary of Agreda. *The Divine Life of the Most Holy Virgin*. Abridgment of *The Mystical City of God*. Abridged by Fr. Bonaventure Amedeo de Caesarea, MC. Trans. from French by Abbé Joseph A. Boullan. Rockford, IL: Tan Books, 1997.

Matraini, Chiara. *Selected Poetry and Prose: A Bilingual Edition*. Ed. and trans. Elaine Maclachlan. Introduction by Giovanna Rabitti. The Other Voice in Early Modern Europe. Chicago: University of Chicago Press, 2007.

McWebb, Christine, ed. *Debating the "Roman de la rose": A Critical Anthology*. New York: Routledge, 2007.

Medici, Lucrezia Tornabuoni de'. *Sacred Narratives*. Ed. and trans. Jane Tylus. The Other Voice in Early Modern Europe. Chicago: University of Chicago Press, 2001.

Montpensier, Anne-Marie-Louise de, Duchesse d'Orléans. *Against Marriage: The Correspondence of La Grande Mademoiselle*. Ed. and trans. Joan DeJean. The Other Voice in Early Modern Europe. Chicago: University of Chicago Press, 2002.

Moore, Dorothy. *The Letters of Dorothy Moore, 1612–64: The Friendships, Marriage, and Intellectual Life of a Seventeenth-Century Woman*. Ed. Lynette Hunter. The Early Modern Englishwoman, 1500–1750: Contemporary Editions. Aldershot: Ashgate, 2004.

Morata, Olympia. *The Complete Writings of an Italian Heretic*. Ed. and trans. Holt N. Parker. The Other Voice in Early Modern Europe. Chicago: University of Chicago Press, 2003.

Mullan, David George. *Women's Life Writing in Early Modern Scotland: Writing the Evangelical Self, c. 1670–c. 1730*. Aldershot: Ashgate, 2003.

Myers, Kathleen A., and Amanda Powell, eds. *A Wild Country Out in the Garden: The Spiritual Journals of a Colonial Mexican Nun*. Bloomington: Indiana University Press, 1999.

Nogarola, Isotta. *Complete Writings: Letterbook, Dialogue on Adam and Eve, Orations*. Ed. and trans. Margaret L. King and Diana Robin. The Other Voice in Early Modern Europe. Chicago: University of Chicago Press, 2004.

O'Malley, Susan Gushee, ed. *"Custome Is an Idiot": Jacobean Pamphlet Literature on Women*. Afterword by Ann Rosalind Jones. Urbana: University of Illinois Press, 2004.

Ostovich, Helen, and Elizabeth Sauer, eds. *Reading Early Modern Women: An Anthology of Texts in Manuscript and Print, 1550–1700*. New York: Routledge, 2004.

Ozment, Steven. *Magdalena and Balthasar: An Intimate Portrait of Life in Sixteenth-Century Europe Revealed in the Letters of a Nuremberg Husband and Wife*. New York: Simon and Schuster, 1986; reprint, New Haven: Yale University Press, 1989.

Pascal, Jacqueline. *A Rule for Children and Other Writings*. Ed. and trans. John J. Conley, SJ. The Other Voice in Early Modern Europe. Chicago: University of Chicago Press, 2003.

Petersen, Johanna Eleonora. *The Life of Lady Johanna Eleonora Petersen, Written by Herself*. Ed. and trans. Barbara Becker-Cantarino. The Other Voice in Early Modern Europe. Chicago: University of Chicago Press, 2005.

Poullain de la Barre, François. *Three Cartesian Feminist Treatises*. Ed. Marcelle Maistre Welch. Trans. Vivien Bosley. The Other Voice in Early Modern Europe. Chicago: University of Chicago Press, 2002.

Pulci, Antonia. *Florentine Drama for Convent and Festival*. Ed. and trans. James Wyatt Cook. The Other Voice in Early Modern Europe. Chicago: University of Chicago Press, 1996.

Riccoboni, Sister Bartolomea. *Life and Death in a Venetian Convent: The Chronicle and Necrology of Corpus Domini, 1395–1436*. Ed. and trans. Daniel Bornstein. The Other Voice in Early Modern Europe. Chicago: University of Chicago Press, 2000.

Roches, Madeleine and Catherine des. *From Mother and Daughter*. Ed. and trans. Anne R. Larsen. The Other Voice in Early Modern Europe. Chicago: University of Chicago Press, 2006.

Salazar, María de San José. *Book for the Hour of Recreation*. Ed. Alison Weber. Trans. Amanda Powell. The Other Voice in Early Modern Europe. Chicago: University of Chicago Press, 2002.

Sarrocchi, Margherita. *Scanderbeide: The Heroic Deeds of George Scanderbeg, King of Epirus*. Ed. and trans. Rinaldina Russell. The Other Voice in Early Modern Europe. Chicago: University of Chicago Press, 2006.

Schurman, Anna Maria van. *Whether a Christian Woman Should be Educated and Other Writings from Her Intellectual Circle*. Ed. and trans. Joyce L. Irwin. The Other Voice in Early Modern Europe. Chicago: University of Chicago Press, 1998.

Schütz Zell, Katharina. *Church Mother: The Writings of a Protestant Reformer in Sixteenth-Century Germany*. Ed. and trans. Elsie McKee. The Other Voice in Early Modern Europe. Chicago: University of Chicago Press, 2006.

Scudéry, Madeleine de. *Selected Letters, Orations, and Rhetorical Dialogues*. Ed. and trans. Jane Donawerth and Julie Strongson. The Other Voice in Early Modern Europe. Chicago: University of Chicago Press, 2004.

———. *The Story of Sappho*. Ed. and trans. Karen Newman. The Other Voice in Early Modern Europe. Chicago: University of Chicago Press, 2003.

Shepherd, Simon, ed. *The Woman's Sharp Revenge: Five Women's Pamphlets from the Renaissance*. New York: St. Martin's Press, 1985.

Sidney, Robert, and Barbara Gamage Sidney. *Domestic Politics and Family Absence: The Correspondence (1588–1621) of Robert Sidney, First Earl of Leicester, and Barbara Gamage Sidney, Countess of Leicester*. Ed. Margaret P. Hannay, Noel J. Kinnamon, and Michael G. Brennan. The Early Modern Englishwoman, 1500–1750: Contemporary Editions. Aldershot: Ashgate, 2005.

Siegemund, Justine. *The Court Midwife*. Ed. and trans. Lynne Tatlock. The Other Voice in Early Modern Europe. Chicago: University of Chicago Press, 2005.

Tarabotti, Arcangela. *Paternal Tyranny*. Ed. and trans. Letizia Panizza. The Other Voice in Early Modern Europe. Chicago: University of Chicago Press, 2004.

Teresa of Avila, Saint. *The Collected Letters of St. Teresa of Avila*, vol. 1: *1546–1577*. Trans. Kieran Kavanaugh. Washington, DC: Institute of Carmelite Studies, 2001. Volume 2 is forthcoming.

———. *The Life of Saint Teresa of Avila by Herself*. Trans. J. M. Cohen. New York: Viking Penguin, 1957.

Tilney, Edmund. *The Flower of Friendship: A Renaissance Dialogue Contesting Marriage*. Ed. Valerie Wayne. Ithaca: Cornell University Press, 1993.

Travitsky, Betty, ed. *The Paradise of Women: Writings by Englishwomen of the Renaissance*. Westport, CT: Greenwood Press, 1981.

Travitsky, Betty, and Anne Lake Prescott, eds. *Female and Male Voices in Early Modern England: An Anthology of Renaissance Writing*. New York: Columbia University Press, 2000.

Villedieu, Madame de. *Memoirs of the Life of Henriette-Sylvie de Molière: A Novel*. Ed. and trans. Donna Kuizenga. The Other Voice in Early Modern Europe. Chicago: University of Chicago Press, 2004.

Vives, Juan Luis. *The Education of a Christian Woman: A Sixteenth-Century Manual*. Ed. and trans. Charles Fantazzi. The Other Voice in Early Modern Europe. Chicago: University of Chicago Press, 2000.

Weyer, Johann. *Witches, Devils, and Doctors in the Renaissance: Johann Weyer, De praestigiis daemonum*. Ed. George Mora with Benjamin G. Kohl, Erik Midelfort, and Helen Bacon. Trans. John Shea. Binghamton, NY: Medieval and Renaissance Texts and Studies, 1991.

Wiesner-Hanks, Merry, ed. *Convents Confront the Reformation: Catholic and Protestant Nuns in Germany*. Trans. Joan Skocir and Merry Wiesner-Hanks. Women of the Reformation. Milwaukee: Marquette University Press, 1996.

Wilson, Katharina M., ed. *Medieval Women Writers*. Athens: University of Georgia Press, 1984.

———, ed. *Women Writers of the Renaissance and Reformation*. Athens: University of Georgia Press, 1987.

Wilson, Katharina M., and Frank J. Warnke, eds. *Women Writers of the Seventeenth Century*. Athens: University of Georgia Press, 1989.

Wollstonecraft, Mary. *A Vindication of the Rights of Men; with a Vindication of the Rights of Women*. Ed. Sylvana Tomaselli. Cambridge: Cambridge University Press, 1995.

———. *The Vindications of the Rights of Men, The Rights of Women*. Ed. D. L. Macdonald and Kathleen Scherf. Peterborough, Ontario, Canada: Broadview Press, 1997.

Women Writers in English, 1350–1850. Projected 30-volume series suspended. 15 volumes published. Oxford: Oxford University Press.

Wroth, Lady Mary. *The Countess of Montgomery's Urania*. Ed. Josephine A. Roberts. 2 parts. Tempe, AZ: Medieval and Renaissance Texts and Studies, 1995, 1999.

———. *Lady Mary Wroth's "Love's Victory": The Penshurst Manuscript*. Ed. Michael G. Brennan. London: Roxburghe Club, 1988.

———. *The Poems of Lady Mary Wroth*. Ed. Josephine A. Roberts. Baton Rouge: Louisiana State University Press, 1983.

Zayas y Sotomayor, María de. *The Disenchantments of Love*. Trans. H. Patsy Boyer. Albany: State University of New York Press, 1997.

———. *The Enchantments of Love: Amorous and Exemplary Novels*. Trans. H. Patsy Boyer. Berkeley: University of California Press, 1990.

SECONDARY SOURCES

Abate, Corinne S., ed. *Privacy, Domesticity, and Women in Early Modern England*. Burlington, VT: Ashgate, 2003.

Ahlgren, Gillian. *Teresa of Avila and the Politics of Sanctity*. Ithaca: Cornell University Press, 1996.

Åkerman, Susanna. *Queen Christina of Sweden: The Transformation of a Seventeenth-Century Philosophical Libertine*. Leiden: E. J. Brill, 1991.

Akkerman, Tjitske, and Siep Sturman, eds. *Feminist Thought in European History, 1400–2000*. London: Routledge, 1997.

Allen, Sister Prudence, RSM. *The Concept of Woman: The Aristotelian Revolution, 750 B.C.–A.D. 1250*. Grand Rapids, MI: William B. Eerdmans, 1997.

———. *The Concept of Woman*, vol. 2: *The Early Humanist Reformation, 1250–1500*. Grand Rapids, MI: William B. Eerdmans, 2002.

Altmann, Barbara K., and Deborah L. McGrady, eds. *Christine de Pizan: A Casebook*. New York: Routledge, 2003.

Amussen, Susan D. *An Ordered Society: Gender and Class in Early Modern England*. Oxford: Basil Blackwell, 1988.

Amussen, Susan D., and Adele Seeff, eds. *Attending to Early Modern Women*. Newark: University of Delaware Press, 1998.

Anderson, Karen. *Chain Her by One Foot: The Subjugation of Women in Seventeenth-Century New France*. New York: Routledge, 1991.

Andreadis, Harriette. *Sappho in Early Modern England: Female Same-Sex Literary Erotics, 1550–1714*. Chicago: University of Chicago Press, 2001.

Arcangela Tarabotti: A Literary Nun in Baroque Venice. Ed. Elissa B. Weaver. Ravenna: Longo Editore, 2006.

Armon, Shifra. *Picking Wedlock: Women and the Courtship Novel in Spain*. New York: Rowman & Littlefield, 2002.

Atkinson, Clarissa W. *Mystic and Pilgrim: The Book and the World of Margery Kempe*. Ithaca: Cornell University Press, 1983.

Backer, Anne Liot. *Precious Women*. New York: Basic Books, 1974.

Bainton, Roland H. *Women of the Reformation in France and England*. Minneapolis: Augsburg, 1973.

———. *Women of the Reformation in Germany and Italy*. Minneapolis: Augsburg, 1971.

Ballaster, Ros. *Seductive Forms*. New York: Oxford University Press, 1992.

Barash, Carol. *English Women's Poetry, 1649–1714: Politics, Community, and Linguistic Authority*. New York: Oxford University Press, 1996.

Bardsley, Sandy. *Venomous Tongues: Speech and Gender in Late Medieval England*. Middle Ages Series. Philadelphia: University of Pennsylvania Press, 2006.

Barker, Alele Marie, and Jehanne M. Gheith, eds. *A History of Women's Writing in Russia*. Cambridge: Cambridge University Press, 2002.

Barstow, Anne L. *Joan of Arc: Heretic, Mystic, Shaman*. Lewiston, NY: Edwin Mellen Press, 1986.

Battigelli, Anna. *Margaret Cavendish and the Exiles of the Mind*. Lexington: University of Kentucky Press, 1998.

Beasley, Faith. *Revising Memory: Women's Fiction and Memoirs in Seventeenth-Century France*. New Brunswick: Rutgers University Press, 1990.

———. *Salons, History, and the Creation of Seventeenth-Century France*. Aldershot: Ashgate, 2006.

Becker, Lucinda M. *Death and the Early Modern Englishwoman*. Burlington, VT: Ashgate, 2003.

Beilin, Elaine V. *Redeeming Eve: Women Writers of the English Renaissance*. Princeton: Princeton University Press, 1987.

Bell, Rudolph M. *Holy Anorexia*. Chicago: University of Chicago Press, 1985.

Bennett, Lyn. *Women Writing of Divinest Things: Rhetoric and the Poetry of Pembroke, Wroth, and Lanyer*. Pittsburgh: Duquesne University Press, 2004.

Benson, Pamela Joseph. *The Invention of Renaissance Woman: The Challenge of Female Independence in the Literature and Thought of Italy and England*. University Park: Pennsylvania State University Press, 1992.

Benson, Pamela Joseph, and Victoria Kirkham, eds. *Strong Voices, Weak History? Medieval and Renaissance Women in Their Literary Canons: England, France, Italy*. Ann Arbor: University of Michigan Press, 2003.

Berman, Constance H., ed. *Women and Monasticism in Medieval Europe: Sisters and Patrons of the Cistercian Reform*. Kalamazoo: Western Michigan University Press, 2002.

Berry, Helen. *Gender, Society and Print Culture in Late Stuart England*. Burlington, VT: Ashgate, 2003.

Berry, Philippa. *Of Chastity and Power: Elizabethan Literature and the Unmarried Queen*. New York: Routledge, 1989.

Bicks, Caroline. *Midwiving Subjects in Shakespeare's England*. Burlington, VT: Ashgate, 2003.

Bilinkoff, Jodi. *The Avila of Saint Teresa: Religious Reform in a Sixteenth-Century City*. Ithaca: Cornell University Press, 1989.

———. *Related Lives: Confessors and Their Female Penitents, 1450–1750*. Ithaca: Cornell University Press, 2005.

Bissell, R. Ward. *Artemisia Gentileschi and the Authority of Art*. University Park: Pennsylvania State University Press, 2000.

Blain, Virginia, Isobel Grundy, and Patricia Clements, eds. *The Feminist Companion to Literature in English: Women Writers from the Middle Ages to the Present*. New Haven: Yale University Press, 1990.

Blamires, Alcuin. *The Case for Women in Medieval Culture*. Oxford: Clarendon Press, 1997.

Bloch, R. Howard. *Medieval Misogyny and the Invention of Western Romantic Love*. Chicago: University of Chicago Press, 1991.

Blumenfeld-Kosinski, Renate. *Not of Woman Born: Representations of Caesarean Birth in Medieval and Renaissance Culture*. Ithaca: Cornell University Press, 1990.

Bogucka, Maria. *Women in Early Modern Polish Society, Against the European Background*. Burlington, VT: Ashgate, 2004.

Bornstein, Daniel, and Roberto Rusconi, eds. *Women and Religion in Medieval and Renaissance Italy*. Trans. Margery J. Schneider. Chicago: University of Chicago Press, 1996.

Brant, Clare, and Diane Purkiss, eds. *Women, Texts, and Histories, 1575–1760*. London: Routledge, 1992.

Breisach, Ernst. *Caterina Sforza: A Renaissance Virago*. Chicago: University of Chicago Press, 1967.

Bridenthal, Renate, Claudia Koonz, and Susan M. Stuard. *Becoming Visible: Women in European History*. 3d ed. Boston: Houghton Mifflin, 1998.

Briggs, Robin. *Witches and Neighbours: The Social and Cultural Context of European Witchcraft*. New York: HarperCollins, 1995; Viking Penguin, 1996.

Brink, Jean R., ed. *Female Scholars: A Tradition of Learned Women before 1800*. Montréal: Eden Press Women's Publications, 1980.

Brink, Jean R., Allison Coudert, and Maryanne Cline Horowitz. *The Politics of Gender in Early Modern Europe*. Sixteenth Century Essays and Studies, 12. Kirksville, MO: Sixteenth Century Journal Publishers, 1989.

Broad, Jacqueline S. *Women Philosophers of the Seventeenth Century*. Cambridge: Cambridge University Press, 2002; reprint, 2007.

Broad, Jacqueline S., and Karen Green. *A History of Women's Political Thought in Europe, 1400–1700*. Cambridge: Cambridge University Press, 2008.

———, eds. *Virtue, Liberty, and Toleration: Political Ideas of European Women, 1400–1700*. Dordrecht: Springer, 2007.

Brodsky, Vivien. *Mobility and Marriage: The Family and Kinship in Early Modern London*. London: Blackwells, 1988.

Broude, Norma, and Mary D. Garrard, eds. *The Expanding Discourse: Feminism and Art History*. New York: HarperCollins, 1992.

Brown, Judith C. *Immodest Acts: The Life of a Lesbian Nun in Renaissance Italy*. New York: Oxford University Press, 1986.

Brown, Judith C., and Robert C. Davis, eds. *Gender and Society in Renaissance Italy*. London: Addison Wesley Longman, 1998.

Brown, Pamela Allen, and Peter Parolin, eds. *Women Players in England, 1500–1660: Beyond the All-Male Stage*. Brookfield: Ashgate, 2005.

Brown-Grant, Rosalind. *Christine de Pizan and the Moral Defence of Women: Reading Beyond Gender*. Cambridge: Cambridge University Press, 1999.

Brucker, Gene. *Giovanni and Lusanna: Love and Marriage in Renaissance Florence*. Berkeley: University of California Press, 1986.

Burke, Victoria E., ed. *Early Modern Women's Manuscript Writing*. Burlington, VT: Ashgate, 2004.

Burns, Jane E., ed. *Medieval Fabrications: Dress, Textiles, Cloth Work, and Other Cultural Imaginings*. New York: Palgrave Macmillan, 2004.

Bynum, Carolyn Walker. *Fragmentation and Redemption: Essays on Gender and the Human Body in Medieval Religion*. New York: Zone Books, 1992.

———. *Holy Feast and Holy Fast: The Religious Significance of Food to Medieval Women*. Berkeley: University of California Press, 1987.

———. *Jesus as Mother: Studies in the Spirituality of the High Middle Ages*. Berkeley: University of California Press, 1982.

Cahn, Susan. *Industry of Devotion: The Transformation of Women's Work in England, 1500–1660*. New York: Columbia University Press, 1987.

Callaghan, Dympna, ed. *The Impact of Feminism in English Renaissance Studies*. New York: Palgrave Macmillan, 2007.

Campbell, Julie DeLynn. "Renaissance Women Writers: The Beloved Speaks Her Part." Ph.D diss., Texas A & M University, 1997.

Catling, Jo, ed. *A History of Women's Writing in Germany, Austria, and Switzerland*. Cambridge: Cambridge University Press, 2000.

Cavallo, Sandra, and Lyndan Warner, eds. *Widowhood in Medieval and Early Modern Europe*. New York: Longman, 1999.

Cavanagh, Sheila T. *Cherished Torment: The Emotional Geography of Lady Mary Wroth's Urania*. Pittsburgh: Duquesne University Press, 2001.

Cerasano, S. P., and Marion Wynne-Davies, eds. *Readings in Renaissance Women's Drama: Criticism, History, and Performance, 1594–1998*. London: Routledge, 1998.

Cervigni, Dino S., ed. *Women Mystic Writers. Annali d'Italianistica* 13 (1995).

Cervigni, Dino S., and Rebecca West, eds. *Women's Voices in Italian Literature. Annali d'Italianistica* 7 (1989).

Charlton, Kenneth. *Women, Religion, and Education in Early Modern England*. London: Routledge, 1999.

Chojnacka, Monica. *Working Women of Early Modern Venice*. Baltimore: Johns Hopkins University Press, 2001.

Chojnacki, Stanley. *Women and Men in Renaissance Venice: Twelve Essays on Patrician Society*. Baltimore: Johns Hopkins University Press, 2000.

Cholakian, Patricia Francis, and Rouben Charles Cholakian. *Marguerite de Navarre: Mother of the Renaissance*. New York: Columbia University Press, 2006.

Cholakian, Patricia Francis. *Rape and Writing in the Heptameron of Marguerite de Navarre*. Carbondale: Southern Illinois University Press, 1991.

———. *Women and the Politics of Self-Representation in Seventeenth-Century France*. Newark: University of Delaware Press, 2000.

Clogan, Paul Maruice, ed. *Medievali et Humanistica: Literacy and the Lay Reader*. Lanham, MD: Rowman & Littlefield, 2000.

Clubb, Louise George. *Italian Drama in Shakespeare's Time*. New Haven: Yale University Press, 1989.

Clucas, Stephen, ed. *A Princely Brave Woman: Essays on Margaret Cavendish, Duchess of Newcastle*. Burlington, VT: Ashgate, 2003.

Coakley, John W. *Women, Men, and Spiritual Power: Female Saints and Their Male Collaborators*. New York: Columbia University Press, 2006.

Conley, John J., SJ. *The Suspicion of Virtue: Women Philosophers in Neoclassical France*. Ithaca: Cornell University Press, 2002.

Cook, Ann Jennalie. *Making a Match: Courtship in Shakespeare and His Society*. Princeton: Princeton University Press, 1991.

Cox, Virginia. *Women's Writing in Italy, 1400–1650*. Baltimore: Johns Hopkins University Press, 2008.

Crabb, Ann. *The Strozzi of Florence: Widowhood and Family Solidarity in the Renaissance*. Ann Arbor: University of Michigan Press, 2000.

Crawford, Patricia. *Women and Religion in England, 1500–1750*. London: Routledge, 1993.

Crowston, Clare Haru. *Fabricating Women: The Seamstresses of Old Regime France, 1675–1791*. Durham: Duke University Press, 2001.

Cruz, Anne J., and Mary Elizabeth Perry, eds. *Culture and Control in Counter-Reformation Spain*. Minneapolis: University of Minnesota Press, 1992.

Datta, Satya. *Women and Men in Early Modern Venice*. Burlington, VT: Ashgate, 2003.

Davis, Natalie Zemon. *Society and Culture in Early Modern France*. Stanford: Stanford University Press, 1975.

———. *Women on the Margins: Three Seventeenth-Century Lives*. Cambridge: Harvard University Press, 1995.

Davis, Natalie Zemon, and Arlette Farge, eds. *Renaissance and Enlightenment Paradoxes*. Vol. 3 of *A History of Women in the West*. Cambridge: Harvard University Press, 1993.

Dean, Trevor, and K. J. P. Lowe, eds. *Marriage in Italy, 1300–1650*. Cambridge: Cambridge University Press, 1998.

DeJean, Joan. *Ancients against Moderns: Culture Wars and the Making of a Fin de Siècle*. Chicago: University of Chicago Press, 1997.

———. *Fictions of Sappho, 1546–1937*. Chicago: University of Chicago Press, 1989.

———. *The Reinvention of Obscenity: Sex, Lies, and Tabloids in Early Modern France*. Chicago: University of Chicago Press, 2002.

———. *Tender Geographies: Women and the Origins of the Novel in France*. New York: Columbia University Press, 1991.

D'Elia, Anthony F. *The Renaissance of Marriage in Fifteenth-Century Italy*. Cambridge: Harvard University Press, 2004.

Demers, Patricia. *Women's Writing in English: Early Modern England*. Toronto: University of Toronto Press, 2005.

Diefendorf, Barbara. *From Penitence to Charity: Pious Women and the Catholic Reformation in Paris*. New York: Oxford University Press, 2004.

Dinan, Susan E. *Women and Poor Relief in Seventeenth-Century France: The Early History of the Daughters of Charity*. Women and Gender in the Early Modern World. Burlington, VT: Ashgate, 2006.

Dixon, Laurinda S. *Perilous Chastity: Women and Illness in Pre-Enlightenment Art and Medicine*. Ithaca: Cornell University Press, 1995.

Dolan, Frances, E. *Whores of Babylon: Catholicism, Gender, and Seventeenth-Century Print Culture*. Ithaca: Cornell University Press, 1999.

Donovan, Josephine. *Women and the Rise of the Novel, 1405–1726*. New York: St. Martin's Press, 1999.

Dreher, Diane Elizabeth. *Domination and Defiance: Fathers and Daughters in Shakespeare*. Lexington: University Press of Kentucky, 1986.

Dyan, Elliott. *Proving Woman: Female Spirituality and Inquisitional Culture in the Later Middle Ages*. Princeton: Princeton University Press, 2004.

Eccles, Audrey. *Obstetrics and Gynaecology in Tudor and Stuart England*. Kent, OH: Kent State University Press, 1982.

Eigler, Friederike, and Susanne Kord, eds. *The Feminist Encyclopedia of German Literature*. Westport, CT: Greenwood Press, 1997.

Emerson, Kathy Lynn. *Wives and Daughters: The Women of Sixteenth-Century England*. Troy, NY: Whitson, 1984.

Erdmann, Axel. *My Gracious Silence: Women in the Mirror of Sixteenth-Century Printing in Western Europe*. Lucerne: Gilhofer and Rauschberg, 1999.

Erickson, Amy Louise. *Women and Property in Early Modern England*. London: Routledge, 1993.

Evangelisti, Silvia. *Nuns: A History of Convent Life, 1450–1700*. New York: Oxford University Press, 2007.

Ezell, Margaret J. M. *The Patriarch's Wife: Literary Evidence and the History of the Family*. Chapel Hill: University of North Carolina Press, 1987.

———. *Social Authorship and the Advent of Print*. Baltimore: Johns Hopkins University Press, 1999.

———. *Writing Women's Literary History*. Baltimore: Johns Hopkins University Press, 1993.

Farrell, Michèle Longino. *Performing Motherhood: The Sévigné Correspondence*. Hanover, NH: University Press of New England, 1991.

Ferguson, Margaret W. *Dido's Daughters: Literacy, Gender, and Empire in Early Modern England and France.* Chicago: University of Chicago Press, 2003.

Ferguson, Margaret W., Maureen Quilligan, and Nancy J. Vickers, eds. *Rewriting the Renaissance: The Discourses of Sexual Difference in Early Modern Europe.* Chicago: University of Chicago Press, 1987.

Feroli, Teresa. *Political Speaking Justified: Women Prophets and the English Revolution.* Newark: University of Delaware Press, 2006.

Ferraro, Joanne M. *Marriage Wars in Late Renaissance Venice.* Oxford: Oxford University Press, 2001.

Fisher, Will. *Materializing Gender in Early Modern English Literature and Culture.* Cambridge: Cambridge University Press, 2006.

Flandrin, Jean-Louis. *Families in Former Times: Kinship, Household, and Sexuality in Early Modern France.* Trans. Richard Southern. Cambridge: Cambridge University Press, 1979.

Fletcher, Anthony. *Gender, Sex, and Subordination in England, 1500–1800.* New Haven: Yale University Press, 1995.

———. *Growing Up in England: The Experience of Childhood, 1600–1914.* New Haven: Yale University Press, 2008.

Franklin, Margaret. *Boccaccio's Heroines: Power and Virtue in Renaissance Society.* Women and Gender in the Early Modern World. Burlington, VT: Ashgate, 2006.

Froide, Amy M. *Never Married: Singlewomen in Early Modern England.* Oxford: Oxford University Press, 2005.

Frye, Susan, and Karen Robertson, eds. *Maids and Mistresses, Cousins and Queens: Women's Alliances in Early Modern England.* Oxford: Oxford University Press, 1999.

Gallagher, Catherine. *Nobody's Story: The Vanishing Acts of Women Writers in the Marketplace, 1670–1820.* Berkeley: University of California Press, 1994.

Garrard, Mary D. *Artemisia Gentileschi: The Image of the Female Hero in Italian Baroque Art.* Princeton: Princeton University Press, 1989.

Gelbart, Nina Rattner. *The King's Midwife: A History and Mystery of Madame du Coudray.* Berkeley: University of California Press, 1998.

George, Margaret. *Women in the First Capitalist Society: Experiences in Seventeenth-Century England.* Urbana: University of Illinois Press, 1988.

Gibson, Wendy. *Women in Seventeenth-Century France.* New York: St. Martin's Press, 1989.

Gies, Frances. *Joan of Arc: The Legend and the Reality.* New York: Harper & Row, 1981.

Giles, Mary E., ed. *Women in the Inquisition: Spain and the New World.* Baltimore: Johns Hopkins University Press, 1999.

Gill, Catie. *Women in the Seventeenth-Century Quaker Community.* Burlington, VT: Ashgate, 2005.

Glenn, Cheryl. *Rhetoric Retold: Regendering the Tradition from Antiquity through the Renaissance.* Carbondale: Southern Illinois University Press, 1997.

Goffen, Rona. *Titian's Women.* New Haven: Yale University Press, 1997.

Goldberg, Jonathan. *Desiring Women Writing: English Renaissance Examples.* Stanford: Stanford University Press, 1997.

Goldsmith, Elizabeth C. *Exclusive Conversations: The Art of Interaction in Seventeenth-Century France.* Philadelphia: University of Pennsylvania Press, 1988.

———, ed. *Writing the Female Voice*. Boston: Northeastern University Press, 1989.

Goldsmith, Elizabeth C., and Dena Goodman, eds. *Going Public: Women and Publishing in Early Modern France*. Ithaca: Cornell University Press, 1995.

Grafton, Anthony, and Lisa Jardine. *From Humanism to the Humanities: Education and the Liberal Arts in Fifteenth- and Sixteenth-Century Europe*. London: Duckworth, 1986.

Grassby, Richard. *Kinship and Capitalism: Marriage, Family, and Business in the English-Speaking World, 1580–1740*. Cambridge: Cambridge University Press, 2001.

Greer, Margaret Rich. *Maria de Zayas Tells Baroque Tales of Love and the Cruelty of Men*. University Park: Pennsylvania State University Press, 2000.

Grossman, Avraham. *Pious and Rebellious: Jewish Women in Medieval Europe*. Trans. Jonathan Chipman. Waltham: Brandeis/University Press of New England, 2004.

Gutierrez, Nancy A. *"Shall She Famish Then?" Female Food Refusal in Early Modern England*. Burlington, VT: Ashgate, 2003.

Habermann, Ina. *Staging Slander and Gender in Early Modern England*. Burlington, VT: Ashgate, 2003.

Hacke, Daniela. *Women, Sex, and Marriage in Early Modern Venice*. Burlington, VT: Ashgate, 2004.

Hackel, Heidi Brayman. *Reading Material in Early Modern England: Print, Gender, Literacy*. Cambridge: Cambridge University Press, 2005.

Hackett, Helen. *Women and Romance Fiction in the English Renaissance*. Cambridge: Cambridge University Press, 2000.

Haigh, Christopher. *Elizabeth I*. London: Longman, 1988.

Hall, Kim F. *Things of Darkness: Economies of Race and Gender in Early Modern England*. Ithaca: Cornell University Press, 1995.

Hamburger, Jeffrey. *The Visual and the Visionary: Art and Female Spirituality in Late Medieval Germany*. New York: Zone Books, 1998.

Hampton, Timothy. *Literature and the Nation in the Sixteenth Century: Inventing Renaissance France*. Ithaca: Cornell University Press, 2001.

Hanawalt, Barbara A. *Women and Work in Pre-Industrial Europe*. Bloomington: Indiana University Press, 1986.

Hannay, Margaret, ed. *Silent but for the Word*. Kent, OH: Kent State University Press, 1985.

Hardwick, Julie. *The Practice of Patriarchy: Gender and the Politics of Household Authority in Early Modern France*. University Park: Pennsylvania State University Press, 1998.

Harness, Kelley Ann. *Echoes of Women's Voices: Music, Art, and Female Patronage in Early Modern Florence*. Chicago: University of Chicago Press, 2006.

Harris, Barbara J. *English Aristocratic Women, 1450–1550: Marriage and Family, Property and Careers*. New York: Oxford University Press, 2002.

Harth, Erica. *Cartesian Women. Versions and Subversions of Rational Discourse in the Old Regime*. Ithaca: Cornell University Press, 1992.

———. *Ideology and Culture in Seventeenth-Century France*. Ithaca: Cornell University Press, 1983.

Harvey, Elizabeth D. *Ventriloquized Voices: Feminist Theory and English Renaissance Texts*. London: Routledge, 1992.

Hawkesworth, Celia, ed. *A History of Central European Women's Writing*. New York: Palgrave Press, 2001.

Hegstrom, Valerie, and Amy R. Williamsen, eds. *Engendering the Early Modern Stage: Women Playwrights in the Spanish Empire*. New Orleans: University Press of the South, 1999.

Heller, Wendy. *Emblems of Eloquence: Opera and Women's Voices in Seventeenth-Century Venice*. Berkeley: University of California Press, 2004.

Hendricks, Margo, and Patricia Parker, eds. *Women, "Race," and Writing in the Early Modern Period*. London: Routledge, 1994.

Herlihy, David. "Did Women Have a Renaissance? A Reconsideration." *Medievalia et Humanistica*, n.s., 13 (1985): 1–22.

Hibbert, Christopher. *The Virgin Queen: Elizabeth I, Genius of the Golden Age*. Reading, MA: Addison-Wesley, 1991.

Hill, Bridget. *The Republican Virago: The Life and Times of Catharine Macaulay, Historian*. New York: Oxford University Press, 1992.

Hills, Helen, ed. *Architecture and the Politics of Gender in Early Modern Europe*. Burlington, VT: Ashgate, 2003.

Hirst, Jilie. *Jane Leade: Biography of a Seventeenth-Century Mystic*. Burlington, VT: Ashgate, 2006.

Hobby, Elaine. *Virtue of Necessity: English Women's Writing, 1646–1688*. London: Virago Press, 1988.

Hogrefe, Pearl. *Women of Action in Tudor England: Nine Biographical Sketches*. Ames: Iowa State University Press, 1977.

Hopkins, Lisa. *Women Who Would Be Kings: Female Rulers of the Sixteenth Century*. New York: St. Martin's Press, 1991.

Horowitz, Maryanne Cline. "Aristotle and Women." *Journal of the History of Biology* 9 (1976): 183–213.

Houlbrooke, Ralph A. *Death, Religion, and the Family in England, 1480–1760*. Oxford Studies in Social History. New York: Oxford University Press, 1998.

Howe, Elizabeth. *The First English Actresses: Women and Drama, 1660–1700*. Cambridge: Cambridge University Press, 1992.

Howell, Martha C. *The Marriage Exchange: Property, Social Place, and Gender in Cities of the Low Countries, 1300–1550*. Chicago: University of Chicago Press, 1998.

———. *Women, Production, and Patriarchy in Late Medieval Cities*. Chicago: University of Chicago Press, 1986.

Hufton, Olwen H. *The Prospect before Her: A History of Women in Western Europe*, vol. 1: *1500–1800*. New York: HarperCollins, 1996.

Hull, Suzanne W. *Chaste, Silent, and Obedient: English Books for Women, 1475–1640*. San Marino, CA: Huntington Library, 1982.

Hunt, Lynn, ed. *The Invention of Pornography: Obscenity and the Origins of Modernity, 1500–1800*. New York: Zone Books, 1996.

Hurlburt, Holly S. *The Dogaressa of Venice, 1200–1500: Wife and Icon*. New Middle Ages. New York: Palgrave Macmillan, 2006.

Hutner, Heidi, ed. *Rereading Aphra Behn: History, Theory, and Criticism*. Charlottesville: University Press of Virginia, 1993.

Hutson, Lorna, ed. *Feminism and Renaissance Studies*. New York: Oxford University Press, 1999.

Ingram, Martin. *Church Courts, Sex and Marriage in England, 1570–1640*. Cambridge: Cambridge University Press, 1987.

Ives, E. W. *Anne Boleyn*. London: Blackwells, 1988.
Jaffe, Irma B., with Gernando Colombardo. *Shining Eyes, Cruel Fortune: The Lives and Loves of Italian Renaissance Women Poets*. New York: Fordham University Press, 2002.
James, Susan E. *Kateryn Parr: The Making of a Queen*. Burlington, VT: Ashgate, 1999.
Jankowski, Theodora A. *Women in Power in the Early Modern Drama*. Urbana: University of Illinois Press, 1992.
Jansen, Katherine Ludwig. *The Making of the Magdalen: Preaching and Popular Devotion in the Later Middle Ages*. Princeton: Princeton University Press, 2000.
Jardine, Lisa. *Still Harping on Daughters: Women and Drama in the Age of Shakespeare*. Totowa, NJ: Barnes and Noble, 1983.
Jed, Stephanie H. *Chaste Thinking: The Rape of Lucretia and the Birth of Humanism*. Bloomington: Indiana University Press, 1989.
Jones, Ann Rosalind. *The Currency of Eros: Women's Love Lyric in Europe, 1540–1620*. Bloomington: Indiana University Press, 1990.
Jones, Ann Rosalind, and Peter Stallybrass. *Renaissance Clothing and the Materials of Memory*. Cambridge: Cambridge University Press, 2000.
Jones, Michael K., and Malcolm G. Underwood. *The King's Mother: Lady Margaret Beaufort, Countess of Richymond and Derby*. Cambridge: Cambridge University Press, 1992.
Jordan, Constance. *Renaissance Feminism: Literary Texts and Political Models*. Ithaca: Cornell University Press, 1990.
Kagan, Richard L. *Lucrecia's Dreams: Politics and Prophecy in Sixteenth-Century Spain*. Berkeley: University of California Press, 1990.
Karant-Nunn, Susan C., and Merry E. Wiesner-Hanks, eds. *Luther on Women: A Sourcebook*. Cambridge: Cambridge University Press, 2003.
Kehler, Dorothea, and Laurel Amtower, eds. *The Single Woman in Medieval and Early Modern England: Her Life and Representation*. Tempe, AZ: Medieval and Renaissance Texts and Studies, 2002.
Kelly, Joan. "Did Women Have a Renaissance?" In *Women, History, and Theory: The Essays of Joan Kelly*. Chicago: University of Chicago Press, 1984. Also in *Becoming Visible: Women in European History*, ed. Renate Bridenthal, Claudia Koonz, and Susan M. Stuard. 3rd ed. Boston: Houghton Mifflin, 1998.
———. "Early Feminist Theory and the *Querelle des Femmes*." In *Women, History, and Theory: The Essays of Joan Kelly*. Chicago: University of Chicago Press, 1984.
———. *Women, History, and Theory: The Essays of Joan Kelly*. Women in Culture and Society. Chicago: University of Chicago Press, 1984.
Kelso, Ruth. *Doctrine for the Lady of the Renaissance*. Foreword by Katharine M. Rogers. Urbana: University of Illinois Press, 1956, 1978.
Kendrick, Robert L. *Celestical Sirens: Nuns and Their Music in Early Modern Milan*. New York: Oxford University Press, 1996.
Kermode, Jenny, and Garthine Walker, eds. *Women, Crime, and the Courts in Early Modern England*. Chapel Hill: University of North Carolina Press, 1994.
King, Catherine E. *Renaissance Women Patrons: Wives and Widows in Italy, c. 1300–1550*. Manchester: Manchester University Press, 1998.
King, Margaret L. *Women of the Renaissance*. Foreword by Catharine R. Stimpson. Chicago: University of Chicago Press, 1991.
King, Thomas A. *The Gendering of Men, 1600–1700: The English Phallus*. Vol. 1. Madison: University of Wisconsin Press, 2004.

Klapisch-Zuber, Christiane. *Women, Family, and Ritual in Renaissance Italy*. Trans. Lydia G. Cochrane. Chicago: University of Chicago Press, 1985.

———, ed. *Silences of the Middle Ages*. Vol. 2 of *A History of Women in the West*. Cambridge: Harvard University Press, 1992.

Kleiman, Ruth. *Anne of Austria, Queen of France*. Columbus: Ohio State University Press, 1985.

Knott, Sarah, and Barbara Taylor. *Women, Gender, and Enlightenment*. New York: Palgrave Macmillan, 2005.

Kolsky, Stephen. *The Ghost of Boccaccio: Writings on Famous Women in Renaissance Italy*. Late Medieval and Early Modern Studies 7. Turnhout: Brepols, 2005.

Krontiris, Tina. *Oppositional Voices: Women as Writers and Translators of Literature in the English Renaissance*. London: Routledge, 1992.

Kuehn, Thomas. *Law, Family, and Women: Toward a Legal Anthropology of Renaissance Italy*. Chicago: University of Chicago Press, 1991.

Kunze, Bonnelyn Young. *Margaret Fell and the Rise of Quakerism*. Stanford: Stanford University Press, 1994.

Labalme, Patricia A., ed. *Beyond Their Sex: Learned Women of the European Past*. New York: New York University Press, 1980.

Lalande, Roxanne Decker, ed. *A Labor of Love: Critical Reflections on the Writings of Marie-Catherine Desjardins (Mme de Villedieu)*. Madison, NJ: Fairleigh Dickinson University Press, 2000.

Lamb, Mary Ellen. *Gender and Authorship in the Sidney Circle*. Madison: University of Wisconsin Press, 1990.

Laqueur, Thomas. *Making Sex: Body and Gender from the Greeks to Freud*. Cambridge: Harvard University Press, 1990.

Larsen, Anne R., and Colette H. Winn, eds. *Renaissance Women Writers: French Texts/American Contexts*. Detroit: Wayne State University Press, 1994.

Laven, Mary. *Virgins of Venice: Broken Vows and Cloistered Lives in the Renaissance Convent*. New York: Viking, 2003.

Ledkovsky, Marina, Charlotte Rosenthal, and Mary Zirin, eds. *Dictionary of Russian Women Writers*. Westport, CT: Greenwood Press, 1994.

Lehfeldt, Elizabeth A. *Religious Women in Golden Age Spain: The Permeable Cloister*. Burlington, VT: Ashgate, 2005.

Leonard, Amy. *Nails in the Wall: Catholic Nuns in Reformation Germany*. Women in Culture and Society. Chicago: University of Chicago Press, 2005.

Lerner, Gerda. *The Creation of Feminist Consciousness, 1000–1870*. New York: Oxford University Press, 1994.

———. *The Creation of Patriarchy* New York: Oxford University Press, 1986.

Levack. Brian P. *The Witch Hunt in Early Modern Europe*. London: Longman, 1987.

Levin, Carole, and Jeanie Watson, eds. *Ambiguous Realities: Women in the Middle Ages and Renaissance*. Detroit: Wayne State University Press, 1987.

Levin, Carole, Jo Eldridge Carney, and Debra Barrett-Graves. *Elizabeth I: Always Her Own Free Woman*. Burlington, VT: Ashgate, 2003.

Levin, Carole, et al. *Extraordinary Women of the Medieval and Renaissance World: A Biographical Dictionary*. Westport, CT: Greenwood Press, 2000.

Levy, Allison, ed. *Widowhood and Visual Culture in Early Modern Europe*. Burlington, VT: Ashgate, 2003.

Lewalski, Barbara Kiefer. *Writing Women in Jacobean England*. Cambridge: Harvard University Press, 1993.

Lewis, Gertrud Jaron. *By Women, for Women, about Women: The Sister-Books of Fourteenth-Century Germany*. Toronto: University of Toronto Press, 1996.

Lewis, Jayne Elizabeth. *Mary Queen of Scots: Romance and Nation*. London: Routledge, 1998.

Lindenauer, Leslie J. *Piety and Power: Gender and Religious Culture in the American Colonies, 1630–1700*. London: Routledge, 2002.

Lindsey, Karen. *Divorced, Beheaded, Survived: A Feminist Reinterpretation of the Wives of Henry VIII*. Reading, MA: Addison-Wesley, 1995.

Liss, Peggy K. *Isabel the Queen: Life and Times*. Rev. ed. Philadelphia: University of Pennsylvania Press, 2004.

Loades, David. *Mary Tudor: A Life*. Cambridge: Basil Blackwell, 1989.

Lochrie, Karma. *Margery Kempe and Translations of the Flesh*. Philadelphia: University of Pennsylvania Press, 1992.

Longfellow, Ewrica. *Women and Religious Writing in Early Modern England*. Cambridge: Cambridge University Press, 2004.

Lougee, Carolyn C. *Le Paradis des Femmes: Women, Salons, and Social Stratification in Seventeenth-Century France*. Princeton: Princeton University Press, 1976.

Love, Harold. *The Culture and Commerce of Texts: Scribal Publication in Seventeenth-Century England*. Amherst: University of Massachusetts Press, 1993.

Lowe, K. J. P. *Nuns' Chronicles and Convent Culture in Renaissance and Counter-Reformation Italy*. Cambridge: Cambridge University Press, 2003.

Lux-Sterritt, Laurence. *Redefining Female Religious Life: French Ursulines and English Ladies in Seventeenth-Century Catholicism*. Burlington, VT: Ashgate, 2005.

MacCarthy, Bridget G. *The Female Pen: Women Writers and Novelists, 1621–1818*. Preface by Janet Todd. New York: New York University Press, 1994. Originally published by Cork University Press, 1946–47.

Macfarlane, Alan. *Marriage and Love in England: Modes of Reproduction, 1300–1840*. New York: Basil Blackwell, 1986.

Mack, Phyllis. *Visionary Women: Ecstatic Prophecy in Seventeenth-Century England*. Berkeley: University of California Pres, 1992.

Maclean, Ian. *The Renaissance Notion of Woman: A Study of the Fortunes of Scholasticism and Medical Science in European Intellectual Life*. Cambridge: Cambridge University Press, 1980.

———. *Woman Triumphant: Feminism in French Literature, 1610–1652*. Oxford: Clarendon Press, 1977.

MacNeil, Anne. *Music and Women of the Commedia dell'Arte in the Late Sixteenth Century*. New York: Oxford University Press, 2003.

Maggi, Armando. *Uttering the Word: The Mystical Performances of Maria Maddalena de' Pazzi, a Renaissance Visionary*. Albany: State University of New York Press, 1998

Marshall, Sherrin, ed. *Women in Reformation and Counter-Reformation Europe: Public and Private Worlds*. Bloomington: Indiana University Press, 1989.

Masten, Jeffrey. *Textual Intercourse: Collaboration, Authorship, and Sexualities in Renaissance Drama*. Cambridge: Cambridge University Press, 1997.

Matter, E. Ann, and John Coakley, eds. *Creative Women in Medieval and Early Modern Italy*. Philadelphia: University of Pennsylvania Press, 1994.

McGrath, Lynette. *Subjectivity and Women's Poetry in Early Modern England*. Burlington, VT: Ashgate, 2002.

McIver, Katherine A. *Women, Art, and Architecture in Northern Italy, 1520–1580: Negotiating Power*. Women and Gender in the Early Modern World. Burlington, VT: Ashgate, 2006.

McLeod, Glenda. *Virtue and Venom: Catalogs of Women from Antiquity to the Renaissance*. Ann Arbor: University of Michigan Press, 1991.

McSheffrey, Shannon. *Gender and Heresy: Women and Men in Lollard Communities, 1420–1530*. Philadelphia: University of Pennsylvania Press, 1995.

McTavish, Lianne. *Childbirth and the Display of Authority in Early Modern France*. Burlington, VT: Ashgate, 2005.

Medwick, Cathleen. *Teresa of Avila: The Progress of a Soul*. New York: Doubleday, 1999.

Meek, Christine, ed. *Women in Renaissance and Early Modern Europe*. Dublin, Ireland: Four Courts Press, 2000.

Mendelson, Sara, and Patricia Crawford. *Women in Early Modern England, 1550–1720*. Oxford: Clarendon Press, 1998.

Merchant, Carolyn. *The Death of Nature: Women, Ecology, and the Scientific Revolution*. New York: HarperCollins, 1980.

Merrim, Stephanie. *Early Modern Women's Writing and Sor Juana Inés de la Cruz*. Nashville: Vanderbilt University Press, 1999.

Messbarger, Rebecca. *The Century of Women: The Representations of Women in Eighteenth-Century Italian Public Discourse*. Toronto: University of Toronto Press, 2002.

Midelfort, Erik H. C. *Witchhunting in Southwestern Germany, 1562–1684: The Social and Intellectual Foundations*. Stanford: Stanford University Press, 1972.

Migiel, Marilyn, and Juliana Schiesari. *Refiguring Woman: Perspectives on Gender and the Italian Renaissance*. Ithaca: Cornell University Press, 1991.

Miller, Nancy K. *The Heroine's Text: Readings in the French and English Novel, 1722–1782*. New York: Columbia University Press, 1980.

Miller, Naomi J. *Changing the Subject: Mary Wroth and Figurations of Gender in Early Modern England*. Lexington: University Press of Kentucky, 1996.

Miller, Naomi J., and Gary Waller, eds. *Reading Mary Wroth: Representing Alternatives in Early Modern England*. Knoxville: University of Tennessee Press, 1991.

Miller, Naomi J., and Naomi Yavneh. *Sibling Relations and Gender in the Early Modern World: Sisters, Brothers and Others*. Burlington, VT: Ashgate, 2006.

Monson, Craig A., ed. *The Crannied Wall: Women, Religion, and the Arts in Early Modern Europe*. Ann Arbor: University of Michigan Press, 1992.

Monson, Craig A. *Disembodied Voices: Music and Culture in an Early Modern Italian Convent*. Berkeley: University of California Press, 1995.

Monter, E. William. *Witchcraft in France and Switzerland: The Borderlands during the Reformation*. Ithaca: Cornell University Press, 1976.

Montrose, Louis Adrian. *The Subject of Elizabeth: Authority, Gender, and Representation*. Chicago: University of Chicago Press, 2006.

Mooney, Catherine M. *Gendered Voices: Medieval Saints and Their Interpreters*. Philadelphia: University of Pennsylvania Press, 1999.

Moore, Cornelia Niekus. *The Maiden's Mirror: Reading Material for German Girls in the Sixteenth and Seventeenth Centuries*. Wiesbaden: Otto Harrassowitz, 1987.

Moore, Mary B. *Desiring Voices: Women Sonneteers and Petrarchism*. Carbondale: Southern Illinois University Press, 2000.

Mujica, Barbara. *Women Writers of Early Modern Spain*. New Haven: Yale University Press, 2004.

Murphy, Caroline. *The Pope's Daughter: The Extraordinary Life of Felice Della Rovere*. New York: Oxford University Press, 2005.

Musacchio, Jacqueline Marie. *The Art and Ritual of Childbirth in Renaissance Italy*. New Haven: Yale University Press, 1999.

Nader, Helen, ed. *Power and Gender in Renaissance Spain: Eight Women of the Mendoza Family, 1450–1650*. Urbana: University of Illinois Press, 2004.

Nevitt, Marcus. *Women and the Pamphlet Culture of Revolutionary England, 1640–1660*. Women and Gender in the Early Modern World. Burlington, VT: Ashgate, 2006.

Newman, Barbara. *God and the Goddesses: Vision, Poetry, and Belief in the Middle Ages*. Philadelphia: University of Pennsylvania Press, 2003.

Newman, Karen. *Fashioning Femininity and English Renaissance Drama*. Chicago: University of Chicago Press, 1991.

Novy, Marianne. *Love's Argument: Gender Relations in Shakespeare*. Chapel Hill: University of North Carolina Press, 1984.

O'Donnell, Mary Ann. *Aphra Behn: An Annotated Bibliography of Primary and Secondary Sources*. 2nd ed. Brookfield: Ashgate, 2004.

Okin, Susan Moller. *Women in Western Political Thought*. Princeton: Princeton University Press, 1979.

Ozment, Steven. *The Bürgermeister's Daughter: Scandal in a Sixteenth-Century German Town*. New York: St. Martin's Press, 1995.

———. *Flesh and Spirit: Private Life in Early Modern Germany*. New York: Penguin Putnam, 1999.

———. *When Fathers Ruled: Family Life in Reformation Europe*. Cambridge: Harvard University Press, 1983.

Pacheco, Anita, ed. *Early [English] Women Writers: 1600–1720*. New York: Longman, 1998.

Pagels, Elaine. *Adam, Eve, and the Serpent*. New York: Harper Collins, 1988.

Panizza, Letizia, ed. *Women in Italian Renaissance Culture and Society*. Oxford: European Humanities Research Centre, 2000.

Panizza, Letizia, and Sharon Wood, eds. *A History of Women's Writing in Italy*. Cambridge: University Press, 2000.

Pantel, Pauline Schmitt. *From Ancient Goddesses to Christian Saints*. Vol. 1 of *A History of Women in the West*. Cambridge: Harvard University Press, 1992.

Pardailhé-Galabrun, Annik. *The Birth of Intimacy: Privacy and Domestic Life in Early Modern Paris*. Philadelphia: University of Pennsylvania Press, 1992.

Park, Katharine. *The Secrets of Women: Gender, Generation, and the Origins of Human Dissection*. New York: Zone Books, 2006.

Parker, Patricia. *Literary Fat Ladies: Rhetoric, Gender, and Property*. London: Methuen, 1987.

Perlingieri, Ilya Sandra. *Sofonisba Anguissola: The First Great Woman Artist of the Renaissance*. New York: Rizzoli, 1992.

Pernoud, Regine, and Marie-Veronique Clin. *Joan of Arc: Her Story*. Rev. and trans. Jeremy DuQuesnay Adams. New York: St. Martin's Press, 1998. French original, 1986.

Perry, Mary Elizabeth. *Crime and Society in Early Modern Seville*. Hanover, NH: University Press of New England, 1980.

———. *Gender and Disorder in Early Modern Seville*. Princeton: Princeton University Press, 1990.

———. *The Handless Maiden: Moriscos and the Politics of Religion in Early Modern Spain*. Princeton: Princeton University Press, 2005.

Perry, Ruth. *The Celebrated Mary Astell: An Early English Feminist*. Chicago: University of Chicago Press, 1986.

Peters, Christine. *Patterns of Piety: Women, Gender and Religion in Late Medieval and Reformation England*. Cambridge: Cambridge University Press, 2003.

Petroff, Elizabeth A., ed. *Medieval Women's Visionary Literature*. New York: Oxford University Press, 1986.

Phillippy, Patricia Berrahou. *Painting Women: Cosmetics, Canvases, and Early Modern Culture*. Baltimore: Johns Hopkins University Press, 2006.

Plowden, Alison. *Tudor Women: Queens and Commoners*. Rev. ed. Thrupp, Stroud, Gloucestershire: Sutton, 1998.

Poor, Sara S., and Jana K. Schulman. *Women and Medieval Epic: Gender, Genre, and the Limits of Epic Masculinity*. New York: Palgrave Macmillan, 2007.

Price, Paola Malpezzi, and Christine Ristaino. *Lucrezia Marinella and the "Querelle des femmes" in Seventeenth-Century Italy*. Madison, NJ: Fairleigh Dickinson University Press, 2008.

Prior, Mary, ed. *Women in English Society, 1500–1800*. London: Methuen, 1985.

Quilligan, Maureen. *The Allegory of Female Authority: Christine de Pizan's "Cité des Dames."* Ithaca: Cornell University Press, 1991.

———. *Incest and Agency in Elizabeth's England*. Philadelphia: University of Pennsylvania Press, 2005.

Rabil, Albert. *Laura Cereta: Quattrocento Humanist*. Binghamton, NY: Medieval and Renaissance Texts and Studies, 1981.

Ranft, Patricia. *Women in Western Intellectual Culture, 600–1500*. New York: Palgrave, 2002.

Rapley, Elizabeth. *The Dévotés: Women and Church in Seventeenth-Century France*. Kingston, Ontario: McGill-Queen's University Press, 1989.

———. *A Social History of the Cloister: Daily Life in the Teaching Monasteries of the Old Regime*. Montreal: McGill-Queen's University Press, 2001.

Raven, James, Helen Small, and Naomi Tadmor, eds. *The Practice and Representation of Reading in England*. Cambridge: Cambridge University Press, 1996.

Reardon, Colleen. *Holy Concord within Sacred Walls: Nuns and Music in Siena, 1575–1700*. Oxford: Oxford University Press, 2001.

Reid, Jonathan Andrew. "King's Sister—Queen of Dissent: Marguerite of Navarre (1492–1549) and Her Evangelical Network." Ph.D diss., University of Arizona, 2001.

Reiss, Sheryl E., and David G. Wilkins, eds. *Beyond Isabella: Secular Women Patrons of Art in Renaissance Italy*. Kirksville, MO: Truman State University Press, 2001.

Rheubottom, David. *Age, Marriage, and Politics in Fifteenth-Century Ragusa*. Oxford: Oxford University Press, 2000.

Richards, Earl Jeffrey, ed., with Joan Williamson, Nadia Margolis, and Christine Reno. *Reinterpreting Christine de Pizan*. Athens: University of Georgia Press, 1992.

Richardson, Brian. *Printing, Writers, and Readers in Renaissance Italy*. Cambridge: Cambridge University Press, 1999.

Riddle, John M. *Contraception and Abortion from the Ancient World to the Renaissance*. Cambridge: Harvard University Press, 1992.

———. *Eve's Herbs: A History of Contraception and Abortion in the West*. Cambridge: Harvard University Press, 1997.

Robin, Diana. *Publishing Women: Salons, the Presses, and the Counter-Reformation in Sixteenth-Century Italy*. Chicago: University of Chicago Press, 2007.

Robin, Diana, Anne R. Larsen, and Carole Levin, eds. *Encyclopedia of Women in the Renaissance: Italy, France, and England*. Santa Barbara, CA: ABC Clio, 2007.

Roelker, Nancy L. *Queen of Navarre, Jeanne d'Albret, 1528–1572*. Cambridge: Harvard University Press, 1968.

Roper, Lyndal. *The Holy Household: Women and Morals in Reformation Augsburg*. New York: Oxford University Press, 1989.

Rose, Mary Beth. *The Expense of Spirit: Love and Sexuality in English Renaissance Drama*. Ithaca: Cornell University Press, 1988.

———. *Gender and Heroism in Early Modern English Literature*. Chicago: University of Chicago Press, 2002.

———, ed. *Women in the Middle Ages and the Renaissance: Literary and Historical Perspectives*. Syracuse: Syracuse University Press, 1986.

Rosenthal, Margaret F. *The Honest Courtesan: Veronica Franco, Citizen and Writer in Sixteenth-Century Venice*. Foreword by Catharine R. Stimpson. Chicago: University of Chicago Press, 1992.

Rublack, Ulinka, ed. *Gender in Early Modern German History*. Cambridge: Cambridge University Press, 2002.

Ruggiero, Guido. *Binding Passions: Tales of Magic, Marriage, and Power at the End of the Renaissance*. Oxford: Oxford University Press, 1993.

———. *The Boundaries of Eros: Sex Crime and Sexuality in Renaissance Venice*. New York: Oxford University Press, 1985.

Russell, Rinaldina, ed. *Feminist Encyclopedia of Italian Literature*. Westport, CT: Greenwood Press, 1997.

———. *Italian Women Writers: A Bio-bibliographical Sourcebook*. Westport, CT: Greenwood Press, 1994.

Sackville-West, Vita. *Daughter of France: The Life of La Grande Mademoiselle*. Garden City, NY: Doubleday, 1959.

Safley, Thomas Max. *Let No Man Put Asunder: The Control of Marriage in the German Southwest: A Comparative Study, 1550–1600*. Kirksville, MO: Sixteenth Century Journal Publishers, 1984.

Sage, Lorna, ed. *Cambridge Guide to Women's Writing in English*. Cambridge: University Press, 1999.

Sánchez, Magdalena S. *The Empress, the Queen, and the Nun: Women and Power at the Court of Philip III of Spain*. Baltimore: Johns Hopkins University Press, 1998.

Sankovitch, Tilde A. *French Women Writers and the Book: Myths of Access and Desire*. Syracuse: Syracuse University Press, 1988.

Sartori, Eva Martin, and Dorothy Wynne Zimmerman, eds. *French Women Writers: A Bio-bibliographical Source Book*. Westport, CT: Greenwood Press, 1991.

Scaraffia, Lucetta, and Gabriella Zarri. *Women and Faith: Catholic Religious Life in Italy from Late Antiquity to the Present*. Cambridge: Harvard University Press, 1999.

Scheepsma, Wybren. *Medieval Religious Women in the Low Countries: The "Modern Devotion'," the Canonesses of Windesheim, and Their Writings*. Rochester, NY: Boydell Press, 2004.

Schiebinger, Londa. *The Mind Has No Sex? Women in the Origins of Modern Science*. Cambridge: Harvard University Press, 1991.

———. *Nature's Body: Gender in the Making of Modern Science*. Boston: Beacon Press, 1993.

Schofield, Mary Anne, and Cecilia Macheski, eds. *Fetter'd or Free? British Women Novelists, 1670–1815*. Athens: Ohio University Press, 1986.

Schroeder, Joy A. *Dinah's Lament: The Biblical Legacy of Sexual Violence in Christian Interpretation*. Philadelphia: Fortress Press, 2007.

Schutte, Anne Jacobson. *Aspiring Saints: Pretense of Holiness, Inquisition, and Gender in the Republic of Venice, 1618–1750*. Baltimore: Johns Hopkins University Press, 2001.

———, Thomas Kuehn, and Silvana Seidel Menchi, eds. *Time, Space, and Women's Lives in Early Modern Europe*. Kirksville, MO: Truman State University Press, 2001.

Seelig, Sharon Cadman. *Autobiography and Gender in Early Modern Literature: Reading Women's Lives, 1600–1680*. Cambridge: Cambridge University Press, 2006.

Seifert, Lewis C. *Fairy Tales, Sexuality, and Gender in France, 1690–1715: Nostalgic Utopias*. Cambridge: Cambridge University Press, 1996.

Shannon, Laurie. *Sovereign Amity: Figures of Friendship in Shakespearean Contexts*. Chicago: University of Chicago Press, 2002.

Shemek, Deanna. *Ladies Errant: Wayward Women and Social Order in Early Modern Italy*. Durham: Duke University Press, 1998.

Shepherd, Simon. *Amazons and Warrior Women: Varieties of Feminism in Seventeenth-Century Drama*. New York: St. Martin's Press, 1981.

Slater, Miriam. *Family Life in the Seventeenth Century: The Verneys of Claydon House*. London: Routledge and Kegan Paul, 1984.

Smarr, Janet L. *Joining the Conversation: Dialogues by Renaissance Women*. Ann Arbor: University of Michigan Press, 2005.

Smith, Hilda L. *Reason's Disciples: Seventeenth-Century English Feminists*. Urbana: University of Illinois Press, 1982.

———. *Women Writers and the Early Modern British Political Tradition*. Cambridge: Cambridge University Press, 1998.

Snook, Edith. *Women, Reading, and the Cultural Politics of Early Modern England*. Brookfield: Ashgate, 2005.

Sobel, Dava. *Galileo's Daughter: A Historical Memoir of Science, Faith, and Love*. New York: Penguin Books, 2000.

Sommerville, Margaret R. *Sex and Subjection: Attitudes to Women in Early-Modern Society*. London: Arnold, 1995.

Soufas, Teresa Scott. *Dramas of Distinction: A Study of Plays by Golden Age Women*. Lexington: University Press of Kentucky, 1997.

Spencer, Jane. *The Rise of the Woman Novelist: From Aphra Behn to Jane Austen*. Oxford: Basil Blackwell, 1986.

Spender, Dale. *Mothers of the Novel: One Hundred Good Women Writers before Jane Austen*. London: Routledge, 1986.

Sperling, Jutta Gisela. *Convents and the Body Politic in Late Renaissance Venice.* Foreword by Catharine R. Stimpson. Chicago: University of Chicago Press, 1999.

Staley, Lynn. *Margery Kempe's Dissenting Fictions.* University Park: Pennsylvania State University Press, 1994.

Steinbrügge, Lieselotte. *The Moral Sex: Woman's Nature in the French Enlightenment.* Trans. Pamela E. Selwyn. New York: Oxford University Press, 1995.

Stephens, Sonya, ed. *A History of Women's Writing in France.* Cambridge: Cambridge University Press, 2000.

Stephenson, Barbara. *The Power and Patronage of Marguerite de Navarre.* Burlington, VT: Ashgate, 2004.

Stevenson, Jane. *Women Latin Poets: Language, Gender, and Authority, from Antiquity to the Eighteenth Century.* New York: Oxford University Press, 2005.

Stocker, Margarita. *Judith, Sexual Warrior: Women and Power in Western Culture.* New Haven: Yale University Press, 1998.

Stone, Lawrence. *Family, Marriage, and Sex in England, 1500–1800.* New York: Weidenfeld & Nicolson, 1977; abridged edition, New York: Harper & Row, 1979.

Straznacky, Marta. *Privacy, Playreading, and Women's Closet Drama, 1550–1700.* Cambridge: Cambridge University Press, 2004.

Stretton, Timothy. *Women Waging Law in Elizabethan England.* Cambridge: Cambridge University Press, 1998.

Strinati, Claudio M., Carole Collier Frick, Elizabeth S. G. Nicholson, Vera Fortunati Pietrantonio, and Jordana Pomeroy. *Italian Women Artists: From Renaissance to Baroque.* Ed. National Museum of Women in the Arts, Sylvestre Verger Art Organization. New York: Skira, 2007.

Stuard, Susan Mosher. *Gilding the Market: Luxury and Fashion in Fourteenth-Century Italy.* Middle Ages Series. Philadelphia: University of Pennsylvania Press, 2006.

Summit, Jennifer. *Lost Property: The Woman Writer and English Literary History, 1380–1589.* Chicago: University of Chicago Press, 2000.

Surtz, Ronald E. *The Guitar of God: Gender, Power, and Authority in the Visionary World of Mother Juana de la Cruz (1481–1534).* Philadelphia: University of Pennsylvania Press, 1991.

———. *Writing Women in Late Medieval and Early Modern Spain: The Mothers of Saint Teresa of Avila.* Philadelphia: University of Pennsylvania Press, 1995.

Suzuki, Mihoko. *Subordinate Subjects: Gender, the Political Nation, and Literary Form in England, 1588–1688.* Brookfield: Ashgate, 2003.

Tatlock, Lynne, and Christiane Bohnert, eds. *The Graph of Sex and the German Text: Gendered Culture in Early Modern Germany, 1500–1700.* Amsterdam: Rodopi, 1994.

Teague, Frances. *Bathsua Makin, Woman of Learning.* Lewisburg, PA: Bucknell University Press, 1999.

Thomas, Anabel. *Art and Piety in the Female Religious Communities of Renaissance Italy: Iconography, Space, and the Religious Woman's Perspective.* New York: Cambridge University Press, 2003.

Thompson, John Lee. *John Calvin and the Daughters of Sarah: Women in Regular and Exceptional Roles in the Exegesis of Calvin, His Predecessors, and His Contemporaries.* Travaux d'Humanisme et Renaissance 259. Geneva: Librairie Droz, 1992.

Tinagli, Paola. *Women in Italian Renaissance Art: Gender, Representation, Identity.* Manchester: Manchester University Press, 1997.

Todd, Janet. *The Secret Life of Aphra Behn*. London: Pandora, 2000.

———. *The Sign of Angelica: Women, Writing, and Fiction, 1660–1800*. New York: Columbia University Press, 1989.

Tomas, Natalie R. *The Medici Women: Gender and Power in Renaissance Florence*. Burlington, VT: Ashgate, 2004.

Traub, Valerie. *The Renaissance of Lesbianism in Early Modern England*. Cambridge: Cambridge University Press, 2002.

Valenze, Deborah. *The First Industrial Woman*. New York: Oxford University Press, 1995.

Van Dijk, Susan, Lia van Gemert, and Sheila Ottway, eds. *Writing the History of Women's Writing: Toward an International Approach*. Proceedings of the Colloquium, Amsterdam, 9–11 September. Amsterdam: Royal Netherlands Academy of Arts and Sciences, 2001.

Vickery, Amanda. *The Gentleman's Daughter: Women's Lives in Georgian England*. New Haven: Yale University Press, 1998.

Vollendorf, Lisa. *The Lives of Women: A New History of Inquisitional Spain*. Nashville: Vanderbilt University Press, 2005.

———, ed. *Recovering Spain's Feminist Tradition*. New York: MLA, 2001.

Waithe, Mary Ellen, ed. *A History of Women Philosophers*. 3 vols. Dordrecht: Martinus Nijhoff, 1987.

Walker, Claire. *Gender and Politics in Early Modern Europe: English Convents in France and the Low Countries*. New York: Palgrave, 2003.

Wall, Wendy. *The Imprint of Gender: Authorship and Publication in the English Renaissance*. Ithaca: Cornell University Press, 1993.

Walsh, William T. *St. Teresa of Avila: A Biography*. Rockford, IL: TAN Books, 1987.

Warner, Marina. *Alone of All Her Sex: The Myth and Cult of the Virgin Mary*. New York: Knopf, 1976.

———. *Joan of Arc: The Image of Female Heroism*. Berkeley: University of California Press, 1981.

Warnicke, Retha M. *The Marrying of Anne of Cleves: Royal Protocol in Tudor England*. Cambridge: Cambridge University Press, 2000.

———. *Mary Queen of Scots*. Routledge Historical Biographies. New York: Routledge, 2006.

———. *The Rise and Fall of Anne Boleyn: Family Politics at the Court of Henry VIII*. Cambridge: Cambridge University Press, 1989.

———. *Women of the English Renaissance and Reformation*. Westport, CT: Greenwood Press, 1983.

Warren, Nancy Bradley. *Women of God and Arms: Female Spirituality and Political Conflict, 1380–1600*. Philadelphia: University of Pennsylvania Press, 2005.

Watt, Diane. *Secretaries of God: Women Prophets in Late Medieval and Early Modern England*. Cambridge, England: D. S. Brewer, 1997.

Weaver, Elissa B. *Convent Theatre in Early Modern Italy: Spiritual Fun and Learning for Women*. New York: Cambridge University Press, 2002.

Weber, Alison. *Teresa of Avila and the Rhetoric of Femininity*. Princeton: Princeton University Press, 1990.

Weinstein, Donald, and Rudolph M. Bell. *Saints and Society: The Two Worlds of Western Christendom, 1000–1700*. Chicago: University of Chicago Press, 1982.

Welles, Marcia L. *Persephone's Girdle: Narratives of Rape in Seventeenth-Century Spanish Literature*. Nashville: Vanderbilt University Press, 2000.

Whitehead, Barbara J., ed. *Women's Education in Early Modern Europe: A History, 1500–1800*. New York: Garland, 1999.

Wiesner-Hanks, Merry E. *Christianity and Sexuality in the Early Modern World: Regulating Desire, Reforming Practice*. New York: Routledge, 2000.

———. *Gender, Church, and State in Early Modern Germany: Essays*. New York: Longman, 1998.

———. *Gender in History*. Malden, MA: Blackwell, 2001.

———. *Women and Gender in Early Modern Europe*. Cambridge, UK: Cambridge University Press, 1993.

———. *Working Women in Renaissance Germany*. New Brunswick, NJ: Rutgers University Press, 1986.

Willard, Charity Cannon. *Christine de Pizan: Her Life and Works*. New York: Persea Books, 1984.

Wilson, Katharina, ed. *Encyclopedia of Continental Women Writers*. 2 vols. New York: Garland, 1991.

Wiltenburg, Joy. *Disorderly Women and Female Power in the Street Literature of Early Modern England and Germany*. Charlottesville: University Press of Virginia, 1992.

Winn, Colette, and Donna Kuizenga, eds. *Women Writers in Pre-Revolutionary France*. New York: Garland, 1997.

Winston-Allen, Anne. *Convent Chronicles: Women Writing about Women and Reform in the Late Middle Ages*. University Park: Pennsylvania State University Press, 2004.

Woodbridge, Linda. *Women and the English Renaissance: Literature and the Nature of Womankind, 1540–1620*. Urbana: University of Illinois Press, 1984.

Woodford, Charlotte. *Nuns as Historians in Early Modern Germany*. Oxford: Clarendon Press, 2002.

Woods, Susanne. *Lanyer: A Renaissance Woman Poet*. New York: Oxford University Press, 1999.

Woods, Susanne, and Margaret P. Hannay, eds. *Teaching Tudor and Stuart Women Writers*. New York: MLA, 2000.

Wormald, Jenny. *Mary Queen of Scots: A Study in Failure*. London: George Philip Press, 1988.

Zinsser, Judith P. *Men, Women, and the Birthing of Modern Science*. DeKalb: Northern Illinois University Press, 2005.

INDEX OF PEOPLE AND PLACES

INDEX OF ALLEGORICAL PERSONIFICATIONS AND MYTHOLOGICAL AND FICTIONAL CHARACTERS